LEARNING TO LEAD

THE MAKING OF A CHRISTIAN LEADER IN AFRICA

RICHARD J. GEHMAN

OASIS INTERNATIONAL LTD

Wheaton, Illinois
USA

Jos, Plateau State
Nigeria

INSIGHT
AFRICAN ISSUES
AFRICA'S AUTHORS
BOOKS

TABLE OF CONTENTS

Preface vii
Acknowledgements xii
Abbreviations xiii

Part One
ADVICE FROM CHRISTIAN LEADERS
1. The Sweet and Sour in Leadership 4
2. The Secret of Success 10
3. Skills of Christian Leadership 17
4. Challenges in Leadership 21
5. Lessons Learned in Leadership 29

Part Two
BASICS FOR CHRISTIAN LEADERS
6. The Church and her Leaders 37
7. Spiritual Disciplines 47
8. The Sovereign Rule of God 57
9. A Forgiving Spirit 63
10. Perseverance of Leaders 71

Part Three
HUMILITY OF CHRISTIAN LEADERS
11. The Necessity of Humility 79
12. The Problem of Pride 87
13. Humility in Leadership Styles 95
14. Servant Leadership 105
15. The Supreme Model of Humility 113

Part Four
LOVE OF CHRISTIAN LEADERS
16. Self Esteem in Leaders 121
17. Jealousy: The Opposite of Love 127
18. Anger: The Opposite of Love 135
19. The Attributes of Agape Love 143
20. The Supreme Model of Agape Love 153

"Dr. Gehman is well qualified to write this book about Christian leadership in Africa. Firstly, he has been vitally involved in training leadership in East Africa for over three decades. Secondly, he is a careful and thoughtful student of African culture and the challenges of church leaders. And thirdly, Dr. Gehman is a biblical scholar permeating his writing with biblical illustrations and scriptural teaching. After interviewing over 175 African church leaders, Dr. Gehman has presented two vital traits that are crucial to leadership within the African church – character and competence – with the greater emphasis on character.

"By careful listening to African voices and through diligent library research, Dr. Gehman is now offering an excellent textbook for leadership courses in Bible colleges, seminaries and graduate schools of theology within Africa and a helpful read for missionaries preparing themselves for teaching within continental Africa. Such a book would have greatly enhanced my own teaching on leadership within Ethiopia."

E. Paul Balisky (PhD), former instructor at the
Ethiopian Graduate School of Theology, Addis Ababa, Ethiopia

"Here is an excellent book, one that is timely for those who lead God's people, and those who desire to lead; and those who train others to lead. God has given us his 'master plan' for leadership in the Bible for us to follow. The author is bold enough in point out the right qualifications to be an accomplished and godly leader."

Rev. Isaac Simbiri, former General Secretary of the Evangelical Fellowship of Kenya;
former Director of the Christian Education Department of the Africa Inland Church in Kenya;
Principal of Ahero Evangelical School of Theology

"One special characteristic of this book is its splendid and pervasive practicality. Another is the gentle, generous tone throughout. A third distinguishing strength of the book is its African texture, exemplified especially in the extensive interview materials with African pastors, and in the African proverbs interspersed throughout. These uniquely African components of the discussion richly enhance the whole."

Paul Bowers (PhD Cantab.), founding coordinator, Accrediting Council
for Theological Education in Africa (ACTEA); managing editor, BookNotes for Africa:
A Review Journal; lecturer, George Whitefield College, Cape Town, South Africa

"Church growth in Africa is overwhelming. How then will these large numbers, who attend churches, be managed so that they will grow spiritually? The answer to this question is found in this book, *Learning to Lead: The Making of a Christian Leader in Africa.* Spiritual leadership by African Christian leaders will produce the results God intended, 'that we may present everyone perfect in Christ' (Col 1:28f). For this reason, I strongly recommend that every leader should get a copy of this book to use in the work of the Lord."

Titus Kivunzi (D.Min), former Principal of Scott Theological College;
former Bishop of the Africa Inland Church, Kenya;
instructor and department head for Pastoral Studies at the
Nairobi Evangelical Graduate School of Theology, Kenya

Learning to Lead

ISBN: 978-1-59452-090-7
ISBN: 1-59452-090-9

Cover design by Robyn Martins

Oasis International is a ministry devoted to growing discipleship through publishing African voices.

Oasis is: *Satisfying Africa's Thirst for God's Word.* For more information, go to oasisinternational.com.

Printed in India.

Part Five

HOLINESS OF CHRISTIAN LEADERS

21. Holy to the Lord 161
22. Integrity 167
23. Purity 175
24. Honesty 183
25. The Pure in Heart 189

Part Six

ATTRIBUTES OF CHRISTIAN LEADERS

26. The Nature of Christian Leadership 203
27. The Marks of an Effective Leader 211
28. Mistakes of Christian Leaders 221
19. The Leader as a Change-Agent 225
30. Nehemiah: A Model Leader 231

Part Seven

MANAGEMENT SKILLS OF CHRISTIAN LEADERS

31. Developing Relationships 243
32. Planning 251
33. Organising 259
34. Shepherding, Part One 267
35. Shepherding, Part Two 277

Part Eight

ISSUES FOR CHRISTIAN LEADERS

36. A Balanced Lifestyle 287
37. Self-Discipline 297
38. Maintaining Unity 303
39. Growing as a Leader in Character 309
40. Growing as a Leader in Competence 317

Select Bibliography 325
Additional Books Written or Edited by the Author 336

DEDICATION

To my former students
who have taught me more about Christian leadership
than I ever taught them.

PREFACE

The purpose of this book is to answer two basic questions: 'What kind of Christian leader do we need according to the Scriptures?' and 'How do we prepare this kind of Christian leader?'

For thirty-six years God granted Florence and me the marvelous privilege of training Church leaders in Africa. For most of those years we served at Scott Theological College in Kenya. After training students, we followed their lives with keen interest and prayers as they scattered throughout all of Kenya and into nine other African countries. We kept in touch with many. Over the years we worked with some and visited others in their ministries. With great joy and admiration we observed many prosper and succeed in ministry, but with sadness we saw some stumble and fall.

What made the difference?

Effective Christian leadership requires both character and competence. Almost none of our graduates failed because of incompetence. Whenever failure occurred, it was in the area of character.

Competence is important! Ministry in the Church requires competence in preaching and teaching, evangelizing, discipling and counseling. It also requires competence in leadership skills and management principles.

However, competence is not the most basic requirement for Christian leadership. From your experience, would you agree? From my observation I am convinced that both character and competence are needed. Leaders can have a relatively acceptable ministry with limited competence, but they are utter failures with flawed character. Without character, no leadership will ever succeed in God's sight. Under a charismatic, gifted and competent leader the Church may prosper outwardly with growing numbers, but wherever the leader's character is defective, the ministry will ultimately suffer and the leader will fall into disgrace.

Christian leaders are not limited to bishops and chairpersons. This book is designed for every Christian leader in Africa: the pastor, elders and lay leaders of the local congregation; the overseers and heads of Church districts, regions and departments; the bishops of dioceses and denominations; teachers and principals in pastoral training institutions, and Christian leaders in para-Church organisations. We may say that since the fundamentals of Christian leadership are the same everywhere and for every one, even Christian parents can benefit from the principles contained in this book as they lead and teach their children.

Is this book practical?

This is not a book on the theory of Christian leadership; it was born out of the practical experience of African leaders who have demonstrated Christian leadership skills. African pastors and bishops, Bible School/College teachers and principals have helped shape this book and made distinctive contributions through their observations and advice. Therefore, the book has very practical value. It reflects the lessons learned about successful ministry.

Two years prior to our retirement God gave the desire to visit as many of our Scott graduates as possible. What followed was one of the most memorable experiences of our entire lives. By God's grace I was able to visit over 175 graduates, mostly in their own homes all over Kenya; and together with my dear wife we visited many in six other countries in Africa. God opened the door for us to spend three months visiting some of our finest graduates in Tanzania, Zambia, Swaziland,

Malawi, Uganda and Ethiopia. We shared their joys and sorrows, their victories and challenges as we interviewed them. Many times in Kenya and elsewhere I felt a tug of grief when leaving them because in all probability I would not be able to visit them again in their homes and enjoy their fellowship. Their interviews filled 500 type written pages.

Although this book has utilized many western sources in research, the framework and application is always the African context – the African culture and Churches. The topics of most units have been derived from the feedback of African Church leaders. However, the author is responsible for shaping and developing these seed thoughts. A few emphases of the book are solely the discretion of the author.

What do we mean? *The Making of a Christian Leader in Africa.*

A preliminary word must be said about the title of the book. In some respects leaders are born and not made; leadership is a gift endowed by God. If you are not gifted as a leader, you cannot be trained to be a leader nor will you lead successfully. You may have a position of leadership, but a leadership position does not make a leader. Gifted leaders are born with leadership abilities but their gifts must be developed. Hence the title: *Learning to Lead.*

The Making of a Christian Leader in Africa: The sub-title emphasises this point of learning to lead. People who are born leaders must also learn the way to become effective Christian leaders. Since leadership is an art, all born leaders must learn and grow in their leadership skills; and they must grow to become truly Christian leaders. No leader can be made in an institution or within a four year course of study. Leadership development is a life-long process. You learn to lead by leading. Learning to be a leader is hard work. You may be gifted as a musician but any successful musician will tell you that competence requires hard work. This is a book about the process of making a Christian leader.

Although this book should help 'Christian leaders in training' in Bible Schools, Colleges and graduate schools, it is also intended for experienced Christian leaders in the field who need to grow to be more successful Christian leaders. A major crisis arises whenever Christian leaders think they are beyond the need for further learning. The worst ignorance possible for Christian leaders is not to know that they don't know. Growth is essential. Unless you realise that you don't know, you cannot learn to know. This book should be helpful in the process of continued growth through in-service training or personal study.

The Making of a Christian Leader in Africa: This book is all about 'leadership.' It is not about preaching or teaching or counseling. It is about the topic of becoming an effective Christian leader. But who is a leader? Many have attempted a definition.

Leadership by definition is someone with influence and authority; someone with followers. According to various scholars, leadership is:

- 'The ability to make things happen' (Ted Engstrom).[1]
- 'The ability of one person to influence others' (Oswald Sanders).[2]
- 'Influence. Anyone who influences someone else to do something has led that person.' 'A leader takes people where they would not go on their own' (Hans Finzel).[3]
- 'Getting others to want to do something that you are convinced should be done' (Vance Packard).[4]

This book will outline many basic principles for becoming an effective leader. But there are many kinds of leaders. This book is not just about leadership but about Christian leadership. The world has their own standards for politicians and leaders in the corporate world. This book, however, is not about secular leadership but Christian leadership.

The Making of a Christian Leader in Africa: In the latter days of Israel the leaders were self-centered, seeking personal gain from their leadership positions.[5] Instead of serving God, they were serving themselves. The princes were like 'roaring lions' who devoured the people, taking their possessions. The priests violated the very law which they were entrusted to teach the people, and in the process they profaned God. The prophets announced 'false visions and lying divinations' to please the people. The officials were 'like wolves tearing their prey,' all for personal gain. Sound familiar? So God declared: *'I looked for a man[1] among them who would build up the wall and stand before me in the gap on behalf of the land so I would not have to destroy it, but I found none.'*[6]

Do you feel that we live in a time when there is a dearth of capable Christian leaders? You are not alone. Ezekiel also found an absence of godly leaders. There were many men filling positions of leadership. But they missed the mark; they lived self-centred lives. Hence, God cried out, 'I looked for a man among them who would build up the wall and stand before me in the gap on behalf of the land…but I found none.' The standards for Christian leaders are extremely counter-cultural, totally contrary to natural human thinking. But God is looking for men and women who meet his standards to stand in the gap.

Too many Christian leaders today are imitating the leadership style and standards of unbelievers, even as Jesus' disciples were tempted to do. James and John were struggling for positions, but Jesus rebuked them saying:

> 'You've observed how godless rulers throw their weight around,' he said, 'and when people get a little power how quickly it goes to their heads. It's not going to be that way with you. Whoever wants to be great must become a servant. Whoever wants to be first among you must be your slave'[7]

If God is calling you to stand in the gap and serve faithfully in Christian leadership, this book is for you so that you can become a Christian leader.

Basically, what distinguishes a Christian leader from all other leaders is this: *First, a Christian leader is a servant of God.* He may lead people but he is accountable to God who has called him, has sent him and empowers him. In many ways Moses was an autocratic leader but he was repeatedly called 'a servant of the Lord';[8] so were Joshua, David and all the prophets. Unless Christian leaders recognise that they are servants of the Lord and ultimately responsible to him for their exercise of leadership, they will fail in ministry. The bottom line is not what people think of you as a leader; the bottom line is what God thinks of you. Some day every Christian leader will give an account of his leadership to the living God, the Judge of all mankind.

---

* This is an appropriate place to explain the use of 'man' and the masculine third person pronoun (he or him). In this book we make no judgement whether women can be leaders or not. But for simplicity and ease of writing, we will often use 'man' in the generic sense of 'mankind' or 'human being.' The English language has some limitations. The third person singular can either be masculine (he or him), feminine (she or her) or neuter (it). In a day of gender sensitivity it becomes cumbersome to write, 'he or she' or 'he/she.' So we often use 'man' and the masculine pronoun third person singular to refer to 'mankind' or a human being which includes both male and female (cf. Ge 1:27).

Secondly, a Christian leader is a servant of the Church. This topic will be discussed at greater length in Chapter 13. Without diminishing the leadership role of a Christian leader, service to the people is a style of leadership that should inform and enlighten all Church leadership. The purpose and goal in Christian leadership is not personal kingdom-building or self-advancement. It is ultimately serving the living God who chose you; and secondly, it is serving God's people and not yourself. It's all a question of the goal and purpose of leadership. A successful Christian leader is one who is commended by God for obeying him and for serving the needs of his Church.

For thirty-five years John Stott has traveled the world visiting many countries and observing Churches and their leaders. As a result he writes: 'It is my firm conviction that there is too much autocracy in the leaders of the Christian community, in defiance of the teaching of Jesus and his apostles, and not enough love and gentleness.' He goes on to say,

> Our model of leadership is often shaped more by culture than by Christ. Yet many cultural models of leadership are incompatible with the servant imagery taught and exhibited by the Lord Jesus. Nevertheless, these alien cultural models are often transplanted uncritically into the Church and its hierarchy. In Africa it is the tribal chief, in Latin America the machismo (exaggerated masculinity) of the Spanish male, in South Asia the religious guru fawned on by his disciples, in East Asia the Confucian legacy of the teacher's unchallengeable authority, and in Britain the British Raj mentality – the overbearing pride associated with the period of British rule until Indian independence in 1947. It is easy for Christian leaders to assimilate one or other of these models without realizing it. But we need to determine that there is no place in the Christian community for the guru or the Confucian teacher or the African chief, for British Raj mentality or Spanish machismo. These models are not congruous with the spirit of love and gentleness.[9]

As a teacher, let me give you a little assignment. Imagine you are in a position to choose a Christian leader for your Church or *Christian* institution. List the qualifications you desire for this Christian leader in the order of their priority. How do these qualifications compare with those of secular leaders in your country today? Is there a difference between the Christian leaders and secular leaders you already have? This book will help you think through this issue of the kind of leader we need for our churches and Christian ministries.

The Making of a Christian Leader in Africa: The principles of Christian leadership mentioned in this book are universal—they apply to Christians on all continents. But the context and application of these principles is with Africa in mind. Though the author is not an African, his whole ministry vocation has been in Africa. The book has grown out of interviews with African leaders. After writing half the book the author felt a deep need to return to Kenya and further clarify certain particularly sensitive issues in African leadership. Thirty-five more interviews with Christian leaders focused on this central question: How do leaders develop and maintain relationships while at the same time accomplish goals? More to the point, are building relationships and achievement of goals compatible? This is discussed extensively in Part Seven.

Anyone conversant with books on leadership in the west will know that of the writing of books on leadership, there is no end. Calvin Miller says, 'No subject has been more explored in our day than leadership.'[10] While the same thing cannot be said of books on leadership in the African context, the concern of many in Africa is the need for better leaders. Leadership is a hot topic in Africa. Many of the problems within the Churches and African countries are rooted in the kind of leaders that have been chosen to lead.

It is our prayer that this book will make a distinct contribution to the Church in Africa so that Christian leaders, biblically defined, may lead from strength to strength.

Can you accept the counsel of your elders?

Traditional African culture highly esteems the advice of the elders. A proverb of the Ngoreme in Tanzania says: *"If you refuse the elder's advice you will walk the whole day."* The Kiswahili version of this proverb says: *"The person who does not listen to an elder's advice gets his or her leg broken."*

These proverbs assume that the elders have witnessed many events in the past and so they have experience to judge wisely. This experience provides wisdom and counsel for the young and inexperienced. But some either ignore the advice or forget the counsel and they end up suffering as a result – so they walk the whole day and break a leg in the process of not taking counsel.

The advice found in this book is offered by those in the field who have served the Lord for many years. We offer the counsel so that you need not walk the whole day or break your leg. As Solomon taught: *"Listen to advice and accept instruction, that you may gain wisdom in the future."*[11]

What are the contents of the book?

The book begins with *Part One*: 'Advice' from seasoned Christian leaders in Africa. These first five chapters are largely quotations of their counsel and observations from their first hand experiences in leadership.

Part Two lays a foundation for Christian leadership with several basic issues. What does the Bible say about the nature of the Church and the qualifications of her leaders? What spiritual disciplines are necessary for effective leaders? Several other fundamental basics are explored for leadership.

Parts Three to *Five* are on character formation of *humility, love, holiness.*

Parts Six through *Eight* discuss the skills for Christian leaders. Part Seven discusses the various principles of management in Africa, including building relationships, planning, organising and shepherding the team toward the accomplishments of goals

Each chapter concludes with questions for study, discussion and reflection. These may be used during in-service seminars, class discussion or assignments in institutions of learning, or for private reflection and study.

May God raise up godly and competent leaders to guide his people, leaders who are spiritual and sacrificial, who know where they are going and are able to lead their people to fulfill God's purposes.

1 Engstrom 1979: 20
2 Sanders 1980: 31
3 Finzel 1994: 16
4 Vance Packard as found in Barna 1997: 21
5 Ez 23:23-30
6 Ez 23:30
7 The Message, Mk 10:42-45
8 Jos 1:1f
9 Stott 2002:113
10 Miller 1987
11 Pr 19:20

ACKNOWLEDGEMENTS

This book could not have been written or published without the valuable contributions of many.

Dr. Samuel Linge contributed invaluable counsel in assessing the book in its formation. Others gave their later assessment and counsel: Dr. Titus Kivunzi, Dr. Paul Bowers, Dr. Fabian Maganda, Rev. Isaac Simbiri, Dr. Paul Balisky, Dr. Daniel Mwailu, Dr. Ted Barnett, Mwalimu Adams Mutonga, Dr. Raymond Wolfe and Rev. Roger Coon. My dear wife, Florence, proof read the final document.

Following are the Christian leaders, former students of ours, whom we visited in seven African countries and interviewed on leadership before the writing of this book. Their lives, testimonies and faithfulness in ministry left an indelible impression and form the background for this book.

Abraham Chebunett
Abraham Koech
Agnes Kyalo
Agnes Kyengo
Agnes Mungwika
Alfred Muli
Amos Lwaya
Andrew Mulandi
Ann Nguku
Anna Ndebe
Alfred Dladla
Andrew Kendagor
Beatrice Kalya
Benedict Mutiso
Benjamin Kamende
Benjamin Mathaka
Bernard Nzioka
Bernice Njenga
Beth Njarambe
Catherine Ndeto
Charles Kababu
Charles Kimwele
Charles Muting'a
Daniel Kilonzo
Daniel Masesi
Daniel Muinde
Daniel Nungwana
David Kieti
David Mulwa
Dawit Yanna
Dinah Nyamai
Dorothy Obengo
Elijah Kalii
Elizabeth Timothy
Elizabeth Mutua
Emmanuel Falanta
Enock Shamapani
Ephraim Dlamini
Erastus Ngene
Esther Kibor
Eunice Bett
Fabian Maganda
Felicien Nemeyimana
Francis Kaunange
Frederick Mati
Geoffrey Muiru
George Opiyo
Gideon Karanja
Gladys Mpeta-Phiri
Isaac Kasema
Isaac Mulinge
Isaac Mutuvya
Isaac Mutwa
Isaac Simbiri
Hannington Kyengo
Jack Kamiruka
Jack Obongo
Jacob Kibor
James Kadanya
James Kombo
Japheth Muvengei
Jared Inzoberi
Jeddy Dladla
Jeremiah Muoki
Job Konzi
Joel Nyabinda
Joel Simbiti
John Karihe
John Moi
John Mondi
John Njoroge
John Njuru
Jonathan Maithya
Johnson Manda
Jonathan Mbuvi
Jonathan Mukote
Jonathan Mutunga
Joseph Imakando
Joseph Kahiga
Joseph Katwa
Joseph Kitur
Joseph Maswai
Joseph Mavulu
Joseph Mbunga
Joseph Ndebe
Joseph Onyango
Josephat Lumumba
Joshua Mutisya
Julius Kalya
Julius Musyimi
Julius Muthengi
Julius Mutwota
Justus Katoo
Justus Musyoka
Kamugu Mungai
Kibii Maiyo
Lawrence Bomett
Lillian Mwaka
Lydia Mwesa
Mary Mutetei
Mary Ndung'u
Mary Waita
Maruice Mpeta-Phiri
Mesfin Woldammanuel
Michael Mwaka
Michel Ngabonzima
Mike Mutua
Milcah Mukoma
Moses Njenga
Musa Magwesela
Mvula J. Mvula
Nancy Muli
Nathan Nzyoka
Nathaniel Kendagor
Ndeto wa Katunga
Noah Thananga
Pastory Masasila
Patterson Maimak
Paul Isayi
Paul Kisau
Paul Mutinda
Paul Njenga
Paul Ombati
Peninnah Kivunzi
Peres Akinyi
Peter Kitula
Peter Maina
Peter Mutisya
Peter Nakola
Peter Ngugi
Peter Ngule
Peter Njoroge
Philbert Nangale
Philip Muia
Philip Mutetei
Philip Osenya
Pierre Celestin
Rachel Ombati
Rebecca Celestin
Richard Muteto
Richard Sunza
Ruth Bomett
Samson Bett
Samson Jele
Samuel Gituka
Samuel Linge
Samuel Maritim
Samuel Munywoki
Shadrack Mukoma
Shadrack Mpanalehi
Shem Abuto
Silas Yego
Simeon Adera
Simeon Lellei
Simeon Otiende
Stanslaus Ndambuki
Stanley Mativo
Stanley Mutangili
Stephen Kitoo
Stephen Lentoror
Stephen Melly
Stephen Munyoki
Stephen Nduto
Stephen Sanya
Thomas Fumbuka
Timothy Kendagor
Timothy Mwangangi
Titus Kivunzi
Tom Obengo
Vundi Nason
Washington Were
William Kipkoros
Zipporah Wainaina

ABBREVIATIONS

Abbreviations for Bible Translations

AV	Authorized Version of 1611 (King James)
ESV	English Standard Version
GNB	Good News Bible (The Bible in Today's English Version)
NASB	New American Standard Bible
NEB	The New English Bible
NLT	The New Living Translation
NIV	The New International Version
RSV	Revised Standard Version
NRSV	New Revised Standard Version

Abbreviations for the Books of the Bible

Genesis .... Ge
Exodus................ Ex
Leviticus .... Lev
Numbers .... Nu
Deuteronomy...... Dt
Joshua .... Jos
Judges .... Jdg
Ruth .... Ru
1 Samuel............ 1 Sa
2 Samuel............ 2 Sa
1 Kings .... 1 Ki
2 Kings .... 2 Ki
1 Chronicles .... 1 Ch
2 Chronicles .... 2 Ch
Ezra .... Ezr
Nehemiah .... Ne
Esther .... Est
Job .... Job
Psalms................. Ps
Proverbs .... Pr
Ecclesiastes .... Ecc
Song of Songs .... SS

Isaiah .... Isa
Jeremiah............. Jer
Lamentations ..... La
Ezekiel .... Eze
Daniel .... Da
Hosea .... Hos
Joel...................... Joel
Amos .... Am
Obadiah............. Ob
Jonah .... Jnh
Micah .... Mic
Nahum .... Na
Habakkuk........... Hab
Zephaniah .... Zep
Haggai .... Hag
Zechariah .... Zec
Malachi.............. Mal
Matthew .... Mt
Mark.................. Mk
Luke .... Lk
John .... Jn
Acts .... Ac

Romans............... Ro
1 Corinthians...... 1 Co
2 Corinthians...... 2 Co
Galatians .... Gal
Ephesians .... Eph
Philippians.......... Php
Colossians........... Col
1 Thessalonians ... 1Th
2 Thessalonians ... 2Th
1 Timothy........... 1 Ti
2 Timothy........... 2 Ti
Titus .... Tit
Philemon .... Phm
Hebrews .... Heb
James .... Jas
1 Peter .... 1 Pe
2 Peter .... 2 Pe
1 John .... 1 Jn
2 John .... 2 Jn
3 John .... 3 Jn
Jude...................... Jude
Revelation........... Rev

PART ONE

ADVICE FROM CHRISTIAN LEADERS

Part One contains the advice from 175 experienced Christian leaders in Africa whom we interviewed in person. Each chapter will deal with different questions posed. Commentary will be interspersed. Solomon gave sound advice in his book of Proverbs:

'Whoever gives heed to instruction prospers...'
(Pr 16:20)

'Instruct a wise man and he will be wiser still...'
(Pr 9:9)

'Listen to advice and accept instruction,
and in the end you will be wise.'
(Pr 19:20)

'The way of a fool seems right to him,
But a wise man listens to instruction.'
(Pr 12:15)

1
THE SWEET AND SOUR IN LEADERSHIP

'Take [the little scroll] and eat it. It will turn your stomach sour,
but in your mouth it will be as sweet as honey.'[1]

Christian leadership is both sweet and sour.

The revelation of God to John seems to promise bliss – the scroll is sweet in the mouth; but he soon realises that it also involves severe trials – it is bitter in the stomach. In the ministry there are opportunities and responsibilities that are sweet to the taste – just plain enjoyable! Then there are experiences that are a bit sour – some which are necessary and part of the ministry, but for various reasons a bit unpleasant. It leaves a sour taste in the mouth.

Do Christian leaders really enjoy being 'Leaders'?

The question we asked was very open ended: 'What have you enjoyed most in *ministry*?' 'Ministry' was left undefined. The respondents were free to say anything. Interestingly, very few chose 'leadership' as something in ministry they enjoyed. A handful enjoyed 'administration' and only one volunteered that he enjoyed 'leadership.'

In contrast, a fair number said they *disliked* leadership.

- *'I don't like being in leadership. Leadership is time wasting, sitting in councils which are endless. I prefer training in the Church.'*
- *'I do not wish to be a leader. These power struggles, these wrangles! I have not wanted that.'*
- *I dislike being locked up in offices – in administration and committees. Offices are a way of getting me away from people.'*
- *'I don't like high leadership. There are always collisions in high powered leadership.'*

- *'I dislike the issue of being a leader, not because leadership is bad but because the devil has his way of bringing division in leadership. You are victimized or disciplined if you say something is wrong. Prayer is not in elections so Church leadership is in trouble. We should not fight for leadership and then pretend God has answered prayer.'*

These comments are revealing. First, pastors and missionaries, Bible School teachers and Christian Education workers are not considered 'leaders.' This is a major misunderstanding. Elders and pastors of the local Church are very much leaders. Through their lives and ministry they 'influence others,' 'make things happen' and 'get others to want to do something that you are convinced should be done.' They are simply not recognised or esteemed as Christian leaders with any recognition of power in the present structure of the Church.

Secondly, the reason many faithful Christian leaders dislike high positions of Church leadership is because such positions are associated with leadership wrangles, fights and quarrels. Indeed, numbers of faithful servants of God have voluntarily stepped aside to avoid the bitter divisions. They prefer to be Christian leaders in the local Church, shepherding the flock.

Given the negative features of high level positions of leadership, it is revealing what aspects of ministry are preferred.

The Sweet and the Sour

What are the sweet elements of ministry?

The vast majority of those interviewed loved preaching and teaching. 'Preaching! That is my biggest strength, especially expository preaching.' 'I enjoy teaching God's Word. It is a thrill and a great joy.' 'I can preach for hours and hours without getting tired.'

What a privilege it is for a servant of God to study the Scriptures and declare God's Word to the people. It is so rewarding and so desperately needed.

The next greatest preference in ministry is people-centred ministry, including evangelism and discipleship, home visitation and counseling.

They love to be with people: *'I enjoy being with people and ministering to people.' 'I've enjoyed mostly being with people in ministry. I don't want to separate myself from them. I want to visit them and share.' 'I have enjoyed as pastor being accepted by members of a Christian home. I am a member of that family under my care, in grief and in joy.'*

They love to see people coming to Christ: *'The most encouraging thing is to see people accepting Jesus Christ as Lord, after preaching or door-to-door visitation – to see people surrendering their lives to Christ. That is one of my greatest joys, and then to see them grow.'*

They love to see lives changed and growing in the Lord: *'I've enjoyed seeing the members growing in the Lord. As I see members rising up to serve, I see growth.'*

They love visitation because it brings them close to the people, as one said: *'Discipleship means impacting the lives of others. This is through informal fellowship, visiting, talking with them about their problems, through Bible studies, teaching and music. We have the ability to make close friends.'*

They love to counsel people: *'After counseling they return and tell me how helpful I've been.'*

People oriented ministry also includes conducting married couples seminars. *'In my Marriage*

Seminars many people do not understand what marriage is, so many have problems. My people are destroyed because of lack of knowledge. I go to these Married Couples Seminars and come back excited. When I hear questions, I know that they need help. They tell me, "Pastor, if it were not for this seminar, my marriage would have fallen apart."' Pastors are busy marrying couples. One such pastor, who has conducted over 1,000 weddings said: '*People from all over come for weddings.*' And beforehand he always conducts pre-marital counseling.

Just the privilege of ministering to people brings great joy. *'I have enjoyed serving my people, especially teaching in the Bible College and in the Church, because people are willing to be ministered unto. I think, "Imagine, all these people are waiting on me to serve them." This gives me incentive to do well. People are ready to be ministered unto.'*

One excited Christian leader enthused: '*I feel so happy, contented and fulfilled even with the little I have in life. The Church pays the least. I do not look at that, but to the service I can render.*'

There are other sweet elements in ministry: the joy of Church planting, seeing progress and success in ministry. '*In Church I trained the elders to preach and when I left they were doing a wonderful job.*'

Just the joy of being in God's appointed place, doing the ministry which God gifted and called you to do, that is reward in itself. '*I have enjoyed a sense of peace in my heart at every place I served because that is where God wanted me to be at that particular time, even though the circumstances may not be easy.*' '*I know I am working in God's will, carrying out the vision God gave me. There is great joy to fulfill the ministry given me by God.*' Truly, there is joy unspeakable in serving the living God. As one person said: '*Oh, the joy and deep satisfaction in my heart in serving the Lord!*'

Are there any sour elements in leadership?

By all means! Though we have stressed the sweet taste of being Christian leaders, there is a sour side as well. No one should enter the ministry blindly.

Among the negatives in leadership are Church policies that need attention. For example, many complain over the transfer of pastors suddenly, unnecessarily and without good reason. '*I dislike moving or transferring from Church to Church. You cannot achieve much if you are moved. It is not fair. One begins a project, and then he cannot continue with it. Some transfers are not for good. He does well and is replaced by one who cannot do better. Quick transfers are not properly organised.*'

'You stay in a Church for one or two years and then you are transferred. You have no problems in the Church and you have not gotten to know the people yet. But they don't consult you. It is because of a hidden agenda. Once you get popular, they want to take you to another area.'

'I dislike it when I am placed by other people in the wrong place by the posting committee. I dislike being in a place I feel is not the Lord's choice.'

More thought must be given to the great number of councils. '*When coming out of councils I have a headache. They are long and people generally do not agree in councils. There are so many councils in the Church. Everything must be done in a council.*'

'You may take minutes but no one follows them. You waste time and money and nothing is implemented. I see these councils as a waste of time. You keep talking and talking for years and nothing happens.'

'I don't like committee meetings because people don't discuss the most serious issues. Having many meetings leads to many quarrels and fights. Those in the committee are illiterate or not born again or they are retirees. So they just fight. The more meetings, the more fighting!'

However, the primary reason for a sour taste in ministry is *sin*, pure and simple. In fact, the reason behind the unhappiness over sudden transfers and committee meetings mentioned above is frequently impure motives.

Power struggles: *'Pastors want to be leaders. They try to fight to be a leader. This is because of the privileges they get when becoming chairman. I hate this. Around here they do not want to study, but they want to be leaders. They have nothing to give to the people.' 'I do not like conflict. The spirit of not forgiving others! It really gives me difficulty.'*

'I hate the power struggles in the Church. It hinders the growth of the ministers and the Church itself. This is something I hate. It leads to divisions and spiritual stagnation if two aim at one seat. It is better to stay a full time pastor or teacher. We leave the biblical principles that teach us to count others better than ourselves. We become a burden, not a blessing.' 'They hurt other brothers and destroy the character of another brother in order to get a seat.'

Church politics *'changes our vision and mission. I dislike pastors who forget the community and only think of themselves. It is envy. I'd like to see a team of pastors as shepherds who know the flock.'*

Church wrangles: *'I hate Church wrangles because most of them are between pastors themselves.'*

Conflict in councils: *'I dislike arguments and ill treatment in councils.'*

Hypocrisy – especially in leadership! *'I like being honest. But when you talk to a person and he is not honest, I feel irritated. Of late, many tell lies and they do not feel guilty. People need to be transparent.' 'A person appears as an angel of light and then you find he is an evil person. He comes as a dear brother and praises the Lord, and then he betrays you.'*

Unfaithfulness: *'I've learned that some pastors are not faithful... They have affairs with women and girls. Others are liars. Some pastor tells you something and you find that he is intentionally lying. I'm finding that really bad. It affects the ministry.'*

Discrimination: A surprising number of women feel frustrated in ministry for they are treated differently from the men. Thought should be given to this issue because women are trained in the institutions for ministries that are not afforded them in the Church. *'As a woman you are not given the opportunity to exploit the training and ability God has given you. You feel underused. Something needs to be done to point out exactly what a woman from a Bible School is able to do in the Church. For me, this has been a real struggle.'*

'I dislike when people think I am just a woman and all I can do is to work. I am a single woman. I do all the work and they take the credit for it. All I ask is for people to know we are co-workers...I need to be encouraged and helped. Many [women servant-leaders] quit because they are loaded and pastors do not understand. They feel we are donkeys and do all the work and then they get the credit.'

Gossip: *'I dislike gossip and slander among ministers, for example, talking behind one's back.' 'The most difficult thing for me is gossip without the facts. That is what has caused me a lot of pain.'*

CONCLUSION

The joys and delights in serving God are such powerful motives for Christian leaders in ministry that they find grace to persevere despite the down-sides. Discouragements are always there. We serve in the Church Militant, not the Church Triumphant. We are in a spiritual struggle. Sin of one degree or another has dogged God's faithful shepherds from time immemorial.

But we remember the words of Christ: '*Blessed are you when others revile you and persecute you and utter all kinds of evil against you falsely on my account. Rejoice and be glad, for your reward is great in heaven, for so they persecuted the prophets who were before you.*'[2]

In fact these trials and buffets in ministry are opportunities of personal growth. Paul rejoiced in his sufferings because it produced deeper character in him.[3] His great desire was to identify with Christ in his sufferings.[4] Our greatest thrill was to find Christian leaders who persevered in ministry despite the many discouragements that come along. Their reward in heaven is great!

This chapter has served to remind those in training and those experienced in the ministry that Christian leadership (of all kinds) has both a sweet and sour taste. 'To be forewarned is to be forearmed.' The purpose of the book is to give counsel and advice so that the servants of God can be faithful in ministry.

The next chapter will offer the advice from these same servants of the Lord on *how* to succeed in ministry. Many do succeed to the glory of God. Success is not measured by human standards but by God's standards. The following chapter will offer their insights to help us all move forward in fulfilling our high calling in Christ Jesus.

SEARCHING THE SCRIPTURE WITH APPLICATION

1. Do you agree that 'leadership' only refers to 'high positions' of oversight over other pastors and Churches? Defend your answer with reasons.
2. Do you believe 'elders' and 'pastors' are recognised as church leaders? If not, why do you believe 'elders' and 'pastors' are not recognised as 'leaders'?
3. If you are an 'elder' or 'pastor' and others do not look up to you or hold you in esteem; or, if you are a trained pastor but for years the Church does not ordain you, how can you persevere with joy in ministry?
4. What aspects of your leadership in ministry have you enjoyed most?
   a. How does this compare or contrast with what others have said, according to what was reported in this chapter?
   b. Why do you think you find such joy in those elements of ministry?
5. What aspects of your leadership in ministry have you disliked? Why?
   How are your comments similar to or different from the ones mentioned in this unit?
6. Read 1 Co 15:58; Mt 25:14-23. On the basis of these verses, why should a servant of the Lord find joy and delight in being a Christian leader even when there are external discouragements that come in ministry?

7. Where should a Christian leader find his greatest joy and delight, from his leadership in ministry or from elsewhere? Read Php 4:4-7; Ro 5:13; Ps 63.
8. From your observation or experience, would you enjoy the opportunity and responsibility that comes from being appointed to a 'high position' of leadership?
   a. Should you 'seek' it in the sense of 'campaigning' for it? Why?
   b. What should your motives be in a 'high position' of leadership?
9. From your observation, how have other 'leaders' (including elders and pastors) handled those who have sinful motives in leadership?
10. How should you or the Church help them?
11. 'All that needs to happen for evil to prevail is for good men to do nothing.' If 'good' Church leaders refuse office for personal reasons of not wanting conflict, what will happen to the Church?
12. How should 'good' Church leaders help to restore godliness to the Church leadership?

Endnotes

[1] Re 10:9
[2] Mt 5:11,12
[3] Ro 5:3f
[4] Php 3:10

2
THE SECRET OF SUCCESS

'This Book of the Law shall not depart from your mouth,
but you shall meditate on it day and night, so that
you may be careful to do according to all that is written in it.
For then... you will have good success.'[1]

Why do Christian leaders succeed in ministry?

To find out, I posed an open ended question: 'In your opinion, what are the three major reasons why people succeed in ministry?' In response more than 550 explanations were given. These were carefully collated and assembled together. These answers form the basis for this chapter.

The Secret of Success in Christian Leadership

Born Again and Called to Ministry

Not a large number mentioned these requirements for success. No doubt they were taken for granted. But we mention this at the beginning because without conversion and a call to ministry, no one can succeed in ministry.

'You should have the conviction that God has called you. Because of the things one goes through in the ministry, it requires a strong sense of call.'

'You need assurance of the call to the ministry. You may be appointed by people but you are not called by people.'

'If you are called, you will even go without food to serve the Lord.'

'Know why you are in the ministry; know whom you serve. Then you can succeed. Be sure that God is your Master. You trust him to show you what to do. You know the work is not yours.'

Dependence on God in Prayer with the Word

This category comprises many diverse responses but references to 'dependence on God' and 'prayer' are the largest number of responses in the survey. Here are some of their explanations for the secret of success in ministry:

'Faith in God! Unless we see things in God's perspective, it is easy to be sight oriented and make decisions that will harm us.'

'Prayer! I don't see any other reason. Number two and three are still prayer. It is in prayer that you develop a deep relationship with God. You could include the Word of God. In prayer you talk with God. In the Word of God, he speaks to you. I see only prayer [and the Word]. I have an open Bible when I pray so that the two go together.'

'Without prayer and the Word of God, one cannot succeed; without being in tune with God – and this means prayer – one will fail.'

'Prayer has been a great help to me; not just prayer but extra ordinary prayer. I've learned to know God better. My faith is strengthened through prayer. Through prayer I have lots of power to continue on when I feel so discouraged and weak.'

'Intimacy with the Lord in prayer; walking with the Lord.'

'Personal devotional life! I noticed when I am going on well in personal devotions, the ministry also goes on well.' 'One's relationship with the Lord.'

'A close walk with the Lord! The more your focus is away from God, the more you fail.' 'A close relationship with the Lord. This is the Lord's ministry and we must work for him. If there is a close walk with him, listening to his voice, communicating with him, having a close fellowship, God will bless.'

'Devotion to the Lord – someone serious with the Lord. In Psalm 42 we read of a deer panting after water. One needs to thirst after the Lord. One should not take the Lord lightly.'

'One's relationship with the Lord. Success comes first and foremost from God.' 'A daily walk with the Lord.'

'I have never met anyone in ministry who is successful apart from prayer. They all say, "prayer." I spend much time in prayer. In one week I spend one day per week in prayer. I go to the top of the hill to pray and see God dramatically helping.'

Not all the respondents expressed this idea in the same way, namely, 'dependence on God' or 'prayer' or the Word of God. They expressed the same sentiment with different words. One pastor commented:

'At times I have felt, "I know." But knowledge has not made me succeed. But when I trust the Lord, I succeed. When called to ministry, there was no money for my education but I went ahead anyway, trusting the Lord. People advised me not to quit my work. No one supported me for fees. But I quit and went to Scott and God provided. I learned that when I trust God, he provides. For example, one day I prayed with another student at Scott because he had no money. Soon afterwards, God provided. In the youth ministry, I've seen demons leave the children and youth, not by my power.'

Under this category there were other related comments, such as:

Fear of God: 'This is clearly seen when you are challenged to do evil. People recognise you as God fearing. You do not fear loosing a seat but you fear God. Like Joseph who feared God and not the wife of his master.'

Commitment to Know Christ: 'Christ is the Vine and we are the branches. If we are cut off from him...One can be very good intellectually but he doesn't bear fruit. The secret of victory is to abide in him. He is the source of life. Jesus Christ is the One doing it. Abiding in Christ is number one. This involves meditation on the Word of God and prayer.'

Complete Surrender to God: 'Sometimes you seek recognition and honour, but if you surrender to the Lord, he helps you succeed.' 'Abandoning yourself and letting the Holy Spirit use you.'

The Spiritual Life: 'Personal integrity comes from the overflow of one's spiritual life. Once a leader's spiritual life goes down, his managerial skills and relationships also go down. You feel it if you preached a sermon in the power of the Spirit or if you preached it out of routine.'

Knowing the Owner of the Work: 'Have a clear understanding of the Owner of the work – who God is and what kind of God we serve. This is crucial. It is a question of conscience. Knowing that we are God's ministers – sinners saved by grace, without strength, facing the ministry with lots of humility, knowing that we are made from dust. This helps you not to fight.'

Obedience to the Word of God: 'To practice and obey what the Word of God says. To be doers of what we teach. People are after a model, not just words.' 'Sticking to the Word of God so that it changes your character and gives you direction.'

Faithfulness

Faithfulness to God, to the ministry and to one's family was counted as very important in success. Half the respondents mentioned that faithfulness is essential.

'Faithfulness, that is key. One may be godly but not faithful in preparation. Faithfulness in labours is rewarded.'

'Faithfulness, both in money and in ministry! There are lots of temptations. No one supervises you. How do you use your time? Also, one should be faithful to your family; faithfulness in so many areas.'

'Faithfulness to God and to the people! You don't bend the law because of a person. If you say no to sin, let it be no to the senior deacon.'

'Faithfulness to God; love for God; obedience to the Lord – reading the Bible and hearing his voice every day. Anything that has value must have a set of rules. God has a way that we must follow to succeed in ministry.'

'Pastoral work is not like other work. It has no supervisor. It is you to plan visitation and time to study. One must be faithful to God.'

'Many pastors are not faithful. They may be given two Churches; then they go away without informing the Churches. Or they come to preach on Sunday and go away immediately. Some are not faithful in finances. A leader has all power. He has the signature to the bank account and can use the money for his own purposes. Some are not faithful to the flock; nor are they faithful to their own family.'

'Being faithful with God's time, handling God's money with honesty is so important; being faithful to the family and your wife. I find it helpful to have my wife with me so that people know.'

Humility

Two-thirds of all respondents considered humility a most important character trait. So important are their comments that Part Three in this book is devoted to this topic where their words are quoted. Here we will mention other comments related to humility.

Servant-heart: *'He must have a servant's heart.' 'We tend to become bosses, instead of being servants.'*

'The attitude of serving the interests of others! Even Christ came not to serve himself but to serve others.'

'I see how I failed in humility. I failed to serve others. I feared to be seen last. I desired to be seen at the top. Servant leadership has given me the right perspective of all that is involved in leadership.'

'Doing minor work that a pastor should not do.'

'A leader must not have a boss's heart. Sometimes people hurt you. You blame the people saying, "You are not paying enough." But God's work done in God's way has God's provision. Don't think the rich will supply your needs, or that the Church will collapse when the rich become upset. God does not depend on us. We should not boast. If you fail, whenever you leave, God will raise up another donkey. A Spirit filled life is not one of perfection but the ability to apologize, to ask forgiveness. Members easily detect when things are not right, when there is fighting in the Church like in Corinth.'

Teachable: *'You should be able to listen carefully to others and accept their advice. We are not perfect. We don't have all the answers.'*

'You should not feel you know everything. Some elders are not willing to attend Bible study. They cannot be challenged because they don't respect the opinions of others.'

'Make yourself vulnerable, open to criticism and advice.'

'You must be open to rebuke in order to learn.' 'Seek advice.'

Accountable: *'You should not be on your own. You need to be accountable to God, to your superiors and to your wife. Don't act as though you are free in this world.'*

'Accountability, especially in the area of finance! Groups of people need to be involved. One must be transparent. Even in life, one must be accountable.'

'You need to identify a person who can be consulted, possibly a prayer partner, to be accountable to on a daily basis, one who is completely naked before you. No one can say, "I've arrived." You need someone to share your joys and frustrations.'

Godly Character

Under this category we have placed a variety of character traits necessary for success in ministry. At the same time we have excluded such godly character traits as humility, faithfulness, patience and love which are being treated separately elsewhere.

Godly character is essential for anyone to succeed in ministry. *'Leaders must lead by example. Those in a congregation will see him and watch him. This cannot be over emphasised. You are an example by what you say and do; for instance, one must be an example in your prayer life.' As others have said: 'You lead by your life'; 'People want to imitate your life.' A Bible School teacher observed: 'Character surpasses knowledge and skills in ensuring success.' Therefore, one said: 'You must take your character seriously.'*

Various topics under 'godly character' include:

Personal Integrity: *'Personal integrity comes from the overflow of one's spiritual life. Once a leader's spiritual life goes down, his managerial skills and relationship also go down. You feel it if you preached a sermon in the power of the Spirit or if you preached it out of routine.'*

So important is personal integrity that this ranked among the top characteristics of a successful leader.

'We all need to work on this area of integrity in the areas of finance, women and pride. This is a great need. I have seen many Christians and ministers have problems in this area. I know a young pastor who is out of the ministry for seven years because of this. When one is caught with one of these sins, he is usually caught up with other sins as well.'

'Be truthful.' 'Be honest to God and to the people.'

'Say what you mean, and mean what you say.'

'You should be a man of honesty; one that can be trusted.'

'Keep your word. Do what you say. Be responsible.'

'Develop a good name; be above reproach.' 'I would advise that they live what they preach. It helps if you are an example to others.'

'Many leaders do not have an iota of integrity. They are involved in the community's corrupt deals. In fact, I had to reprimand some for being involved in bribery.'

Holiness of Life: *'People may become like the world. Most people live just like the others. It is rare to find a model to follow.'*

'Obedience to the Word of God! It is God's work you are doing.'

'One must hate all sin, especially lying; one must be faithful and not greedy for power.' 'Keep away from all sin.'

'Be a testimony of what you say.' 'Show the way by being an example, having an exemplary life.'

Freedom from Hypocrisy: *'There is a lot of hypocrisy in the Church, a lot of pretense. People pretend. "I love you," they say. People show a different picture outwardly from what they are inwardly. We pretend to love, but we don't.' 'Live what you preach; don't preach what you don't live.'*

Sincerity of Heart: *'Sincerity in ministry. You must do the ministry you sincerely believe God has called you to do. You think, talk, dream of your ministry and are willing to die for it.'*

'You need to have sincerity of heart.'

'You need to be practical in life. Do I practice what I preach? I need to be an example.'

Controlled by the Spirit: *'Being led by the Spirit.'*

'There are divisions and in-fighting in the Church, rushing to the courts or to the police to arrest a colleague. All this is due to Church leaders not being led by the Spirit. Any disagreement in the Church they rush to the police to arrest another pastor. One bishop actually used guns, firing them to scare the people.'

Truthfulness: *'Speaking truth in line with the Word of God. Being truthful has really helped me in my ministry. If I speak the truth, it may create heat and conflict, but people know it and it heals. For example, one pastor took money; he actually put other pastors in prison. The Bishop knew about it but in the Central Church Council it was covered up. I tabled it. The truth was spoken. There was lots of heat. We insisted that those pastors be taken out of the cells who were wrongly accused.'*

Perseverance and Patience

If one is to persevere, he must have patience. If one has patience, he will persevere. Therefore, we shall consider these together. Well over half the respondents considered perseverance and patience vital in success.

'Leadership needs lots of patience. Decide to be nothing. Always prepare to be a loser. This is the situation and there is no other solution.'

'Sometimes you decide on doing things and they are not done. People give excuses. You must be patient with people or you will give up.'

'Bear with people. Be patient in serving. Some things are very hard.'

'Be able to hold on and not give up.' 'You need staying power.'

'The pastor handles different kinds of people and he needs patience.'

'One person I know was tested in many ways. The key has been patience and forbearance. He was falsely accused but he continued and is now blessed.'

Patience is required to persevere; without perseverance you will quit.

'You need perseverance when things are difficult; you keep on persevering.'

'You need staying power. There have been so many discouragements but the Lord has kept me going. I should have quit a long time ago. The pastor has a very difficult ministry; so many do not appreciate him. What do you do? Quit? No, you stay.'

'Our Church lacked funds for two months so the pastors were not paid for two months. The District Church Council was not to be blamed because the little they collected was used in official matters. Some felt like giving up the ministry and going into business. A good number were about to leave. They complained a lot. Others did not complain; they persevered. They waited until the time they were paid. It was a tough situation. Those who *persevered recalled those pastors in the 1930's who were not paid. Given money or not, they continued in ministry.'*

Love for the People

Interpersonal relationship skills are essential for success in leadership. At the heart of this is a deep love for the people. As one said, *'People must feel the love of their leaders. They must love people. Leaders must always go the extra mile for people even when it hurts. Leaders must not always listen to their feelings. The feelings of the leader must come second and the feelings of the others must come first.'*

'One must love people, welcoming them without discrimination.' 'One must have a warm personality, and be warm towards people.' 'Do everything in love, even correcting people in love.' 'Speak the truth in love.' 'Love people despite their character. Hatred destroys the Church. Some pastors and people do not speak to one another.'

'They should have a burden for people. They should see the need of people and learn how to help them. A 'burden' is love shown in action. Leaders must have love for the people.'

There is much more to say about inter-personal relationships which are reserved for Part Four in the book.

CONCLUSION

The fascinating fact is this. When experienced servants of the Lord in the field were asked: 'In your opinion, what are the three major reasons why people succeed in ministry?' The overwhelming number mentioned the above character traits. *Character* is of utmost importance for success in leadership.

Scattered responses referred to leadership or management skills, such as planning, decision making, organising, controlling, delegating or leadership. They were mentioned but they were only a fraction of all other emphases on the spiritual nature of leadership. And that is the way it should be because that is the biblical emphasis as well.

However, many did indicate the importance of skills in leadership. This will be the topic for the next chapter.

SEARCHING THE SCRIPTURE WITH APPLICATION

1. Why do you think the vast majority of reasons for success in ministry are spiritual? Mention several reasons for this.
2. In the light of Jn 15:1-8, why is the devotional life of the servant-leader so important?
3. Evaluate your own devotional life of prayer and Bible meditation.
   a. Do you regularly meet with God in prayer and Bible meditation daily?
   b. Do you feel in your heart that you are meeting with God and growing in the Lord? Or do you have devotions out of a sense of duty?
   c. Are you growing in the Lord or do you feel stagnant spiritually?
   d. Do you truly depend on the Lord for guidance and help in ministry?
4. What steps should you take to grow in your dependence on God?
5. Can a Church expand and grow under leadership without spiritual qualifications? What are the consequences according to 1 Co 3:10-15?
6. Why is faithfulness to God of such great importance according to the following Scriptures? 1 Co 4:1-6; Mt 24:36-51 (esp. v 45); Lk 16:1-15.
7. Humility is essential for a servant of the Lord who 'made himself nothing, taking the form of a servant…' (Php 2:7). In addition, there are practical considerations.
   a. Why must a Christian leader with more education be extra concerned about humility when serving with lesser trained elders or pastors?
   b. How does pride affect relationships (Php 2:3,4)?
   c. What practical steps can you take to demonstrate from the heart a spirit of humility before others with whom you serve?
8. Integrity is 'soundness of moral character; honesty.'
   a. What kinds of behaviour do Christian leaders sometimes engage in that shows lack of integrity?
   b. What steps can you take to ensure 'sound moral character'?
9. According to Heb 12:1-3, what is the secret of running life's race with perseverance?
10. Why is love so important and critical in leadership positions (as well in Christian living) according to the following passages?
   (a) 1 Co 13:1-3;
   (b) Ro 13:8-10;
   (c) Gal 5:13-15

Endnote [1] Jos 1:8

3
SKILLS OF CHRISTIAN LEADERSHIP

'We have different gifts, according to the grace given us...; if it is leadership, let him govern diligently.'[1]

Why is this chapter so short on skills for Christian leadership?

The significance of this chapter is twofold: first, it is the shortest of all. This reflects the answers from the Christian leaders interviewed. The question was very open ended: 'In your opinion, what are the three major reasons why people succeed in ministry?' The vast majority of answers dealt with spiritual qualifications of character. We could have doubled the size of Chapter 2. In fact, large numbers specifically mentioned 'humility,' 'patience' and 'integrity;' but nothing similar occurred with reference to skills of leadership. The total number of all comments on skills (gifts) of leadership was few compared to character traits. Therefore, this unit is brief, reflecting that reality.

The second significance of this chapter, however, is that it is found here. Though dependence on God and godly character are the bedrock of leadership, that is not all that is required of Christian leaders. Someone who is very godly but lacking gifts and skills for leadership cannot be an effective leader. As one respondent said, '*The gift of leadership is important for success. Many leaders are simply elected to the position because of wealth and relationships.*'

The structure of this book has been shaped by this reality. More attention is devoted to the spiritual aspect of leadership than skills of leadership. But a significant portion is devoted to leadership skills. Many emphasised: '*You must receive good academic training; you must know many things.*'

'*Training is important. One cannot minimise academic preparation; but this can be counterproductive. If your walk with the Lord is not right, education cannot make you successful in the ministry.*'

What skills must Christian leaders have to succeed in ministry?

Christian Leaders Need Managerial Skills

The managerial skills, mentioned by the leaders, include:

Planning: *'A visionary leader. One needs to have a vision. "Where there is no vision, the people perish."'*

'You need a dream. If you have no vision, you go in a vicious circle. To have a vision makes life exciting. You know where you are going. Working with people can be difficult when there is criticism, but you persist with your dream.'

'You need a clear focus. What do you want to achieve? What are you there for? Do you have a clear idea of where you are going? Do you have direction and a reason for being in the ministry? Vision includes goals.'

'Understand your work and plan for it. In my first church we made a five year plan to know where we were going. If there is no plan, the leader will stumble. In the next church I discussed with the elders, to make a plan, where to take the people in worship, evangelism and education. Where do we want to go? We made a five year plan. We had two prayer meetings, the one in the church had 4-8 people attending and the one in a home had 20. Yet the church had 580 members. I felt there was a need for 20 prayer groups. The elders laughed. The church was there since 1969 and had only two prayer meetings. How could they develop 20 within five years? I told them we will evangelise, bring 50 more people into church. They thought this was impossible. In five years we had 10 prayer groups with 350 attending. The Sunday service grew from 580 people to 1,200. I taught seminars on evangelism. We had seminars for leaders every month. We established Biblical Education by Extension and there was none before. After five years they said, 'This is amazing.' It was because of planning.'

Decision Making: Respondents indicated that decision making must be wise and firm. '*Wisdom is needed, what to say and how to handle problems.*' '*Decisiveness in decision making is important; being firm in knowing what is true.*' '*Godly wisdom and discernment are important.*'

Organising: '*You need to be organised and skilled in management. Some church members have higher qualifications than you have as the pastor.*'

'In ministry you need to plan and organise how you are to do the ministry. Pray to God to actualise your plans.'

'Periodic evaluation is needed after six months to see where you have succeeded or failed. Many pastors do not evaluate what they have done. My training did not show everything to do. This came from within me.'

Delegation: In order to accomplish a goal one needs to train others and delegate responsibility to them. '*I've learned that it is so rewarding to equip people to do something, instead of doing everything myself. Don't get trapped in the busy syndrome. I got into the same problem. I was so busy but not producing. I went around putting out fires, but after I left, the fire broke out again. I asked, "What am I doing?" I decided to let people do it. I only counseled and preached.*'

Christian Leaders need Leadership Skills

Many random statements were made, pointing to different character traits that lead to success in leadership and ministry.

Diligence: The Scripture says that if you have the gift of leadership you should '*govern diligently.*'[2] It is of interest that more respondents mentioned the importance of *diligence* in leadership than any other character trait. As one said, '*One must have a sense of responsibility and not be careless.*'

'*When called to the ministry you should do it happily and with all your energy. You should not take it as a part time job.*'

'*Diligence and hard work are essential – with aggressiveness.*'

'*Commitment to one's assignment is essential; dedication to the ministry.*'

'*Commitment and eagerness to serve are important; one must work hard.*'

Self-discipline: '*I struggle with keeping time – taking care of my devotional life, staying on schedule to follow a series of messages. There are things no one sees you are doing.*' Therefore, success requires one to be '*self-driven.*' One must have '*determination to succeed.*' '*Discipline and devotion are essential; a resolve to act according to our knowledge of who God is and who we are.*'

Motivation: Self-discipline is a character trait that is strengthened by proper motivation. '*Having the right motivation is essential. Whether you are rewarded or not, to know that you are serving God should motivate you.*' Another motivation is '*the conviction of being in the will of God.*' '*If one doubts that you are in the will of God, you cannot put your all into it.*'

Enthusiasm: '*You must maintain zeal and enthusiasm in the ministry.*' '*You should be a "go-getter." If you just follow, it will never happen.*'

Time conscious: '*Don't waste your time.*' '*Be a good manager of time.*'

Manages family well and has a faithful wife: This was indicated by many.

'*If the family breaks down, you are hurt. You need a family that works.*'

'*Success of a pastor depends on his relationship with his wife and children. If she does not share his vision, it becomes a tug of war. You have someone dragging you back.*'

'*A united family is essential. If the family is torn, there can be problems. When love is in the family, one can work hard.*'

CONCLUSION

These Christian leaders interviewed appreciated their training in college but they felt a need to keep growing. '*We did get a good education at College but you can't go with the idea that you know it all. You must go out to learn.*' '*Learning is a process. It doesn't end with graduation. Much learning continues afterwards.*' With this thought in mind, this book has been designed to help make you into an effective Christian leader with leadership skills.

We further probed these Christian leaders to learn what kind of problems they actually faced in ministry. 'To be forewarned is to be forearmed.' Surprises can be devastating, especially when someone is unprepared. The following chapter lays out the challenges these Christian leaders faced in ministry.

SEARCHING THE SCRIPTURE WITH APPLICATION

1. Spiritual qualifications and leadership skills are both essential. In order to develop leadership skills, education is important. Consider the following comments by leaders: '*Without a Bible School education leaders do not understand the deeper things of the Word of God. Or he does not understand the contemporary issues facing the church, such as HIV/AIDS. Without knowledge, what can he do?*' '*Training is very, very important.*' '*One must be as well equipped as he can be.*'
   In light of the above statements, consider the following example:

'A lay leader, with basic primary school education up to Class 4, worked with the church in evangelism. The church did not pay him. He devoted himself to God. Now he is very old. He is one of the most successful ministers I know. God sustained him. God blessed his family materially. He is still strong in the gospel and respected by the people in his village. You learn the fear of God in him. His children are highly placed in business and also God fearing. One son said that he showed his father his beautiful house. The father replied, "Can you imagine if this were your house in heaven?" He was so God conscious. The son said, "That changed my life completely and made me want to invest in heaven."'

   a. What does all this suggest about the relative importance of spiritual qualifications and education?
   b. No doubt the man mentioned above with Standard IV education was gifted by the Spirit, and perhaps with a keen intellect he picked up ideas informally along the way.

   Does this example disprove the need for training in leadership skills? Why?

2. Consider the following biblical examples:
   a. '*Now when they saw the boldness of Peter and John, and perceived that they were uneducated, common men, they were astonished*' (Ac 4:13).
   And yet these apostles had been in the School of Christ for three years; furthermore, they learned by doing, practicing on their preaching tours. So they were uneducated by some standards but were they really uneducated? Why?
   b. Moses was one of the outstanding leaders of the Old Testament. Read Ac 7:20-22. How did God use the education he received in Pharaoh's court?
   c. Paul was one of the outstanding leaders in the New Testament. Paul declared, 'Under Gamaliel I was thoroughly trained in the law of our fathers…' (Ac 22:3). Gamaliel was the most honoured rabbi of the first century in the city of Jerusalem. Describe the ways Paul's education helped him in ministry?
3. Do you have proven gifts of leadership? What steps can you take to grow?

Endnotes

[1] Rom 12:6f *NIV*

[2] Rom 12:8

4
CHALLENGES IN LEADERSHIP

'Let us run with perseverance the race marked out for us.
Let us fix our eyes on Jesus... who for the joy set before him endured the cross, scorning its shame,
and
sat down at the right hand of the throne of God.'[1]

Must Jesus bear the cross alone and we have none to bear?

Serving the Lord is a glorious privilege; this includes the privilege of bearing the cross with Jesus. 'If anyone would come after me,' Jesus said, 'let him deny himself and take up his cross and follow me.'[2] But everyone's cross is shaped differently, just as the running lanes of the race are marked out differently for each person. 'The race marked out for us' may not be what we would choose; it most certainly is different from others. But it is what God has sovereignly planned for his glory and our good. In preparing for the role of Christian leadership, we should not venture forth in ignorance but with full understanding of the challenges involved.

Each one of the Christian leaders we interviewed was asked this question: 'Describe one or more problems [challenges] you have faced in the ministry which have caused you personal pain.' Following are their answers.

The Challenges in Leadership

Financial Challenges

The one-word answer most frequently heard was *finance*, with 34% mentioning this challenge. Pastors, Bible School and College teachers, Church workers, missionaries and other Church leaders lack adequate support. Some do not have adequate housing near their ministry; others lack transportation to their ministry, or finance to pay for public means of transport, hence they walk long distances; others lack books for study. They comment:

'The most painful part is the finance. This causes us pain. We are paid so little that we cannot meet our needs. You are only given enough to eat today and you do not know about tomorrow. We have visitors and as a pastor we must feed them.'

'One big problem upper-most is financial. It is a big problem to serve the Lord in Church when you don't have support; it is very painful. What we receive is not enough for basic living expenses. You don't have enough to pay for medical expenses and education of the children. But God has helped us.'

'Most ministers of the Church say the same thing – lack of support. You discuss this with the administration but they do not see it. There is no change. The pastor is to be an example to the flock in giving of offering and tithe. One must also pay for public transport. But little money is received compared to the expenses. You just wonder. I talk to the leaders but there is no change. Sometimes I feel like moving from the Church. It is not easy, but I pray. Sometimes the pain ceases.'

'The pastor's support is not enough to support a family with two children in Secondary School. We strive to pay for their fees. Sometimes traveling is difficult. But 'pain' seems to be an extreme word. It has not been that serious.'

Relational Challenges

Although *finance* was the one word most frequently mentioned as a challenge, 67% of respondents reported pain in relational challenges. Following are some of the challenges mentioned.

Jealousy: *'The greatest challenge is jealousy. People see your competence and they feel bad. They feel threatened, so they try to suppress and finish you.'*

'One of the biggest problems of those ministers more highly educated is that people see you as too learned because of your level of education. There is misunderstanding and jealousy as a result. Because you are led by people without a vision, they frustrate you. If you are from a higher level institution, you are never ordained but those from lower level Bible Schools are ordained.'

'Opposition from Church ministers is a major challenge. I noticed that education is very important; but the more you have, the more threatened some leaders feel.'

'Just before graduation, my home Church leaders were not ready to receive me. They said that they have no position for a person with a degree. That was near the time of elections. They were afraid of not being elected. They asked me what my plan was. They wanted me to stay at home. Now that I am teaching in the Bible School, some people are happy that I am out of their way. Being rejected by my own people was so painful. My expectation was that they would receive me. It was so painful in my heart. The Church leaders did not come to my graduation. Now that I teach in the Bible School I can talk to them because I am out of their system.'

'The Principal of the Bible School felt that he was incompetent and that I was a threat to him. We found that we could not stay in the Bible School, though the students appreciated us so much. The Church leaders feared that I would become the Chairman of the District Church Council. You could tell the pastors were not happy with me but the ordinary people were happy. This has been one of the most challenging things we have faced in life.'

Suspension and Rejection: Official licensing and ordination are withheld.

'Twice I've been stopped from preaching in Church because of jealousy. This has caused a lot of pain because people misunderstand us. Why are you treated so? Once a pastor is terminated, people quickly think it is because of immorality. People are suspicious; they gossip. This causes a lot of pain. Also, you are without support.'

'It is a paradox. Graduates from upper level schools preach nicely and people love them. But graduates from other schools feel threatened. I am not officially licensed yet after fifteen years of ministry. Others from low level Bible Schools are licensed to give communion in two years. Then during Church elections they say I cannot hold office because I am not ordained.'

Leadership Struggles: *'Church politics with leadership struggles is so painful. When people colluded to say that I was not doing well, it was just for the purpose of protecting their positions. They sacked me, terminated my services from the Church for fourteen months. It gave me great pain.'*

'There is a lot of Church politics when one is a Church leader; we are attacked. It was just the same with our Lord Jesus Christ who was attacked unreasonably.'

'When I was pastoring a Church I was purged with much pain. The Chairman heard praise of my competence. He felt threatened so he sent me to serve in a distant place. He tried to tame me. In my new Church I visited every family and people came back to Church so the Church was full. They really supported me. I knew all the people by name. Then the Chairman called me from that place to tame me. He assigned me to be a pastor where he could oversee me. I had to gain permission from the Chairman to visit anyone. He said I could never visit a family unless he accompanied me, but he was never available to accompany me. I desired to start a youth ministry, but he never put it on the agenda for the business meeting. I recommended that we make a preaching programme with preachers appointed to speak on different topics. The Chairman rejected this because that would mislead the Church. He feared that only a few would come to hear him. He never told me when I would preach until Friday. On Sunday the Chairman came fifteen minutes late. I thought he was not coming so I gave the Scripture reading for my message to the man who read the Scripture. Then the Reverend (Chairman) came fifteen minutes late and gave the Scripture reading to the same one to read. This hurt me so much because I thought I was preaching.'

Misunderstanding: A pastor's wife was misunderstood and this brought much pain. *'Generally, in Church the pastor's work is not understood. We put our family first. I did voluntary work in Church. As a mother of young children I was not able to be away from home for a long time. 'Don't give me any post,'* she said to the district Church leaders. *'But they did not understand me. They complained. I was really hurt because the other ladies were older and had no small children. I was a young mother.'*

'Most pastors with whom we work are from different Bible Schools and Bible classes. Sometimes it is very hard to discuss with them serious problems facing the Church. It is easy to be misunderstood by them.

They are graduates of Primary Schools. I find it hard to help them understand some issues. Sometimes we discuss and we differ due to the gap of education.'

'There was a lack of understanding by the elders. When I started in the Church ministry, I was a threat to the leaders. There was a lot of insecurity with those people to the extent that they did not want to hear me or to help me.'

Falsely Accused: Many reported that they were slandered by fellow workers. One pastor was accused of immorality so that another pastor could replace him in leadership; another was accused because the senior pastor was unhappy that he was loved by the youth.

'Being accused of what you have not done is so painful. I was falsely accused of having two wives and also of negligence.'

'This is a very emotional question. Some years back we were shocked to receive a letter from so-called "all the pastors of the Church." That letter was addressed to me, saying that I had not conducted myself well. They said that I had won the elections because I had washed in charms. That caused a lot of pain. Up to this point my wife and I found it difficult to accept and wondered how any one would have thought of that. They further accused me of having a child out of wedlock, one who is now eleven years old and that I was feeding it with a long spoon. I could not have a child out of wedlock and I said I would love to see that child. They said that they did not know but they were continuing their investigation. They never found any child. I never washed in charms. It was just a rumour. This was very painful to me.'

'There was a rumour that spread some years back which I heard through my wife. "What is your relationship with the wife of so-and-so?" she asked. She knew the rumour was not true. It went to the District Church Council and another Church department. It was a rumour that I had a love affair with another woman. The rumour said that the wife's husband caught me and and forgave me once. At mid-night he found me sleeping again. The second time he tied me and asked me to give enough money to release him. I had 3,000/shillings in my pocket, the rumour said, and I gave this to him. But he was not satisfied. He went to my father for money. It was reported that my father said I was a bad son and he was tired of me, so he gave a cow. I was so stunned by the report from my wife that I could not speak for thirty minutes. That reported rumour is what is done culturally when a man finds his wife unfaithful. But the person is tied up and beaten but that did not happen. After thirty minutes I spoke. "It sounds true," I said. "You are my witness. I never keep 3,000/shillings in my pocket. I have never stayed out after 8:00 P.M. If a cow was given, you are witness." I congratulated her that she had kept quiet for three months and investigated the matter. She knew it was not true.'

Divisions: Divisions can be so great that pastors cannot pray together.

'Disagreements are a major challenge. There is always someone who has a contrary idea, especially among Church elders. Some desire to take a different direction. Everyone has different conceptions on issues.'

'The division that occurred in our Church caused me great pain. One thing that I thought we would always understand was that we should never take a Christian brother to court. This has caused me pain; it has affected my family relationships. It has affected me so greatly. At one point I thought it best to leave our Church. Then I realised that there is no perfect Church.'

Hostility of Co-workers: *'Opposition from my co-workers is a major problem. The people I thought would support me have not.'*

'Hostility from my co-pastors is a challenge. Some even hate me. They see my gifts and are jealous. I've been denied ordination. They fear that if I am ordained I will get their seat. Lay people want me to be ordained so I can marry them, but leaders oppose this.'

'Some time after my graduation my denomination chose me to be Assistant General Secretary but this was a threat to the General Secretary. They assigned me a particular job and the sponsor in UK requested that someone should be sent there for a visit. The Church recommended me to go to UK. But the General Secretary was not happy. "Why not just send a delegate?" So he wrote a nasty letter to the donor in UK and said I was not the head of the Church, that I knew little and that he was the head. After returning from UK, after many days of prayer and seeking counsel from others, I thought it best to see the General Secretary. He said that I was arrogant and not giving him due respect as the General Secretary. It was painful because he had also written to the Mission. This was very painful.'

Interaction with People: *'Interaction with people is not easy. Some groups don't accept you because of age. They don't appreciate what you are doing.'*

'All the men in the Church were with me – except for one old man who never saw it the same way. He was very negative; he could not appreciate anything. It hurt when people did not understand.' 'In any Church you must encounter one troublemaker.'

'Working with people always has its ups and downs. We've had opposition when we stand for the truth. We have been forced out of a local Church because some people didn't like what we preached.'

Tribalism: Tribalism and clanism are mentioned as problems in ministry by numbers of Christian leaders. One pastor said, *'Tribalism has caused me personal pain. I came here to serve but I find tribal feelings.'* The Church leaders threatened that he would never be ordained and that they would even follow him to his home area to prevent him from being ordained.

Gender Challenge

For the women who enter ministry there is an additional challenge that arises from the gender gap and marital status. Single women may be misunderstood in ministry. Moreover, women trained for ministry feel frustrated because they are not free to use their gifts and training.

'Because of my status as a single woman, people do not accept my recommendations. There is a gender problem in the Church. They do not accept leadership positions for women. Although there is something you are able to do, they feel a woman should not do that. It is painful at times, because I feel I can do it but they choose men.'

'In our Churches people expect to be recognised for the work they do. But a lady graduate is not recognised. Their support is little compared to men.'

'It is not easy to be a pastor's wife. Members of the Church often have specific expectations for the pastor's wife and it can be very frustrating to try to live up to them. Some may feel threatened by a pastor's wife who is very active and wants to be involved. Others may ridicule a pastor's wife who feels not very competent for a leadership role. Others view you as a superhuman being since you are married to the pastor and you supposedly live in a utopia kind of home. I was counseling one lady who told me that I cannot understand her problems since I am married to the pastor.'

'It is a bad experience to know that my boss looks down on me because I am a woman and he thinks a

woman cannot excel. It is a cultural thing to think that women are like children and cannot do anything worthwhile.'

Leadership Challenges

There are many challenges that stem from leadership. Frustration can result because of poor leadership skills of those leaders above you.

A pastor may train members to do certain things, but they prove unable to do it or don't want to do it or they are negligent. People can be slow to learn.

A leader may try to keep time but the people delay, causing great frustration. Meetings are scheduled but they begin several hours late.

Leaders find loneliness in the ministry – no one to share and pray with. '*Sometimes you get so involved in the work that you almost become lonely.*'

Opposition arises from the Church against vigorous mass evangelism.

Cultural problems arise so that when troubles come, Christians fall away.

Ecclesiastical Challenges

Additional challenges may be classified as *ecclesiastical challenges.*

Rigid Elders: On the one hand, trained pastors should learn how to relate well with their elders, and learn to appreciate them. On the other hand, the elders should value and respect their pastor who, though he may lack some experience, has learned much for the ministry. Rigid elders can be painful.

'Some elders feel that they know more than the pastor and they challenge you in the ministry. It is not easy to work with elders. It has been so painful. Elders never went to Bible School, but they feel they know the Bible more than you do. It is not easy. As a pastor you should be a resource person for them. Yet they feel they know more than you do. You reach a point where you may feel you are not being used in the right way.'

'Elders are strong on tradition; for example, clapping of hands or singing choruses are problems with them. We need lots of wisdom.'

'These elders! You know they are not saved. They are a hindrance to the ministry. They block everything. You hear of an elder who wants to move you. One year two elders said they wanted to throw me out.'

'When the pastor opposes wrongdoing, the elders oppose him. The Church elders are stronger than the pastors so the pastors are frustrated.'

Councils: *'Our Church always has people going to councils. But rarely do they put into practice or carry out the decisions of the councils. They just talk. Next time they talk around the same thing.'*

'The pain I have is administration. The spiritual aspect is overtaken by social activities. The emphasis is not on Church growth or spiritual things but more on administration, councils and finance. This is painful.'

Transfers: *'There are constant transfers and changes of duties.'*

'If they see you excel and do well, they move you to a smaller Church.'

'When you are sent to a Church, you want to start a project. Then you are plucked away prematurely. This is painful.'

CONCLUSION

After one reads these comments on the challenges in Christian leadership, one might collapse and give up. The faithful servants of God in ministry, however, have learned the secret of persevering:

'In the ministry, we need perseverance because of the challenges of many kinds. Perseverance and trust in God are the keys.'

'I've learned that if I am called by God, there is no quitting. Regardless of what comes my way – slander, suffering, discouragement, and unhappiness – I must not quit. I must not be distracted from my focus which is on Jesus Christ. I must keep on going. This is not easy. To be a Christian – the name is a very nice word – but to live it is not easy. I must live the name I have.'

Christian leaders cannot dwell on these challenges; they must fix their eyes on Jesus who saved them, called them and will reward their faithfulness.

Through years of experience they have learned valuable lessons that can benefit those who would listen. The following chapter surveys the valuable lessons these Christian leaders have learned from these challenges. Growth in grace comes only through pain and suffering.

SEARCHING THE SCRIPTURE WITH APPLICATION

1. Financial struggles are real and cannot be dismissed lightly. Read the following passages inthe Bible and discuss how those principles might help guide someone who struggles with inadequate financial support.
   a. Php 4:19. How does one distinguish between 'need' and 'desire'? How should one respond to the promise of Php 4:19?
   b. Php 4:11-13. What does Paul imply when he says he 'learned' to be content? Is it natural and human to be content or to be discontent?
   c. How does one learn to be 'content' in 'whatever the circumstances,' especially when financial 'need' prevails?
   d. 2 Co 6:3-11, especially v. 10. From your own experience, how can one be 'poor' and yet 'make many rich'? How can one 'have nothing' and yet 'possess everything'?
   e. Ac 18:1-3; 20:33-35; 1 Co 4:11-12; 1 Th 2:9. When and why did Paul decide to work with his hands, making tents, in addition to preaching the gospel?
   f. How have you handled your financial struggles?
   g. What lessons learned from Scripture should help you in the future?
2. What lessons can be learned from the attitude of Paul towards those who preached 'out of envy and rivalry'? Php 1:15-18.
3. What should be our motivation in service despite all the challenges in leadership? Compare the motive of Paul according to Ac 20:22-24.
4. Why do you think there is sometimes hostility towards co-workers in the Churches? See Gal 5:19-22; Eph 4:25-32; Col 3:5-17.
5. What steps should be taken to eliminate hostility among Church leaders and promote greater love?

6. Are Church leaders justified in their attitude towards women Church workers? What should be done to resolve this discrimination among women Church leaders?
7. Misunderstanding is common in social groupings. What actions should be taken to resolve those misunderstandings?
8. What is the chief cause for strife and divisions and power struggles among Church leaders? What steps should Church members and leaders take to eliminate division and promote love and unity among the brethren?

Endnotes

[1] Heb 12:1f

[2] Mt 16:24

5
LESSONS LEARNED IN LEADERSHIP

'Although he was a son, he learned obedience through what he suffered.'[1]

How profound! Jesus *learned* obedience through what he suffered.

He never disobeyed; nor was he inclined to do so. Jesus was the spotless, sinless Lamb of God. Nevertheless, as new challenges came his way, he *learned* to obey. Even so the servants of God *learn* many lessons through the painful trials which God leads them through so they may be perfected in his likeness.

Following up the previous chapter of study, these Christian leaders were asked, '*What practical lessons have you learned from these painful experiences*?' Taking a cue from these responses, many whole chapters later in this book will focus on in-depths study of the issues mentioned here.

Lessons Learned

Following is a summary of their comments.

Perseverance

The largest number of leaders responded that *perseverance* and *patience* are the lessons they learned. Briefly, we mention some of their comments.

'God allows these things to make me trust him so that I will persevere.'

'I've learned to be very, very patient.'

'Endurance; be slow to speak; be patient and let God deal with the matter. Some things that seemed hard are now possible. For example, like this house. I could not imagine being able to build a house because of my low income. When I graduated I could not believe that I could be a Church leader and Chairman

of a District. I'm trying to give positions away. Through patience and humility it came. I never struggled for it.'

When these experienced Christian leaders offered advice to those beginning in ministry, they vigorously affirmed the importance of perseverance. *'We need to persevere. There are painful things in the ministry, slander and rejection, but we need to look to God and keep on going.'*

Trust in the Lord

Dependence on God is a major lesson learned. Here are a few comments.

'I have learned to trust God and to serve him despite people.'

'One day I will face God and give a report. We trust in God for direction, what to do. He is our Supplier.'

'When I look to myself, I can only be depressed. But when I look to the Lord and ask for his enablement, I find help. I go to him with a heavy heart and he gives me joy. On some occasions I have not trusted him, even grumbling or retaliating or using my authority; but all I get is more resentment. I have learned every time I go to my Good Shepherd, he graciously provides.'

'I have learned that the Lord will never leave me nor forsake me.'

'I have learned to depend on God for our support. We learned not to trust an organisation but to trust God who is Jehovah Jirah. Whether there is a salary or not, God is our support as long as we are in his will.'

'I've learned to depend on God and not on people who have money. Our ministry is biblical. We knocked and knocked on doors for funds but people did not give. I learned I must depend on God. Since then he has provided up to now. We always learn to trust in God. When a problem arises, we sit and pray and see God answering.'

'I've learned to trust God in finance. Initially, I was terribly fearful. I kept praying. God taught me to trust. I don't struggle. I see God providing through the month.'

'It is absolutely important at all times to let go and let God have his way. We are not able to succeed in our wisdom. God does bring change in his own way.'

These Christian leaders unanimously declare that trust in God is the foremost requirement to persevere through the many challenges.

'Foremost, you go into ministry serving God directly. You need to trust him in all that you do in your daily needs and work, because things will be hard. The main thing is to trust the Lord. That is the foremost thing I would say.'

'I've learned to trust God in every situation. No matter how dark it is, God is in control. God has seen me through difficult situations. The more I've been in ministry and face challenges, I know I can do it with God's help. I am not scared as I used to be. God will see me through every situation. Keep on plodding on. I know God is there to lift me and to carry me through.'

Prayerfulness

Another major lesson learned from challenges is to turn to God in prayer.

'The more problems, the more you depend on prayer. Prayer is essential. It is always my support. The more problems you have, the more you go down on your knees and pray to God.'

'When you have problems, you move closer and closer to God.'

'What helped me most was that I kept on praying. Once I went to Machakos for one week to pray and call upon the Lord for direction. It was not in vain. It removed my bitterness. We have kept on track; only reconciliation and forgiveness will keep a person. So we were not overly broken because we kept in tune with the Lord.'

'One always needs to go to God for encouragement. Unless one keeps his relationship with God, one would be discouraged. To overcome discouragement, one must be near God.'

Nothing can exaggerate the importance of prayer in the thinking of these Christian leaders. Time after time, person after person, all stress the importance of the devotional life with God in prayer and the Word.

'What I've learned is that the best child of God is the one closest to God. That means there is need for constant reading of the Word of God and prayer and seeking him. I found that wisdom is not in books. It is from God. If you lack wisdom, ask God. I don't belittle books. I buy books all the time. Most of my money is spent on good books. God the Holy Spirit uses books. But being close to God and reading the Word of God, that is it.'

Humility

Without humility no servant of the Lord will survive with grace and love.

'Humility has been a very tough lesson. By serving in a place where I am threatened and ostracised because of my tribe, I have been humbled more than ever before.'

'I've learned to keep quiet. When co-workers oppose me, I don't oppose them.'

'We should not assume we are learned. I have learned not to show myself as a threat. I serve humbly. I've learned to be so humble, so I can be of help to them. I try to be simple and cooperative. I have come not to threaten them but to be a co-worker.'

'I have learned to have shock absorbers. We are all human beings and have failures. As I see them fail, they see me fail. We need humility, forgiveness and patience.'

'I've learned to work without someone recognising or appreciating what I do. I realised that they never tell you. The result of my work is not for the applause of people but for the praise of God.'

Forgiveness

No one can succeed in leadership without a forgiving heart.

'From the human point of view, one can become bitter. The Lord taught me a lesson of forgiveness. I did not do anything wrong; but I will leave it to God. He is the righteous Judge. I felt peace in my heart.'

'I've learned the whole lesson of forgiveness. I went through a period of disillusionment and trauma. But the Lord told me to forgive. I went to the Chairman and I told him I have nothing against him.'

'If you fail to forgive, you will always fight. Forgiveness is especially important.'

'Without love and forgiveness, it would be very hard to minister. Many step on your toes and sin against you.'

'If I don't forgive, I don't feel well in the ministry. One big lesson is to develop a forgiving heart. This has helped me. I felt so much pain. This has helped me as I pray for them and I see God coming in to help.'

'Forgiveness is a lesson I learned. To forgive the sins of violence from the tribal clashes was a real task. To preach on forgiveness and reconciliation was the hardest sermon to communicate to those who suffered from the brutal tribal clashes. It was very hard; we shed tears.'

God's Faithfulness

Experience confirms to all of God's servants that God truly is faithful.

'Let them go into the field, not afraid of what they will eat. God is faithful. They should not doubt God. They have chosen a noble job. It is the highest calling one can receive. If I would start all over again, I would be a pastor again. I want to assure them that God is faithful. My wife and I can testify to this. We have never gone hungry.'

'When we remain faithful to God, he will always remain faithful to us. Not only does he give me more, he gives me peace. You don't have enough but you feel satisfied and settled. You can serve faithfully.'

'God has not forsaken us as a family. Even when there was no job, he provided.' 'God is always with us.'

Contentment

'Learn to be content with what the Lord provides us.'

'I've learned to lean on God for provision. I was getting 600/sh. ($8) per month after graduation. Through being satisfied with what I got, I said, let it be sufficient for me. I will live in my budget. The Lord has provided for my needs.'

Acceptance

'Learn from the situation and adjust to it in a positive way.'

'Tolerance; I've learned to accept people the way they are.'

'I've learned to live with leaders who are jealous and offend me. It is not easy but by faith I've learned to do it.'

'I am still in pain from frustration of being in the ministry as a woman. Apart from trusting the Lord, I learned just accepting it. It takes a long time for people to know things have changed. I've learned to do what I can, and take it as it is. Some in the Church are learning. It will take time.'

Wisdom

Wisdom is needed for many situations. Singles need to take care when reaching out to others in ministry; men need wisdom when counseling women.

'I've learned to be very cautious, especially when making a promise, when relying on the promise of others. Before I promise, I see if I can fulfill it.'

'Not all those people who speak positive things about you are with you. Those you regard as your close friends may be bitter with you.'

Pain Universal

'Just as Jesus said, we will have trouble and pain from family or ministry. Pain is bound to come.'

'As a family we've always had it good. Now my eyes are open to see life, that it has pain. These are the realities of life – to see what people go through.'

Practical Lessons

The lessons in character, heretofore mentioned, are practical and relevant to life. But there are also other *practical lessons* of how one should adjust.

Plan better: Learn how to plan so as to eliminate unnecessary expenses.

Prepare a budget: Learn to prepare a budget based on what one has – a simple budget that meets the real needs. '*Sometimes I am forced to omit some things in order to squeeze the budget to meet the real needs.*'

'Tent making': Learn to support oneself through '*tent making*.'

Never complain: Learn to do your own part without complaint even when others do not do their part.

Flexibility: Learn flexibility to avoid conflict and accommodate people.

Seminars: Learn the value of seminars to gain important skills and lessons.

Books: Learn to read from good books on the challenging issues.

CONCLUSION

When students graduate from Bible College, they expect '*automatic respect and help from the leadership.*' Such expectations are soon dashed to the ground. A learning attitude is indispensable. '*I've learned that some challenges prepare us for fruitful ministry.*' More than that, '*One must be fully decided to serve the Lord. If not for that, you would forget about serving in the ministry.*'

Focusing on God who saved and called you to ministry is the key. '*If I would ponder the problems, I would not serve the Lord. But by focusing on God we can serve cheerfully. The Lord has always been with us. We have never lacked.*' True servants of the Lord do not serve God with mere endurance; they serve with joy. '*I've learned the lesson to serve with joy. They return the same to you when you serve with joy. I've learned that if you serve with annoyance, that will be returned to me.*'

The purpose of *Part One* of the book has been to offer advice from those with rich experience of Christian leadership, providing profound instruction from their experiences in Church leadership. The remainder of the book will point the way toward becoming an effective Christian leader.

SEARCHING THE SCRIPTURE WITH APPLICATION

1. What challenges have you faced in life and ministry which have been deeply painful?
2. What lessons have you learned from those challenges? Or have you succumbed to them? Or perhaps you have only learned lessons partially?
3. Describe some challenge that God gave you and the grace to overcome.
    a. What life changing lessons have you learned from that challenge?

    b. Or do you still have lingering resentment from that challenge?
4. Describe the natural reactions to a financial challenge. How can one find God's grace to overcome the naturally sinful reaction and what steps should one take to make a faith reaction instead?
5. Describe the natural reactions to some challenge which seems so unfair and unjust. How can one find God's grace to overcome the naturally sinful reaction and make a faith reaction instead?
6. The primary lessons learned by these Christian leaders interviewed were: perseverance, trust in God, his faithfulness, prayerfulness, humility, forgiveness, contentment, acceptance, wisdom and universality of pain.
    a. Show how many of these lessons learned are interrelated. For example, the lesson of trusting the Lord entails numerous other lessons learned as well.
    b. As you survey these various lessons, what great over-riding common denominator binds them together? For example, why is it that if you learn perseverance you have learned many of the other lessons as well?
7. God is the Creator and Designer of human beings made in his image. He has so structured human nature that obedience to his Word leads upward to 'life' and disobedience leads downward to 'death.' [We define 'life' as that quality of life manifest in 'the fruit of the Spirit' (Gal 5:22-23) and 'death' as that quality of life manifest in 'the works of the flesh' (Gal 5:16-21).]
    a. Reflect how 'life' is the end result from learning the lessons mentioned in this chapter.
    b. Show how 'death' is the end result from failure to accept and submit to the lessons mentioned in this chapter.
    c. Explain how it is to one's own best interest (let alone, to the glory of God) to seek the way of 'life' by trusting God, praying to God, humbling oneself before God and others, forgiving others, persevering in doing God's will, being content, filled with joy and accepting one's lot in life humbly?

Endnote

[1] Heb 5:8

PART TWO

BASICS FOR CHRISTIAN LEADERS

Part Two deals with five basic issues in *The Making of a Christian Leader in Africa.* To be an effective Christian leader, one must understand *the nature of the Church* and the *qualifications for Church leadership.* To become a leader after God's own heart, one must engage in *spiritual disciplines* for spiritual growth. In the midst of success and challenges in ministry, one must rely on *the sovereign rule of God* in all circumstances. When so many wrongs are done to the leader, he must learn the virtue of *a forgiving spirit* of others. Without *perseverance* a Christian leader will fail when experiencing the challenges in ministry. These are basics to learn.

6
THE CHURCH AND HER LEADERS

'God has placed everything under the power of Christ
and has set him up as head of everything for the Church.
For the Church is his body, and in that body lives fully the one who fills the whole wide universe.'[1]

The Church is an organism, not an organisation; yet she is organised.

If you desire to be a Christian leader in the Church, you need to understand the nature of the Church. Leadership in the Church is not like any other organisation, for the Church is not a mere organisation; the Church is a living organism, 'the Body of Christ.' And yet the Church is organised visibly as an institution. Herein lays much confusion. Exactly, what is the Church?

The Nature of the Church

What is the Church?

The Church is spiritual in her nature, evidenced by the various metaphors.

The Church is the Body of Christ: When anyone is born again of the Spirit, that person is 'baptised by one Spirit into one body.'[2] That body is the Body of Christ.[3] Even as the human body needs many different members, so the body of Christ needs different kinds of gifted members to contribute to the growth of this dynamic and growing Body.

The Church is the Temple of the Holy Spirit: Believers are described as 'members of the household of God, built on the foundation of the apostles and prophets, Christ Jesus himself being the corner-stone, in whom the whole structure, being joined together, grows into a holy temple in the Lord. In him you also are being built together into a dwelling place for God by the Spirit.'[4]

The Church is apostolic in the sense that it is built on the authoritative teaching of the 'apostles and prophets;' it is Christo-centric in the sense that Jesus Christ is the 'cornerstone.' The Church is dynamic and growing by the Spirit who indwells the Church as 'a holy temple.'

The Church is both visible and invisible: The Invisible Church is a spiritual organism, and the Visible Church is an institutional organisation.

The Church *Invisible* is the 'the Holy Catholic Church,' that is, the Church Universal. It is the Body of Christ of which Jesus Christ is the Head and every member, born of the Spirit, is an integral part of the Body. This spiritual or invisible Church incorporates all the elect, those who know Jesus Christ as their Lord and Saviour. Thus the Body of Christ is an *organism*, called 'the Church.'

The distinction between the Invisible Church and the Visible Church was made to distinguish between what we see as an imperfect, visible Church and the Church which is the Body of Christ. This distinction first appeared in the writings of Augustine and then was taught by the Protestant Reformers.

The *visible* Church refers to professed believers in Jesus who are organised together in local assemblies where believers and unbelievers assemble together for worship. By definition, *only* the elect are members of the invisible Church. But the visible Church is comprised of believers and unbelievers, wheat and tares, and is imperfect in its life and testimony.

The *visible* Church should reflect the Body of Christ. For this to occur, however, the visible Church must be marked by the following characteristics: (1) submission to the lordship of Jesus Christ as the Head of the Church; (2) the faithful preaching of the Word of God; (3) obedience to the Lord in baptism and the Lord's Supper; (4) the dynamic working of the Holy Spirit within the Body as members contribute in unity to the building up of the Body of Christ; and (5) faithful discipline to preserve the unity and purity of the Church of Jesus Christ.

Who are the Leaders of the Visible Church?

Christ as the Head of the Church 'gave' to the visible gathered Church leaders 'to equip the saints for the work of ministry, for the building up the body of Christ'[5]

Elders, also known as bishops, are the designated leaders of the Churches: The New Testament Churches were governed by *elders* chosen by the Christians in each local assembly. Deacons in the New Testament are noted for their serving while elders ruled. In the transitional apostolic Church the apostles or their representatives sometimes appointed the elders.[6] There is no hint, however, of any hierarchy of clergy in the early Church with leaders above the elders (apart from the apostles, who with the prophets, formed the foundation of the Church[7]).

The two Greek words for leaders in the Church, *episcopos* (translated in the Authorized Version as *bishop*; also translated as *overseers*) and *presbuteros* (translated as *elder*) are the bases for two different forms of Church government: the Episcopal form, governed by bishops, and the Presbyterian form, governed by elders. In the New Testament, however, these two words are used interchangeably and without distinction.[8] Furthermore, the 'original usage [of *episcopos*], at least until the time of Ignatius, was restricted to those who exercised oversight in the local Church.'[9] Bishop David Gitari of the Anglican Church in Kenya notes that, 'It was not until the fourth century that a single Bishop took charge of a Diocese or group of churches.'[10]

The Role of the elders/bishops in the Churches: The elders (also referred to as bishops/overseers) are to be 'shepherds of the flock of God.'[11]

And most importantly, elders/bishops are to serve under 'the chief Shepherd' to whom they are responsible and to whom they will give an account of their service.[12] Church leadership is not autocratic but 'body leadership' – leaders who facilitate the growth of the Church by equipping the saints with differing gifts so they can function as members of the Body.

The shepherds of God's people in Old Testament Israel were unfaithful. God's judgement fell upon them. The Lord God said to them: 'I am against the shepherds and will hold them accountable for my flock.'[13] Leadership in the Church is a great privilege, but it is also a great responsibility for which every one will be held accountable by the Lord.

Qualifications for Church Leaders

The qualifications and requirements of Church leaders are laid out by the Lord and should be followed by the Church members and overseers. The qualifications for deacons and elders are essentially the same, so in our discussion we shall refer to the qualifications of Church leaders, whether they are deacons or elders. What is the most important qualification for Christian leaders?

Character

Leadership is a gift;[14] not everyone is able or called to lead. It is significant that the qualifications laid down for Church elders in the Bible are not primarily about skills or gifts but about *character.*[15] The character of the leader is the foundation of leadership. Without godly character, the most gifted leader will fail. A prominent leader's observation has confirmed mine:

> We have watched with astonishment as one effective leader after another has crashed and burned, resulting in public humiliation for the leader, their families, as well as the organisations to which they gave leadership…After much inquiry and investigation into the causes of these public leadership failures, it has been discovered that the primary culprit in virtually every case has been a flaw in the failed leader's personal foundation. Though the leader may have been gifted, intelligent, and apparently extremely effective, there were fissures in the foundation that had either escaped notice or had been purposely ignored.[16]

This is our observation. What is yours? What is the main reason for failure in Christian leadership as you see it?

What is character? Someone has said that *character* is what you are when no one is watching; it is what you do in the dark. It is not the same as reputation or success. *Character* is what you are down deep inside, not what others think of you; it is the core of the person. *Character* is 'the essential "stuff" he or she is made of, the inner reality in which thoughts, speech, decisions, behavior, and relations are rooted. As such, character determines behavior just as behavior demonstrates character.'[17] *Character* pertains to the moral qualities and ethical standards of a person that have grown over time. As it has been said, 'Sow a thought, reap an action; sow an action, reap a habit; sow a habit, reap a character; sow a character, reap a destiny.'[18]

Phillips Brooks defined preparation for ministry as 'nothing less than the making of a man.' 'No matter what kind of ministry God gives us – preaching, teaching, counseling, supervising, encouraging – we can never give to others what we do not have ourselves. To ignore character is to abandon the foundation of ministry.'[19]

Effective leaders first learn to lead themselves; only afterwards are they capable of leading others. For any leader to neglect his own life is to prepare for his own failure. The purpose of this book is to assist in *the process of making* Christian leaders, beginning with character.

The remainder of this chapter will examine the biblical qualifications of a spiritual leader laid down in 1 Timothy 3:1-7 and Titus 1:5-9.

Should people desire to be Christian Leaders? '*If anyone aspires to the office of overseer* [traditionally, a bishop], *he desires a noble task.*'[20] Does Paul advocate ambition for leadership? When fallen human beings are ambitious for leadership, selfish gain is all too often the motive. That is why Jeremiah admonishes: 'And do you seek great things for yourself? Seek them not…'[21] Jeremiah warns against selfish ambition, of seeking '*great things for yourself.*'

Here in 1 Timothy Paul recommends *the desire of serving* as an overseer of the Church, a noble desire when accompanied by noble motives. In the early Church, leadership was a dangerous responsibility, associated with hardship, contempt and rejection. During persecution of the Church, the leaders of the Church were singled out and brutally treated; even as it happens today with the persecuted Church in Communist and Muslim countries. Paul is encouraging potential elders not to flee the privilege of leading the Church but to embrace the responsibility since it is a noble work. In contrast today, many seek high offices for personal gain, recognition and fame; and to grasp such positions they use the worldly means of politics with campaigning and bribery. As Bishop Gitari observes, 'To crash other candidates on one's way to the top or to bribe the voters is unchristian and unworthy of the ambition to become a church leader.'[22]

Motives are all important. Addiction to power is an evil like addiction to alcohol. So much harm is done to the Church because of leaders intoxicated with a thirst for power! As Oswald Sanders comments:

> Our word *ambition* derives from a Latin word meaning 'canvassing for promotion.'…Ambitious men enjoy the power that money or authority brings. Such carnal ambitions were roundly rebuked by the Lord. The true spiritual leader will never canvass for promotion.[23]

A man's ambition must fit into God's plan. His eye must always be on the Lord. Paul reminds us that when God places his hand on someone to lead, that person should not shrink back but with courage accept the responsibility with humility and dependence on the Lord.

What then are the qualifications of a spiritual leader of the Church?

A Christian Leader must have a reputation beyond reproach

The overseer/elder '*must be above reproach.*'[24] Further, '*he must be well thought of by outsiders, so that he may not fall into disgrace, into a snare of the devil.*'[25] Reputation is all important. Paul begins the list of qualifications with a categorical assertion, '*It is necessary*' (an emphatic conjunction in the Greek) that the leader be '*above reproach.*' After listing the other qualifications he concludes, '*he must be well thought of by outsiders.*' In other words, an elder must be of blameless character and known for that among the unbelievers. No leader should be charged with a sin, a sin that can be substantiated by two or three witnesses.

> We need to see leadership as a calling. Church leadership is not a political position to be sought for oneself. It is a burden that some must accept. Leaders are not determined by popularity. They must be the kind of men profiled here by Paul to Timothy. And the Church must recognize who they are.[26]

Extensive research by the Association of Theological Schools in America in 1975 identified two of the top three characteristics of effective leaders to be (1) *personal integrity* and a (2) *Christian example.* Paul declared the same two-thousand years ago. 'Integrity – soundness of moral principle and character, uprightness, and honesty – is the essential characteristic for effective spiritual leadership. One who lacks integrity is not to be selected for leadership and invested with its authority and responsibility.'[27]

Leaders serve as models. A Church leader represents Christ and the Body of Christ. Whatever he speaks or does reflects on Christ and the Church. Terrible reproach falls upon Christ and his Church when the leader fails. No leader can demand respect; he can only earn it through his or her character.

> Leaders…must be chosen carefully for the very qualities of Christ-likeness that they are able to demonstrate as examples. It is no wonder that the writer to the Hebrews urges the Church, 'Remember your leaders, and imitate their faith' (Heb 13:7). It is no wonder that Paul, speaking of attitude, can say to the Corinthians that they should follow his example (1 Co 11:1), or, speaking of the deepest motives that guided his choice, can remind the Thessalonians that he does not try to please or manipulate men, but always to please God, 'as you know' (1 Th 2:1-5). As the leaders live among God's people, their total character is to be open and exposed.[28]

A Christian Leader must be spiritually mature

Emotional and spiritual maturity is prerequisite for effective leadership. '*He must not be a recent convert or he may become puffed up with conceit and fall into the condemnation of the devil.*'[29] Paul adds, '*And let them also be tested first.*'[30] In this context, maturity has more to do with spiritual maturity than age. Someone can be old in years yet immature spiritually. When a spiritually immature person gains a position of leadership, he can be blinded and deluded with a sense of self-importance; and become 'puffed up' with pride.[31] The leader then becomes a major problem for the Church.

A spiritually mature person is '*upright* and *holy*,' a '*lover of good*'[32] and '*faithful in all things.*'[33] God is righteous for he conforms to the law which he gave to the human race.[34] Jesus Christ is 'the Righteous One.'[35] As a representative of God in the Church of Jesus Christ, every Christian leader is required to live a life that is 'just' and 'righteous,' 'conforming to the law of God.'[36] He is to be 'devout, pious, pleasing to God, holy.'[37]

Spiritual maturity is so important for leadership. How will he react to criticism? How will he handle his position of authority over others? How faithful will he be when no one is looking? How will he behave in differing situations including his association with women? Can you think of any situation where a spiritually immature Christian might be acceptable as a Christian leader? There can be no substitute for spiritual maturity. Without it, the Church will be greatly troubled and ashamed.

A Christian Leader must have edifying speech

A leader with a loose tongue is divisive and troublesome. He should be '*not quarrelsome,*'[38] '*not double-tongued [insincere],*'[39] and '*not a slanderer.*'[40] Some individuals love to pick a fight, start a quarrel, and argue their point; others are insincere, speaking falsely or misleading. Still others slander people behind their back. The word translated, 'slanderer,'[41] is literally, 'the devil' (*diabolos*). To elect someone to Church leadership who is like the devil, someone who destroys the reputation of others, is to destroy the Church. No Church can survive or grow with a leader who speaks in these ways.

Words are powerful; they can build up and they can tear down. If a word is misspoken, apologies should be made and forgiveness requested. But words leave impressions that cannot be erased. '*Not many of you should become teachers,*' advises James, because it is so easy to stumble when speaking.[42] The leader must learn the self-discipline of controlling his speech. '*The more talk, the less truth; the wise measure their words. The speech of a good person is worth waiting for; the blabber of the wicked is worthless.*'[43]

A Christian Leader must be self-controlled

To become a Christian leader one must be self-controlled. A spiritual leader must be '*sober minded,*'[44] '*self-controlled,*'[45] '*not quick-tempered,*'[46] '*not violent but gentle,*'[47] and '*not a drunkard*'[48] or '*not addicted to much wine.*'[49]

Sober minded can refer to the use of alcohol but here it more likely means temperate in emotions. The Christian leader should be free from rash actions; he must master his emotions and exercise self control in the use of his words, the decisions he makes and the actions he takes. A *self-controlled* person is temperate in his disposition, always keeping his emotions under control.

Not quick-tempered refers to self-control of the emotions so that the leader does not quickly react in anger. A quick-tempered person speaks rashly. When the temper is lost, anger pours forth. Anger disqualifies for Church leadership.

Not violent – not 'a bruiser' or 'ready with a blow;' not 'contentious' or a 'quarrelsome person.'[50] Bauer translates this, not 'a bully.' In contrast, Christian leaders must be gentle and patient with full control of the emotions.

Not a drunkard. In New Testament times, the drinking of naturally fermented wine was customary in the absence of purified water. Although one had to drink much more than today to become drunk, people did get drunk. Self-restraint was an essential characteristic of leaders. Drunkenness is listed with other 'works of the flesh.'[51]

A Christian Leader must be content

The disqualification for leadership is not wealth but '*a lover of money.*'[52] He must not be '*greedy for dishonest gain;*'[53] or not even '*greedy for gain.*'[54]

'Godliness with contentment is great gain...People who want to get rich fall into temptation and a trap and into many foolish and harmful desires that plunge men into ruin and destruction.'[55] As we read in Ezekiel 34:1-10, pastors (shepherds) sometimes pay more attention 'to the fleece than to the flock.' The tragedy is that many Church leaders who fall into this trap are not properly disciplined. 'If a man is drunk on wine, you'll throw him out. But if he is drunk on money, you'll make him a deacon.'[56]

A Christian Leader must be respectable in conduct

Elders must be '*respectable*';[57] the deacons 'likewise' must be '*dignified.*' These are not only cultural values among the Greeks and Romans, and the Africans, but they are biblical norms for leadership. Christian leaders must not be frivolous, silly or childish. Rather, they should be 'respectable' and 'honorable,' conducting themselves in a 'dignified' manner.

A Christian Leader must be sociable

The Christian leader should be '*hospitable;*' literally, he should have '*love for strangers.*'[58] One mark for all Christians is 'to seek to show hospitality.'[59] Literally, Christians are to 'pursue' or 'chase' a love for strangers. Leaders should love to show hospitality, and not fulfill this as a reluctant duty. Hospitality is to be done 'without grumbling.'[60] (Churches also have a responsibility to support their leaders so that they will be able to feed their guests. Without support, hospitality can be a burden.)

In the early Church traveling evangelists depended on Christian hospitality for there were no motels or hotels.[61] Hospitality in the Old Testament was a virtue. Christian leaders cannot be introverts who shun others and cling to their own privacy. A love for people, shown by a love for hospitality, should mark a leader within the Church.

A Christian Leader must be faithful in marriage

Christian leaders should be '*the husband of one wife.*'[62] Is this qualification directed against polygamous men, or widowers, or single unmarried young men, or divorced men? The phrase means literally 'a one-woman man' or 'a man of one woman.' In other words, the emphasis is that a Christian leader should be faithful to his one wife. There should be no other woman in his life. He should not flirt with another woman.

This qualification does not make marriage a requirement for Church leadership because Paul himself was single,[63] and elsewhere commended the single state.[64] Rather, it is directed against unfaithful married men. The leader must be known for his faithfulness to his one wife.

A Christian Leader must have skills for ministry

While most of the qualifications for leaders in the Church pertain to character, two things are said of leadership skills for the Church. The first is about management and the second about teaching.

Management skills: A Christian leader '*must manage his own household well, with all dignity keeping his children submissive, for if someone does not know how to manage his own household, how will he care for God's Church?*'[65]

In the patriarchal families of ancient times, similar to Africa, the man was the overseer of the family members in the house (*oikos* in the Greek), even as the elders were overseers of the Church (also known as the *oikos* of God)[66] which met in the houses of believers – house-Churches.

A qualification of all Church leaders is that they must demonstrate their leadership skills and paternal care by rearing their children well. Dignity of leadership in the home was to be manifest by overseeing the family affairs. If someone was unable to lead the family in his own house, he was disqualified from leading the house of God which is the Church.

It should be observed that the word for 'managing' of his children in 1 Timothy 3:12b (*proistamai*) is the same word used for the gift of leadership in Romans 12:8. As the 'head' of the house, he was to 'rule' and 'direct' by managing and caring for the members in the household. His success or failure in the home qualified him or disqualified him for leadership in the Church. No one should assume leadership in the Church without proven experience. The proving ground for management skills in the Church is in the home.

Teaching skills and knowledge of 'The Faith': One other skill is required of a leader in the Church, the ability '*to teach.*'[67] Bauer translates this, '*skillful in teaching*.'[68] But this is more than the 'gift of teaching.' 'In classical Greek, the word *didaktikos* meant "teachable." In essence, a person who is "able to teach" demonstrates a sense of security, teachability and a non-threatening response to those who may disagree.'[69]

A person able to teach is also teachable. He holds his knowledge and understanding with humility so that he is open to further light. Knowledgeable people can be proud; but Church leaders '*must not be arrogant.*'[70] In the context of 1 Timothy 3, this person with skills of teaching is also 'gentle, not quarrelsome;' he is 'self-controlled' and 'respectable.'

But the requirement is beyond skills of teaching; Paul points to the need for a full grasp of and commitment to The Faith: '*They must hold the mystery of the faith with a clear conscience.*'[71] '*He must hold firm to the trustworthy word as taught, so that he may be able to give instruction in sound doctrine and also to rebuke those who contradict it.*'[72]

A Christian leader must be a student of the Word; someone who reads it, compares Scripture with Scripture, and understands it. Moreover, he must '*hold firm to the trustworthy words as taught.*' Any person who is untaught or unclear about the gospel or unconvinced of the truth of the Word should not be a leader. He must then be able to communicate the Word in public. The Pastoral Epistles make clear that these Christian leaders must be able to stand up and defend the faith, but with gentleness and not quarreling.[73]

CONCLUSION

Some Christian leaders try to grow their Churches through the force of a charismatic personality. Whenever such leadership is divorced from godly character and spiritual maturity, sooner or later the charisma wears thin and everything falls apart. Weakness of character will be revealed some day.

On the other hand, 'We honor Christian leaders because their lives command respect; we trust them because they are honest; we love them because they are caring; we want to emulate them because their lives are exemplary.'[74]

Which kind of leader would you like to be? A gifted charismatic leader who draws crowds of followers, but with a flawed character? Or a spiritually mature person with Christ-like character that is faithful to Christ?

If you desire to be a spiritually mature shepherd who pleases the Chief Shepherd, the following chapter will guide you in knowing the spiritual disciplines that one must follow to be a Christian leader beyond reproach.

SEARCHING THE SCRIPTURE WITH APPLICATION

1. Read and study 1 Corinthians 12.
    a. Why does Paul compare the Church with 'a body'?
    b. What do the more prominent parts of the body often feel about themselves? Why? Is there any member of the body that is unimportant? Why?
    c. Why should members not feel superior to others? (cf. 12:11, 18, 28)
2. Why must a Christian leader have a reputation that is beyond reproach?
    a. What effect does this have on the Church and on the Name of Christ, when a Church leader has a spoiled reputation?
    b. Generally, in what areas do Christian leaders often fail?
    c. What should be done to correct this problem?

Endnotes

[1] Eph 1:22f from *The New Testament* Translated by J.B. Phillips
[2] 1 Co 12:13
[3] 1 Co 12:27
[4] Eph 2:19f
[5] Eph 4:12
[6] Ac 14:23; Tit 1:5; Jas 5:1
[7] Eph 2:20
[8] Ac 20:17,28; Tit 1:5-7; cf. 1 Ti 3:1-7
[9] Guthrie 1977:79
[10] Gitari 2005:28
[11] 1 Pe 5:2; Ac 20:28
[12] 1 Pe 5:4
[13] Eze 34:10 *NIV*
[14] Ro 12:8
[15] 1 Ti 3:1ff; Tit 1:7ff
[16] Rima 2000:16
[17] Guinness 2000:15f
[18] Guinness 2000:13
[19] Phillip Brooks as found in Wiersbe 1980:82
[20] 1 Ti 3:1
[21] Jer 45:5
[22] Gitari 2005:3
[23] Sanders 1980:14

[24] 1 Ti 3:2a
[25] 1 Ti 3:7
[26] Hughes 2000:82
[27] Means 1989:32f
[28] Richards 1980:121
[29] 1 Ti 3:6
[30] 1 Ti 3:10
[31] Marshall 1999:482
[32] Tit 1:8
[33] 1 Ti 3:11c
[34] Ro 3:26
[35] Ac 7:52; 1 Jn 2:1
[36] *dikaios*
Bauer 1957:195
[37] *hosios*
Bauer 1957:589
[38] 1 Ti 3:3c
[39] 1 Ti 3:8
[40] 1 Ti 3:11
[41] 1 Ti 3:11
[42] Jas 3:1
[43] Pr 10:19f
The Message
[44] 1 Ti 3:2, 11
[45] 1 Ti 3:2; Tit 1:8
[46] Tit 1:7
[47] 1 Ti 3:3; Tit 1:7b
[48] 1 Ti 3:3a
[49] 1 Ti 3:8
[50] Thayer 1983:517
[51] Gal 5:21
[52] 1 Ti 3:3c
[53] 1Ti 3:8b
[54] Tit 1:7c
[55] 1 Ti 6:6ff
[56] Hughes 2000:80
[57] 1 Ti 3:2
[58] 1 Ti 3:2b; Tit 1:8
[59] Ro 12:13
[60] 1 Pe 4:9
[61] 3 Jn 5-8
[62] 1 Ti 3:2a, 12; Tit 1:6
[63] 1 Co 7:7,8
[64] 1 Co 7:1,32-35
[65] 1 Ti 3:4,5; cf. 3:12b; Tit 1:6
[66] 1 Ti 3:15
[67] 1 Ti 3:2b
[68] Bauer 1957:190
[69] Barna 1997:93
[70] Tit 1:7
[71] 1 Ti 3:9a
[72] Tit 1:9
[73] 2 Ti 2:24f
[74] Wofford 1999:108

7
SPIRITUAL DISCIPLINES

'Discipline yourself for the purpose of godliness;
for bodily discipline is only of little profit, but godliness is profitable for all things,
since it holds promise for the present life and also for the life to come.'[1]

Paul writes, 'Keep *a firm grasp* on both your character and your teaching;'[2] and that takes *discipline.*

It is not enough for servants of the Lord to be well trained in biblical theology and gifted for teaching and ministry – and having a charismatic ministry. 'Charisma without character leads to catastrophe,' Peter Kuzmic reminds us. More leaders collapse and fail in ministry because of *faulty character*, and more Churches splinter and divide because of *character flaws. Discipline* to be a true *disciple* of Christ is essential.

Discipline in Leadership

Many a Church leader is more diligent in ministry than in keeping 'a firm grasp' on character. They are more concerned with *doing* the work of ministry than *being* a godly person. 'Leadership is not something one does but something one is.' Ministry grows out of character, not vice versa; and character grows out of a deep and personal relationship with God.

Leadership places one in a vulnerable position. The greater one's sphere of influence, the greater will be the impact when mistakes in judgement are made or when sin is committed. There is a reason James warns not many should become teachers (and leaders) because the greater the influence, greater the judgement.[3] After forty years of faithful service, Moses forfeited the privilege entering the Promised Land because of just one sin.[4] 'To whom much [responsibility and privilege] is given, much is required.'[5]

We bless our God forever and ever for his gracious gift of a Saviour who bore our sins in his own body on the cross. Jesus Christ accomplished what we could never have done – pay the atonement for our sins. No one is saved apart from pure grace – '*For by grace you have been saved through faith. And this is not your own doing; it is the gift of God, not a result of works, so that no one may boast.*'[6] This is the gospel (good news) of Jesus Christ.

But this grace is not cheap. True, grace is free. No one can offer God any good works that merit salvation; it is all by grace. But grace was neither cheap for the Lord Jesus who paid dearly for our salvation; neither is it cheap for his disciples who have been called to a life of discipleship. Being reconciled to God and entering into a personal relationship with Jesus Christ is only by grace through faith alone. But following conversion every believer, how much more, every Church leader is called into a rigorous discipline to grow in godliness.

Discipline for godliness

Paul instructed a minister in training, '*Discipline* yourself for the purpose of godliness.'[7] That word for *discipline* comes right out of the world of sports in the Greco-Roman empire. It means literally, 'exercise naked, train,'[8] and is derived from the noun meaning 'naked.' Youth who trained their bodies in gymnastic sports, such as boxing and running, trained strenuously to make their bodies fit; and they did so in a naked condition to avoid any impediments in their running. Greek athletes were required to train for ten months prior to the race. Then before the games they practiced in the gymnasium under the direction of the judges who had instructed them for ten months. Horace commented: 'The youth who would win in the race hath borne and done much; he hath sweat and been cold; he hath abstained from love and wine.'[9]

Paul's command to 'discipline yourself' is in the present tense and indicates a continuous activity. As any athlete knows, the body deteriorates when not continually exercised. To be in top performance requires *continuous* bodily exercise. 'Bodily training' (ESV) or 'bodily discipline' (NASB) in 1 Timothy 4:8 translates the Greek word from which our English word, *gymnasium*, is derived. *Discipline* in Bible School is insufficient. The servant of the Lord who fails to discipline himself continually, 'for the purpose of godliness,' will fail.

Clearly, godliness will not happen without discipline. Every disciple of the Lord must learn to discipline himself for the purpose of godliness. How much more, those who are Christian leaders! No discipline – no godliness!

The many allusions to athletic events in the writings of Paul suggest that he was an avid spectator who attended these athletic events; indeed, athletic stadiums were found in many of the Roman cities where Paul planted Churches. The athletic allusions emphasise the strenuous discipline necessary for godliness. Even as an athlete must 'train hard,' so the disciple of Jesus Christ must 'train hard' in the spiritual disciplines in order to achieve God's purpose for life. Listen to Paul's comments in *The Message*, taken from 1 Corinthians 9:24-27:

You've all been to the stadium and seen the athletes race. Everyone runs; one wins. Run to win.

> *All good athletes train hard.* They do it for a gold medal that tarnishes and fades. You're after one that's gold eternally.
>
> I don't know about you, but I'm running hard for the finish line. I'm giving it everything I've got. No sloppy living for me! I'm not going to get caught napping, telling everyone else all about it and then missing it myself [italics added].

The purpose of this unit is to lay out the spiritual disciplines that are required for growth in godliness. However, we caution that these disciplines should not become soul-killing rules and regulations. Jesus warned the religious leaders of his day about their legalism.[10] The scribes and Pharisees cultivated external righteousness such as prayers, fasting, tithing and keeping the traditions of the fathers, thinking that such external observance would gain favour with God. The end result is death to the spirit. Anyone who engages in these spiritual disciplines in order to be a successful Church leader has started the race on the wrong foot. Success is not possible.

Focus on loving God

All spiritual discipline must have as its focus a love for God, a thirst for him. When one becomes a child of God, that means the person is reconciled to the Father and is brought into a personal relationship with the Triune God.[11] David exhibited this relationship when he wrote: '*As a deer pants for flowing streams, so pants my soul for you, O God. My soul thirsts for God, for the living God.*'[12] Again he wrote: '*O God, you are my God; earnestly I seek you; my soul thirsts for you; my flesh faints for you, as in a dry and weary land where there is no water.*'[13]

Prayer can be deadening and utterly boring without this thirsting for God; meditation on Scriptures can be academic and unfulfilling without a love for the One who gave the Scriptures. Whatever you do in developing spiritual discipline for godliness, let it not spring from duty or pride. Let your devotion spring from the heart and find its centre in the heart of God. Do not despair if you feel like a beginner. For the remainder of life, every disciple is learning like a beginner. Begin and forever continue to thirst for God.

There are many spiritual disciplines that help one to draw near to God but they can all be subsumed under two: prayer and meditation on the Scriptures.

When the Scott graduates were asked, 'Why do people succeed in ministry?' A large number replied, 'prayer.' Said one pastor: 'I have never met anyone in ministry who is successful apart from prayer. They all say 'prayer.' Other Christian leaders said that success came through the 'love of God's Word.'

It is my conviction that you cannot have one without the other. No one can truly pray or pray truly apart from meditation on Scripture; and no one can read/study/meditate on Scripture without prayer. The one feeds the other.

When Ezra and Nehemiah led Israel in a renewal of the covenant after the Babylonian exile, we find this beautiful combination of the Word of God and prayer. For one-quarter of the day they stood, listening to the Word of God read and explained by Ezra. The second quarter of the day they prayed, confessing their sins and worshiping the Lord.[14] The Spirit of God is pleased to stimulate one in prayer when the Scripture is read; and the Spirit of God ministers to the heart in the reading of Scripture as we pray over the Word.

> The Word of God and prayer have always been God's most important tools for ministry…Both are necessary. If we study the Word and never pray, we could have a great deal of light without heat. If we pray but never study, we could become fanatics exhibiting a great deal of zeal but little knowledge…If we use the Word of God and prayer, we will have a balanced, healthy ministry and will do the work of God according to the will of God.[15]

So in this short chapter we shall subsume all other spiritual disciplines under these two essentials without which no one can truly grow into godliness.

Discipline of Prayer

Tokunboh Adeyemo comments:

> We need prayers. God is looking for people who pray. He is not looking for more preachers today. There are so many preachers on the streets of Nairobi. All you need to do is go out during lunch time; you'll find the street-corner preachers. They are in plenty. God is not looking for more preachers; or more miracle workers; nor more social activities; or even evangelists. He is looking for people who can stand in the gap. I believe God is looking for people who pray…[16]

'In nothing more should the leader be ahead of his followers more than in the realm of prayer.'[17] Prayer is so essential for every believer, but especially for the leaders of 'the flock' because prayer is a personal relationship with God. It is God's appointed means of knowing God and growing in grace. As William Carey, the 'father of modern missions,' once said: 'Prayer – secret, fervent, believing prayer – lies at *the root of all personal godliness*' [italics added].[18]

Jesus' example of prayer is the all-compelling reason for underlining the importance of prayer in the life of every servant of the Lord. In Mark 1:21-35 we read of Jesus' extraordinarily busy ministry. He taught in the synagogue one morning; after the synagogue service he cast out an unclean spirit. Jesus went home to Simon's house where he healed Simon's mother-in-law. That evening after sun set the whole village came to Jesus for healing. Morning, noon and evening Jesus was busy. But the following day, '*rising very early in the morning, while it was still dark, he departed and went out to a desolate place, and there he prayed.*'

This was the lifestyle of Jesus. As reports about Jesus spread abroad, 'great crowds gathered to hear him and to be healed of their infirmities. *But he would withdraw to desolate places and pray.*'[19] Before Jesus made the most important decision in his ministry, the choosing of the Twelve including Judas Iscariot, 'he went out to the mountain to pray, and *all night he continued in prayer to God.*'[20] Before his Passion Jesus admonished his disciples, 'Pray that you will not fall into temptation.'[21] While Jesus '*prayed more earnestly*' through the night, the disciples fell asleep. In the end Jesus triumphantly fulfilled the Father's will but the disciples yielded to temptation and forsook their Lord at the moment of his greatest need. 'When we pray, God moves us.'

Prayer as petition: Prayer is an expression of weakness and dependence on God. 'To pray' is 'to ask.' In many languages the word for 'prayer' is the word meaning 'to ask' or 'to beg.' Even in old

English, the word for prayer could be used for anyone 'asking' another for help. What does the word for prayer mean in your mother tongue? People who ask are not self-reliant. God does not pray because he is supremely self-sufficient. In the mystery of the Incarnation, Jesus showed his total dependency on his Father in heaven through a life of prayer.

Prayer includes worship and confession. But the most elemental aspect of prayer is 'asking' for our needs and interceding on behalf of others. When Jesus taught us to pray, 'Give us today our daily bread,' he meant praying for all our material needs, with 'bread' representing that which we need to live in our mortal bodies. The glorious truth is that our Father in heaven loves us even more than our earthly fathers do. God desires us to make known our 'wants and wishes' while trusting God to determine what is best for us.

Martin Luther declared, 'I have so much business that I cannot get on without spending three hours daily in prayer.'[22] For many a forlorn servant of the Lord, however, they loose out in their prayer life because they are too busy. But for Martin Luther, the busier he was, the more time he found necessary to spend in prayer. A servant of the Lord can not do the work of the Lord apart from divine enabling and divine help is available only through prayer. 'You do not have, because you do not ask.'[23] 'The minister who is too busy to study the Word of God and pray is simply too busy. He may be successful in his own eyes, and in the eyes of his peers; but he is a failure in God's eyes – one day everybody will know it. God has not promised to bless methods, but he has promised to bless his Word and to answer prayer.'[24]

Prayer as worship: Prayer is much more than 'asking' and 'beseeching.' Above all else, prayer is offering God our love and devotion, reverence and honour, thanksgiving and praise. Ministering to people is ministering to Christ when done with a heart of love for God. But too often ministry to people has priority over ministry to the Lord in worship. Richard Foster writes: 'If the Lord is to be *Lord*, worship must have priority in our lives...The divine priority is worship first, service second... Service flows out of worship. Service as a substitute for worship is idolatry. Activity is the enemy of adoration.'[25]

Worship in prayer takes many forms. *Thanksgiving* for all of God's blessings is a fundamental duty of all believers. Too often we forget to give thanks in the midst of our dissatisfaction and frustration of life. Like the Israelites who murmured over their diet, so we are prone to focus on the cup that is half-empty rather than the cup which is half-full. *Remembering* with gratitude the ways God has protected and led and guided in the past is a way of honouring God. *Adoration* of the perfections of God is surely a priority. To focus on the gifts and forget the giver is a gross failure. *Submitting* to God's will, 'not my will but *your* will be done,' renders honour to God.

Reflection on the prayers found in the Bible reveals the priority given to worship. When a 'vast army' confronted king Jehoshaphat, he called upon God in prayer. Uppermost in his mind was his petition for divine intervention. But he begins with worship.[26] Moreover, when they went into battle the Levites led the army into warfare with songs of praise – and victory came.

When Nehemiah received the disheartening report of Jerusalem in great trouble, he prayed for help when speaking to King Artaxerxes. But most of his prayer was not petition but worship and praise.[27] In the Lord's Prayer Jesus taught his disciples *how* to prayer. Clearly, one third of the prayer is devoted to worship with adoration and submission.[28] He who does not worship in prayer has not prayed.

Prayer as confession is an integral part of prayer. A good confession should include three things:[29]

(1) Self-examination of conscience: Every leader must be honest with himself and honest before God when examining his conscience. Confession must be specific, not general. Remembering the unkind word, the impure thought, the deceptive deed, or the selfish attitude is so important when offering to God our confession of sin.

(2) Sorrow for sin: Confession must never be a mere recitation of sins done. Deep sorrow should accompany confession; not sorrow that you were caught but sorrow for displeasing the One whom you love. 'For godly sorrow leads to repentance.'[30]

(3) A determination to avoid further sin: Confession is not complete unless there is a determination to avoid those sins again. True, genuine confession leads to forgiveness without number.[31] But genuine confession is accompanied by such sorrow for sin that there is a strong determination to *stop* sinning. Sin is the worst enemy of a Church leader; it is what should be hated most. John Wesley once said: 'Give me one hundred preachers who fear nothing but sin and desire nothing but God… such alone will shake the gates of hell and set up the kingdom of heaven on earth.'[32]

Prayer with fasting has been practiced throughout redemptive history by such illustrious figures as Moses, Elijah, Daniel and Jesus Christ; it has also been practiced throughout Church history by men and women of God. Though fasting is not a command in Scripture, Jesus clearly intimated that fasting would be practiced by his disciples after his departure.[33] Unlike prayer and meditation on Scripture, fasting is optional. But with proper motives fasting can strengthen one's spiritual life for godly living.

Fasting may be brief, from sunrise to sunset, limiting oneself to fruit juices and water; or it may be abstinence of all food for several days. Since bodily functions begin shutting down without water after three days, it is recommended that fasting should include drinking of purified water.

But fasting can be with wrong motives and unacceptable to God. Fasting is no substitute for godly living;[34] fasting may be customary and routine, an empty habit with no value;[35] fasting may be done with pride and vainglory,[36] a form of self-righteousness to gain divine favour.[37] Fasting as works-righteousness is detestable before God.

The motive of fasting is all-important. Is it for self-advancement or is it for the Lord? Fasting should be an act of self-denial before the Lord as a tangible means of expressing humiliation, contrition and utter dependence on the Lord. It is not food that sustains the believer but the living God through his Word. Our true nourishment comes from above and not from this world. Fasting is almost always accompanied by extra-ordinary prayer to plead with God for his mercies and grace.

Discipline of Meditating on Scripture

Sin is the believer's arch enemy. It is important to understand that sin is more than external words and deeds. Sinful deeds spring from the sinful human heart. '*For out of the heart* come evil thoughts, murder, adultery, sexual immorality, theft, false witness, slander.'[38] Transforming the *mind* (a crucial element of the heart) is necessary for godly living.[39] That is why Solomon advises: 'Keep vigilant watch over your heart; that's where life starts.'[40] A godly life pleasing to God begins with the thought life.

Temptation *always* begins in the mind. Living in this fallen world, the Christian is continually bombarded with values contrary to God's thinking. For one to grow in godliness every disciple must engage in a transformation of the mind with its values. This can only be done by the Spirit impressing God's will upon the heart and mind through the Scriptures. To transform the thinking of a believer one must (1) Study the Scriptures, (2) Meditate on the Scriptures, (3) Apply the Scriptures, and (4) Memorise the Scripture.

Study the Scripture: The Bible is the world's masterpiece of literature filled with poetry and prose, history and allegory of world renown. For centuries the Roman Catholic Church feared giving the Scriptures to the common people in their own mother tongue for fear that they would misinterpret it. Only the Church authorities were empowered to read the Bible, so they thought. The marvel of the Bible is that its message is so simple and straightforward that any literate lay person can read and understand its meaning.

Nevertheless, care must be taken to interpret the Scriptures aright and this requires *study*. 'Be diligent,' Paul instructs Timothy, 'to present yourself approved to God as a workman who does not need to be ashamed, *accurately handling the word of truth*.'[41] How important it is for teaching elders and pastors to 'handle the word of truth' accurately. Otherwise the flock under their care will be led astray. This requires some basic tools and instructions.

Vocabulary and grammar must be understood within the context of the Scriptures. Knowledge of the historical and geographical context is important. Since the Bible is inspired by the Holy Spirit the unity of Scripture means that Scripture interprets Scripture. Although every student of the Bible understands that the original manuscripts were written in Hebrew, Aramaic and Greek, a believer should not be intimidated by this but with confidence may study the Bible in the mother tongue, using basic principles of biblical interpretation.

In practice this means it is ever so helpful, if possible, to own and use a Study Bible with cross references so that one can compare Scripture with Scripture, learning how to interpret Scripture by comparing other Scriptures. Various Study Bibles are available, such as *The NIV Study Bible*. Footnotes help to explain difficult terms or passages; introductory studies to each book of the Bible explain the historical background. The main point to remember is that the Word of God that feeds the heart must not be understood allegorically but accurately as the original authors of Scripture so intended.

Meditation of Scripture: Bible study can be all academic – and dry, doing nothing to feed the heart. But meditation of Scripture can be detached from the accurate meaning of the Scriptures. Therefore *study* is important but *meditation* is essential. Blessings are pronounced on the righteous who 'delight' in the 'law of the LORD – 'and on his law he *meditates day and night*.'[42] In fact, such a person thrives in difficult times and, '*In all that he does, he prospers*.'

How does one develop a biblical worldview with values that are alien to culture? How does one think God's thoughts after him? Only by developing a habit of *meditating* on God's Word. The Hebrew words which convey the idea of meditation have various meanings: 'listening to God's word, reflecting on God's works, rehearsing God's deeds, ruminating on God's law...In each case there is stress upon changed behavior as a result of our encounter with the living God. Repentance and obedience are essential features in any biblical understanding of meditation.'[43]

Meditation is on God *through* the reading of Scriptures. The Bible is not an end in itself or a challenge to mastery. Rather, God's Word is a means of grace whereby the Holy Spirit draws us to worship and adore our Creator and Lord. *Meditation* is a sheer delight. 'My soul will be satisfied as with fat and rich food, and my mouth will praise you with joyful lips, when I remember you upon my bed, and meditate on you in the watches of the night.'[44]

Application of Scripture: Whenever a servant of the Lord studies or meditates on Scripture, application to life should be an assumed response. But lest application be overlooked, we make this a special point. When David speaks of 'the law,' 'the statutes,' 'the precepts,' 'the commands' and the 'ordinances' of the Lord, he exults: 'More to be desired are they than gold, even much fine gold; sweeter also than honey and the drippings of the honeycomb. *Moreover, by them is your servant warned; in keeping them there is great reward.*'[45] God's Word was given to teach and to be obeyed. Even the historical record of redemption in the Old Testament is meant to instruct with application to life. Having enumerated various events in the history of Israel Paul says, 'Now these things happened to them as an example, but they were written down for our instruction.'[46]

This truth of applying God's Word is ancient. The Lord commanded Joshua: 'This Book of the Law shall not depart from your mouth, but you shall *meditate on it day and night, so that you may be careful to do according to all that is written in it.* For then you will make your way prosperous, and then you will have good success.'[47] Does anything more need to be said? Great blessing is promised to those who meditate on God's Word and *obey* it. A good practice when reading the Scripture in devotions is to ask this question: How does this apply to my life? Carry that truth throughout the day and witness growth in godliness.

Memorise Scripture: If obedience to the Word of God brings great blessing; if the great challenge is transforming the mind through the Word of God, what better practice is there than to memorise Scripture? As the Psalmist wrote: 'I have stored up your word in my heart, that I might not sin against you.'[48] Moses frequently stresses the importance of keeping God's Word 'in the heart.'[49] The best time to begin memorising Scripture is during the younger years. The older one grows, the more difficult it is to memorise. What better time to memorise Scripture than when one is walking to some destination or waiting in queue. Buy up the wasted time by memorising Scripture.

CONCLUSION

The time and place for daily devotions is all important. Developing a habit is strategic; irregularity will lead to failure. Meeting with God in prayer and Scripture must not be hurried. God is not honoured when we are in a rush and expect God to fit into our schedule. Remember! Prayer and Bible reading are for the purpose of meeting with God; it is not some legalistic routine that fulfills our obligation. The Psalmist writes: 'I have stilled and quieted my heart; like a weaned child is my soul within me.'[50] Spiritual disciplines lead to quiet confidence and assurance in our leadership role.

Tokunboh Adeyemo says, 'I believe the destiny of Africa lies with the people of God who pray.'[51] Equally true is this. The destiny of the Church in Africa lies with Christian leaders who offer their lives as models in the spiritual disciplines of prayer and meditation on the Word of God.

We also need to remember that God is in control. Every leader needs a strong shoulder to lean on. The work is too demanding, the disappointments too painful and the challenges too overwhelming. Sometimes you may wonder, 'Where is God?' 'What has happened to his promises?'

God in his infinite wisdom and for purposes known to him is working out every detail of your life. When the heart is filled with confidence in the sovereign working of God in every aspect of your life, you can gather courage to persevere in ministry. The following chapter teaches the sovereignty of God with the reminder that God is working out every detail of life for his glory and for our good.

SEARCHING THE SCRIPTURE WITH APPLICATION

1. In this chapter we have emphasised a daily time spent with God in prayer and the Scriptures. What further aspect of prayer does 1 Th 5:17 bring out? Compare with Ps 62:8. How does one 'practice the presence of the Lord' throughout each day? How does one 'pray without ceasing'?
2. Prayer should include various elements including: (a) Adoration and praise for who God is; (b) Thanksgiving for what he has done; (c) Confession; (d) Prayer for others; (e) Prayer for personal needs. Examine the following Scriptures and decide which element of prayer these verses refer to: Heb 13:15; Ps 38:18; Jas 1:5; Eph 5:20; 1 Sa 12:23; Ps 51:1-4; Eph 3:14-19; Ps 63:1-8; Ps 16:1.
3. Reflect on your own prayer life. Are you satisfied with your prayer life? Enumerate the aspects of your prayer life you are pleased with and those aspects you are not pleased with.
4. What steps can you take to improve your own prayer?
5. How does the Scripture help the believer according to the following verses: Jer 15:16; Jn 5:39; 2 Pe 1:4; 1 Jn 2:1?
6. Reflect on your practice of reading/studying/applying/meditating/and memorising Scripture. Are you satisfied with your growth in your knowledge of God through his Word? What can you do to improve your Bible reading?

Endnotes

[1] 1 Ti 4:7f *NASB*
[2] 1 Ti 4:16
The Message
[3] Jas 3:1
[4] Dt 32:48f
[5] Lk 12:48
[6] Eph 2:8,9
[7] 1 Ti 4:7
[8] Bauer 1957

9 Horace, as found in Vincent 1972: 781
10 Mt 5:20
11 Jn 17:3
12 Ps 42:1f
13 Ps 63:1
14 Neh 8:1-9:37
15 Wiersbe 1980: 85
16 Adeyemo 1993:26f
17 Sanders 1980: 121
18 William Carey as found in Bounds n.d.: 23
19 Lk 5:15
20 Lk 6:12
21 Lk 22:40
22 Martin Luther as found in Foster 1998:34
23 Jas 4:2
24 Wiersbe 1980: 85f
25 Foster 1998: 160f
26 2 Ch 20:5ff
27 Neh 1:4-11
28 Mt 6:9-13
29 Foster 1998: 151f
30 2 Co 7:10
31 1 Jn 1:9
32 Foster 1998: 152
33 Mt 9:15
34 Isa 58:3-7
35 Zec 7:5
36 Mt 6:16
37 Lk 18:12
38 Mt 15:19
39 Ro 12:2
40 Pr 4:23 *The Message*
41 2 Ti 2:15 *NASB*
42 Ps 1:2
43 Foster 1998: 15
44 Ps 63:5,6
45 Ps 19:10f
46 1 Co 10:11
47 Jos 1:8
48 Ps 119:11
49 c.f. Dt 6:6
50 Ps 131:2

8
THE SOVEREIGN RULE OF GOD

'We know that to those who love God, who are called according to his plan, everything that happens fits into a pattern for good.'[1]

How does one thrive in leadership?

Given all the challenges which a Christian leader faces, what keeps him going? A personal knowledge of Jesus Christ in saving grace is basic; without a divine call to ministry one will falter. The faithful spiritual disciplines of prayer and the Word are non-negotiable.

But effective Christian leaders also manifest a trust in the lordship of Jesus Christ; they exhibit a confidence that he is the Builder of the Church. God is in charge of every detail and is the Blessed Controller of our lives. Discouragement comes when the leader assumes responsibility for the building. Paul knew better. He commented, 'I planted the seed, Apollos watered it, but God made it grow.'[2] Christian leaders are only servants of the Lord, working in the Lord's vineyard.

Every student of the Word of God believes this in some measure. But it is in the details of life that doubts arise. Discouragement arises when pain is experienced: unbelievers are resistant to the gospel; new converts backslide; carnal Christians bicker and complain; a congregation fails to catch the vision of the leader. The list can go on and on: opposition, slander, and backbiting; resistance, lack of cooperation, insufficient support, and unfair treatment.

Is God in control? You cannot read your Bible from cover to cover without noticing that the Bible is God-centred. The Lord God is nothing if he is not the sovereign Lord of the universe who is in control of everything. Believing in the sovereign God is the bedrock of security in ministry.

The purpose of this chapter is to review the many biblical statements which teach God's sovereignty in every detail of life. This is a difficult subject. You may argue with me but you should not argue with God. Therefore, in this chapter we will primarily quote the Scripture and occasionally ask some questions. Think long and hard on the Scripture and apply to your life.

God is the Sovereign King

'The LORD sits enthroned over the flood; the LORD sits enthroned as king forever.'[3] *'The LORD has established his throne in the heavens, and his kingdom rules over all.'*[4]

'For his dominion is an everlasting dominion, and his kingdom endures from generation to generation; all the inhabitants of the earth are accounted as nothing, and he does according to his will among the host of heaven and among the inhabitants of the earth; and none can stay his hand or say to him, "What have you done?"'[5]

'Our God is in the heavens; he does whatever pleases him.'[6]

Think about this: If God is truly sovereign and does whatever pleases him, does anything take place outside his control and will?[7]

God is supreme over the gods

'For the LORD is a great God, and a great King above all gods.'[8] *'For you, O LORD, are most high over all the earth; you are exalted far above all gods.'*[9]

'For I know that the LORD is great, and that our Lord is above all gods. Whatever the LORD pleases, he does, in heaven and on earth, in the seas and all deeps.'[10]

Think about this: If God is sovereign and in control, should any Christian fear when someone else who puts him under a curse; or should he fear the spirits who threaten to attack and destroy?

God governs the nations

'For kingship belongs to the LORD, and he rules over the nations.'[11] *'For the LORD, the Most High, is to be feared, a great king over all the earth. He subdued peoples under us, and nations under our feet…For God is the King of all the earth; sing praises with a psalm! God reigns over the nations; God sits on his holy throne.'*[12] *'The LORD is high above all nations, and his glory above the heavens!'*[13]

'O LORD, God of our fathers, are you not God in heaven? You rule over all the kingdoms of the nations. In your hand are power and might, so that none is able to withstand you.'[14]

Think! Is God in control of every aspect of history; of every detail?[15]

God uses nations to punish others

'Ah, Assyria, the rod of my anger, the staff in their hands is my fury! Against a godless nation I send him and against the people of my wrath I command him to take spoil and seize plunder, and to tread them down like the mire of the streets. But he does not so intend and his heart does not so think; but it is in his heart to destroy and to cut off nations not a few.'[16]

Does God continue to use nations for his own purposes? Is God at work in the world today in every world event, fulfilling his purpose?[17]

God elevates leaders and removes them

'It is I who by my great power and my outstretched arm have made the earth, with the men and animals that are on the earth, and I give it to whomever it seems right to me. Now I have given all these lands into the hand of Nebuchadnezzar, the king of Babylon, my servant, and I have given him also the beasts of the

field to serve him. All the nations shall serve him and his son and his grandson, until the time of his own land comes. Then many nations and great kings shall make him their slave.'[18]

'For not from the east or from the west and not from the wilderness comes lifting up, but it is God who executes judgment, putting down one and lifting up another.'[19]

'...to the end that the living may know that the Most High rules the kingdom of men and gives it to whom he will and sets over it the lowliest of men.'[20]

Think about this: Does God raise up leaders in the Church and remove them? Is God still the sovereign Lord who is in control of everything today, even in the Church?[21]

God is the sovereign potter

'Then the word of the LORD came to me: "O house of Israel, Can I not do with you as this potter has done? declares the LORD. Behold, like the clay in the potter's hand, so are you in my hand, O house of Israel."'[22]

God turns the heart of kings wherever he wills

'[God] turned the heart of the king of Assyria to them, so that he aided them in the work of the house of God, the God of Israel.'[23]

'The king's heart is a stream of water in the hand of the LORD; he turns it wherever he will.'[24]

I ask you, does God continue today to do what he did in the past by shaping history?[25]

God overrules the plans of men

'He frustrates the devices of the crafty, so that their hands achieve no success. He catches the wise in their own craftiness, and the schemes of the wily are brought to a quick end.'[26]

'The LORD brings the counsel of the nations to nothing; he frustrates the plans of the peoples.'[27]

'Many are the plans in the mind of a man, but it is the purpose of the LORD that will stand.'[28]

Think about this! How many plans have you made that God has overruled?

Did God overrule your plans or did others frustrate your good intentions?

Can God's perfect will for your life be frustrated by others?[29]

God gives life and takes away life; God makes rich and makes poor

'See now that I, even I, am he, and there is no god beside me; I kill and I make alive; I wound and I heal; and there is none that can deliver out of my hands.'[30]

'The LORD kills and brings to life; he brings down to Sheol and raises up. The LORD makes poor and makes rich; he brings low and he exalts. He raises up the poor from the dust; he lifts the needy from the ash heap to make them sit with princes and inherit a seat of honor.'[31]

God achieves his purpose through man's sin:

'Surely the wrath of man shall praise you...'[32]

- ***He used the jealousy of Joseph's brothers to achieve his purpose:*** Joseph said, *'And now do not be distressed or angry with yourselves because you sold me here, for God sent me before you to preserve* *life. For the famine has been in the land these two years, and there are yet five years in which there will be neither plowing nor harvest. And God sent me before you to preserve for you a remnant on earth, and to keep alive for you many survivors. So it was not you who sent me here, but God.'*[33]

- ***God used the jealousy of Jewish rulers to fulfill his Word:*** *'This Jesus, delivered up according to the definite plan and foreknowledge of God, you crucified and killed by the hands of lawless men.'*[34] *'And now, brothers, I know that you acted in ignorance, as did also your rulers. But what God foretold by the mouth of all the prophets that his Christ would suffer, he thus fulfilled.'*[35]
- ***God used the injustice of Pilate and Herod to accomplish his will:*** *'For truly in this city there were gathered together against your holy servant Jesus, whom you anointed, both Herod and Pontius Pilate, along with the Gentiles and the peoples of Israel, to do whatever your hand and your plan had predestined to take place.'*[36]
- ***God used imprisonment of Paul to forward the gospel:*** *'I want you to know, brothers, that what has happened to me has really served to advance the gospel…'*[37]

Does God continue to overrule the intentions of sinful men and use them to accomplish his purposes? Even in your life? Today?

God hardens whom he wills and shows mercy on whom he wills

'For he says to Moses, "I will have mercy on whom I have mercy, and I will have compassion on whom I have compassion." So then it depends not on human will or exertion, but on God, who has mercy. For the Scripture says to Pharaoh, "For this very purpose I have raised you up, that I might show my power to you, and that my name might be proclaimed in all the earth." So then he has mercy on whomever he wills, and he hardens whomever he wills.'[38]

God turns events around for his purposes

'So the king [Rehoboam] did not listen to the people, for it was a turn of affairs brought about by the LORD that he might fulfill his word which the LORD spoke…'[39]

CONCLUSION

The mysteries of God's sovereignty and man's responsibility are deep. We will let your theology teachers help you to wrestle with this conundrum. But let me assure you that Christian theology does not teach any form of fatalism. Although the Bible clearly teaches that God is the sovereign King and nothing takes place in this world outside his perfect will, it also teaches that we are fully responsible – to pray and evangelise, to study and prepare for our sermons, to work diligently and faithfully. And when we don't, there are consequences. Christians are not fatalists like the Muslims. How do we reconcile God's sovereignty and man's responsibility? We cannot but these two truths are both biblical. As Joseph said to his brothers, *'You meant it for evil against me, but God meant it for good.'*[40]

Here are some insights from this awesome biblical truth:

a. We have deep joy and peace in knowing that God, who has called us into ministry, is the

Sovereign Lord of the universe who is in control of every minute detail of history and of our own lives. God in his sovereign rule has laid out '*the race that is set before us*.'[41] This may not be our preference but we rest in God's good and wise intentions.

b. We rest in God's promises: '*For my thoughts are not your thoughts, neither are your ways my ways, declares the LORD. For as the heavens are higher than the earth, so are my ways higher than your ways and my thoughts than your thoughts.*'[42]

c. We further affirm that behind every undesirable turn of events is the hand of a wise and loving providence. '*And we know that in all things God works for the good of those who love him, who have been called according to his purpose... Who shall separate us from the love of Christ? Shall trouble or hardship or persecution or famine or nakedness or danger or sword?...No, in all these things we are more than conquerors...*'[43]

d. We believe that behind all secondary causes (the acts of men) is the Supreme First Cause – the loving Supreme Being who rules with wisdom and love.

Embracing God's sovereign will is not something to be accepted with joyless submission to unavoidable circumstances. Christian leaders embrace God's will with joy in Christ. This is basic for all Christian leadership.

Moreover, they learn to love and forgive all who have wronged them. Learning how to forgive others is essential for every Christian leader. Forgiving others is not easy but it is basic. Do you have problems in forgiving others? Forgiving others is the topic for the next chapter of our study.

SEARCHING THE SCRIPTURE WITH APPLICATION

1. Read the story of Joseph in Ge 37-50.
    a. Using your imagination, trace the pain and anguish, the despair and doubts that may have surfaced in Joseph's mind throughout this account.
    b. How do you think Joseph was able to come to the conclusions reflected in Ge 45:5-8 and 50:19-21?
    c. What lessons can we learn from Joseph to help us in ministry?
2. Read the life of Job in the Old Testament book of Job.
    a. Describe the state of Job before and after and the tragic events?
    b. Why did these things happen to Job?
    c. What loftier reason did God have for bringing these trials to Job than simply a desire for Job's comfort and well-being?
    d. What lessons can we learn from Job to help us whenever facing such difficult situations?
3. Read the account of Paul's 'thorn in the flesh' in 2 Co 12?
    a. What experiences did Paul have that preceded the thorn in the flesh?
    b. What was 'the thorn in the flesh'? Make a study of this.
    c. Why did God in his sovereignty bring this affliction to Paul?
    d. Whenever troubles or trials of one kind or another come our way, what should be our attitude?

Endnotes

1 Ro 8:28 from *The New Testament* Translated by J. B. Phillips
2 1 Co 3:6
3 Ps 29:10
4 Ps 103:19
5 Da 4:34f
6 Ps 115:3 *NIV*
7 Also read Dt 4:39;1Ch 29:11f; Ps 29:10;145:13; Lam 5:19.
8 Ps 95:3
9 Ps 97:9
10 Ps 135:5,6
11 Ps 22:28
12 Ps 46:2,3,7,8
13 Ps 113:4
14 2 Ch 20:6
15 Also read Ps 67:4; Isa 40:22,23; Jer 10:10
16 Isa 10:5-7
17 Also read Isa 13:3-5; Jer 51:20-25
18 Jer 27:5-7
19 Ps 75:6,7
20 Da 4:17; c.f. 4:25
21 Also Jer 32:27,28; Da 4:17,25
22 Jer 18:6f
23 Ezra 6:22
24 Pr 21:1
25 Also read 1 Ch 5:26; 2 Ch 36:22f
26 Job 5:12,13
27 Ps 33:10
28 Pr 19:21
29 Also read Ps 127:1; 1 Co 4:19; Lam 3:37
30 Dt 32:39
31 1 Sa 2:6-8
32 Ps 76:10
33 Ge 45:5-8
34 Ac 2:2:23
35 Ac 3:17, 18
36 Ac 4:27,28
37 Php 1:12
38 Ro 9:14-18;
39 1 Ki 12:15
40 Ge 50:20
41 Heb 12:2
42 Isa 55:8,9
43 Ro 8:28-39

9
A FORGIVING SPIRIT

'Be forbearing with one another, and forgiving,
where any of you has cause for complaint:
you must forgive as the Lord forgave you.'[1]

Learning to forgive is so hard but so basic for all Christian leaders.

Those in ministry will tell of the rewards in the service of the King; but they will also tell of *difficult people*. What joy in leadership except for *difficult people!* They come in many stripes. Some reject anything new put forward by the leader – 'We never did this before.' Others are constant critics; they find fault in everything, making mountains out of anthills. Those with inferiority complexes try to bolster their self-image through arrogant talk and behaviour; they are self-willed and domineering opponents of the leader. Still others gossip behind the leader's back, slandering and finding fault. Hard work may be unappreciated and even criticized. 'It is a rare person who reaches adulthood without realizing the inevitability of hurts and disappointments in life.'[2]

As they say: 'To dwell above with the saints in love, Oh that will be glory. But to dwell below with the ones I know, that is another story.' 'If you would lead, know this: Coping with difficult people is a must!...Every great leader has learned that problem people are customary and must be dealt with every day.'[3]

A Forgiving Spirit

The natural response to difficult people is frustration, impatience, anger, bitterness and self-pity. The reality is that any leader whose spirit is ruled by bitterness, grudges and deep resentment will not have an effective ministry. This chapter is meant to help every leader to learn the grace of forgiveness.

What is meant by forgiveness?

The only solution to being trapped in an endless cycle of resentment and bitterness is forgiveness.[1] But what is meant by 'forgiveness'? Many people do not understand what is entailed in forgiveness.

1. What forgiveness is not –

- Forgiveness is *not* denying the offense or its painful effects; nor is it denying the offender's responsibility. Biblical forgiveness recognises all of this but acknowledges other truths as well.
- Forgiveness is *not* a feeling. If you wait until you *feel* like forgiving you may never forgive. Biblical forgiveness is an act of the will, to let go of your right to demand a payback.
- Forgiveness is *not* only with the lips but from the heart.[4]
- Forgiveness is *not* a one-time event but an on-going process, 'a life sentence.' Forgiveness cannot erase painful memories but it requires a continued refusal to dwell on those thoughts.
- Forgiveness is *not* a passive attitude which tolerates further injury or injustice. Biblical forgiveness trusts God for his help and seeks measures to protect and redeem, rather than retaliate with revenge.

2. What forgiveness is –

Old Testament vocabulary: The principle Hebrew word in the Old Testament for persons forgiving others is *nasa* with the underlying meaning, 'to lift, carry, take away.'[5] The offence is carried away so there is no longer any barrier between the offended and the offender.

New Testament vocabulary: In the New Testament the underlying meaning of the Greek word, *aphesis*, is 'to send away.' To forgive is 'to let go' as 'letting go of a debt'; or 'releasing' as 'releasing a prisoner.'[6] When someone *forgives* another, he let's go and releases the offender of any debt owed to him. There is no longer any barrier between the two.

English usage: The English word, *to forgive*, carries the idea of ceasing 'to feel resentment against.'[7] A forgiving person lets go of all resentment because the offender has been released of all guilt and blame. 'Forgetting is the *result* of complete forgiveness; it is never the *means*. It is the final step, not the first.'[8]

This means that a forgiving person:

- Does not take revenge on those who have wronged him,[9] but instead is kind and compassionate toward them,[10] and prays for them that they will be blessed.[11]
- Does not hate those who have wronged him or make them feel guilty, but instead[12] shows love towards them.[13]
- Does not bring up the matter any more to the offender or gossip the matter to others.[14] The issue is finished for it has been forgiven 'from the heart.' Some people say, 'I forgive him but I cannot forget.' That is not forgiveness. Though the memory may linger, we no longer remember in the sense of holding it against him.

---

[1] The emphasis of this study is on 'horizontal' forgiveness, forgiving one another; 'vertical' forgiveness which God grants to sinners will only be treated indirectly.

Forgiving others, however, does not absolve the person of all moral or civil consequences. Committing a criminal act has legal consequences; committing adultery or misappropriating funds has consequences for Christian leaders. Remember David? Forgiveness by God blots out sin so that it is remembered by God no more; but forgiveness does not blot out the temporal consequences of legal infringement, babies born out of wedlock or blemished reputation.

Why should we forgive?

Forgiveness is not natural; revenge is. As Alexander Pope said: 'To err is human, to forgive is divine.' But for a Christian, forgiveness is not an option. Two major reasons support the importance of forgiving others.

1. Forgiveness is mandated by Christ himself. Jesus taught his disciples to pray, 'Forgive us our debts, *as we also have forgiven our debtors.*'[15] This part of the Lord's Prayer is the only one elaborated upon in the following verses. '…but if you do not forgive others their trespasses, neither will your Father forgive your trespasses.' Debtors were cast into prison in ancient times until their debts were paid. Jesus warns that if his disciples refuse to forgive the 'spiritual debts' of others (their offenses and injuries), Christ will not forgive their own sins. A very serious warning indeed! The reason for this stern warning is because of the forgiveness which God has offered to sinful men and women. 'For a Christian to be willfully unforgiving is unthinkable. We who have been forgiven by God Himself have no right to withhold forgiveness from our fellow sinners.'[16]

This truth is vividly illustrated by the 'Parable of the Unforgiving Servant'[17] which is a commentary on the Lord's Prayer. One servant in the parable was deeply in debt; he owed his master 10,000 talents, the largest measure of money. One *denarius* was a fair wage for one day of work, and 6,000 *denari* equaled one talent; hence, 10,000 *talents* represented 60,000,000 days of work! Utterly hopeless! Yet, when the servant pleaded for mercy, the master graciously forgave all his debt.

But then that servant took his fellow servant, who owed him just 100 *denari* (100 days of work), and 'grabbed him and began to choke him,' throwing him into prison until he paid all that he owed. When the master heard this, he called the unforgiving servant and said: '"You wicked servant…I canceled all that debt of yours because you begged me to. Shouldn't you have had mercy on your fellow servant just as I had on you?" In anger his master turned him over to the jailers to be tortured, until he should pay back all he owed.' Jesus concludes by saying, 'This is how my heavenly Father will treat each of you unless you forgive your brother from the heart.' A very serious warning indeed! We cannot press this parable in every detail but it is illustrative of a truth.

> God's punishment is illustrative of how God will discipline unforgiving believers. God will employ harsh measures when necessary to correct a disobedient Christian. As a Father, his love for his children is reflected in his discipline to correct his wayward children. The punishment was not final punishment…Christians will be severely disciplined until they learn to forgive.[18]

How often should we then forgive those who offend us? The human response to offences is revenge. Moses taught in the Old Testament that punishment in the courts should be by the standard of an 'eye for an eye and a tooth for a tooth.' The Jews, however, twisted this to teach personal vengeance. Taking personal vengeance for wrongs done to us makes sense, doesn't it? The rabbis thought that the most one should forgive someone was three times, based on Amos.[19] Jesus' disciples tried to be generous and suggested forgiving seven times.[20] But Jesus replied that the number is unlimited – 7 times 70 (or 490 times). An incredible number! This can only be understood with the background of the extraordinary mercy that God has shown us through Christ.

2. An unforgiving spirit leads to merciless self-destruction. Medical research demonstrates that an unforgiving person destroys himself from within. Could this be the judgement that Jesus warned about? James also teaches: 'For judgement will be merciless to one who has shown no mercy.'[21] A Chinese proverb says: 'The man who opts for revenge should dig two graves.'

An unforgiving spirit leads to a whole array of troubling thoughts that take away peace of mind. Since failure to forgive is sin, the conscience will feel unclean[22] and guilt will weigh heavily on the person.[23] The mind will be taken captive with the endless cycle of reviewing the wrongs done by the person; he becomes captive to feelings of bitterness, resentment, self-pity and ill-feelings.[24] The mind becomes darkened with confusion, ignorant of God's gracious will.[25] Inevitably, an unforgiving spirit leads to broken fellowship and disunity between persons.[26]

An unforgiving person is captive to the past as he dwells on the past wrongs. 'What a helpless, hopeless cycle of feelings bitterness brings. It carries us around and around the same senseless circle. Around and around ourselves…Only forgiveness can intercept our endless orbiting around ourselves and set us free.'[27] The unforgiving person has actually yielded his mind to the control of the very one who injured him. 'We all know bitter people. They have amazing memory for the tiniest detail, and they wallow in self-pity and resentment. They catalog every offense against them and are always ready to show others how much they have been hurt.'[28] Hatred becomes so entrenched that the personality is inextricably marked by hatred; love is no longer possible.

Such a condition begins to take a toll on the physical and mental health of the unforgiving person. Medical scientists believe that anywhere from 60% to 90% of all illnesses today are caused by such emotional conditions as fear, envy, resentment, hatred and sorrow. One doctor told his patient: 'If you don't cut out all your resentments, I will have to cut out your intestines.' Holding a grudge raises the blood pressure, depletes the immune system's resistance to disease, leads to depression and causes enormous stress on the whole body. Psychosomatic diseases are manifestations of the close ties between the inner spirit and the body.

> This close connection between forgiveness and health has recently been noted by medical researchers. Recent research has shown that the experience of receiving forgiveness strengthens the body's immune system and helps us ward off or heal more rapidly from disease. On the other hand, people who have a tendency to hold resentment and a related inability to forgive others are much more likely to develop a range of diseases, including cancer and heart disease.[29]

Resentment poisons and eventually destroys the mind, spirit and the body. Psychiatrists point out that murder and suicide are the results of an unforgiving spirit. Failure to show mercy will lead to suffering without mercy. Alan Patton, the South African anti-apartheid politician, reportedly said, 'There is a hard law that when a deep injury is done to us, we never recover until we forgive.'

How can we forgive?

Forgiving others is costly and difficult. 'True forgiveness is the hardest thing in the universe. Our ideas of justice pull the other way. "He has wronged me. Let him pay," we say.'[30] Given the mandate to forgive and the dire warnings if we don't forgive, what can be done to help the servants of the Lord to forgive? The following is needed:

1. Experience the forgiveness of God. Thomas Merton, a Trappist monk and scholar, said: 'We do not know how to forgive until we know what it is to be forgiven.' The motive and enabling for our forgiveness of others is God's forgiveness of us. Not only does God's forgiveness *require* us to forgive others, as taught in the 'Parable of the Unmerciful Servant'; God's forgiveness should *motivate* us to forgive others. Listen to Paul when he writes:

> Get rid of all bitterness, rage and anger, brawling and slander, along with every form of malice. Be kind and compassionate to one another, *forgiving each other, just as in Christ God forgave you.*[31]

'*As God forgave you*' is the key. Because God forgave us, he *requires* us to forgive others; and this forgiveness *motivates* us to forgive. Experiencing God's forgiveness *enables* us to forgive. If you have trouble forgiving others, meditate and pray over God's forgiveness of your sins. How can you be so small-minded to be unforgiving of others when God has forgiven all your sin?

2. Enter into the feelings of the offender. An ancient proverb says: 'To know all is to forgive all.' Helpful in the process of forgiving is trying to understand the history and the motivations of the offender. We need not agree with the person but understanding does help in forgiving.

This all entails empathy. 'Empathy and compassion enable us to become aware of the humanness of our offenders as people…who, like us, also suffer from stories of painful victimization.'[32] Keeping a distance from the offender only aggravates the problem. By talking to the person and seeking to understand that person with empathy will much more quickly lead to apologies and consequent forgiveness. 'Offenders are more likely to offer apologies in close, satisfying relationships…[33]

3. Demonstrate love for the offender. Love is primarily volitional and not emotional. Love is commanded. Both the first and greatest commandments are 'to love.' Emotions are not commanded; only the will is. Jesus commanded, 'Love your enemies.'[34] Loving enemies is not natural; it does not flow from the heart of emotions. But the command is directed to the will. 'To love one's enemy does not mean to love the mire in which the pearl lies, but to love the pearl that lies in the mire.'[35] Pray for the offender; value the offender; forgive!

When should we forgive?

Some offenses should be forgiven unconditionally; others have conditions.

Unconditional forgiveness: It is impossible to pass through life without offenses coming our way, even from friends. When jokes or humourous comments are made, there may be a barb, or an inferred attack against another; perhaps it was unintentional or unconscious, but the comment hurts. Most people who hurt you don't even think they have done anything against you. A person may feel overlooked or excluded from some social gathering, or may feel slighted or unappreciated or passed over. For friends to be confronting one another for all these 'hurts' would be rather burdensome.

Paul seemed to have these offences in mind when he admonished the Colossian Christians: 'Bear with each other and forgive whatever grievances you may have against one another.'[36] There is no need to 'bear' with each other if there is no burden – if there is nothing unpleasant in the relationship. Friendship requires a generous tolerance of one another's weaknesses. Human relationships can have annoyances but Paul pleads: 'forgive whatever grievances you may have against another.'

'This, then, is the governing rule: Unless an offense *requires* confrontation, unconditional, unilateral forgiveness should cover the transgression. The offended party, in suffering the offense, is following the footsteps of Christ.[37] This is the attitude Christ called for in Matthew 5:39-40.'[38] Jesus manifested this attitude when he prayed, 'Father, forgive them, because they do not know what they are doing.'[39] Most offenses can be forgiven unilaterally within the heart because of Christ's love; and they must be forgiven. To wait for someone to repent first before you forgive will mean a very, very long wait with you nursing a harmful, bitter spirit within you.

But what should you do if you yourself have offended another unintentionally? You meant nothing by it; you feel innocent. What should you do? Eugene Habecker, a Christian university president makes this observation:

> Many times people are offended by something the leader has done, but the leader has no idea that his or her actions have been offensive. In my experience as a leader people rarely tell me directly that I have offended them. Rather, I find out second or third-hand. This lack of directness is unfortunate, but once I know that I have been the source of the offense, the responsibility is still mine to initiate forgiveness.[40]

Conditional forgiveness: If someone has truly sinned in a scandalous way, the Bible does admonish confronting the offender before offering forgiveness.[41] Scripture implies that forgiveness is not always offered until repentance is expressed. John MacArthur offers four criteria for those times when confrontation is necessary before forgiveness can be offered:[42]

- *When observing a serious offense against someone other than you.* Overlooking such wrongs is itself a sin.[43] We have no right to forgive the sins committed against others.
- *When ignoring an offense that might hurt the offender.*[44] Someone may display poor judgement or manifest poor habits which, if left to himself, would seriously hurt that person in ministry, personal relationships or within the Church community. In love such a person should be confronted to save him or her.
- *When a sin is scandalous and damages the Body of Christ.*[45] Any such sin as immorality, lying, stealing or any other breaking of the Ten Commandments must be dealt with before they bring reproach to the Body of Christ.
- *Whenever an offense results in broken relationships, then formal forgiveness is essential to reconciliation.* 'A rift in the relationship between Christians rules out the possibility of the kind of forgiveness that simply overlooks a fault. Whether harsh words have been exchanged or an icy silence prevails, if both sides know that a breach exists, the only way to resolve matters is by the formal granting of forgiveness.'[46]

CONCLUSION

There are so many blessings when we humble ourselves and forgive others, as learned from African traditions. As an African proverb says, '*He who forgives, ends a quarrel.*' Quarrels are costly; forgiveness solves it. Harbouring bitterness and anger solves nothing. As the Idoma proverb says, '*The fly cannot be driven away by getting angry at it.*' The only way to get rid of the problem is to forgive. Before the coming of the gospel the Luhya of Kenya observed: When a man goes to sacrifice he must remain peaceful, without a hot heart. He must stay thus for at least a day. If he quarrels on that day or is hot in his heart he becomes sick and destroys the words of the lineage and of the sacrifice. If the Luhya knew this before the coming of the gospel, how much more should Christians act upon the message of love and forgiveness in Christ.

In the face of difficult people, an effective leader needs more than a forgiving spirit if he is going to succeed. One more basic requirement remains for Christian leaders, namely, *perseverance.* 'Winners never quit, and quitters never win.' After all has been said about basics for Christian leadership, leaders must learn to persevere. Learning how to persevere with the joys and sorrows in leadership is discussed in the following chapter.

SEARCHING THE SCRIPTURE WITH APPLICATION

1. From a biblical perspective, why is the forgiveness of others important?
2. For personal and practical reasons why is the practice of forgiving others so important for a Christian leader? Discuss the reasons why you think so.
3. Discuss what 'forgiveness' includes and what it does not include.
4. If forgiveness is so important, why do Christians find it so difficult to forgive?
5. Using the ideas found in this chapter along with your own observations and experience in life, how can one learn to forgive another who has hurt you?
6. Discuss the various times when you and others need to learn to forgive unconditionally.
7. What is meant by 'conditional forgiveness'? What kind of offenses can justify forgiveness only on condition of meeting certain requirements?
8. The only part of 'The Lord's Prayer' which Jesus commented on was this request, '*Forgive us our debts as we also have forgiven our debtors.*' Read Mt 6:12-15. Why is this teaching so important for Christian leaders?
9. A parable Jesus gave which further elaborates this need for forgiveness is in Mt 18:21-35. Study this and reflect on the reasons forgiving others is so important. How faithfully do you follow Jesus' teaching?

Endnotes

[1] Col 3:12-13 NEB
[2] Benner 1996:87
[3] Miller 1987:102
[4] Mt 18:35
[5] Brown 1983:669
[6] Trench 1953:114
[7] Random House College Dictionary: 1988
[8] Augsburger 1970: 19
[9] Ro 12:17
[10] Eph 4:32
[11] Mt 5:44
[12] Mt 18:35
[13] Mt 5:44
[14] Tit 3:2-3
[15] Mt 6:12
[16] MacArthur 1998: 97
[17] Mt 18:21-35
[18] MacArthur 1998: 111
[19] Am 1:3,6,9,11,13
[20] Mt 18:21f
[21] Jas 2:13 NASB
[22] Ps 51:2,7
[23] Ps 51:8
[24] Ps 51:8
[25] Isa 44:20
[26] Gal 5:15
[27] Augsburger 1970: 30f
[28] Arnold 1997:7
[29] Benner 1996:28
[30] Augsburger 1970: 19f
[31] Eph 4:31-32
[32] Shults 2003: 58
[33] Shults 2003: 58
[34] Mt 5:44
[35] Augsburger 1970: 30
[36] Col 3:13
[37] 1 Pe 2:21-25
[38] MacArthur 1998: 123
[39] Lk 23:24
[40] Habecker 1987: 105
[41] Lk 17:3; Mt 18:15-17
[42] MacArthur 1998: 129-132
[43] Isa 1:17; Je 22:3; La 3:35f
[44] Gal 6:1, 2
[45] Heb 12:15, 24
[46] MacArthur 1998: 132

10
PERSEVERANCE OF LEADERS

'Therefore…be steadfast, immovable, always abounding in the work of the Lord, knowing that your toil is not in vain in the Lord.'[1]

With perseverance the Christian leader can succeed in ministry.

In fact, a Nigerian proverb says, 'With patience you can cook stones.' No doubt you have heard the story of the tortoise and the rabbit? The rabbit has the natural ability to outrun any tortoise. But the folklore tells of the patient, plodding and persevering tortoise winning the race because the rabbit got side-tracked and lost his focus. In his cocky, self-assurance the rabbit lost out to the patient, persevering tortoise.

Perseverance with patience will help the Christian leader succeed in ministry because of the inevitable obstacles in the race of life. Without a patient, persevering spirit, the leader will eventually despair and give up.

Perseverance among successful people

> Throughout the course of history this one principle has proven true: Success comes to the committed. Volumes of books could be filled with stories of businesses, inventions, wars, and relationships that were on the verge of failure when a single courageous, persistent person refused to raise the white flag. One more day of business, one more experiment, one more battle, and one more try at communicating a vision proved to be the ticket to success.[2]

A careful study was made of two very successful men: Thomas Edison, the prolific inventor of many things, including the electric light bulb; and Henry Ford, the inventor and engineer of a self-propelled vehicle with a gasoline engine, the Ford automobile, which helped America in the early 1900s to become a nation on wheels. The researcher concluded: 'I found no quality save *persistence*, in either one of them that even remotely suggested the major source of their stupendous achievements [italics added].'[3]

Thomas Edison failed thousands of times in trying to invent the electric light bulb. When he began experimenting, he said it would only take him a few weeks to invent the light bulb. In fact it took him two years. He tried over 6,000 different carbonized plant fibers, looking for a carbon filament for his light bulb. After thousands of failed efforts, he commented: 'I haven't failed. I've identified 10,000 ways this doesn't work.' When working on the nickel/iron storage battery, he performed 10,296 experiments. Edison never gave up.

One of the greatest Presidents of the United States was Abraham Lincoln, who led the nation through a civil war in order to emancipate the African slaves. Without perseverance he would never have reached that pinnacle of success.

- He failed in business in 1831.
- He was defeated for legislature in 1832.
- He failed in business again in 1833.
- He suffered a nervous breakdown in 1836.
- He was defeated for speaker in 1838.
- He was defeated for elector in 1840.
- He lost his bid for Congress in 1843.
- He lost his run for Senate in 1855.
- He was defeated for Vice President in 1856.
- He lost another run for the Senate in 1858.
- He was elected President in 1860.

Perseverance in African tradition

Perseverance has been a traditional virtue in African cultures. Many African proverbs reveal the traditional wisdom on this subject.

'*By persevering the egg walks on legs*,' say the Oromo and Amhara in Ethiopia. In other words, patience enables one to succeed.

'*The hurry-hurry person eats goat; the one who takes his or her time eats beef*,' say the Sesotho in Lesotho of South Africa. Almost nothing in life is ever accomplished in a hurry; surely, nothing of eternal value.

'*The wasp says that several regular trips to a mud pit enables it to build a house*,' report the Ewe in Ghana. Persistence yields results, even with small achievements; small steps result in a big step.

'*One who enters the forest does not listen to the breaking of the twigs in the brush*,' according to the Bemba in Zambia. Anyone who fears a slight obstacle will fail. Success comes by ignoring distractions.

Perseverance among Christian leaders

Anyone who has experienced the realities of Christian leadership throughout history can testify to the need of a patient spirit that perseveres under trials.

In the 13th century Bonaventure was selected to be the governor-general of the Franciscan monastic movement. He wrote, 'The head [of the monasteries] needs a great deal of patience.' Note how similar his reasons are for needing patience to our own experiences today.

The first reason a head of an organisation needs patience is the many responsibilities which are time-consuming and tiring.

> *Second*, a head also needs patience when he sees how little he gets for all his labor. Even though he wears himself out, he will not see much spiritual growth in the community. He may try many things and finally, after much labor, find the people under him beginning to improve a little. But so many obstacles stand in the way of spiritual progress that they will be easily delayed again. A head is tempted to despair of ever seeing a return for his labors; he is like a farmer who sows much but reaps a poor harvest.
>
> *A third reason* why a head needs patience is the ungratefulness of those he works and cares for. His charges are scarcely ever satisfied with him; rather, they always feel put upon, because they are sure that he could do things differently, and better, if he wished. Often one is perplexed, not knowing whether to yield to their constant demands and allow everything they want, or to hold firmly to the course of action that one believes will do more good. Many things that a head does are twisted by his people and given a bad interpretation. They murmur at his decision, make accusations against him, reveal his faults, and derive matter for scandal from things that he did out of a sense of duty to God and to them. It is almost impossible to escape the fact that whatever one determines or does, it will upset some of the brethren.[4]

Sound familiar? Human nature has not changed in the past eight hundred years. Christian leaders still need patience if they are to persevere and succeed. Those who have experienced the realities of Christian ministry in recent days in Africa have the following advice for those who follow in their footsteps:

'*We need to persevere. There are painful things to the ministry, slander and rejection, but we need to look to God and keep on going.*' (Pastor)

'*Before anyone enters the ministry, they should prepare for action. The ministry is not easy with human strength, but with God we can make it. Ministry needs patience. I've learned the fruit of the spirit of patience.*' (Teacher)

'*Let them go into the field, not afraid of what they will eat. God is faithful. They should not doubt God. They have chosen a noble job. It is the highest calling one can receive. If I would start all over again, I would be a pastor again. I want to assure them, that God is faithful. My wife and I can testify to this. We have never gone hungry.*' (Pastor)

'*I've learned that if I am called by God, there is no quitting. Regardless of what comes my way – slander, suffering, discouragement, and unhappiness – I must not quit. One must not be distracted from my focus which is on Jesus Christ. I must keep on going. This is not easy. To be a Christian – the name is a very nice word – but to live it is not easy. I must live the name I have. I must be serious with what I profess.*' (Bible School Teacher)

'There is need for patience and humility, because if you want things to happen quickly you will be discouraged, because people may not understand the ideas you come up with and cannot accept them.' (Pastor)

Patience contributes to perseverance

Patience is not identical to perseverance but they are interrelated; patience contributes to perseverance. Without patience, one would not persevere. *Patience* refers to calm endurance and long-suffering whenever confronted with opposition, suffering or provocation. *Perseverance* refers to steadfastness and persistence in following a course of action. Leaders who persist in their calling are patient when experiencing problems of one sort or another. You cannot have perseverance without patience. In fact, the Greek words for *patience* and *perseverance* are the same.

One such word, *makrothumia*, refers to 'long-suffering'. Patience (*makrothumia*) has a 'long-temper' and refrains from anger whenever aggravated by people. God 'suffers long';[5] He holds back his wrath until 'the day of wrath.' Christ displayed his 'unlimited patience' when he showed mercy to Saul, 'the worst of sinners.'[6] The patient person is not easily provoked; nor does he blaze into anger with those who disagree with him;[7] he has learned to control his emotions.

Paul urged the Christians in Ephesus to live 'with all humility and gentleness, *with patience, bearing with one another in love*, eager to maintain the unity of the Spirit in the bond of peace.'[8] Living and working with people can test one's patience. But the Christian leader must learn to develop a 'long-suffering' spirit, patiently bearing with difficult people. Instead of exploding in anger or frustration, the patient, 'long-tempered' leader calmly endures and patiently persists in the ministry.

A synonym of *makrothumia* is the Greek word, *hupomone*, translated by *patience* and *perseverance*; it means literally, 'to remain under.' Whereas, *makrothumia* refers to patience with people, *hupomone* refers to patience under adverse circumstances; he 'remains under' the unpleasant circumstances and perseveres.[9] Whenever a leader is under a siege of trials, he or she bears up, does not lose heart but perseveres. Comparing the Christian life with an athletic race, Paul urges: 'let us run with *endurance* the race set before us.'[10] In life we soon discover that our own 'running track' is different from others. God in his sovereignty chooses to place us in a particular 'running track' ('the race set before us'). With God's grace we are commanded to run 'with endurance,' 'remaining under' the difficult circumstances with our eyes fixed on Jesus who saved us and called us to Christian ministry.

Development of patience

James writes to the Hebrew believers during persecution.

> When all kinds of trials and temptations crowd into your lives, my brothers, don't resent them as intruders, but welcome them as friends! Realize that they come to test your faith and to produce in you the quality of ***endurance***. But let the process go on until that ***endurance*** is fully developed, and you will find you have become men of mature character with the right sort of independence.[11]

Trusting in the sovereign control of the loving God, James urges believers to endure 'all kinds of trials and temptations,' seeing them as 'friends' who are sent by God for blessing. Even though trials may be frustrating, annoying and even painful, believers should 'count it all joy' when trials come because of what God will do in their character through them. Trials are like the crucibles of fire which purified gold. Even as the fire melted away the dross and produced pure gold, so the painful fire of 'all kinds of trials' produces mature character that is marked by *endurance*. Patience and perseverance are not learned in the classroom with academic instruction; they are learned in the University of Experience. Without difficult people and trying circumstances no opportunity is found to develop and grow a patient and persevering spirit.

Therefore, whenever you meet a difficult person who opposes your vision or when you encounter a frustrating circumstance, 'count it all joy' that you have opportunity of maturing in your character to become more patient.

Motivation for perseverance

James concludes the letter to the Hebrew Christians with these words:

__Be patient__, therefore, brothers, until the coming of the Lord. See how the farmer waits for the precious fruit of the earth, __being patient__ about it, until it receives the early and the late rains. You also, __be patient__...As an example of suffering and __patience__, brothers, take the prophets who spoke in the name of the Lord. Behold, we consider those blessed who __remained steadfast__. You have heard of the __steadfastness__ of Job, and you have seen the purpose of the Lord, how the Lord is compassionate and merciful.[12]

In this context perseverance is needed when you must wait (farmers wait for a harvest); when you are mistreated (the prophets suffered persecution); and when things happen and you just don't know why (even as Job suffered the loss of his material wealth, the loss of his health, and the loss of support from his friends and even his own wife without knowing why).

The motivation for perseverance is twofold:

- Faith in the compassionate purpose of God who is in sovereign control and will prove faithful to one steadfast to his calling.
- Hope in the future reward at the return of Christ. Even as Jesus 'endured the cross, despising the shame' because of 'the joy that was set before him,' so the servant leader endures much suffering for Christ's sake because of the joyful expectation of God's reward and future blessing – 'Well done, good and faithful servant...Enter into the joy of your master.'[13]

CONCLUSION

Blessed is the Christian leader who never quits; he will reap a great reward. Also blessed is the Christian leader who serves with humility. Without humility God's favour is impossible. 'Humility' is the topic for all of *Part Three.*

SEARCHING THE SCRIPTURE WITH APPLICATION

1. Describe the common reasons for the need of patience and perseverance in Christian ministry. How are these similar to or different from the situations calling for patience in secular employment?

2. In Scripture God is called 'the God of patience' (Ro 15:5).
   a. Why did God show patience according to Ro 2:4?
   b. Describe the circumstances of God's patience in 1 Pe 3:20?
   c. What benefit did God's patience offer us in 2 Pe 3:15?
   d. What lessons can we learn from God's patience and how can we apply this to our own lives and ministry?
3. Christian leaders are specifically called upon to pursue patience.
   a. Read 1 Ti 6:11 and the context, 1 Ti 6:6-16. In this context, why is endurance/steadfastness/perseverance (*hupomone*) so important to Timothy, a 'man of God,' in the ministry? (Notice that perseverance is included with the list of other important qualifications for ministry – 'righteousness, godliness, faith, love... and gentleness.')
   b. Read 2 Ti 3:10 and the context, 2 Ti 3:10-17. (Notice that both patience [*makrothumia*] and perseverance [*hupomone*] are mentioned in 3:10.) Do you have a Timothy or Timothys whom you are discipling and mentoring? Why is it so important that they see in your life evidence of perseverance? What can they point to that indicates your patience and perseverance in ministry?
   c. Read 2 Ti 4:2 and the context, 2 Ti 4:1-6. Why is it so important whenever you 'reprove, rebuke and exhort' that you do it with 'patience'? What evidence is there in your life of patience or impatience when teaching or confronting others with the gospel truth?
4. Read Ro 5:1-5. Proven character that is essential for effectiveness in Christian leadership can only be developed with trials and troubles.
   a. Why should anyone rejoice in trials?
   b. How do trials produce character that is approved or proven?
   c. Why is character that has stood the test (Ro 5:1-5), so important?

Endnotes

[1] 1 Co 15:58 NASB
[2] Perkins 2000:73
[3] Engstrom 1979:116
[4] Bonaventure 1993:39-41
[5] Ro 2:4
[6] 1 Ti 1:16
[7] 2 Ti 4:2
[8] Eph 4:2,3
[9] Trench 1953: 198
[10] Heb 12:1
[11] Jas 1:2-4 *The New Testament* Translated by J.B. Phillips
[12] Jas 5:7-11
[13] Mt 25:21

PART THREE

HUMILITY OF CHRISTIAN LEADERS

Part Three is devoted to the topic of *humility*, deemed by Christian leaders to be most essential for any effectiveness in leadership. After considering the *necessity of humility*, we consider the opposite of humility, namely, *pride*. Pride is the cause of most failure in Christian leadership and therefore it must be starved and slain because it is a beast that will devour God's servants. Various *leadership styles* are examined with emphasis on humility needed to shape Christian leadership. *Servant leadership* is studied as the crowning style for leadership. The life and ministry of Jesus Christ is finally examined as *the supreme model of humility*.

11
THE NECESSITY OF HUMILITY

'Whoever exalts himself will be humbled,
and whoever humbles himself will be exalted.'[1]

Humility is the 'treasure house in which all other graces are contained.'[2]

Bernard of Clairvaux was asked which were the four cardinal virtues. His reply: 'Humility, humility, humility and humility.'[3] To put it simply: without humility, no Christian virtue can exist. Can you name any virtue that can thrive without humility? It has been observed that, 'half the harm that is done in this world is due to people who want to feel important.'[4]

Humility – A *Christian* Virtue

Jesus Christ turned the ethics of this world on its head, transforming a despised attitude into a virtue second to none. In Greek culture 'humility' was held in contempt. It was a virtue alien to ancient ethics.

'Humility' among the Greeks: Words for 'humility' were used by the Greeks but without Christian content. *Tapeinos* means 'lowly,' 'insignificant,' 'weak,' and 'poor,' in the sense of 'groveling.' The word was used disparagingly of someone being 'servile.'[5] The basic sense of the verb is 'to stoop low.' The lion does not 'stoop' (is not 'humble') before its prey but the sheep flees and 'bows down.' The verb in the active voice means 'to harass' or 'to oppress.'

'Humility' referred to the lowly social position of those who were oppressed and downtrodden by rule. 'Thus, to be low on the social scale, to know poverty, or to be socially powerless was seen as shameful. Only seldom in classical Greek do these words have a positive tone…'[6] The lower classes, 'the humble,' are set over against the upper, ruling class. 'Humility' was the 'lowly disposition of insignificant people.' The 'humble' were subjected to 'all strenuous physical labour and all paid work,' unfit for the ruling classes. 'Humility' was synonymous with poverty and lack of public influence. The way out of 'humility' was upward social mobility.[7]

Over against 'humility' was the virtue of 'pride' (or being 'high-minded'). This referred to 'self-sufficient' people who had no need for help from anyone but who were able to lend support to others. In short, the 'self-sufficient' were found among those in high positions.

Humility in the Old Testament: The Greek translation of the Old Testament (the Septuagint) uses various Greek words to translate Hebrew words meaning 'low,' 'flat' and 'under.' Following Greek usage, *tapeinos* may convey the negative sense of 'bow,' 'mean,' 'small,' and 'base' in the Old Testament.[8]

But the Old Testament does not speak of 'humility' in an utterly hopeless and demeaning sense but attributes a positive sense to the 'lowly,' 'contrite' and 'humble' in spirit.[9] Humility is praised.[10] God requires humility of his people[11] and upholds humility as a virtue.[12] God also chooses to dwell with the humble.[13]

Humility in Jesus' teaching

What transformed the concept of *humility* was Jesus Christ who reversed the pagan thinking. Jesus was the master teacher; he practiced what he taught. Through his teaching and example he elevated humility to a level unknown among the ethics of mankind. He taught humility on many occasions with the most powerful lessons given in the midst of the turmoil of life.[14] Jesus continually confronted the Pharisaical conceit and warned the people of their pride. They teach but do not practice.

The humble practice what they preach: The Pharisees 'preach, but do not practice.'[15] But Jesus practiced what he preached, even as the humble do today.

The humble do not publicise their good deeds: The Pharisees 'do all their deeds to be seen by others; for they make their phylacteries broad and their fringes long.'[16] They 'love to pray standing in the synagogues and on the street corners to be seen of men.'[17]

The humble take the lower seats: The proud 'love the place of honour at feasts and the best seats in the synagogues.'[18] They claimed the 'exalted' seats for themselves during a feast. When Jesus noticed at a wedding feast 'how they chose the places of honour,' he advised: "But when you are invited, go and sit in the lowest place…'[19]

The humble do not claim titles: The Pharisees loved the 'greetings in the marketplaces and being called rabbi by others.'[20] But Jesus taught, 'Whoever exalts himself will be humbled, and whoever humbles himself will be exalted.'[21]

The humble do not consider themselves great: The sense of Jesus words in Matthew 18:4 is not so much that one should 'humble himself *as this little child,'* but rather that he should 'humble himself *until he is like this little child.'* A child does not recognise himself as being 'great.' Neither will humble people think of themselves as great.

The humble do not seek great positions for themselves: After three years of instruction by the master teacher, James and John manipulated their mother to request the 'highest seats' with Jesus in the

Kingdom. So his disciples began arguing among themselves 'as to which of them was to be regarded as the greatest.' What vanity! Jesus replied: 'Let the greatest among you become as the youngest, and the leader as one who serves. For who is the greater, one who reclines or the one who serves? Is it not the one who reclines at table? But I am among you as the one who serves.'[22]

Even today, after three years of Bible School training, Church leaders follow in the footsteps of James and John rather than Jesus. We need to follow Jesus who came to serve rather than seeking seats of position. 'For even the Son of Man came not to be served but to serve, and to give his life as a ransom for many.'[23]

Humility in the apostolic teaching

In view of the teaching and example of our Lord, the apostles continued to emphasise the priority of living and serving with all humility. The one Greek word for humility that was never used in classical Greek nor used in the Septuagint is *tapeinophrosune.* This became the New Testament word for Christian 'humility,' meaning 'lowliness of mind.'[24]

Paul described his ministry among the Ephesians as that of humble service. 'You yourselves know how I lived among you…serving the Lord with all *humility* and with tears and with trials…'[25] Paul served with selflessness, without any desire to rule over them. He served the Lord by serving the Ephesians and enduring tears and trials.

After Peter exhorts the elders in their conduct, he admonishes the younger to be subject to the elders. Then he addresses both the young and the old, both the elders and those they lead, 'Clothe yourselves, all of you, with *humility* toward one another, for God opposes the proud but gives grace to the *humble.*'[26] Humility towards others is reciprocal. Not only should the younger manifest humility toward their elders but the elders should display humility to the younger. No doubt Peter had learned the searing lesson of humility from Jesus when the Lord wrapped a towel around his waist, stooped down before his disciples and washed their feet. Such a lesson in humility could never be forgotten. So Peter says, 'clothe yourselves' with the towel of humility.

Humility – The Counterfeit and the True

Humility is not feeling inferior: Many confuse humility with feeling inferior. But an inferiority complex is a counterfeit of humility. Such people think lowly of themselves, deny their self worth and hold to a negative self-image. To have a low opinion of oneself is not humility. It is important that every child of God have a positive self-evaluation, recognising the goodness of God in bestowing on them the rich grace of God.

'Humility is thinking less *about* yourself, not thinking less *of* yourself.'[27] Thinking little of yourself is not humility. Paul admonishes everyone 'not to think of himself more highly than he ought to think, but to think with sober judgement.'[28] A humble person should engage in reflection on his life before God. He should be capable of recognising God's gracious gifts in his life. To deny or demean those God-given gifts is no sign of humility.

Humility is not being weak: Many confuse humility with weakness. The counterfeit humility is being a coward, lacking conviction, being nice but not strong. But meekness is not weakness. A meek person is gentle, patient, forbearing and self-controlled. A gentle person is in fact strong. 'Gentleness is power placed under control.'[29] A humble person holds to strong conviction and has courage to stand up for the right; but he does so graciously and kindly.

Humility is being God-centred and God-conscious: The decisive characteristic of humility is that one always acknowledges that all achievements are by the grace of God. Humility is 'self-forgetfulness that exalts the glory of God.'[30] God, not self, is at the centre of thoughts. Bernard of Clairvaux observes: 'It is therefore necessary to know both what you are and that you are not of yourself, lest you either glory not at all or glory vainly.'[31] The humble child of God should indeed glory, but only in God, not in self.

A humble person first recognises that he was made in the image of God's glory and is the object of God's love and favour. Humility proceeds to boast and glory, but only in God. Paul admonishes, 'God chose what is low and despised in the world…so that no human being might boast in the presence of God…Therefore, as it is written, "Let the one who boasts, boast in the Lord."'[32] Boasting in Christ in all things is true humility. Self-centred, proud people boast of their own achievements.

Characteristics of humility: Let us list some of the traits of true humility:

(1) Humility is unconscious of its humility. If someone thinks he is humble, he probably is not.

(2) 'Humility is remembering that the gifts we have come *through us* but not *from us*. We have nothing that we have not received from above, and we give them back to God to use [italics added].'[33]

(3) Humility suffers in silence, submitting to God's providence without complaint, confident that God is in control.

(4) Humility does not seek to dominate, control or manipulate. Humility does not strive for position and power.

(5) Humility is unselfish. The humble person is primarily concerned for the welfare of others, not his own. He does not seek fame, does not look for 'better seats' or 'better service,' does not desire fancy offices and lofty titles.

(6) Humility is focused on service and not 'professional' ministry. Humility seeks to help others rather than receive rewards for service.

(7) Humility responds to criticism with grace, without defensiveness. Humility is open to correction and rebuke; it never takes revenge.

(8) Humility sees his own sins worse than others. 'When it's *our* sins that most grieve and offend us and are the ones we most want to avoid, then we demonstrate a real measure of humility.'[34]

Advice from Christian Leaders

When seeking the counsel of African Christian leaders we found that 'humility' was ranked one of the most important character traits of a leader. Dependence on God, a life of prayer, and faithfulness were ranked higher. But next to those, these leaders considered humility of the greatest importance.

Humility is manifested in the following ways:

Admit making mistakes: *'When someone goes wrong, you must be humble enough to say, "I am wrong." "I did not do well here." You need to take responsibility as the leader and the topic is closed. People are very appreciative when a leader is open and honest to admit a mistake.'* (Bishop) *'Humility is willingness to accept when you are wrong. You last longer when you accept when you are wrong. Humility is first in importance.' 'Remember that you are also a human being. You make mistakes too. You cannot say, "I know." We are all learning until we go to the grave.'* (Pastor)

Listen to every person: *'A leader must listen to other people's viewpoints, because it is very possible in an African context, once the leader says something, the discussion is finished. No one else wants to say something. So the leader must be humble enough to listen to even the smallest viewpoint in coming to resolutions. For example, there may be two or three opinions. You may be able to draw something out of the least important things said. You must be humble enough to acknowledge the opinions of each person. In many cases you agree by consensus and therefore every little contribution is valuable. I feel this is very helpful. People value their views being appreciated when the leader acknowledges the contribution being made. Even when you feel it is not important, you should find something important in it. This is another sign of humility.'* (Bishop)

'Be careful not to be a dictator. Be open to other people's opinions.'

Be slow to speak: *'I learned this the hard way in the African context. A leader should be slow to speak. I would come into a Board meeting and think I would contribute like any other Board member. But I got my fingers burned because my contribution was taken as the direction, which the leader wants the Board to take. So they stopped talking. The next day they said, "This is what we were told we should do." I said, "Wait a minute. I was just contributing like another member." I learned it a very hard way that the leader must be slow to speak. I should let the others speak and then deduce from them which viewpoints are helpful. Then they talk further which decision to make. When the leader speaks, it is like a chief speaking and the discussion ends there because the chief has spoken. I have learned to be slow to speak unless I have other information which they do not have. When you push your own ideas as a leader, when it does not work out well, it becomes your own problem to solve later. But if a decision is not good but it was made by consensus, everyone will participate in correcting the mistake that was made. It becomes your common problem. The leader does not then take it as his personal problem because everyone has contributed in making the decision. I found this to be very helpful.'* (Church Leader)

Never boast: *'Leaders should not boast. If there is any praise, let others speak it. Once you boast, the chances of falling are great. This temptation is in the Church. "I have started this," someone says, "so this is mine. So I can do what I want." The story is told of people who went hunting. They killed an elephant. As they were pulling it to the village, they kept saying, "Ours," "ours," "ours." But when they came near the village the one who had speared it said, "Mine," "mine," "mine." So the others left it in the bush and the one who speared it could not pull it. It was left there to rot.'* (Kenyan Missionary)

Never be proud of your education: *'Training should not make you puffed up, thinking that people will accept you more than those without training. One must not be aloof. You must mix with them. One pastor said, "You are a layman but I am educated." But he was a dictator. He got a PhD and thought the world was in his hand; but he failed. People said, 'We don't need him.' He thought the country needed him. He was proud of his education. He was pushed out of the Church. He desired to divide the Church. He didn't respect* *anyone. He left the country and went to the U.S.A and pastored a Church there, but ended up marrying someone's wife. He was proud and did not guard his heart.'* (Educator)

'Church leaders really need humility. This has helped me. Educated Church leaders are suspected because we are people who change the Church and bring in new practices. People accuse us of being proud because of higher learning. Humility has helped me to get closer to people and to bridge the gap. This is required from the Scriptures. All servants of God in the Bible were required to be humble. I pray that I might fit in with old women and young people because of humility. I'm not different from others. I tried to develop an attitude that I am not different.' (Church Leader)

Come down to the common person: *'Humility is the key. People fear learned people. We need to come down and follow Jesus.' 'Most African leaders aspire to be western. They are programme oriented, not people oriented. They need to come down to the level of other people.'* (Pastors)

'Humble yourself before others. Follow the example of the Lord as we read in Philippians 2. Serve under the District Chairman who may be trained at a low level Bible School. This is crucial. For example, I find it important to humble myself and keep my cool. Some people in Church feel they know. The elders challenge me, saying, "If you do this…" They speak with a lot of anger. If I raised my voice like that, it would lead to a fight. I must be humble. Such men are wealthy with high positions and they wear better clothes. They put their pastor down and humble him.' (Pastor)

'There is a pastor whom no Church wants. When he goes to a Church, he knows too much. "I have come here and you know nothing." He is a young person but he knows. He cannot humble himself and say, "I don't know." He thinks a pastor knows everything. He cannot humble himself under elders who never went to school. During the month when pastors were posted to Churches, his Church refused this pastor. They said, "Transferring him to another Church is like sweeping dirt from one room to another."' (Educator)

Avoid power struggles: *'I've seen many leaders being proud. But being humble brings unity. When you are down, others see that you are not competing for their seats. Then you can serve.'* (Pastor) *'He must not fight for leadership.'* (Pastor)

Serve others as a leader: *'In Africa once you are a leader, it is a position of honour. But one must be a servant. Leadership is a position of serving others.'* (Church Leader) *'The Church leader should be a servant like Jesus Christ when he came not to be ministered unto but to minister. He humbled himself even to the point of the cross.'* (Educator)

Move slowly in making changes: *'They should be ready to work with people. They should implement slowly and they will succeed. Those who go to Church to change things, those who think they have excellent knowledge and others know little, they end up in conflict. They should deliberately bend to the level of other people.'* (Pastor)

Be patient when others humiliate you: *'I found it very helpful, though not easy, to remain humble when being humiliated. I chose to be silent and speak when I must, especially when things were going wrong. Those who were my enemies provoked me to speak. Then they found reason to accuse me. So I thought it best to be patient.'* (Pastor)

CONCLUSION

Humility does not come naturally, for by nature we are all proud and self-centred human beings. But Jesus made it abundantly clear: '*whoever humbles himself will be exalted.*' Rich rewards and blessings from God, the only One who really counts, are promised to those who learn to serve him with humility.

Conversely, '*whoever exalts himself will be humbled.*' Pride persists by motivating and influencing many Christian leaders. The future of the proud, if not in this life then in the life to come, is to be brought low before God. This destructive cancer of pride in Christian leaders will be the subject of the following chapter.

SEARCHING THE SCRIPTURE WITH APPLICATION

1. Enumerate the promises God makes to the humble: Ps 9:12; 10:17; 25:9; 37:11; 138:6; 147:4; Pr 3:34; 11:2; 15:33; 22:4; 29:33; Jas 4:10.
2. If these promises are true, why do so many believers disobey God and follow a lifestyle of pride?
3. Nimrod, 'the mighty hunter,' established the first world empire and ruled it. But his own ambitious plan in building the Tower of Babel was in defiance against God's declared will (Ge 10:8-14; 11:1-9). In contrast to the self-seeking of Nimrod, Abram was submissive in his obedience to God (Ge 12:1-9). Contrast the pride and humility of these two men and their end.
4. Moses enjoyed the privileges of the Egyptian palace and was an heir to Pharaoh's throne but was forced to flee into the desert for his life. Moses had not learned humility in Pharaoh's palace where he felt important. Read Ex 2:1-3:27. How did Moses' desert experience contribute to his ability to lead Israel? (c.f. Nu 12:3)
5. How does the prayer of the 'tax collector' manifest a spirit of humility that pleases God in contrast to the Pharisee's prayer of pride (Lk 18:9-14)? How does our attitude, if not our prayers, resemble that of the Pharisee? Why is God pleased with the tax collector's prayer?
6. Read Mt 18:1-4. What are the characteristics of 'humility' that are manifest in a little child? According to verse 4, who is 'the greatest in the kingdom of heaven'? How should we become more like a child?

Endnotes

1 Mt 23:12
2 Trench 1953:148
3 Bernard as found in Kreeft 1986: 99
4 T.S. Eliot, Bibliographical source unknown to author.
5 Groundmann 1972: 1
6 Richards 1985: 347
7 Wengst 1988: 4-8
8 Groundmann 1972: 9
9 Ps 131:1,2; 147:6; 149:4
10 Pr 25:6,7; 27:2; 30:32; Jer 45:5
11 Mic 6:8
12 Pr 15:33; 16:19; 22:4; 29:23
13 Isa 57:15; 66:2
14 Mt 5:3,5; 18:2ff; 20:26f; 23:12; Lk 1:52; 14:10; Lk 17:10; 18:13f; 22:24-27
15 Mt 23:3
16 Mt 23:5
17 Mt 6:5
18 Mt 23:6
19 Lk 14:10
20 Mt 23:7
21 Mt 23:12
22 Lk 22:25-27
23 Mk 10:45
24 Ac 20:19; Eph 4:2; Php 2:3; Col 2:18, 23; 3:12; 1 Pe 5:5
25 Ac 20:19
26 1 Pe 5:5
27 Kreeft 1986: 100
28 Ro 12:3
29 MacArthur 1998b: 34
30 Hunter 1990: 951
31 Bernard 1940: 50
32 1 Co 1:28f
33 Ford 1991: 85
34 MacArthur 1998:40f

12
THE PROBLEM OF PRIDE

'Arrogance and pride – distinguishing marks in the wicked — are just plain sin.'[1]

Pride is the cardinal sin which damns the human race because it exalts self and is the root for all other sins.

The Problem of Pride

Who is proud?

The greatest blight of people is their *pride*; the second greatest is their *ignorance* of pride. We are not aware of pride because it is such an intrinsic part of our fallen, human nature. Pride is like spectacles; we see through them without being conscious of them. Pride is pervasive in our cultures. We live and move in our pride without being aware of it. As C.S. Lewis wrote:

> There is one vice of which no man in the world is free; which every one in the world loathes when he sees it in someone else…There is no fault which makes a man more unpopular, and no fault which we are more unconscious of in ourselves. And the more we have it ourselves, the more we dislike it in others.[2]

Greek culture eulogised pride. Pride for the Greeks was a belief in their superiority over others. They believed that Greeks were *better* than all others, so they coined the word *barbarians* to refer to all other peoples – those who did not speak Greek. The Greek philosopher, Aristotle, taught that pride was 'the justified love of oneself,' with the emphasis on *justified*. To be proud is to love yourself more than others because you are truly better than others.

When the British colonised Africa, like all other European colonizers, they justified their colonial rule by their apparent superiority. The sun never set on the British empire; they were the undisputed master of the seas. In their eyes the Africans were primitive – ignorant of the wheel, unable to read or write and without modern technology. Their arrogant demeanor said everything.

America is likewise a proud nation. Americans love to say that America is 'the envy of the world' and 'the only superpower.' Politicians flaunt their pride by asserting: 'America is the greatest nation in the world' and 'The American military is the most powerful in world history.'

What of Africa? When we closely examine the peoples of Africa we find no difference, whether one is Gikuyu or Masai, Swazi or Tonga, Somali or Turkana, they are all *proud* peoples. They believe that humility is cowardice and therefore a weakness.

But surely, there must be a difference in the Christian Church! We would hope to see a shining example – humble, gracious and loving leaders who serve others! But alas, pride is destroying the fabric of the Churches. Many Church leaders have '"the pride of grace" – they are proud of something that they did nothing to deserve.'[3] They are proud of gifts and accomplishments from God.

When we speak with individuals, we discover that Christians are often not conscious of this endemic sin of pride in their lives. Students often struggle to find some moral weakness which needs correction. Pride is seldom mentioned as a character flaw and only with hesitation.

As a missionary teacher for many years I was aware of the general existence of pride in my life but not aware of its pervasive and corrosive effect on me. Other sins were more serious, I thought; but pride was a lesser problem. Not until years of maturity brought me to a painful awareness that in my nature, down, down, deep in my fallen, sinful, human nature is this resilient and persistent monster of pride.

When asked for the reasons why people fail in ministry, our graduates listed *pride* more than any other reason. Examples of pride are many.

When God blesses the ministry, a pastor can easily become proud, thinking '*I* am doing it.' One pastor commented, 'I am the only person educated,' a very dangerous attitude. Many people are selfish, always wanting to be the central person. Self-centred thinking is all about me, myself, and I – 'the sin of the first person singular.' One pastor commented, 'If anything happened and I go home to glory, the Church would collapse.'

Pride destroyed a close friend of a pastor. 'Why don't you come down?' the pastor asked. He was so gifted in Greek and exegesis, but pride destroyed him. He moved from one Church to another and then to another and today he is nowhere. Another pastor believed that he had learned enough to lead the Church. He needed no further reading of the Bible or prayer. He did not need to prepare for sermons. In a few years he lost his purpose. He had no messages for the people. Because of pride, he felt he needed no help from others.

One pastor was so gifted and could really preach well but he was so critical of others. The elders talked with him but he blasted them. Pride set in. He thought he knew it all. When he became involved with the young people an allegation surfaced that he was moving around with a certain lady. But he refused to humble himself and admit his sin. Today, he moves from one denomination to another, even though he is gifted. He refuses to confess because he fears people will look down on him.

What is Pride?

Pope Gregory the Great around AD 600 suggested that all sin could be traced back to 'Seven Cardinal Sins,' later called 'Seven Deadly Sins.' These 'Seven Cardinal Sins' are: pride, lust, envy, greed, gluttony, anger, and sloth (or laziness). Pride heads the list of sins because it reflects 'the Church's judgement that the other sins spring ultimately from pride and are not possible until pride has first established itself.'[4]

What is pride?

- Pride is exalting self, receiving the honour belonging to God alone.
- Pride is the excessive belief in one's own ability that does not recognise God as the source of those abilities. Pride is 'inordinate self-esteem; an unreasonable conceit of superiority in talents, beauty, wealth, rank etc.'[5]
- Pride is self-exaltation in contempt of God. When we become self-centred and focus on self, comparing ourselves with others, we become puffed up, conceited, blinded to our own weaknesses; pride is arrogance in word or deed; pride is haughtiness and an undue sense of our own self importance.
- Pride is idolatry for in the final analysis it makes self into a god to be praised, adored, honoured and served. 'An idol is something within creation that is inflated to function as a substitute for God.'[6] Pride says '*My* will be done,' instead of submitting to God, saying '*Your* will be done.' Fallen human beings are 'idol factories' that elevate self and demote the Creator God.
- Pride is the feeling of being superior to others – 'I am better than…' – I am better educated…; I have more experience than…; I am older than…; I have a more influential position than…
- Pride is the feeling of being entitled to something – 'I deserve more than…' – I deserve a better salary than..; I deserve a better seat than …; I deserve more respect than...

Is all pride sinful?

Can pride ever be legitimate? People may speak of pride in a positive vein. We may talk of being 'proud of our children,' 'proud of our college education,' 'proud of our accomplishments,' or 'proud of our country.' Can we ever be 'proud' and not sin? Even Paul in the Holy Scriptures speaks of being proud of his 'work for God.'[7]

The difference between legitimate pride and sinful pride is the reference point. If the focus is on self and personal accomplishments, that is sin; but if the focus is on God who graciously provides, enables and empowers, that is joy in God's grace. Whenever Paul felt a positive pride, it was with reference to what God had done in and through him. We might better speak of 'gratitude,' for Paul 'was careful to explain that his success was entirely due to God's gifts... Thus [Paul's] boasting "in Christ" was tantamount to thanking God…Pride is legitimate only when it remembers to attribute all honour to God.'[8]

Pride as a self-exalting attitude is wrong. But God wants us to take a healthy pride, and to find joy, in what he is doing in our lives. As arrogance, pride is a source of sin, for only the humility that keeps us responsive to the Lord and his Word is appropriate in our relationship with the one who is truly the living God.[9]

What are the manifestations of pride?

Pride manifests itself in similar ways throughout the centuries though the historical context and culture do mark differences.

Pride among 'saints' in AD 1115: Saint Bernard, Abbot of the monastery of Clairvaux in Europe in AD 1115, vividly describes the steps of pride as he observed them among the monks nearly 900 years ago. These graphic descriptions of pride by Bernard in his monastery have their counterpart today.

> *Boastfulness:* But when increasing vanity begins to make the windbag swell, then the wind must be belched out through a larger opening, a wider passage, else it will burst…He hungers and thirsts after hearers, to whom he may vaunt his vanities, to whom he may pour forth all his feelings, to whom his character and greatness may become known…Opinions fly around, weighty words resound. He interrupts a questioner; he cuts short his fellow speaker's unfinished words. [His only concern is] to know that you know that he knows.[10]
>
> *Singularity:* It is disgraceful for him who vaunts himself above other men if he does not do something more than other men by which he may appear superior to other men…He does not long to lead a better life, but to seem to surpass, so that he may say, *I am not as other men are…*At dinner he keeps constant look around the tables, and if he sees anyone eating less than himself, he grieves that he is beaten and begins mercilessly to deprive himself of even that food which he had planned to allow as indispensable, fearing the damage to his reputation more than the pangs of hunger. If he discovers anyone more haggard, anyone more cadaverous, he despises himself, he gets no rest…But although these things he does with singularity but without sincerity raise his reputation among the more innocent, who praise the works they see without discerning whence they proceed, the poor wretch is grievously deceived when they call him blessed.[11]
>
> *Conceit:* He believes all they say, he approves his own way, his motives do not matter. He forgets his own motives, and embraces their opinion of him...[I]n the depths of his heart he believes that he is more holy than other men. And whatever he hears praised about himself he conceitedly ascribes, not to the ignorance or benevolence of the speaker, but to his own merits.
>
> *Audacity:* Must not he who thinks himself superior to others be more forward than others? In assemblies he is seated first, in councils he speaks first. He comes unsummoned, he intrudes unbidden…He judges his abbot to be either jealous or deceived. If some petty obedience is assigned to him, he indignantly disdains it, thinking that he ought not to be occupied with lesser things when he knows himself capable of greater ones.[12]

Excusing of sins: There are many ways of making *excuses in sins*. For he who excuses himself may say, I did not do it; or, I did it indeed, but it was right; or, if wrong, it was not very wrong; or, if very wrong, it was not with bad intent. If nevertheless he is convicted of it, like Adam and Eve, he attempts to excuse himself on the ground that he was beguiled by someone else.[13]

Pride among Christian leaders in AD 2000: Nine hundred years later pride still plagues the Church. Inquiry was made from many African Church elders to learn the 'signs' or 'evidences' of pride among Christian leaders today. These are ***the signs of pride*** which they gave:

- Struggles for leadership and power, using bribes and campaigning.
- Public giving of contributions in *harambees* so as to be seen. When offerings are not announced publicly, they contribute very little.
- Assigning others to do manual work in Church while they stand and watch, or pretending to work with meaningless activities.
- Not rendering service without assurance of pay; a love of money.
- Desiring to be served rather than serving.
- Flaunting oneself before the congregation, giving themselves as examples. 'You see, Church, we need to be faithful in tithing, like myself, I give a tithe of 10,000/sh. ($145.00) every month. Amen!'
- Overruling the wishes of the people and making decisions without consultation. 'I am the chairman of ... and so I have the final say.'
- Flaunting education and degrees.
- Believing they are 'big' people, they have no time to 'go down' to minister to the poor; they only associate with their own class.
- Desiring people with problems to come to them rather than the leader stooping down to go to them; this enhances their position.
- Attributing to themselves the credit for new people in Church.
- Desiring to be recognised whenever they attend meetings.
- Wanting to be boss, they divide the Church with their pride.
- Boasting of the influence and respect they have in the congregation, and the big size of the Churches they are leading.
- Bragging and telling people of personal and family achievements.
- Adopting big names, such as 'prophet,' 'apostle,' 'miracle worker' or 'a mighty preacher'; being elevated as a 'reverend' while looking down on the 'pastors' or 'evangelists' not ordained.
- Using disrespectful words when addressing elders older than them.
- Wearing special dress to distinguish them from others.

Is pride identified with any culture?

Pride is not a specialty of any race or culture. All cultures, being the products of proud human beings, are expressions of proud people. Cultures, apart from grace, are not neutral but are morally bankrupt. Cultures provide channels for proud people to express their true self-interests.

In western countries pride is more individualistic, flaunting oneself before the neighbours with bigger houses, better cars, all in the attempt to magnify one's elevated significance above others. In Africa the traditional context of pride was within the social structures of the community. Having observed 'humble' students grow into 'proud' leaders has stirred my interest. A Kenyan friend offered a suggestion which has been confirmed by others.

African society is stratified with peoples ranked in different age groups. Those in a low social rank may be mistaken as 'humble' individuals because they are only behaving according to the demands of society for that rank. Children are very subservient; adolescents are modest before their elders. Leaders may appear to be humble in the early stages but as they gain rank they begin to behave according to the entitlement of their rank. When a man marries and has a growing family, when he is granted 'positions' in the Church as 'chairman' or 'secretary' or 'bishop,' his self-image changes. He begins to claim the rights and entitlement to that position. He becomes proud manifestly.

Communities differed in their customs, but generally, the leader was the final person in decision making. Though he may consult others, he could overrule the people's wishes. The leader sat alone, a bit far from the people, on his traditional stool. He enjoyed receiving gifts after succeeding in a mission. Only men were chosen as leaders and they enjoyed making women feel inferior to them. Leaders were proud of their wealth of land and cattle, their children and wives; and they frequently spoke about their possessions.

While these observations may be true, the basic problem is spiritual, for many African Christian leaders do reflect genuine humility. Leaders are cooked from the same pot in each community, growing up in the same culture and trained in the same Bible Schools. The fact that many become servant-leaders while others fall into pride, demonstrates that the issue is deeper than culture; it is a question of a person's obedience and devotion to the Lord.

Where did pride originate?

From whence did all this pride come? It originated in heaven! Before Satan was his dark and rebellious self, he was an exalted angelic being, loving and serving God. Very little is said in the Bible about the fall of the devil, though some biblical scholars find reference to Satan's rebellion in Isaiah 14:12-14 and Ezekiel 28:12-15. Though the primary reference is to the king of Babylon and the king of Tyre, this exalted one, called 'Lucifer' and 'the Anointed Cherub,' became ambitious to be exalted above God. In his pride, Satan drew a great multitude of lesser angelic beings into this rebellion against the authority and glory of the Creator God.

Then in pride Satan tempted Eve in the Garden of Eden.[14] Unlike the animals in the Garden, Adam and Eve, created in the image of God, were endowed with a will by which they could choose to love and obey God, or they could choose to love self more than God. To test the moral will of the first man and woman, God planted a tree in the midst of the Garden and then commanded them not to eat thereof. Satan in the form of a snake seduced Eve with a clever temptation.[15] Casting doubt on the character of God, the devil appealed to the 'pride' of Eve – becoming 'like God.' She was not content with God's gracious will, so she and Adam asserted their own will over God's. Supplanting God and becoming little gods has been the vocation of the human race ever since, taking credit for all the good in their lives and feeling superior.

Adam and Eve were perfect human beings when God created them. But with their desire to supplant God, they fell into 'death' with all kinds of aberrations of their personality. Before the fall they were noble and complete, reflecting the glory of God. After the fall they lost their self-esteem and self-worth, being filled with guilt and shame. Pride wrecked the human face.

Divine Judgement on Pride

The Bible is abundantly clear: God will not tolerate proud people but will pour out judgement on them, for pride is the exaltation of self and refusal to acknowledge the supreme glory of the Holy One of Israel.

'God opposes the proud';[16] 'Pride and arrogance…I hate';[17] 'Everyone who is arrogant in heart is an abomination to the LORD';[18] 'Count on it: The day is coming, raging like a forest fire. All the arrogant people who do evil things will be burned up like stove wood, burned to a crisp, nothing left but scorched earth and ash – a black day.'[19]

The haughty looks of a man shall be brought low, and the lofty pride of men shall be humbled, and the LORD alone will be exalted in that day. For the LORD of hosts has a day against all that is proud and lofty, against all that is lifted up – and it shall be brought low…And the haughtiness of man shall be humbled, and the lofty pride of men shall be brought low, and the LORD alone will be exalted in that day.[20]

CONCLUSION

Pride is the cardinal sin of the human race – and of Christian leaders. The wise leader will be honest with himself and before God, wanting to deal with this monster that lives within. Rejoice when others put you down because this is God's redemptive grace to teach you humility. A sure sign of your humility is acceptance of a lower position when others treat you like a servant.

Because pride is a primary characteristic of the fallen, human nature, it is only natural that pride is manifested in leadership styles. In our next chapter we will examine the different styles of leadership and notice how pride is such a dominant feature. For the Christian leader, however, humility should mark the style of leadership.

SEARCHING THE SCRIPTURE WITH APPLICATION

1. 'Pride is the high opinion that a poor, little, contracted soul entertains of itself.' Why do little people (that includes everyone) exaggerate their self importance with high opinions? Why are 'little people' proud? Cf. Gal 6:3.
2. Why does God hate pride? Reflect on Pr 6:16f; 8:13; 16:5.
3. Read Dt 8:11-20. How does wealth even today lead to pride with the same consequences as in Israel?
4. The religious leaders in Jesus' day were rigorous in keeping the law but they manifested pride. What were the signs of pride among the Pharisees according to Mt 23:6-12; Mk 12:38f; Lk 11:43; 20:46? How does pride today manifest itself in similar ways?
5. Can one manifest his pride through his dress? See Isa 3:16-26. Is this always true? What makes the difference between pride and humility in one's dress?

6. Why are most believers unaware of the depths of their pride?
7. Read Mt 7:1-5. It is so easy to suspect pride in others but fail to understand the depths of your own pride. Reflect and pray over the pride in your heart.
8. Why is anyone foolish to be puffed up in pride? 1 Co 4:6-10.
9. '*Pride goes before destruction, and a haughty spirit before a fall*' (Pr 16:18). How does Nebuchadnezzar exemplify this truth? (See Da 4:1-37).
10. Read the story of the rise and fall of King Saul in 1 Sa 9:1-15:35. What noble qualities are found in Saul initially in 9:1-11:15? What evidences of pride can be found in 12:1-15:35? Discuss how this pattern is often followed in Christian leaders today?
11. In view of the great harm that pride has done in the Christian Church, what steps should be taken to reduce and eliminate pride?

Endnotes

1 Pr 21:4
The Message
2 Lewis 1943: 94
3 Bonn 2002: 154
4 Hunter 1990: 951
5 Webster's Dictionar 1959
6 Guinness 1992: 32
7 Ro 15:17; 1 Co 15:31
8 Bromiley 1982: 960
9 Richards 1985: 77
10 Bernard 1940: 205
11 Bernard 1940:209
12 Bernard 1940: 211
13 Bernard 1940: 213
14 Ge 3
15 Rev 12:9
16 Jas 4:6
17 Pr 8:13
18 Pr 16:5
19 Mal 4:1
The Message
20 Isa 2:11-17

13
HUMILITY IN LEADERSHIP STYLES

'Whoever wants to be great must become a servant. Whoever wants to be first among you must be your slave.'[1]

Humility will transform any style of leadership into servant leadership.

Much has been written on leadership styles. 'Style, by definition, is the way a leader carries out his functions and how he is perceived by those he attempts to lead.'[2] The appropriate style is determined in part by the personality of the leader, the history and traditions of the people led, and the culture and context of the particular situation. The purpose of this chapter is to introduce the topic of *servant leadership* and demonstrate that whatever leadership style one adopts, it must be transformed into *servant leadership*.

Leadership Styles

Western styles of leadership

There is a wide range of leadership styles among western leaders, ranging from an authoritarian approach to hands-off. Following is an abbreviated summary[3] of differing leadership styles on a 'leadership continuum':

Leader-Dominant			**Worker-Dominant**
Authoritarian	*Consultative*	*Participative*	*Hands-Off*

The Authoritarian* or *Directive Style makes the leader dominant. He may decide and then direct the group, or he may seek to persuade the group to accept his decision, or he may present the decision and invite questions. But he is always in charge with no in-put from others. This approach may be appropriate when the leader alone has the expertise which the group members lack. The Authoritarian Style may lead to swift accomplishments but it has serious drawbacks. At best, group members may be unenthusiastic and at worst, they may resist and be uncooperative; and there is no development of members.

The Consultative Style provides greater give-and-take between the leader and the group. The leader may present the decision to the group with the possibility of revision based on their feed-back; or he may explain the problem to the group, invite their suggestions for the solution, and then the leader makes the decision. With a consultative style of leadership, the leader does not make a decision without consultation. The leader asks the group to brainstorm and offer alternative suggestions. The leader regularly seeks ideas from the group.

There are many advantages to the consultative style of leadership. '*The more a person is involved in developing a plan, the more he will do to accomplish it.* This aspect of human nature occurs because when a leader asks another individual for his thoughts, he is validating that person. Natural responses to such validation are esteem, loyalty, and reciprocal love.'[4] Another benefit of this style is that decision making involves the contributions of many individuals. Since no one has full understanding and insight and everyone has something to contribute, the decisions made with a consultative style are usually better. Another important principle of leadership is that a Church leader's responsibility is to *facilitate* ministry processes, not to do them himself. There are few drawbacks to this leadership style.

The Participative Style of leadership moves towards the other end of the 'leadership continuum' which is 'worker-dominant.' The non-directive leader delegates responsibilities and authority to a group and lays out the boundaries of their authority. The leader may or may not choose to be part of the group decision making process. Through discussion the group reaches a consensus. If the leader chooses to be part of the group, he must take care of what he says for that may distort the consensus of the group as they 'follow the leader.'

The advantages of this style are many. The more people who contribute to the decision making process, the more creative and effective will be the plan. The members develop and grow because of exercising their gifts, although they can also make mistakes. More work is accomplished because everyone feels a part of the decision which they own.

The Hands-off Style of leadership is at the extreme end with the workers totally dominant. With this approach the leader does not get involved with the group nor does he exercise authority over the decision making process. He may provide useful information to the group but allows the decisions and resultant consequences to play out as they will.

While there are advantages in certain situations, this style leads to the abdication of leadership. This may grow out of laziness of the leader. The end results are underperformance and failure to contribute to the mission goals of the institution or group.

Traditional African styles

Scholars have discerned two types of political systems in traditional Africa; hence, two styles of leadership.[5]

Top-Down Leaders: Those societies which have centralised authority are ruled by monarchs or chiefs who act like monarchs. They rule from the top-down with an authoritarian style of leadership. The leadership class possesses wealth, privilege and status in contrast to the subordinates. The king was the richest man in the community. The leader inherited his role and his word was final.

> 'In Africa it may be said that the king is the executive head, the legislator, the supreme judge, the commander-in-chief of the army, the chief priest and even perhaps the principal capitalist of the whole community.'[6]

Setting the leader apart from others were the symbols of office: leopard skin cloaks, ivory or copper bracelets, bead necklaces or a scepter (*rungu*). The official titles used when the subjects addressed the king or chief included 'lion,' 'great wild beast,' 'devourer of people,' or 'lord of the soil.'[7]

The societies in which authoritarian rulers lead are complex and large. Among the Zulu of South Africa, for example, the hundreds of clans were united by their submission to the absolute rule of the king who owned all the land. Ruling under the king were many chiefs. Though the king was supposed to follow the advice of his council, no one dare place himself in the position of contradicting the king. 'It seems that in fact the king did consider his councilors' views and did not act autocratically.'[8]

Bottom-Up Leaders: Those societies which lack central authority are ruled more by a participative style, what might be called 'a group-democracy.' These societies are smaller and lack a sharp division of rank, status or wealth. Though kinship plays an important role throughout Africa, kinship plays a major role in governing smaller societies. In very small societies such as hunters and gatherers, 'the political relations are coterminous with kinship relations and the political structure and kinship organization are completely fused.'[9] The leadership patterns tend to be non-formal with decisions reached by consensus.

While the Pygmies, Hottentots and Bushmen had the least central authority, many others fall into the category of 'group-democracy.' The leaders of the Agikuyu of Kenya[10] earned their position which was not inherited. They emerged as leaders in each stage after the rite of passage, in early childhood, boyhood, youth, and manhood. The council of elders was the supreme ruling body which made their decisions through consensus.

The role of the father in Luhya tradition is representative. Many traditions set the father apart from the others as the head of the home. He sat on a traditional three-legged stool. No other family member could sit on that chair. His spear and walking stick were specially prepared for him; and when walking with his wives and children, the father always walked ahead. The father's clothes were different from other family members. The skin of an antelope was designed with a unique style and could not be worn by any other family member. When eating, the father sat alone. When his sons were circumcised, they could sit together with him but the father was given his own separate food. Certain parts of an animal were reserved for the father; for example, the gizzard of a chicken. His eating utensils were special. The father was very authoritative. He could not consult his wife or children for suggestions or advice. His word was final in all matters concerning the home and property.

All other family members had to obey him, though he may seek advice from his age mates or the clan council. Limits were set for him so that if he overstepped and was too cruel to his wives or children, parents and uncles could step in.

In these societies where the family lineage structure serves as the framework for overall government, the rule of the father in extended families is all important. The strong, authoritarian rule of the patriarchal head is the mirror image of leadership in Africa. Also, the ranking through the age-sets determined the status of the Agikuyu and others, their seniority, equality or juniority. Some men are 'sons,' some are 'brothers' and others are 'fathers.'

What proportion of African societies are 'authoritarian' or 'group-democratic' is difficult to say. What is clear is that African leadership may also be ranked on a 'leadership continuum.' Even the most authoritarian style of leaders was moderated by councils giving advice; and even the most non-directive form of leadership was strengthened by patriarchal authority.

Added to the collective memory of the African traditional leadership styles is the colonial legacy. Under colonialism the 'chief' was no longer guided by the councils and was 'no longer for the people, but was subordinate to the colonial government' through the colonial policy of 'indirect rule.' Chima claims that, 'The making of decisions in common and in a participative way has long been recognized as a major characteristic of African policy.'[11] However, under colonialism an alien system of leadership developed whereby the 'chief' 'lost some of his traditional authority but gained *power*.'[12] Although colonialism is now history, 'its mental creations of "bwana" (master) have not disappeared from the African scene.'

The fact is that societies worldwide are marked by a significant emphasis on authoritarian style of leadership. Among the Chinese, the Confucius ideal reigns supreme.[13] 'Filial piety' with deep respect for the elders in the family was extended to the regional leaders, the emperor and ultimately to the 'living-dead.' The same can be found in Korea. 'Authoritarianism was deeply rooted in the value from Confucianism of respect for elders.'[14]

Christian leadership styles

Inevitably, the traditional patterns of leadership have their effect on Church leadership. The ways of leading Christian Churches around the world have been profoundly affected by their cultures. The hierarchy of the Roman Catholic Church with the 'infallible' pope and authoritarian bishops and the separation of clergy and laity can be traced back to the Roman Empirical government, to:

> ...such events as the declaration of Emperor Theodosius in 380 A.D. that Christianity would be the official religion of the empire, and that clergy would be endowed with a civil rank corresponding to their status within the Church. The growing 'clericalisation' of the Church was reflected also in the liturgy, where signs of civil dignity were accorded the clergy: candles, thrones, certain kinds of clothing, kisses, incensing.[15]

The Korean culture has impacted the style of leadership in the Korean Christian Church. 'Authoritarian leadership has influenced almost every aspect of the Korean Church community.'[16] Church leaders exercise strict control over the members and do not like to share power or authority with other pastors.

'Because these secularized Christian leaders normally adopted leadership models from secular perspectives the underlying motivation of their leadership was selfish ambition and self-glorification. They tended to be competitive rather than cooperative, divisive rather than unifying, jealous rather than generous, destructive rather than constructive, unforgiving rather than forgiving, authoritarian rather than democratic, judgemental rather than understanding, materialistic rather than spiritual, and proud rather than humble.'[17]

The same may be said of the Churches in Africa. Growing out of the hierarchy of traditional society with the chief at the top, status and prestige are driving forces in Church leadership.[18] 'Professional leaders,' with specialised training, do the work of the ministry rather than equipping the people to do the ministry alongside of the Church leaders. This leads to 'clericalism' of the privileged few who are leaders over the people. The pastor directs and the people follow uncritically. An elitism develops through education. Copying the pattern of society, the more education one receives the higher status he gains.

Janvier observes that if leaders follow the cultural patterns and not the biblical patterns, then the Church leader will resemble an African chief. For example a Church leader:

- May desire to be served rather than serve. The Church becomes a chiefdom not a place of service.
- He may demand respect even if he has not earned it.
- Leaders may misuse power to gain personal wealth. They seek positions for self advancement not service.
- Administratively, the leaders' policies are not changed or challenged. Elders are never wrong.
- Younger men are not considered for leadership positions or training simply due to age. They cannot exercise their gifts. People are elected by age and not qualifications or experience.
- Lobbying, campaigning, bribing, and wooing for offices are sometimes used.
- Usually a hierarchy model of leadership is established.[19]

Ken Harder did a study of the *leadership styles found in the Africa Inland Church, Kenya.*[20] In his analysis there are five leadership styles:

The first style of leader decides what should be done and tells the people his decision, and then expects the people to help him accomplish the decision.

The second style of leader decides what should be done but offers the people an explanation and invites questions. But the leader's decision is final.

The third style of leader seeks advice before making a decision. The pastor then makes the final decision, based on the advice and expects them to follow.

The fourth style of leader calls the decision-making council together to discuss and decide. While the pastor retains hold of the facilitative responsibility, he does let the council make the final decision on their own.

The fifth style of leader is to do nothing but let events take their course. He does nothing and waits for things to happen on their own.

Contextualizing Christian leadership is tricky business. Church history is replete with tragic examples of Christians shaping Christian practices and leadership by the values of culture. Without proper biblical training in Christian leadership, Church leaders simply follow the pattern of their culture. Carl George, former Director of the *Charles E. Fuller Institute of Church Growth*, observes:

> 'Many [pastors] are not taking the trouble to educate themselves in needed areas of management [leadership]. Almost all ministers are well educated theologically. Most seminary graduates have more to teach than anybody wants to learn. Meanwhile, the serious deficiencies are in management and leadership skills [and principles].'[21]

Following cultural leadership styles is not bad when those leadership styles are not contrary to biblical teaching. The problem is that following culture is not always following God's way. Westermann gives several examples. Being decisive as a leader is considered the essence of good leadership. But this too often means that the leader should make the decisions by himself without due consultation. A good leader leads the pack but this may become a top-down organisational structure without utilizing the gifts of all believers. Seeking to be more democratic in leadership style may lead to majority rules. But the majority may be wrong!

If we desire to be biblical in the way we lead as Christians, we need to understand the biblical pattern of servant leadership.

The Biblical Leadership Styles

Can we say that there is only one biblical style of leadership? Few would agree. If one examines the Scriptures, you can find examples of many authoritarian styles. Can anyone find a better example of a godly leader than Nehemiah? Yet he was a total top-down, authoritarian leader. Who today has followed Nehemiah's example when he said, 'I rebuked them and called curses down on them. I beat some of the men and pulled out their hair.'[22]

And yet as disciples of Jesus Christ, we have been elevated to something new. 'Servant leadership' with humility is the style of Christian leadership that should inform and enlighten all kinds of leadership. '[T]he ultimate test of the biblical accuracy of any approach to leadership is whether or not it is marked by *service* and *selflessness* [italics added].'[23] Though some writers insist on participative styles; though some more authoritative approaches may be used, the Christian style of leadership must be marked by the selflessness of the leaders who serve the One who called him and others entrusted to their care. Gottfried Osei-Mensah states, '...humble service to one another is, in fact, the main purpose for which the Lord appoints office-bearers in his church...'[24]

Servant Leadership rooted in the life of Jesus Christ: A nagging question bothers us. Why do we lead our Churches today so differently from Jesus' teaching and example? When James and John implored Jesus to be granted preeminence in sitting on the right hand and left hand of Jesus in the Kingdom, the other disciples became indignant. Jesus replied:

> You know that *those who are considered rulers of the Gentiles lord it over them, and their great ones exercise authority over them. But it shall not be so among you. But whoever would be great among you must be your servant...*[25]

Jesus here teaches two different types of leadership: the disciples of Jesus are to *serve*, following the example of Christ himself, while the unbelieving peoples of the world *lord it over* others, exercising an authoritarian rule. Two ways: leading through service or leading through authoritarian rule.

The Bible presents two kingdoms: the kingdom of light and the kingdom of darkness, the kingdom of God and the kingdom of Satan. Conversion entails the transfer of a person *from* the power of Satan *to* the reign of God.[26] These two kingdoms have two diametrically opposite patterns of behaviour[27] and two different kinds of leaders.

Satan is a murderer and a liar from the beginning.[28] His followers develop a style of leadership characterised by deception and lies. They lack integrity and transparency in their lives. These leaders dominate through manipulation and fear.

> [T]he leadership of domination operates by force and control. An unrighteous leader has an insatiable appetite for control. He wants to direct, he wants to guide, but deep in the reservoir of his being is a lust to control others. He wants to be in charge, and finds it difficult, if not impossible to step away from that position. His leadership is a reinforcement of his longing for power and status. To give it up is to give up his primary ambition in life.[29]

Jesus Christ, on the other hand, is *The Servant*. 'For the Son of Man came not to be served but to serve.'[30] The implications are many. Jesus was not 'me' centred but 'other' centred. Strictly speaking, he was 'God-centred,' for he came to this world in obedience to the Father to do the Father's will. Jesus was mission oriented. He came to accomplish the purpose for his coming.

When Jesus' followers emulate their Master, they are mission centred. Whatever is best for the building of the Church, they will do. Jealousy does not distract them from accomplishing the purpose of their reason for being. They work tirelessly for others and for the glory of God, thinking not of themselves and their rights. 'Me' centred people care not for the flock but themselves; not for the growth of the Church but for their profit; not for the salvation of the lost but for their ease and comfort.

Jesus Christ is the *Light*. This implies purity with a holy life. It also points to transparency and honesty before others. Jesus lived openly and in the light. What he was in public, he was in private. He spoke truthfully and with power.

The servant of Jesus Christ also lives a life of humility, acknowledging weaknesses and failures. His followers are honest and open. They develop a style of leadership reflecting the glory of their Lord, lives of transparency and honesty. They do not pretend or wear a mask. Their motive in life is service out of love which was exemplified by Christ. Just as Jesus is holy, so his followers lead with integrity and purity.

Servant Leadership rooted in biblical theology: One distinguishing feature of biblical theology is the absolute distinction made between God and the creation.[31] The Creation account of Genesis portrays the eternal Word of God speaking the word and bringing forth the heavens and the earth out of nothing. What had never existed came into being through the creative word of God who is fundamentally separate and distinguished from his creation.

The consequence of this truth is that mankind is always responsible to God. The highest tribute for someone in the Old Testament was to be called 'a servant of the Lord.'

Ancient myths of the peoples in the Middle East tell of the origin of the heavens, earth and the gods 'from one and the same original substance.' There was either no distinction or a blurred distinction between God and man. The result was profound. The Pharaohs of Egypt considered themselves to be the incarnation of the sun god. The ancient rulers of Babylon were direct representatives of the gods. They spoke with absolute authority and the people never questioned their authority.

According to Bediako, 'political authority in traditional Africa was equally considered sacred, absolute and therefore incontestable.'[32] This tradition is rooted in the blurred distinction between the divine and human. The various specialists in African society, including the chief, exerted their leadership through their unique relationship with the spirit world which was more or less close to the Creator.

Not so in Israel. Yahweh was their King. When Israel desired a king 'like all the nations,' Samuel warned them: 'The king should obey his God, who remains the only one who is King by nature, and if the earthly representative did not obey, he would be judged like his people (1Sa 12:14,25)'[33] The prophets in Israel were God's spokesmen who boldly criticised the kings. In Israel there was only one King and that was Yahweh. Israel's 'kings' were subject to the King of kings.

What is so important today in the Christian Church is to 'desacralise' the Church leadership. They do not have any privileged access to God more than the people of God. Neither do they exercise unchallenged authority but they are accountable to God. They serve under God and are accountable to the people of God. God alone through his people appoints leaders to serve. These leaders humbly relinquish those positions at the appointed time.

Servant Leadership rooted in biblical models: The greatest figure in the Old Testament was Moses. Humanly speaking, we would want to be remembered for some heroic work, some outstanding achievement when our obituary is written. Perhaps we would write, 'Moses, the Lord's miracle worker, is dead.' Sounds contemporary! 'Moses, the Lord's statesman, is dead.' Possibly, 'Moses, the Lord's lawgiver, is dead.' But instead God declares to Joshua, 'Moses my servant is dead.'[34] Moses is known principally as a servant.

Moses was not a weak leader. In every way he was a strong leader who exercised authority. But he was a bondservant of God. He did not seek his own glory but the glory of God. When he attempted to follow his own way in a fit of anger, God poured out judgement on him. Moses was a servant leader.

The greatest figure in the apostolic church was Paul. As an apostle of Jesus Christ and by his authority, he wrote to the Galatians, 'If anyone is preaching to you a gospel contrary to the one you received [from me], let him be accursed.'[35] Such talk does not reflect weak leadership. He led as an apostle. But Paul considered himself as a 'servant.' In defense of this strong talk to the Galatians, Paul affirms that he speaks thus not to please men. 'If I were still trying to please men, I would not be a servant of Christ.'[36]

Servant leadership is not a weak kind of leadership. Cultural features of leadership style can be adopted by the Church if they are not contrary to biblical principles. But a truly Christian leader should be a servant leader who is a bond servant of Christ, obeying and glorifying God in all things, and serving the people of God rather than seeking personal gain.

CONCLUSION

It is only natural that Church leadership is influenced by the cultural styles of leadership in which the Church members live. Instead of conforming to cultural norms, Christians should be transformed by the Word of God. Scripture teaches that Christians should be 'light' and 'salt' in society, displaying the counter-cultural values rooted in the Christian faith. Theologians may point to many biblical texts to support their leadership style. As Christians, however, we must be guided by the teachings of Christ and his example. The Christian ethic has been raised to a new level, far surpassing the standards under the Old Covenant. And Jesus' teaching points to the need for humility to dominate whatever leadership style one may adopt culturally.

In the next chapter we shall explore more deeply the nature of 'servant leadership.' The Christian leader truly shows forth a humble spirit when he conducts his leadership as a servant of God.

SEARCHING THE SCRIPTURE WITH APPLICATION

1. Research the traditional styles of leadership among your people in the past. (Was it 'top-down' with an authoritarian style? Did the leaders consult with the people? Was the governing structure 'bottom-up,' or a participative style, or a 'group democratic' style of leadership based on consensus?)
2. What styles of leadership are found in your own Church?
3. How do the styles of Church leadership today differ from or are similar to the traditional styles of leadership?
4. Read and study Lk 22:24-30 and 1 Pe 5:1-7. What biblical principles should transform the leadership patterns in the Christian Church, based on these Scriptures?
5. Read Eze 34:1-24.
   a. Who were the 'shepherds of Israel' in this chapter?
   b. How did they behave as shepherds over Israel? (vss 1-19)
   c. How are they different from or similar to many Church leaders today?
   d. What is God's attitude towards these shepherds? (vss 7-10)
6. How does a 'servant leader' actually lead? (1 Pe 5:3; Lk 22:26)
   a. How does leading by example and service work out in practice?
   b. Does a 'servant leader' take a passive, non-directive approach in leadership? How does he exert his authority?
7. Explore the strengths or limitations of this concept of 'servant leadership.' How can a leader lead if he is a servant?

Endnotes

[1] Mk 10:43 *The Message*
[2] Engstrom 1979: 67
[3] Westermann 1997:13ff
[4] Westermann 1997:16
[5] Fortes & Evans-Pritchard 1940
[6] Janvier & Thaba 1997:14
[7] Kofele-Kale 1978:438
[8] Fortes 1940:33
[9] Fortes 1940: 6,7
[10] Kamau 1996
[11] Chima 1984:333
[12] Chima 1984:334
[13] Branner 1983: 57ff
[14] Hwang 1992: 103
[15] Chima 1984: 332
[16] Hwang 1992:104
[17] Hwang 1992: 105
[18] Kohls 1998:110ff
[19] Janvier 1997: 15
[20] Harder 1984: 11
[21] Carl George as found in Westermann 1997:243
[22] Ne 13:25
[23] Love 1994: 109
[24] Osei-Mensah 1990:12
[25] Mk 10:42-45
[26] Ac 26:18
[27] Eph 5:8-14
[28] Jn 8:44
[29] Boehme 1989:58
[30] Mk 10:45
[31] Van den Toren 2004: 166
[32] Kwame Bediako as found in Van den Toren 2004: 169
[33] Van den Toren 2004:167
[34] Jos 1:2
[35] Gal 1:9
[36] Gal 1:10

14
SERVANT LEADERSHIP

'My servant Caleb thinks differently and follows me completely.'[1]

Can any *leader* be a '*servant* leader'?

The term, 'servant leader,' was first coined in 1970 by Robert Greenleaf.[2] Ever since, there has been debate because 'servant leader' is an oxymoron, that is, an apparent contradiction in terms. How can one be a leader and still be a servant? In this chapter we explore a 'servant leader.'

It is of interest that the King James Bible has only 6 references to 'leader' or 'leaders' in the entire Scriptures, but it has 1,452 references to 'servant' and 'service.'[3] 'Servant' has a negative connotation today; no one desires to be one. But many want to be leaders. The biblical worldview of leadership is counter cultural. The 'leaders' of the Old Testament, such as Moses and Joshua, are called 'my servant' and the prophets of Israel are repeatedly called 'my servants the prophets'; never are they called 'my leaders.' The concept of 'servant leader' is as old as the Bible, even though the term was coined in recent years.

The Meaning of a Servant Leader

'Servant leadership' is perplexing to many because they confuse 'leadership' with a certain kind of power. A position of leadership does bestow power, influence and authority. Being the 'head' means that one may be empowered to overrule another and make the final decision. The leader has status and prestige as others recognise his authority and address him respectfully. How then can a 'leader' also be the 'servant'?

The '*servant leader*' has power but it is a certain kind of power exercised with humility. Worldly power demands and dictates; spiritual power is soft and humble. The Chinese philosopher Laotzu wrote in 600 B.C.: 'Water is fluid, soft, and yielding. But water will wear away rock, which is rigid and cannot yield. As a rule, whatever is fluid, soft and yielding will overcome whatever is rigid and hard. This is another paradox: what is soft is strong.'[4]

'Servant leaders' cannot escape the use of power. They have responsibilities of authority but this must not be patterned after the world. Osei-Mensah in his excellent book, *Wanted: Servant-Leadership*, declares:

> 'If the tradition of a particular society is such that there is no room for people to exercise their gifts, then let our traditions be shattered to pieces! Let us look for other structures which will make it possible for God's people to use their gifts.'[5]

'Cultural leadership' is all about power; 'servant leadership' is all about facilitating the growth of others so that they can help build the Church.

What is a 'servant leader'?

'Servant Leaders' are bondservants of the LORD: The principle word for 'servant' in the Old Testament was *'ebed*[6] which occasionally meant 'slave,' 'servant of servants' or 'the humblest of servants.' In the land of Egypt the Israelites were in 'the house of slavery,'[7] a bitter experience indeed. But in ancient Israel the 'slaves' were elevated above the servile condition of their counterparts in neighbouring countries.

The principle significance of 'servanthood' among the Hebrews was *submission* to their masters. Servants were 'subjects,' being absolutely submissive to the chief, the military, the king – and to God. 'As applied to men serving God in a particular capacity, the word denotes (1) submission and (2) the honour of being chosen for service.'[8]

Those who served God, including the Levitical singers in the temple, were called 'servants.' The people of Israel were 'servants.' The Messiah is 'The Servant of the Lord.' For Moses to be designated a 'servant of God'[9] was an honourable and elevated position. For God to call his spokesmen, 'my servants the prophets,'[10] is to emphasise their submission and absolute obedience to the Lord; and also the honourable privilege of being chosen for this service.

The Greek Septuagint used several Greek words to translate the Old Testament idea of servant; these words are again used in the New Testament. The most prominent one is *doulos* which in Greek and Roman culture was a menial slave who had a permanent relationship of servitude to the master.

But once again, this terminology of 'bond servant' is elevated when the apostles called themselves 'slaves of God'[11] and 'slaves of Christ Jesus.'[12] 'Slaves of God' are those who submit to God and serve him to execute his will. What a privilege to serve the Lord! The Psalmist wrote, 'I would rather be a doorkeeper in the house of my God than dwell in the tents of wickedness.'[13]

Christ has purchased us from slavery to sin for his own possession by his own precious blood. As Paul wrote, 'You are not your own; you were bought with a price.'[14] In this new relationship of total submission and obedience to the Saviour, God has chosen certain ones to be his 'servant leaders.'

We conclude that a 'servant leader' is a servant of the Lord in the fullest biblical sense. In addition, being a 'slave of Christ,' Paul considered himself a servant of the Corinthians to whom he preached.[15]

'Servant Leaders' serve God's people: '*Leadership*' is about someone's *role* among people. By definition, a leader is a person who leads, guides, directs and is the head; he has a vision and knows where he wants to lead the people. Presidents, Prime Ministers, Chairmen, Principals, Head-Teachers, Vice Chancellors and Bishops – all these people pop into our heads when we think of leaders. But 'leadership' is at different levels, ranging from leadership in the home to lay leadership in the local Church to ecclesiastical administrative leadership over districts, regions and nations.

'*Servant*' on the other hand is about the *character* of the leader. How should a Christian lead? The fundamentals of leadership are not about charisma, gifts or personality. The bed rock of leadership is *character*. And the kind of character needed for a Christian leader is that of being a '*servant*.'

> Charles Spurgeon [that gifted preacher in England during the 19th century] spoke of a man who preached so well but lived so badly that when he was in the pulpit everybody said he ought never to come out again, and when he was out of it, they all declared he ought never enter it again. No gifts or abilities can make up for a lifestyle that belies one's profession.'[16]

As Jesus taught, the unbelievers 'lord' it over others and 'exercise authority' over them. '*But it shall not be so among you.* But whoever would be great among you must be your servant.'[17] 'Servant' describes the *humility* by which a leader conducts himself in his role of leadership. To be a 'servant' of the Lord is a noble calling and an honourable position. As Martin Luther King Jr. commented, 'Everyone can be great, because everyone can serve.'[18]

'True servant leaders allow themselves (their gifts, talents, and abilities) to be properly used for the benefit of others and the organization as a whole. It's as simple as that. The greater your responsibility to lead, the greater your responsibility to serve.'[19] In the pattern of Christ, everyone has been created to serve. Winston Churchill, a former Prime Minister of England, observed: 'You make a living by what you get. You make a life by what you give.'[20] If an unbeliever can say that, how much more should a servant of the Lord!

The ministry of a 'servant leader' is much more than doing deeds of service; it is manifesting *a spirit* of servanthood. One can be reluctant or grudging in service; one can even be self-serving. A leader can even give away all his wealth for deeds of charity but discover in the end of the day that the service was empty and without divine favour because of poor motives.[21]

> A servant leader is easily spotted: If his position is taken away, he doesn't fight for it. And when it's given, he doesn't make a big deal about it. The servant leader is committed to serving God and serving people and leaves the authority and positioning to God.[22]

Characteristics of a 'Servant Leader'

The 'servant leader' acknowledges and practices dependence on God: Education is important when developing competent leaders. Developing confidence through training and experience is also desirable. But a subtle danger arises when the leader becomes *self*-confident. Yes, there is that measure of 'self-confidence' which is gained through education and experience. Leaders know what to do and how to do it because of their training and experience. But this can soon grow into a *self*-reliance and pride; they no longer feels a need for God's help. Highly trained leaders may fall into complacency, depending on their knowledge and abilities rather than relying on God. 'Servant leaders' must always *feel* needy, utterly dependent on the Lord.

An educated leader must be conscious of the danger of giving the appearance of pride (an appearance of excessive self-confidence), even when he may not be proud. He must also learn how to relate to others who have lesser academic credentials. For those less educated and less confident may take offence and accuse the competent leader of pride. The ideas of these educated leaders are so far above the people that they are considered proud.

This places a heavy burden on the competent and 'self-confident' leader. He must ever be conscious of his own spiritual weakness and inclination to pride. He must ever walk humbly before others so that they do not misinterpret an air of competence as a sign of vanity and conceit. And above all, he must always remember that he is first and foremost a *servant of the Lord*. God is the One who saved him and called him into ministry; God is the One who gifted him and empowers him for ministry. As a *servant of the Lord* he always relies on God and gives him the glory for all success that takes place. His mouth should always be filled with words of utter dependence on God for his help and words of praise for God's enabling.

The 'servant leader' is motivated by the glory of God: The focus is not on self but on the glory of God, loving him and obeying him in all things. In this he is humble. He bows before God and does his will. All of life is devoted to glorifying God – 'whatever you do, do all to the glory of God.'[23]

Motivation is everything. Two pastors labour hard to build the Church; one does it for self-glorification and the other does it for the glory of God. Two pastors do extensive evangelism; one for vain glory and the other for God's glory. The 'servant leader' is motivated with his eyes fixed on his Lord. He strives for nothing more than God's kingdom and glory.

In many traditions pride is achieved through leadership. A person is recognised and made famous because of leadership. This tradition has been brought into the Church and leads to in-fighting for leadership and seats on councils so that they can be known, recognised and praised. In public they draw attention to their positions and achievements.

But a true 'servant leader' is one whose whole ambition in life is to serve and glorify the Lord who is the Saviour and Head of the Church. Instead of being motivated by self, the 'servant leader' is motivated by his devotion to the love of his life. The king of Israel prayed, 'Because your love is better than life, my lips will glorify you.'[24] Again David wrote, "I said to the LORD, 'You are my Lord; apart from you I have no good thing.'"[25]

The 'servant leader' hopes and trusts in God: Leaders who are concerned about themselves look over their shoulders nervously to see who may be challenging their position. Not so with the 'servant leader' for his hope and trust is in God. Confident in the sovereign rule of the Lord, he knows 'that for those who love God all things work together for good, for those who are called according to his purpose.'[26] Nothing can separate them from the loving sovereign care of their Father,[27] neither the threatening Reverend or Bishop, nor a jealous pastor or disgruntled elder. An unexpected transfer or unfair demotion is all part of God's plan. He is content to serve in the place of God's appointment, even under difficult leaders. Although he does not understand why God allows certain things to happen, he submits to the all-wise, all-loving Sovereign Lord who will reward faithfulness and judge sin.

Many a pastor or Church leader feels like quitting from time to time. The work is endless and thankless, the people lack appreciation, criticism is rampant, jealousy and division hurt. 'Even youths shall faint and be weary, and young men shall fall exhausted; but they who *wait for the LORD* shall renew their strength.'[28] The implication of *waiting* is *hoping* and *trusting* as other versions translate it. 'Those who look to the LORD will win new strength' (NEB) as they trust in him (GNB). These 'servant leaders' have an inner strength that is not threatened by circumstances or people.

The 'servant leader' exercises power through weakness: The thirst for power has shaped the history of our world as leaders fight for more power. More intoxicating than alcohol and more addictive than drugs is the drive for power. King Uzziah, king of Judah, became powerful and successful. 'And his fame spread far, for he was marvelously helped, till he was strong.' It was then, 'when he was strong, he grew proud' and fell into grievous sin.[29] Worldly power leads to pride; and pride is fatal, going before a fall.

Sadly, this sinful ambition is found in the Church with clergy seeking to build the largest sanctuaries with the largest congregations. The dream of building huge empires drives many Church leaders. They may thrive as 'leaders,' even 'Church leaders,' but they can never be 'servant leaders.' Motive is everything.

Paul learned humility through his weaknesses. God in his grace teaches all of his servants their weakness in order that God may exercise his power through weakness. Before enumerating all of his problems, Paul wrote: 'But we have this treasure in jars of clay, to show that *the surpassing power belongs to God and not to us.*'[30] Given our sinful nature, we are quickly lifted up in pride. Many afflictions come to teach us humility.

God took steps to keep Paul humble. Because of God's gracious and marvelous revelations, God gave him a thorn in the flesh to humble him. When Paul pleaded for God's touch, God replied, 'My grace is sufficient for you, for *my power is made perfect in weakness.*'[31] God may do the same with us today.

A 'servant leader' recognizes his weakness and limitations; in fact, he rejoices in his weakness, for he then learns to depend entirely on God's grace and power to work in and through him. When God does bless, he gives God the glory and takes no credit for himself. He is ever praising God and never boasting of his accomplishments.

The 'servant leader' is under authority: Every 'servant leader' understands that he is *under* another who is superior in rank and has authority over him.

> If you have not learned to be a good follower, you are not qualified to be a good leader. Leaders who are not good followers almost always become tyrants. Rebellion and independence is within them, and this combined with egotism can be deadly. The true servant leader willfully places himself under the care and authority of others. This is easy because he is a broken man who knows the depravity of his own heart all too well. He gladly submits to others because he needs them to walk the pathway Christ has laid out for him.[32]

The 'servant leader' develops a transparent relationship: The leader is *among* those he leads, not *over* them. Instead of *telling* them, he *models* by his own example.[33] He lives a transparent life before them.

A 'cultural leader' separates himself from others and does not mingle with those below his status. He operates from the vantage of authority, speaking down to others. But a 'servant leader' mingles with his people, visits them, and enters into their joys and sorrows. Even as Jesus became incarnate, identifying with his people, so the 'servant leader' identifies with the people. As Jesus felt and showed compassion toward the peoples, so does the 'servant leader.'

Distance protects the leader from scrutiny. People do not see the blemishes. Serving *among* the people exposes the leader's own weaknesses; the 'servant leader' becomes vulnerable. But a true 'servant leader' is so confident in his relationship with God that he admits his own weaknesses and is open to criticism. He lives a transparent life and is held accountable by those whom he serves. What a powerful influence the 'servant leader' can be in his mentoring when he becomes transparent and vulnerable by sharing his own personal struggles. In this relationship the leader identifies with the people as they struggle and grow in their Christian lives.

The 'servant leader' mentors others for ministry: 'Success without a successor is failure.'[34] One of the great leadership failures is failure to mentor others to become leaders. Out of that pool of mentored leaders, a successor may come. Effective ministry is not a 'one-man show.' The more who minister, the greater growth takes place. It is biblical for the pastor/teacher to train all of God's people to do the work of ministry.[35] But the 'I, only I' leader 'hugs leadership responsibilities to himself, sure that no one else could carry them.'[36]

Many feel threatened if someone emerges who is more effective. 'The greatest portion of a man's self-identity and sense of worth is from his job...For many a leader, the job is the very essence of his or her self-worth. To lose that role of leadership is to lose all confidence and identity.'[37] One indication of a 'servant leader' is the ability to focus on the mission instead of self. The desire and ability to prepare others to do the work of ministry is a true indication of a servant. Leaders cannot prepare successors unless they are 'servant leaders' who 'do not consider their own status or ambitions but set their attention on the means that will meet the needs of their followers.'[38]

A 'servant leader' is not upset when others are doing well in ministry. Jealousy does not strike fear in his heart. Instead, a 'servant leader' trains them for ministry. The 'servant leader' sees potential in others, tolerates their mistakes and weaknesses and is patient in training. Great patience is needed because it takes a whole life time to develop a 'servant leader.' Just look at yourself in the mirror and realize how much more you need to grow until you are a mature, wise 'servant leader.' Be patient! As you do this, discover how this enhances your own power. By empowering others to lead you receive power back. 'Leaders who divest themselves of power and invest in others will find that the initial investment has grown.'[39]

Defects in Servant Leaders

Why are some Church leaders *not* 'servant leaders'? We interviewed several dozen Church elders about their thoughts. Their comments are very revealing. In their observation many Church leaders are *not* 'servant leaders' because:

- They are not born again; chosen only because of being active in Church.
- They are not called to ministry; or they enter with wrong motives.

- They seek leadership positions for wrong reasons, such as material gain.
- They fail to understand whom they are serving; they serve people, not God.
- They seek to please people, not God; they want to be popular with people.
- They are selfish and seek power and respect.
- They love themselves more than others, and more than God.
- They are caught up in arrogance because of their high education.
- They love money and are seeking material things.
- They are 'know-it-all' types; they are not ready to learn from others.
- They are influenced by culture; culturally, a leader is not a 'servant.'

It also takes humility to understand that others do not see us as servant leaders. May we seek God's grace to humbly accept counsel from these elders!

CONCLUSION

The concept of 'servant leader' is not only difficult to comprehend because it is so foreign to our cultural understanding; 'servant leadership' is difficult to accept because it goes against our proud, sinful human nature.

We must turn our gaze on Jesus who is the best model. 'He was a great leader yet a truly sacrificing servant. He rendered service to all in need, and people hung on His every word. He served but He did so from a position of confidence and strength.'[40] The following chapter is devoted to 'The Model of Servant Leader.'

SEARCHING THE SCRIPTURE WITH APPLICATION

1. 'Servant leaders' are first servants of God. 'Servant leaders' are also stewards of time, talents and opportunities entrusted to them by God. Read Lk 19:11-27. What lessons can you learn from this parable?
2. Read Nu 14:1-38. One translation of 14:24 reads, 'My servant Caleb *thinks differently* and follows me completely.'
   a. Describe how Caleb thought differently from the majority.
   b. Why did Caleb think differently?
   c. Thinking precedes actions; a mind-set precedes 'the walk' and 'the talk' of life. What must you do to 'think differently' like Caleb did?
   d. What evidence can you offer to show that *you* think differently?
3. Do you (and others) think of yourselves as stewards in the Church or as owners of the Church? (c.f. Mt 16:18) What actions or words show the thinking of Church leaders, whether they see themselves as 'owners' of the Church or a 'stewards' who serve in the Church?
4. '*No worker can serve two bosses: He'll either hate the first and love the second, Or adore the first and despise the second. <u>You cannot serve both God and the Bank</u>.*' (Lk 16:13 *The Message*)
   a. What are the different 'bosses' that leaders often serve instead of God?
   b. Describe the consequences of this wrongful service?
   c. What steps should you take to make sure you serve only God?

d. What steps should the Church take to make sure their leaders (elders, pastors and overseers) are truly 'servant leaders'?

Endnotes

1 Nu 14:24 New Century Version
2 Spears 1998:15
3 Strong n.d.
4 Perkins 2000: 187
5 Osei-Mensah 1990:17
6 Brown 1983:713
7 Ex 13:14
8 Harrison 1960:480
9 Nu 12:7
10 Jer 7:25
11 Jas 1:1
12 Ro 1:1
13 Ps 84:10
14 1 Co 6:20
15 2 Co 4:5
16 Means 1989: 49
17 Mk 10:43
18 Martin Luther King as found in Martin 2002:2
19 Martin 2002: 3
20 Winston Churchill as found in Martin 2002:3
21 1 Co 13:3
22 Boehme 1989: 209
23 1 Co 10:31
24 Ps 63:3
25 Ps 16:2
26 Ro 8:28
27 Ro 8:31-39
28 Isa 40:30f
29 2 Ch 26:15,16
30 2 Co 4:7
31 2 Co 12:7,9
32 Boehme 1989: 204f
33 Richards 1980: 106f
34 Finzel 1994: 160
35 Eph 4:11,12
36 Osei-Mensah 1990:15
37 Finzel 1994: 165
38 Wofford 1999: 161
39 Ford 1991: 199
40 Wofford 1999 159

15
THE SUPREME MODEL OF HUMILITY

'For even I, the Son of Man, came here not to be served but to serve and to give my life as a ransom for many.'[1]

Jesus not only taught us to be servant leaders; he was a servant leader.

We have only two choices: to bow before Jesus Christ as our Saviour *and Lord*, or to reject him as our *Lord* and Saviour. Jesus Christ cannot be the Saviour of anyone who does not also submit to his lordship in their lives. The teaching and modeling of Christ is clear: Jesus taught 'servant leadership' and he modeled it. For anyone to be a disciple of Christ, that person must submit to his lordship in this matter.

The two greatest examples of 'servant leadership' are of Jesus' washing the disciples' feet and Jesus' death on the cross. These examples are the subject of this chapter.

Jesus' Washing the Disciples' Feet

When did this take place?

John 12 concludes the public ministry of Christ. John 13:1 ushers us into the concluding days of Jesus' life. John 13:1 affirms the motive of all that transpired in the Upper Room and on Calvary.

> Now before the Feast of the Passover, when Jesus knew that his hour had come to depart out of this world to the Father, *having loved his own who were in the world, he loved them to the end.*

It was Jesus' love that led him to wash his disciples' feet, not duty. The oriental custom of hospitality meant that the host should arrange for someone to wash the feet of his guests after a hot, dusty journey on dirt roads. This was a menial task, only performed by servants or lesser people.

When John the Baptist described his feeling of unworthiness to baptise Jesus he referred to the task of stooping down, removing the sandals from Jesus' feet and holding them in his hands.[2]

Jesus and his disciples had come from Bethany on sandy, dusty roads with only sandals to protect their feet. Their feet were dirty and uncomfortable. In the Upper Room where the disciples met to celebrate the Passover, there was no servant. Which of the disciples would stoop to perform this menial task? Certainly not James and John who earlier desired to have the highest seats next to Jesus.[3] None of the disciples was willing since they were arguing who was to be regarded as 'the greatest' only a few hours earlier.[4] 'Service' was incompatible with 'greatness.' Service is rendered *for* the 'the great' and not *by* 'the great.' So the disciples thought! All peoples and cultures teach and practice this.

Jesus demonstrated his love toward his own disciples. '*His own*' applied first to his twelve apostles, including Judas Iscariot who was there with them; but secondly it applies to all those who should later believe.[5] By stooping down and *serving* his disciples he demonstrated his love to them (and to us), even as a mother stoops down and cleans her little ones.

Jesus' love is magnified when John informs us that Judas Iscariot was at the meal and that Satan had already prompted Judas to betray Jesus. Jesus knew all this and yet Jesus showed his love toward Judas and all the *Big People* reclining around the table.

What did Jesus do?

[Jesus] rose from supper. He laid aside his outer garments and taking a towel, tied it around his waist. Then he poured water into a basin and began to wash the disciples' feet and to wipe them with the towel that was wrapped around him.[6]

> The 'outer garments' refer to both long, flowing garments. These he laid aside and, like an Oriental slave, he stooped down to wash the disciples' feet with only a loin-cloth. Truly, Jesus 'took the form of a servant.'[7]

The graphic, detailed description of this act indicates the vivid memory John had of this incident. Jesus, stooping on the floor, took a wash basin and a pitcher of water and placed it right behind the men whose feet he was to wash. The disciples were reclining on couches around the table with their feet projecting outward. Then Jesus began to wash the feet, one by one, using the linen cloth tied around his waste to dry the feet after washing them with his hands.

Why did Jesus do this?

When Jesus had finished the washing and putting on his outer garments, he returned to his place and asked,

> Do you under understand what I have done to you? You call me Teacher and Lord, and you are right, for so I am. If I then, your Lord and Teacher, have washed your feet, you also ought to wash one another's feet. For I have given you an example, that you also should do just as I have done to you.[8]

'Do you understand what I have done to you?' The disciples did not, and those who have believed on Jesus thereafter surely have not either. Otherwise, there would be no power struggles for leadership within the Church, less ruling by lording it over others, more transparency and accountability – more humility in the exercise of leadership.

Jesus' washing of the disciples' feet was truly part of his humiliation. But it was also intended as a graphic, visual lesson on humility – *an example* – 'that you also should do just as I have done to you.' This was not the institution of an ordinance for his followers to practice 'foot washing.' Rather it was an *example* to do *as* (not *what*) Jesus did, that is, offer humble service to others.

To *wash one another's feet* means the disciples of Christ are obligated to offer others the lowliest of service from love and humility. 'We are bound by our tie to Christ to be tender and considerate towards our fellow-Christians, to serve them by love; pride, superiority, rank have no place in the Church of Christ. The only rank there is the rank of service. What the Lord and Master condescended to do, we may and must do.'[9]

Jesus' Death on the Cross

What is Jesus' greatest example of humility?

The greatest example of humility given to mankind was the humbling of Jesus 'by becoming obedient to the point of death, even death on the cross.' This example was offered by Paul because of quarrels and divisions in the Church at Philippi. The paraphrase from *The Message* will bring this to life.

> Agree with each other, love each other, be deep-spirited friends. Don't push your way to the front; don't sweet-talk your way to the top. Put yourself aside, and help others get ahead. Don't be obsessed with getting your own advantage. Forget yourselves long enough to lend a helping hand.
>
> Think of yourselves the way Christ Jesus thought of himself. He had equal status with God but didn't think so much of himself that he had to cling to the advantages of that status no matter what. Not at all! When the time came, he set aside the privileges of deity and took on the status of a slave, became *human*! Having become human, he stayed human. It was an incredibly humbling process. He didn't claim special privileges. Instead, he lived a selfless, obedient life and then died a selfless, obedient death – and the worst kind of death at that: a crucifixion.[10]

Talking about status, Jesus had it all. He was God with all the rights and privileges that pertain thereto. But in humility Jesus 'did not count equality with God a thing to be grasped.' What symbols of deity did Jesus hold on to? His high and exalted throne? His unending songs of praise by the seraphim? The brilliant light that surrounded the throne? Think of all the *Big Men* who insist on their privileges and symbols of status and honoured greetings! But Jesus laid it all aside, 'made himself nothing, taking the form of a servant.' More than that, '*he humbled himself* by becoming obedient to the point of death, even death on a cross.'

Why did Jesus humble himself?

The purpose of this lofty treatise on the humiliation of Christ was to provide an example of humility to the Church in Philippi. Disunity had erupted. Disagreements broke out between servants of the Lord.[11] Paul urges them to 'Do nothing from rivalry or conceit, but in humility count others more significant than yourselves. Let each of you look not only to his own interests, but also to the interests of others.'[12]

The description of the broken relationships in Philippi sounds so familiar. Human nature never changes. What is needed is a change of the mind. All behaviour begins in the mind. Our minds are naturally cultivated by our own self-centred nature, by our self-seeking friends, and by the values of our culture.

How do you develop a mind-set of humility?

Paul now pleads for a change of mind: '*Have this mind* among yourselves, which is yours in Christ Jesus.' Literally, Paul is saying, 'keep on thinking this among yourselves.' It is a present imperative tense, meaning a command to continually think this way. This amounts to a 'mind-set,' 'a fixed attitude,' 'a set of convictions.' This is a 'mind-set' that is in Christ, namely, humility. The attitude of Christ in verses 6-11 is clearly that of humility and self-renunciation, putting the welfare of others first. This was precisely the problem in Philippi – believers were putting their own interests first. Christ did not. Paul here writes that believers in the congregation should jointly and corporately have 'a set of convictions' and 'fixed attitude' and 'mind-set' which Jesus had.

How is this possible? It will not come naturally. There must be a spiritual exercise and discipline to develop this 'mind-set' through the enabling of the Holy Spirit. Meditation on the example of Christ's humility is a good place to begin; unceasing prayer that God would implant in your heart this attitude of Christ; a humility that recognises when you fall short, followed by confession of sins to God and then confession to those whom you have injured. There is no easy path to change this natural 'mind-set' to a Christ-like 'mind-set.' Reading and memorising Scripture is surely important. Becoming conscious of the ways in which you and others fall short and seeking to show the humility of Christ to others also helps.

It all begins in the mind. 'Do nothing from rivalry or conceit, but in humility count others more significant than yourselves.' Become conscious of the need to do this. Become aware of the times when you fail. If need be, confess to others. At the least, confess to God and seek his help to 'count others more significant than yourselves.' How can you do this? Begin recognising the depths of sin in your own heart – the persistent pride down deep inside. Recognise the gifts that God has given to others. Be honest with yourself and recognise your own weaknesses and deficiencies in your own gifts.

This has nothing to do with self-depreciation, which is unhealthy. But we all need to recognise that all we are is by God's grace. Though God has gifted us, the sun does not rise or set on us because we are extremely limited. Surprisingly, others are also gifted and capable! Besides, it is a command. Do it! 'Count others more significant than yourselves.' You can take very practical steps by obeying Philippians 2:4, 'Let each of you look not only to his own interests, but also to the interests of others.' If this task were easy, it would be commonly practiced after 2000 years. If it were impossible, God would never have given this command. And it all starts with love.

> Let love be genuine...Love one another with brotherly affection. Outdo one another in showing honor...Live in harmony with one another. Do not be haughty, but associate with the lowly.

> Never be conceited. Repay no one evil for evil, but give thought to do what is honorable in the sight of all. If possible, so far as it depends on you, live peaceably with all. Beloved, never avenge yourselves, but leave it to the wrath of God, for it is written, 'Vengeance is mine, I will repay, says the Lord. To the contrary, if your enemy is hungry, feed him; if he is thirsty, give him something to drink; for by so doing you will heap burning coals on his head.[13]

To follow Christ's example of service to others does not diminish our dignity. Christ surely did not lose his dignity when he served others. He forever was the beloved Son of God. Neither will we lose our dignity.

Osei-Mensah implores: 'May we be daily assured of who we are: sons and daughters of the living God, freed from ourselves to give ourselves in humble, loving service to one another. *This is the biblical challenge facing Christian leadership in Africa today* [Italics added].'[14]

Is there a reward for humility?

The biblical truth is this: the way downward is the path upwards to greatness. To go up you must first come down. Honour and blessing and great reward are promised to all who follow in Christ's train. When Jesus obeyed the Father and humbled himself to the point of death, 'God highly exalted him and bestowed on him the name that is above every name…'[15] When Peter alludes to the humiliation of Christ washing the disciples' feet, he connects humility with subsequent exaltation. 'Clothe yourselves, all of you, with humility toward one another, for God opposes the proud but gives grace to the humble. Humble yourselves, therefore, under the mighty hand of God so that at the proper time he may exalt you.'[16]

CONCLUSION

One may ask how Christ, the Second Person of the Trinity, could show humility. He did so by his absolute submission to the Father in his incarnation – 'he made himself nothing, taking the form of a servant…' In this Jesus expressed humility, even as all wise people should. 'He must be the pattern of all humility, of all creaturely dependence; and it is only as a man that Christ thus claims to be *tapeinos* [humble]; his human life was a constant living on the fullness of his Father's love.'[17]

Humility and love go together. Christ could live a life of humility because he knew the deep love of his Father. Love is a fundamental virtue for all Christian leaders. Failure comes when leaders fail to love as Christ loved. *Part Four* will focus on 'The Love of Christian Leaders.'

SEARCHING THE SCRIPTURE WITH APPLICATION

1. '*Do nothing from rivalry or conceit, but in humility count others more significant than yourselves*' (Php 2:3).
    a. How much rivalry or conceit do you observe in the Church?
    b. Do you participate in any of this rivalry yourself?
    c. Why do you and/or others engage in rivalry?
    d. The solution to rivalry and conceit is humility, counting others 'more significant than yourselves.' Why does it take humility to 'count others more significant

than yourselves'? How can you do this? That is, what steps must you take to 'count others more significant than yourselves'?

2. '*Let each of you look not only to his own interests, but also to the interests of others*' (Php 2:4).
    a. Is it wrong for 'servant leaders' to look after their own interests?
    b. When does it become wrong?
    c. When was the last time you 'looked after' the interests of others?
    d. How have you done this? What did you do?
    e. What were your motives? Do you need to reevaluate your motives?
3. '*Have this mind among yourselves, which is yours in Christ Jesus*' (Php 2:5). This is a corporate activity by all members of the Church. 'This mind' refers to a 'mind-set,' a 'set of convictions' or 'attitude.'
    a. How does one change the 'mind-set' of Christians in the Church from a natural 'me first' to 'others first' attitude?
    b. If the natural 'set of convictions' or 'attitude' is not changed, what will be the consequences?
    c. Meditate on the humility of Christ manifested in the washing of the disciples' feet and in his obedience to the Father in dying on the cross. Mention the ways in which Christ's humility is different from our 'pride' and 'self-importance.'
    d. What promise is there for those who do humble themselves before God and before others, even as Jesus did? See Php 2:9-11; 1 Pe 5:5-7.

Endnotes

[1] Mk 10:45 NLT
[2] Mt 3:11
[3] Mt 20:20f
[4] Lk 22:24
[5] Jn 17:9, 20
[6] Jn 13:4,5
[7] Php 2:7
[8] Jn 13:12-15
[9] Reith 1948: II 83
[10] Php 2:2-8
[11] Php 4:2f
[12] Php 2:3,4 ESV
[13] Ro 12:9-20
[14] Osei-Mensah 1990:21
[15] Php 2:9
[16] 1 Pe 5:5-6
[17] Trench 1953:150f

PART FOUR

LOVE OF CHRISTIAN LEADERS

In a perfect world we would love God with all of our hearts and our neighbour as ourselves. But in this fallen world we do not love God supremely; and, therefore, we do not love our neighbour as we should, nor do we accept ourselves as God designed us.

Part Four focuses on love for people which every Christian leader should have. First, we consider *self-esteem* and the importance of every leader accepting and appreciating himself. The following two chapters examine the opposite characteristics of love, namely, *jealousy* and *anger*, which are character flaws that flow from a heart that does not love God supremely. The chapter on the *attributes of agape love* provides a careful examination of divine love. The final chapter concludes with *the supreme model of agape love.*

16
SELF-ESTEEM IN LEADERS

'You shall love the Lord your God with all your heart and with all your soul and with all your mind. This is the great and first commandment. And a second is like it: You shall love your neighbor as yourself.'[1]

Life is not about you; neither is the ministry about you. It's all about God who created you for his glory. *Everything* centres on God.

The paradox is this: when God is the centre, you are affirmed; but when you are the centre, you loose your self-esteem. And when you cannot accept yourself, you cannot accept others. This is a fact of life.

Put another way. When the greatest commandment is *first*, and when the second commandment is *second*, God will affirm you. But when you put self first, you loose all sense of self-worth because a person's worth is in his relationship with God. To be an effective Christian leader one must have a healthy self-respect in order to reach out to others with love. Interpersonal relationship skills are fundamentally all about love.

This chapter is on the importance of self-esteem which is self-acceptance.

Creation and the Fall

Persons created in God's likeness

In the eternal councils of the Triune God, the divine decision was made: 'Let us make man in our image, after our likeness...male and female he created them.'[2] Adam and Eve were 'image bearers,' reflecting the likeness of God; they were not duplicate, carbon copies or 'little gods' but a reflection of God.

The image of God includes personality with life, intelligence, a will with purpose and decision-making capacity, self-awareness, emotional capacity and of course, spirituality.

Adam and Eve were created to have a personal relationship with their Creator – worshipful, dependent, trusting and obedient. As God's children, they respected, loved and looked up to their Father. God was their friend who walked with Adam and Eve in the garden in the cool of the day. They submitted to their Lord as obedient servants.

In this condition Adam and Eve were granted dignity and honour. God ever remained the Lord God while Adam and Eve remained dependent, obedient, trusting and worshipping. Their dignity was in being children of God, holding dominion over the works of God as vassal kings.[3]

Persons affected by the Fall

Everything changed when Adam and Eve chose with pride to invert the order of importance in the universe. Instead of loving God with all their hearts, they chose with pride to love themselves above all else, reversing the divinely established order.[4] Life could not continue as usual. The judgement of death fell on them as God had forewarned.[5]

'And so death passed upon all men.'[6] The whole human race plunged into death. Moreover, the sins of the fathers were visited on their children for generations.[7] Even as the trespass of Adam and Eve affected all their children, ever since, the sins of parents have terrible consequences on their children for generations. Death not only reigned in the spiritual and physical realms but sin brought 'chronic anxiety' to man's personality.

The roots of chronic anxiety are in man's alienation from God; the personal relationship with the Creator had been badly fractured. Because of this spiritual condition, psychological consequences followed. When man was filled with anxiety, he defended himself with the natural means of defense mechanisms.

Among other things man began to experience a low self-esteem that grew out of guilt and shame. When Adam and Eve loved God supremely, they recognised their dependent and obedient relationship with God; they were his children. But when Adam and Eve sought to be preeminent, they felt guilty, shameful, vulnerable, unhappy, anxious and alone.

So Adam and Eve made aprons out of fig-leaves to cover their nakedness, their shame and guilt. Their offspring began doing things that people are doing ever since: seeking to enhance their self-worth through the acquisition of wealth, power and a name, to feel better than others; to be chief.

Nimrod, the 'mighty hunter' who set himself against the authority of God, built a city with a tower reaching to the heavens to 'make a name' for himself.[8] All this was done to enhance himself and make him appear great, because down, deep inside he felt anxious, vulnerable and insignificant. In a word, he had a low self-image, an inferiority complex and a lack of self-esteem because he had rebelled against God and had lost the affirmation from God.

Low Self-Esteem

Cause of low self-esteem

The root cause of low self-esteem is the sin and guilt that has estranged persons from God. Even those who have been redeemed suffer from the Fall because they do not yet have that perfect relationship with God of trust and obedience; they have not yet been glorified.

Furthermore, in our fallen state and without the perfect affirmation from God, a low self-esteem is learned through negative experiences.

Counselors generally agree that the basis for a child's self-esteem is formed during his or her early years. Inferiority and low self-esteem, therefore, often arise in the home. Most parents are inconsistent in their child rearing and feelings about children. Even the most patient parent explodes in criticism at times or withholds acceptance and warmth.[9]

Parents, uncles and teachers criticise, shame, reject and scold a child repeatedly. The father mistreats one of his wives and her children, depriving them of love, respect and support. Parents and teachers set unrealistic standards which are unachievable by the child. Children are punished mercilessly, repeatedly and unjustly. Comments are made of the child's incompetence and stupidity. A child's appearance or shabby clothes are ridiculed. Parents fail to show love through cuddling, hugging or affectionately touching. Whenever parents are overly strict and fail to offer words of praise or commendation, the child grows up with a poor self-image. Peers and age-mates criticise and reject the person, picking on him and making him feel inferior.

Effects of low self-esteem

A person with an inferiority complex may not be inferior at all. In actual fact he may be intelligent, physically attractive and gifted. But the person *feels* inferior. A person arrives at conclusions about himself based on the opinions of others. From parents and family, friends and peers, you derive the impression of who you are. Because of a broken relationship with God, you embrace the opinion of others while not fully experiencing the love of God.

This low self-esteem is manifest in many different ways. Few people have all the following manifestations of low self-esteem, but numbers of the following conditions will be found.

The person feels isolated and unlovable so he withdraws from others. The person unconsciously punishes himself. He is depressed; he lacks self-confidence and inner peace. Feeling sensitive, his feelings are hurt easily. Self-criticism, self-hatred and self-rejection are common experiences. Ironically, a person who is starved for love is often unable to accept compliments or expressions of love. Without self-respect people loose a desire for life. Tribes have perished from this planet because they lost all purpose of living through self-depreciation. The World Health Organization reports that 1,000 people commit suicide every day and 10,000 people *try* to commit suicide daily.[10]

> Our self-hatred would not be quite so serious if its target were only the self, but, unfortunately, that is never the case. Always the hatred includes others as well. In a nutshell, the two hatreds – the hatred of self and hatred of others – always go hand in hand. In fact, whenever we see someone who in one way or another is lashing out at other people, we can be sure of this: deep down, he hates himself.[11]

An inferiority complex has social consequences. The person has difficulty getting along with others. Interpersonal conflicts are common. He is jealous of others and often critical. He will judge others as proud when he observes their self confidence. There is a tendency to complain, argue, and be intolerant, angry and unforgiving. He manifests a drive to gain power, superiority and control over others. Or he may be submissive and dependent on others. An insecure person is obsessed with himself and seeks to draw attention to himself.

Difference between self-esteem and pride

Some Christians believe the emphasis on self-esteem today is unbiblical, for it centres on the 'me' while we should be focused on God. Christians are afraid to 'love themselves' because of fear of being egotistical and even blasphemous. However, this rejection of self-esteem, self-respect and self-love is misguided.

Jesus taught: 'Love others as well as you love yourself.'[12] The truth is that people who hate themselves cannot love others. 'Without self-love there can be no love for others. Jesus equates these two loves, and binds them together, making them inseparable.'[13]

There are two ways of loving yourself: selfishly and unselfishly. A selfish kind of self-love focuses on the self; it is preoccupied with itself with little concern for others; it is egotism illustrated by the Greek myth about Narcissus. He was a youth who, while gazing at his reflection in a well of water, fell in love with himself. Totally engrossed with his own image, he tumbled into the water and drowned. From this myth the English word, *narcissism* is derived.[14] Obviously, this self-love is neither biblical nor healthy, for it always looks inwardly and does not reach out. A narcissistic person does not love God with all his heart; neither can he love others.

But a healthy self-love is unselfish, referring to *self-acceptance.* 'We cannot give what we do not possess. Only when we have accepted ourselves can we become truly self-less and free from ourselves…The word *self-centered* aptly describes us when we revolve only around ourselves.'[15] A healthy self-love must be acquired but a selfish self-love is inherited with our sinful natures.

Growing in Self-Esteem

There is no easy way to overcome the baggage of low self-esteem developed from childhood. No simple prayer will do it. Etched in your subconscious is the feeling of inferiority. Sustained effort must be made to reject your self-rejection and accept your affirmation by God. How do you grow in your self-esteem?

Grow in your relationship with God: Deep seated feelings of inferiority can only be transformed by developing a deep and abiding relationship with Jesus Christ in his Word – knowing God's love for you and his acceptance. John writes: 'We are going to love – love and be loved. First we were loved, now we love. He loved us first.'[16] Paul urges: 'Accept one another, just as Christ also accepted us to the glory of God.'[17] Reflect on God's love for you; thank God in prayer for his many blessings. Remind yourself of the gifts God has given. Although others may have put you down and failed to affirm you, God first loved you; and he continues to love you. Even when fathers and mothers let you down, the Lord is there to lift you up.[18]

Persistent meditation upon Scripture with memorisation is where you must begin. Resist the devil when thoughts of inferiority surface. A healthy self-esteem is rooted in God, not self; it is built on your relationship with God, understanding who you are in Christ. You need to think biblically.

> Self-love…includes the following: (1) accepting myself as a child of God who is lovable, valuable, capable; (2) being willing to give up considering myself the center of the world; (3) recognizing my need of God's forgiveness and redemption. Christian self-esteem results from translating 'I am the greatest, wisest, strongest, best' to 'I am what I am, a person made in God's image, a sinner redeemed by God's grace, and a significant part in the body of Christ.[19]

Grow in your acceptance of yourself: Certain things in life should not be accepted, such as moral weakness, laziness, ignorance, indulgences and lack of discipline. But other things that were given to you through birth and nurture (rearing by parents), those things beyond your control, must be accepted as God's sovereign will, such as limited intelligence, physical weaknesses and handicaps, personality and appearance.

Have you accepted yourself as you are, your body, mind, family background and education? Have you accepted yourself fully and completely with all your limitations? Have you accepted your spouse and your children, your economic situation and your state of health? Self-acceptance is basic to self-love.

Grow in your affirmation of others: A healthy self-image does not dwell on self but on others. Affirm others, congratulate them, praise them, and thank them. As you do this, others will become your friends and you begin to fill your emotional cup with warm acceptance. The more you are loved, the more you gain self-esteem, and the more you can love others.

As you grow in your love for God, the more you feel valued by God. As you grow in your affirming of others, showing love to others, they in turn will respond by loving you. This strengthens your self-image and self-esteem. This becomes a blessed cycle. Only when you can touch the lives of others through your love can you become a successful leader.

CONCLUSION

An Ewe-Mina proverb says, 'The dog does not worry when the chicken runs over to the bones.' A person who feels secure will not feel threatened by the performance or gifts of others. When your cup of God's love is full and overflowing, you can pour out love to others. With self-esteem and self-acceptance, you can reach out to others without feeling threatened

In contrast a jealous person is self-centred and therefore cannot love others. Jealousy, the opposite of love, is the topic of our next chapter.

SEARCHING THE SCRIPTURE WITH APPLICATION

1. How much does God love you? Jn 3:16; Ro 5:8; Eph 2:4,5; 1 Jn 3:1.
2. After reading and meditating on Ro 8:28-39, write down on paper all the blessings that are yours because God chose you in love.
3. God has given every single child of God precious gifts. Read Ro 12:3-8; 1 Co 12:1-30.
    a. Has any believer been bypassed without a gift? (Ro 12:3ff)

b. Does every believer have the same gift? (Ro 12:6)
c. Who chooses what gifts each believer has? (Ro 12:6)
d. Is every gift important for the Body to function properly?
e. In light of all this, how should a person with a low self-esteem change his attitude toward himself and why?

4. Read 1 Jn 4:8-19. How is God's love for us and the command to love others related in this text? Why should you be able to love others?
5. In view of God's matchless love for you, how valuable are you in God's sight? If you reject yourself and hate yourself, what does that tell of your understanding of God's love for you?
6. Describe the differences between a selfish self-love and a selfless self-love.
7. Explain the priorities of a healthy, mature Christian in his relationship to God, others and himself. How much devotion, commitment and attention should one give to God, others and self in relationship to each other?
8. Have you seen Church leaders who have a healthy self-esteem? What evidence do you find that points to a healthy self-image?
9. Have you seen Church leaders who have a low self-esteem? What evidence do you find that points to a low self-image? What should Christians do to help them?
10. Do you have any personal indications of an inferiority complex? If so, what should you start doing to overcome it?

Endnotes

[1] Mt 22:37 *The Message*
[2] Ge 2:26f
[3] Ps 8
[4] Ge 3
[5] Ge 2:17
[6] Ro 5:12
[7] Ex 20:5,6
[8] Ge 10:8-11:9
[9] Collins 1988: 318
[10] Ashford 1977:2
[11] Ashford 1977:5
[12] Mt 22:39 *The Message*
[13] Trobisch 1976:11f
[14] Trobisch 1976:14
[15] Trobisch 1976: 15
[16] 1 Jn 4:19 *The Message*
[17] Ro 15:7 NASB
[18] Ps 27:10
[19] Collins 1988: 315

17
JEALOUSY: THE OPPOSITE OF LOVE

'Love does not envy.'[1]

Can community prevail without love? Can a leader succeed with jealousy?

As an African proverb says, 'Peace is good soil for man to grow.' Love provides that peace but jealousy destroys it. Jealousy even destroys health. Solomon said, 'Envy makes the bones rot.'[2] A Kenyan proverb says, 'Lack of unity spells weakness.' A Ganda proverb says, 'Unity is strength.' But unity is impossible whenever jealousy prevails. An Amharic proverb says, 'You can tie down a lion with a spider's web.' A Swahili proverb says, 'Unity among the cattle makes the lion lie down hungry.' Unity is impossible where jealousy reigns. What is needed is a united community bound together with love.

The Greek and Hebrew words for jealousy refer to a very strong emotion, a passionate desire. The root meaning of the Hebrew is 'to be dyed dark red, black.'[3] It refers to a deep emotion that causes the blood to darken the face. *Zelos* is the Greek word for *jealousy* from which the English word, *zeal*, is derived. The context determines whether the word conveys a positive or negative idea and can be translated either as *jealousy, envy* or *zeal.*

In this chapter we shall consider the biblical teaching on jealousy.

Godly Zeal and Jealousy

Can 'zeal' be shameful?

The English word, *zeal*, carries the notion from the Greek of 'a passionate commitment to a person or cause.'[4] It refers to a deep emotion that can be described as 'ardently active, devoted, or diligent.'[5] A person who is zealous *strives, desires, exerts oneself earnestly, and is dedicated.* He is full of *ardour.*[6] The human capacity for zeal is a reflection of the divine image, for God is passionate in his commitment to his own glory and in his devotion to his own people.

Zeal is often commended. When Jesus manifested intense emotion by driving out the money changers from the Temple, his disciples remembered the Scripture, '*Zeal* for your house will consume me.'[7] Jesus' zealous action was an act of jealousy for the glory of God and the sanctity of the Temple of God. He was deeply fervent in his anger when he said, 'Get these out of here! How dare you turn my Father's house into a market!'[8] The grace of God trains the Christian to be '*zealous* for good works.'[9] A *zealous* spirit caused Epaphras to 'work hard' for the benefit of the Colossian Church. Indeed, fervency and devotion are admirable traits. The sin of the Church in Laodicea was their lukewarm devotion to God. 'So because you are lukewarm, and neither hot nor cold, I will spit you out of my mouth.'[10] To be hot is to be *zealous* in devotion. The Church today needs more *godly zeal* to enliven its witness.

Zeal is often the equivalent of *jealousy.* After the great victory on Mt. Carmel, Elijah fled from Jezebel to a cave on Mt. Sinai. He said to God: 'I have been very *zealous* for the LORD, the God of hosts...And I alone am left; and they seek my life, to take it away.'[11] Elijah was *zealous*, but he was also *jealous* for Yahweh's glory, even as other Bibles translate the word, *jealous* instead of *zealous.*[12]

However, *zeal* is not always a virtue. This 'passionate commitment' can lead to false piety as when Saul (Paul) persecuted the Church because of his *misplaced zeal.*[13] Before conversion he was '*extremely zealous* for the traditions of the fathers.'[14] Moreover, he was '*zealous for God.*'[15] But *zeal* can be 'not according to knowledge.'[16] When the attendant virtues of humility and love are not present, *zeal* exhibits a destructive character. In this case *zeal,* found in the *zealot*, becomes fanaticism which is capable of every kind of violence, all in the name of religion. The Christian Crusades and the present day terrorism in the name of Islam are examples.

Can jealousy be godly?

Jealousy can be either good or bad. Mankind, created in the image of God, has the capacity for the emotions of jealousy and anger since God is a God of jealousy and wrath. In the midst of renewing the Ten Commandments,[17] God warned Israel: 'For you shall worship no other god, for the LORD, whose name is *Jealous*, is *a jealous God.*' Yahweh, the only true and living God, demands exclusive devotion of his people and is intolerant of any rival.

God requires absolute loyalty, even as a man expects total commitment of his wife. The Mosaic Law made provision for a *jealous* husband to find justice over a wayward wife. God commanded, 'If any man's wife goes astray and breaks faith with him...and if the *spirit of jealousy* comes over him and he is *jealous* of his wife who has defiled herself...' then certain rituals were performed to ascertain her guilt or innocence.[18] Jealousy is 'viewed positively as a high level of commitment when it describes the feeling of a person for something that is rightly his or her own.'[19]

References to *God's jealousy* are mostly in the context of a marriage relationship with his people. The Bible represents God being wedded to Israel in a covenant relationship. Even as a husband is jealous over his wife, not wanting any other man to woo her, so God is jealous over Israel, not wanting her to wander from her covenant. When God's people break that bond of covenant love and fall into idolatry, God breaks forth in righteous indignation. 'For they provoked him to anger with their high places; they moved him to *jealousy* with their idols.'[20] Ezekiel describes apostasy as adultery. When *jealousy* is expressed by God it is almost always a question of his relationship with his people. He is *zealous* in rescuing his people from their enemies, or he is *jealous* over his people who have provoked God to anger by their idolatry.

Men of God have been commended for their jealousy. When Israel worshiped Baal at Peor, Phinehas, with a *zealous jealousy*, thrust a spear into an Israelite man having intercourse with a Moabite woman. Then we read: 'Phinehas the son of Eleazor, son of Aaron the priest, has turned back my wrath from the people of Israel, in that he was *jealous* with *my jealousy* among them, so that I did not consume the people of Israel in *my jealousy*.'[21] 'The sense here is a passionate, *consuming zeal* focused on God, or rather on the doing of His will and the maintaining of His honour in face of the ungodly acts of men and nations [italics added].'[22]

Paul by nature was a zealous person. As a non-Christian his zeal led him to persecute the Church.[23] But as a disciple of Jesus Christ he wrote to the Corinthians: 'I feel a *divine jealousy* for you, for I betrothed you to one husband, to present you as a pure virgin.'[24] Godly jealousy is concerned with God's glory and keeping his commandments.

Jealousy versus Envy

In common usage, envy and jealousy are synonyms, used interchangeably. But in reality their meanings are different.

Jealousy is 'an unpleasant apprehension, suspicion, or resentment, arising from fear or mistrust of another.' On the other hand, envy has 'a feeling of grief or repining, with a longing to possess some excellence or good fortune of another.'[25] Thus jealousy focuses on a perceived threat or loss that diminishes one's own self-importance and significance. Jealousy arises because of a threat. On the other hand, envy wants to possess what another has or to diminish the superiority of the other.

A person who feels inferior becomes envious of others because their good qualities are thought to devalue his own self-worth. People tend to compare themselves with one another, seeking to determine their own significance and importance. In so doing, however, the discovery of another person's 'greatness' becomes a threat to their own self-image.

Envy is singularly evil. Augustine called envy 'the supremely diabolical sin.' Other vices tend to provide some pleasure, at least initially. But envy never does. Envy 'begins with a perceived loss of self-worth; rather than leading to actions that enhance self, it seeks to devalue the other.'[26]

Envy is quite different from ambition. An ambitious person strives to attain the good that another has. This can be good, depending on the motive. In the process of their ambition they are neither diminishing the other person nor robbing them of their character traits. But an envious person 'sorrows at another's good,' as Thomas Aquinas observed.[27] Envy feels threatened by another's success. Herein lay the roots of envy. 'Envy is covetousness with anger. Covetousness…is longing for another's possessions. Envy goes beyond this to include resentment toward the owner of the desired object.'[28]

Sinful Jealousy

The difference between a *godly jealousy* and a *sinful jealousy* is motive. Every deep emotion turns sinful when it springs from pride and selfishness. *Zeal* and *jealousy* can be motivated by rivalry or envy which leads to contention and strife. Paul admonishes: 'It is fine to be zealous, provided the purpose is good.'[29] Purpose and motive are everything. The problem with sinful human beings is that most motives are self-centred with the aim of selfish gain. *Jealousy* is a sinful zeal that does not help others but harms them instead. A God-fearing person who seeks only the glory of God will manifest zeal and jealousy for God, but always with love and humility.

A selfishly motivated jealousy is deeply sinful and always listed in the New Testament with the works of the sinful nature. Notice the inclusion of *jealousy* in all the New Testament catalogues of sinful practices.[30] *Jealousy* is a typical attitude of the 'flesh.' *Jealousy* is intertwined and interconnected with these vices. For example: 'quarreling, jealousy, anger, hostility, slander, gossip, conceit, and disorder.'[31] Jealousy is implicated in every one of those vices. A jealous person is conceited, engages in quarrels, becomes angry, is hostile, slanders, gossips and is the cause of disorder. *Jealousy* caused Joseph's brothers to betray him, selling him as a slave in Egypt.[32] *Jealousy/envy* motivated the Jews to call for Jesus' death before Pilate.[33]

According to the Christian leaders we interviewed, the largest number of hurts in the ministry, apart from financial struggles, is jealous Church leaders and pastors. When Church leadership sees a young pastor with higher education, doing commendable ministry, they feel threatened and stifle the pastor. Opposition from Church ministers can be painful.

Another Christian leader said this: 'Being rejected by my own people was so painful. My expectation was that they would receive me. It was so painful in my heart. The Church leaders did not come to my graduation. Now that I teach in a Bible School, I can talk to them because I am out of their system of Church administration and not a threat to them." Fellow pastors do not see you as a brother but as competition. 'Sometimes you are stabbed in the back by someone you worked with for years. It is so painful because your ministry is destroyed which you built with resources and time.'

What is the source of jealousy?

Inferiority complex: The soil from which jealousy sprouts is a threatened ego. In fact, one may say that the primary soil from which jealousy arises is an inferiority complex saturated with pride.

'Inferiority is the primary internal condition that makes it easy for the seeds of jealousy to sprout. Those who believe they "can't compete" are likely to have a great deal of fear.'[34] Such a person with an inferiority complex is suspicious of rivals. Jealousy is manifested in distrust, suspicion, resentment and apprehension.

Pride: Pride lifts up self, claiming the right to be the centre of attention. When the self-image is threatened, jealousy explodes. When others excel because of God given gifts, jealousy arises. A better preacher, a more attractive personality, a more gifted teacher or administrator brings them praise. This is a threat to a proud person who wants to be the most prominent and most important

Rejection of God's will: Unbelief questions God's sovereign will. He does not accept himself as he is; he rejects God's good and perfect plan for his life.

An inaccurate view of gifts and calling: An inaccurate view of one's gifts leads to erroneous conclusions: either self-importance is exaggerated, or feelings of inferiority develop. A self-image that is not accurate or that fails to accept God given gifts humbly will lead to jealousy.

Lack of contentment: A servant of God is content in knowing God and his will for life. Contentment arises out of confidence in God's eternal purposes and plans working themselves out in all circumstances. Knowing that God affirms you builds self-esteem which in turn delights in the gifts and blessings of others. A beautiful person is marked by graciousness that flows from contentment and confidence and does not compare himself with others.

What are the effects of jealousy?

Jealousy hinders church growth: Jealousy is one of the greatest impediments to Church growth. Instead of welcoming young, educated and gifted pastors, they are sidelined, demoted and even removed from ministry. Ordination is withheld for decades to eliminate competition. Instead of building on the strengths that God provides the Church with gifted and educated servants of the Lord, Church leaders seek to protect themselves, even if that means stifling the growth of the Christian Church. Self-promotion is their primary concern, not the glory of God or the building of his Church. Near the time of Church elections, pastors with strengths in ministry are transferred or removed from ministry under false pretexts for one purpose: to eliminate competition in elections and to protect their own seat of authority.

Jealousy creates division: Church politics brews many a squabble and competition. Friendly fellowship vanishes. Churches are sometimes led by people without a vision and direction. One pastor said, 'When I graduated from Bible College I believed that I would work with my home district Church council. They led me to believe that. But after graduation they did not accept me. It made me think there was some deficiency in me, but then I learned that this happens with many others. It was Church politics. Politics leads to a weak Church. They don't want competition.'

Jealousy creates emotional grief: Not only does jealousy harm the Church; it also affects the persons gripped with jealousy. All sinful reactions have consequences that begin in the present. Out of jealousy grows *emotional problems*. Jealousy leads to unhappiness. The heart is filled with fear of loosing something of value. Depression, hurt, anger, suspiciousness, mistrust and loneliness grow from jealousy. *Physical problems* include many stress related diseases, such as ulcers, colitis, twitching and muscular tension. *Relational problems* also occur. Because a jealous person is suspicious and distrusting, relationships are broken and the person becomes less attractive to others. Jealousy breeds hatred and spite.[35]

Jealousy has no practical benefit: Envy is the 'least practical of all vices' because there is no personal reward that comes from it; it only leads to grief. No one becomes happy or satisfied through envy.

> Envy removes joy because envy is the opposite of gratitude, and gratitude is the seedbed of joy... We are always confronted by the half-full, half-empty glass. Our lives and our worlds are finite, never fully filled, never fully empty, so we always have opportunities for gratitude for the half full, or ingratitude, resentment, and bitterness at the half empty and envy of those whose glass is fuller.[36]

Envy develops because of distorted thoughts: 'I cannot be happy unless I have what someone else has.' Envy assumes that significance comes from positions or possessions instead of from being a child of the heavenly Father. It is whose we are, not what we have, that makes us significant.

Overcoming Jealousy

How does one learn to overcome a spirit of jealousy? Since jealousy springs from deep inside our sinful nature, there is no simple, quick cure. Following are guideposts to point the way in loving your neighbour and avoiding jealousy.

Know yourself: Be honest with yourself and humble before God. Admit the sins of jealousy and envy. Without honesty, no help is available.

Grow in your knowledge of God: To know yourself, you must *know God* intimately through the Scripture and in prayer. The more you know God and his ways through a knowledge of Scripture, the more you will know yourself.

Admit the harm done through jealousy: Recognise and acknowledge the damage that is done within the Church and community through the vices of jealousy and envy. Recognise the harm done to yourself. Be honest!

Confess your sin of jealousy: Pray and confess to God your sin. You cannot hide from God; he knows. Even if you fall into jealousy several times a day, continue to confess your sins with a contrite and broken heart. God is gracious.

Pray for God's blessing upon those of whom you are jealous: Begin to pray for the welfare of the others. When you begin to pray sincerely for their wellbeing, you will be surprised how God begins to change your heart, filling it with love.

Give thanks to God for those of whom you are jealous: Thank God for the good which you appreciate in the other. Recognise their gifts and abilities. As you think and pray over the issue, give thanks to God for them.

Tell others about the good you have seen in their lives: Jesus commanded us to love our enemies. Love can only spring up when we begin to recognise the gifts and abilities that they have received from God. Begin to tell others about the good you have seen in the other.

Begin to compliment those of whom you are jealous: Counteract thoughts of suspicion of others with words of praise and compliments for those who seem to excel and threaten you.

Learn to accept yourself with all your strengths and weaknesses: Make an honest self-evaluation. Learn to accept God's loving and sovereign providence. Become content with God's gifts and opportunities granted to you. As Elizabeth Elliot remarked, 'We have nothing to do with the choice of gift. We have everything to do with the use of the gift.'

Cultivate contentment: Develop a thankful spirit for God's providential blessings on you. One servant of the Lord who served under difficult circumstances developed five habits of contentment. If these habits could become part of our worldview and set of convictions they would go a long way to eliminate jealousy and envy from our breasts. (1) Never allow yourself to complain about anything; (2) Never picture yourself in any other circumstance; (3) Never compare your lot in life with that of another; (4) Never allow yourself to wish this or that had been different; (5) Do not dwell on tomorrow – that is God's, not ours.

CONCLUSION

Sinful jealousy is a noble virtue gone badly. Because human beings are made in God's image, they have the capacity of feeling zeal, ardour and fervour. God is pleased when we display this emotion because of our love for him.

But sinful jealousy is self-centred. Instead of loving others and building them up for God's glory, the jealous person tears them down in order to protect self. Jealousy is a self-destructive vice for it does personal harm, emotionally and physically, to the one who is jealous. Furthermore, Christian leaders who become jealous cannot experience God's favour; nor can they build the Church for God's glory. Jealousy is the opposite of love.

Another vice that is the opposite of love is anger. While love builds up, anger tears down. Anger is the topic of the next chapter.

SEARCHING THE SCRIPTURE WITH APPLICATION

1. Discuss what is meant by 'godly jealousy'?
2. Share the times you have observed Christian leaders demonstrating 'godly jealousy'?
3. Read of David and Goliath and Saul's jealousy (1 Sa 17:1-18:30).
    a. Should not Saul have been pleased with David instead?
    b. What harm did Saul's jealousy cause to himself and others?
    c. Why are Church leaders jealous today?
    d. Why should they be pleased instead of being jealous?
    e. What harm does their jealousy do to themselves and others?
4. Read the account of Korah, Dathan and Abiram in Nu 16:1-50.
    a. Who was Korah? Why should he have been grateful for his gifts and calling? C.f. Nu 16:1,8-11; 1 Ch 6:31-33; 9:31,32
    b. Why was he not content? Reflect on the possibilities.
    c. Why are Church leaders today not content with the gifts, calling and opportunities that God has given them?
    d. Did he admit his own jealousy? How did he blame Moses?
    e. What harm did he bring on himself, Moses and Israel?
    f. Make application of this to the Church today.
5. How does an 'inferiority complex' often lead to jealousy?
6. How would you advise someone with an 'inferiority complex' so that he would not be so troubled with feelings of jealousy?

Endnotes

1 1 Co 13:4
2 Pr 14:30
3 Richardson 1950: 115
4 Popkes 1981: 100
5 Random House College Dict., 1988
6 Danker 1979: 427
7 Jn 2:17
8 Jn 2:16 NIV
9 Tit 2:11-14
10 Re 3:16
11 1 Ki 19:10 NASB
12 1 Ki 19:10 ESV
13 Php 3:6
14 Gal 1:14
15 Ac 22:3
16 Ro 10:2
17 Ex 34:14
18 Nu 5:11-31
19 Richards 1985: 358
20 1Ki 14:22
21 Nu 25:11
22 Stumpff 1964: 878
23 Php 3:6
24 2 Co 11:2
25 Webster's Dictionary, 1959
26 Hunter 1990: 359
27 Thomas Aquinas as found in Kreeft 1986: 121
28 Walters 1985: 61
29 Gal 4:18
30 Ro 13:13; 2 Co 12:20; Gal 5:20; Jas 3:14; 1 Ti 6:3-5; Tit 3:3; 1 Pe 2:1.
31 2 Co 12:20
32 Ac 7:9
33 Mt 27:18
34 Walters 1985: 30
35 Walters 1985: 31f
36 Kreeft 1986:122

18
ANGER: THE OPPOSITE OF LOVE

'Never go to bed angry –
don't give the devil that sort of foothold.'[1]

Love builds up; but anger tears down.

A Kenyan proverb says, 'It is the hyena that howls.' Hyenas are the scavengers. They roam the countryside in packs in order to destroy and tear apart. With greed and vicious attacks they devour and eat. Anger does the same. Anger is the opposite of love because love builds up, but anger divides and tears apart for selfish reasons.

Many poisonous emotions spring out of *anger,* including mild annoyance, irritation, exasperation, frustration, bitterness, hurt feelings, resentment, withdrawal, brooding, depression, violent rage – and hatred. 'Anger is the emotion that typically pits you against the person, place or thing that stimulated the emotion. It is the opposite of the feeling of love. Love draws you toward the person; anger sets you against the person.'[2]

What does *anger* look like?

Understanding Anger

Anger is a human emotion like joy, sorrow or fear. The dictionary definition of *anger* sounds familiar: 'A strong passion or emotion of displeasure, and usually antagonism, excited by a sense of injury or insult.'[3] Words similar to anger are *wrath*, *rage* and *fury*. The picture is one of someone out of control.

The Greek root for *anger* used in the New Testament (*thumos*)[4] refers essentially to 'a violent movement.'[5] *Orge*[6] is the second word used for anger in the New Testament and is sometimes used with *thumos*[7]. Though these words are often used interchangeably, they do have distinct meanings.

Thumos is the strongest of all passions and refers to 'the turbulent commotion, the boiling agitation of the feelings' that can eventually subside and disappear; whereas, *orge* is an emotion that is 'more of an abiding and settled habit of mind with the purpose of revenge.'[8] Hence *orge* is used of God's settled attitude toward sin. God's *wrath* is God's abiding judgment[9] and hostility toward everything that violates God's holy character. *Anger* can either be a momentary violent emotion of hostility (*thumos*) or a settled, long standing feeling of animosity with a desire for revenge (*orge*).

Where does *anger* come from? Does it emanate from our sinful nature? Is anger in itself sinful?

The Christian Church has reckoned *anger* to be one of the 'Seven Deadly Sins.' The New Testament lists *anger* with all the other vices to be shunned.[10] No one should ever be chosen as a Church leader who is 'quick tempered.'[11] The Bible is filled with warnings against *anger*. Hear the Proverbs of Solomon:

> 'Whoever is slow to anger has great understanding, but he who has a hasty temper exalts folly.'[12] 'A hot-tempered man stirs up strife, but he who is slow to anger quiets contention.'[13] 'Whoever is slow to anger is better than the mighty, and he who rules his spirit than he who takes a city.'[14] 'Good sense makes one slow to anger, and it is his glory to overlook an offense.'[15] 'Make no friendship with a man given to anger, nor go with a wrathful man, lest you learn his ways and entangle yourself in a snare.'[16] 'Be not quick in your spirit to become angry, for anger lodges in the bosom of fools.'[17]

Clearly, a wise man exercises self-control over his temper. Being quick- tempered makes a person unfit for leadership. But the question remains. Where does the capacity for *anger* emanate? Is *anger* always sinful?

What is the origin and nature of anger?

Those who rely on evolution as the explanation for mankind's origin, believe that *anger* evolved as man's way of protecting himself from danger. *Anger* is a defense mechanism that stimulates the body to fight back in defense. Many studies are based on this theory. Neuroscience teaches that we get angry when we feel threatened.[18]

But a biblical study of anger shows that anger is not only the experience of human beings; God himself becomes angry. Of the 455 times *anger* appears in the Old Testament, 375 times it refers to *God's anger*. In fact, the Bible says, '[God] is angry with the wicked every day.'[19]

The Bible indicates that the capacity for anger is divinely bestowed to people in the image of God; *anger* is not a relic of man's evolution. When God created mankind in his image,[20] that image included his emotional capacity for love and anger. Even as God has the capacity for anger, so do men and women.

Why does God experience *anger*? As humans we associate anger with lack of control, irrational outbursts, hasty and thoughtless rage. Not so with God. God's *anger* and *wrath* manifest God's passionate opposition to all that opposes his glory. When human beings reject God's gracious love and mercy, when they oppose his holy and righteous decrees, then he responds with *anger*.

Gary Chapman suggests that God's anger 'derives from two aspects of God's divine nature: God's holiness and God's love.'[21] 'God is holy'[22] and 'God is love'[23] but nowhere do we read that 'God is anger.' Anger is not part of God's nature but is God's response to anything that is an affront to his holiness and love. Thus the capacity for anger is within the divine nature but the expression of God's anger is due to human sin. 'It is God's concern for justice and righteousness (both of which grow out of His holiness and love) that stimulates God's anger. Thus, when God sees evil, God experiences anger. Anger is His logical response to injustice and unrighteousness.'[24] Repeatedly we read of God's *anger* towards sin and the sinners.

The human race was made to respond toward injustice and unrighteousness in the same way. Jesus as the God-Man expressed *righteous anger*. When the Jews manifested callous hearts and a legalistic mindset in rejecting divine mercy on a sick man, Jesus 'looked around at them with *anger*, grieved at their hardness of heart...'[25] When the holiness of God's temple was desecrated by the priests and Sadducees, Jesus displayed a *righteous anger* by driving out the money changers and declaring the words of his Father, 'My house shall be called a house of prayer, but you make it a den of robbers.'[26] Andrew Lester believes that,

> ...our capacity for anger is one of God's good gifts, intentionally rooted in creation and serving important purposes in human life...Anger is not necessarily contrary to love and can actually function as an expression of love. In fact, *not* being angry in some circumstances (such as in response to injustice and oppression) is to miss God's claim on our lives. Compassionate anger is often necessary for Christians to 'proclaim release to the captives' and 'let the oppressed go free' (Luke 4:18).[27]

John Chrysostom says, 'He who is not angry when he has cause to be, sins. For unreasonable patience is the hotbed of many vices.'[28] John Stott says, 'There is a great need in the contemporary world for more Christian anger...In the face of blatant evil we should be indignant not tolerant, angry not apathetic...If evil arouses [God's] anger, it should arouse ours also.'[29] *Anger* that is expressed on behalf of another who suffers unjustly is a noble expression of *anger*, as when David became *angry* with righteous indignation when Nathan told him of a rich man who unjustly took a poor man's lamb to feed the rich man's guest.[30] 'Anger is a strong force that God built into man *for the purpose* of moving him to biblical action. All emotions are, *per* se, motivating forces. The only question is whether the emotion has been properly used for God's honor.'[31] For Christians to remain apathetic and indifferent in the face of injustice and inhumanity done to others is a failure to show love.

Have you ever exhibited 'righteous anger'? Were all your motives and responses 'righteous'? Why do you consider your anger to be 'righteous'?

The emphasis of the biblical teaching on *anger* is a warning *against anger*, not in support of it. Though anger against injustice *can* be righteous and justified, most anger expressed by people is sinful because it is enmeshed with sinful attitudes and with an impure motive. During an interview with *Decision Magazine*, Robertson McQuilkin, a distinguished Christian leader, had this to say: 'I discovered early on in life that for me to be angry and call it righteous indignation was wrong, because my motives aren't all that pure. I don't claim righteous indignation except at something outrageous, such as people who are destroying the Church from within or the evil of terrorists.'[32]

There is no inconsistency between the universal commendation of God's wrath and the general condemnation of man's anger. God in his perfection of holiness displays anger with perfect love; in his great wisdom he never misinterprets the intentions of others, never acts irrationally, never looses control, and never feels threatened; his anger is pure and holy, always consistent with his love and holiness and always directed against sin and sinners. But man's anger is mostly sinful, arising out of pride and self with wrong attitudes toward others, loss of control, vindictiveness and vengeance.

It is helpful to apply this to our lives. In the past few weeks, have you felt frustration, resentment, anger or antagonism toward someone? What caused you to feel this way? Every Christian leader is wise when being honest with himself as he examines his motives and emotions.

What are the causes of anger?

Don't pretend that you don't get angry or that you are above such feelings. *Anger* is universal among all human beings with *no* exceptions. Our problem is that we restrict our understanding of *anger* to an explosive anger. We may say, 'I'm not angry but only frustrated because the Bishop does not know where he is leading the Church,' or 'I'm not angry but just upset because the Principal does not consult with his teachers.' People who are frustrated, upset, disgusted, hostile, bitter or resentful are exhibiting anger in different forms.

Ellen Norton, a medical doctor and psychiatrist, understands anger as a reaction or response of indignation toward people or a situation when progress toward some desired goal is blocked.[33] Anger erupts when plans or ambitions are thwarted or when dignity or self-esteem are threatened. Many feelings derived from anger include:

- *Frustration:* This arises when some event, person or physical barrier hinders progress toward some goal.
- *Hurt:* Anger with hurt is aroused when someone feels rejected, put down, ignored, humiliated, or treated unfairly.[34]
- *Defensiveness:* A person who fears failure, rejection, loss or insecurity will have defensive anger because he feels threatened.

Anger with irritation, annoyance and vexation can arise when one thinks another is unjustly successful. David counsels those who felt annoyed because the wicked were prospering. The prosperity of the wicked seems contrary to justice.

> 'Be still before the LORD and wait patiently for him; fret not yourself over the one who prospers in his way, over the man who carries out evil devices! *Refrain from anger, and forsake wrath! Fret not yourself; it tends only to evil.'*[35]

Human *anger* most often arises out of a *perceived* threat to oneself. You *think* you are injured, threatened or insulted. *Anger* begins in the mind when the brain interprets an experience to mean that you are in danger of any kind. If someone physically attacks you to rob, you react with *anger* in self-defense. The blood pressure rises, the heart beats faster, the muscles tense and the body temperature rises. In the same manner, if someone does or says anything that is perceived as a threat you respond with similar feelings. People with inferiority complexes often feel threatened by those who exude greater self confidence.

Human *anger* always begins with an event, some experience that is *perceived* as a threat to one's plans, ambitions or self-dignity. In fact, it may not even be a real threat but the person *thinks* it is a threat. The threat may not be physical but an inferred attack on his person, dignity, position, ambitions, or family. People do not respond the same way to potentially anger-producing situations. A strong person with a healthy sense of self-esteem and with confidence in the sovereign control of God can meet those situations with a deep seated confidence in God. His mind is saturated with confidence in God. The person can take a deep breath, step back, and listen without feeling threatened or attacked. If feelings of anger do arise, he has learned to control the anger so that he takes time to think and pray over the incident.

What are the effects of anger?

When the Bible admonishes, 'Never go to bed angry,' profound wisdom is there expressed. 'Anger is a killer.' When not handled wisely, anger kills others or destroys oneself. When allowed to persist, anger is totally destructive.

Explosive anger is violent outrage, aggressive behaviour or patterns of abuse. This anger destroys friendship, breaks relationships and undermines the community. A person who projects his anger outwardly on to others will eventually destroy others and himself because explosive anger is never constructive; it does not build up the community nor does it glorify God.

Many people, however, have learned to control their temper outwardly. Their Christian training cultural values have taught them *not to show anger*, for they have learned that it is wrong; but they still *feel angry*. Personalities and cultural upbringing may minimise angry confrontation with others. But whenever someone *feels angry* and does not deal with it wholesomely, that *anger* becomes self-destructive. Instead of *exploding with anger* they *implode with anger* on themselves. Turning the anger in on themselves can be the most destructive. Milton Layden says that anger,

> ...is the root of many psychological, interpersonal, physical, and spiritual problems. Along with hostility, anger has been called 'the chief saboteur of the mind,' and 'the leading cause of misery, depression, inefficiency, sickness, accidents, loss of work time and financial loss in industry...No matter what the problem – marital conflict, alcoholism, a wife's frigidity, a child's defiance, nervous or physical disease – elimination of hostility is a key factor in its solution.[36]

All the books on counseling say the same. Buried anger is *unresolved anger*. The person broods on the events and persons that brought on the anger. A feeling of injustice and unfairness is rehearsed over and over. Like a video played over and over again, the angry person reviews the unfair episode which led to anger. But the anger is not exhibited; instead it is buried inside, and there it begins to destroy the person.

Just a question: Do you carry in your heart buried bitterness, resentment, hurt feelings or dislike because of some incidents? How long is this unresolved?

Research shows that suppressed anger leads to hypertension, ulcers, colitis, headaches, high blood pressure and heart disease. Moreover, this internalised, suppressed anger leads to psychological and emotional ill-health. Withdrawal from social contacts or verbal and physical attacks on innocent people may result. The person seethes with resentment, bitterness and often hatred.[37] Unresolved anger leads to resentment and bitterness which leads to emotional breakdown, depression and even suicide. 'Bitterness is the result of stored anger, and bitterness is always condemned as sinful in Scripture (For example, see Ac 8:23; Ro 3:14; Heb 12:15).'[38] Anger must be dealt with wisely.

Resolving Anger

Jay Adams, a Christian educator and counselor, claims that 'sinful anger probably is involved in 90 percent of all counseling problems.'[39] Since *anger* is common place among humans and a 'quick tempered' person is ineligible to be a Church leader; since anger takes many forms and can destroy relationships, personal health and peace of mind; it is imperative for Church leaders to know how to handle *anger* in themselves and offer constructive counseling to others.

How do you handle anger that rises up in your heart and mind?

Be honest with yourself: Learn to recognise and admit anger when you experience it. Process your anger in a loving, positive and constructive manner instead of in negative and destructive ways.

'Never go to bed angry:' Deal with your anger day by day and do not allow interpersonal problems to pile up. Be reconciled![40]

Learn to control the temper: If you explode with anger, seek God's help to bring your temper under control. Learn to respond slowly. Count to ten before speaking. Speak slowly; don't raise your voice. Preferably, answer the person only after time to think, pray and reflect on it.

Learn to forgive: If you brood over wrongs done to you with bitter attitudes developing, learn to forgive and let go. Anger destroys. Itemise on paper the reasons for your anger. Is your understanding of the problem correct or is there another way of looking at things?

Empathise with others: Listen carefully and try to understand anyone who accuses you of something. Never respond to an angry person with anger but try to understand his predicament from his perspective.

Never attack others: Never direct your anger towards others in order to hurt them. Never speak 'unwholesome words' to tear others down.[41] Instead of accusing others by saying, 'you,' 'you,' 'you;' use 'I' statements, such as 'I feel frustrated' or 'I feel hurt' or 'I feel angry.'

Love: Learn to confront with love, rather than remaining hurt and angry.

Again and again, learn to forgive the person who slandered you or wronged you in some way. Retaliation is natural but sinful; holding a grudge may seem justified, but this is disobedience and harmful to your health. 'Don't repay evil for evil. Don't retaliate when people say unkind things about you. Instead, pay them back with a blessing. That is what God wants you to do, and he will bless you for it.'[42]

Take appropriate steps to solve the problem when righteous anger arises. Whatever you say or do must be with pure love and under the constraint of the Holy Spirit. Often the Christian who feels a righteous anger ends up committing a sin by expressing anger in a destructive manner. Be constructive, courageous, truthful but always loving, seeking to redeem, restore, and save.

Focus on solutions, not problems: Be solution-oriented rather than problem-oriented. Rather than blaming others or brooding, take steps to solve the problem. This may include rebuking in love but also focuses on solving the problem, not attacking the problem maker.[43]

Reject all self-pity: Stop thinking on wrongs done to you; refuse to indulge in self-pity. Count your many blessings; rejoice in the Lord always. Fill your mind with God's Word. Give thanks but don't blame others. Trust God to right the wrongs and defend yourself. He is the final Judge.

Build a healthy self-concept: 'Hostility and anger, including prolonged hostility, often indicate that a person feels inferior, insecure and lacking in self-esteem or self-confidence. Individuals who are made to feel inferior often react with anger and attempts to assert superiority.'[44] Think God's thoughts. Remind yourself that you are a child of God, loved with an everlasting love, that nothing can separate you from his love. Memorise Romans 8:28-39.

Show compassion and forgiveness towards those who wrong you. It is not easy but it is Christ's command.[45] God will help.

CONCLUSION

No greater challenge faces the Christian leader than to learn how to control the temper and process anger so as not to destroy himself and the ministry. Remember, angry words and actions are like bullets; if anger shoots, damage is inevitable. And if anger is unresolved and internalized, you will be hurt. The wise leader will recognise that his anger can land him into major problems. Whatever must be done, confront the problem and find ways of dealing with it.

For anger is the opposite of love. Only love can build up a community and commend a leader to the people. In the next chapter we shall examine the attributes of *agape* love.

SEARCHING THE SCRIPTURE WITH APPLICATION

1. State in your own words your understanding of anger.
    a. Now think of several times when you experienced this feeling of anger.
    b. How did you handle your anger? Are you pleased with your response?
2. Read the following biblical references and answer these questions:
    a. What caused the anger?
    b. Was the person justified in his anger?
    c. What were the consequences of the anger?
    Cain - Ge 4:1-16; Moses - Ex 32:19; Balaam - Nu 22:22f
    Ephraimites - Jdg 8:1-3; David - 2 Sa 12:5; King Ahab - 1 Ki 21:1-19;
    Namaan - 2 Ki 5:1-14; God - 2 Ki 22:11-13; Jonah - Jn 4:1-9.
3. Study the meaning of Eph 4:26, 27.
    a. Do you think it is wise never to go to bed angry? Why?
    b. Do you hold any resentment or bitterness toward others?
    c. What is the danger of holding resentment in your heart?
4. Have you ever experienced what you might call, 'righteous anger'?
    a. What aroused your anger?
    b. Did you respond well with anger or did you sin in your response?
    c. How could you have done better in glorifying God with your anger?

Endnotes

1 Eph 4:26, 27
The New Testament
J.B. Phillips
2 Chapman 1999: 18
3 Webster's Dictionary, 1959
4 θυμος
5 Buchsel 1965: 167
Cremer 1977
6 οργη
7 Ro 2:8; Eph 4:31; Col 3:8; Rev 19:15
8 Trench 1953:131
9 Mt 3:7; Ro 2:5; 1 Th 1:10
10 2 Co 12:20; Gal 5:19-22; Col 3:8f
11 Tit 1:7
12 Pr 14:29
13 Pr 15:18
14 Pr 16:32
15 Pr 19:11
16 Pr 22:24f
17 Ecc 7:9
18 Lester 2003: 85
19 Ps 7:11 *NLT*
20 Ge 1:26-27
21 Chapman 1999: 19
22 1 Pe 1:16
23 1 Jn 4:8
24 Chapman 1999: 20
25 Mk 3:5
26 Mt 21:13
27 Lester 2003: 3
28 John Chrysostom
as found in Kreeft 1986: 134
29 Stott 1979: 209
30 2 Sa 12:5,6
31 Adams 1973: 355
32 McQuilkin in
Decision Magazine June 2005:21
33 Norton n.d.: 8
34 Collins 1988: 124
35 Ps 37:7,8
36 Milton Layden
as found in Collins 1988: 120
37 Chapman 1999: 82
38 Chapman 1999: 83
39 Adams 1973: 359
40 Mt 5:21-26
41 Eph 4:29
42 1 Pe 3:9 *NLT*
43 Adams 1973: 354
44 Collins 1988:131
45 Lk 6:27-36

19
THE ATTRIBUTES OF AGAPE LOVE

'Love is patient and kind.
Love is not jealous or boastful or proud or rude. Love does not demand its own way.
Love is not irritable,
and it keeps no record of when it has been wronged.'[1]

Leadership is all about people and relationships.

Osei-Mensah writes, 'When we have our priorities right, people will become more and more important to us.'[2] No one can be an effective leader unless he has love for people. Many Christian leaders have administrative skills but lack people skills. Consequently, they are unable to perform effectively in public because they cannot get along with people in private. A leader may be knowledgeable and a capable organizer, but the ministry of a leader is always with people. Leadership is a reciprocal relationship between the leader and his followers. In this area of interpersonal relationships many leaders fail.

The Necessity of Love

Hear the advice of those with practical experience:

'Ministry is people. It is not money or certificate or a degree. Those coming to ministry need to know that they are dealing with people – some sinful and selfish. Until we know how to deal with people in their context, we cannot succeed.' (Pastor)

'Of first importance, ministers must be people oriented, being involved with people. This means understanding and loving people, being concerned with people. If they are not concerned, if they do not listen to people, their ministry will fail. You cannot rush; you must be a good listener. Think of how they feel, feel with them.' (Teacher)

'[Students in Bible College] must be ready to cope with other servants in the ministry. They must fit in with others and have good relationships. If they look down on older pastors and don't respect them, they are in trouble. They must respect them and have fellowship with them. Relationships with people are important.' (Pastor)

A major question is this: How easy is it for you to work with people?

The fact is that people can be difficult to lead. 'The trouble with people is that they can be our greatest joy and source of satisfaction, and at the same time our worst nightmare. I've often thought that ministry would be [easy] if it weren't for people. But then if it weren't for people, there would be no ministry.'[3] *Learning to love the people* we lead and minister to is fundamental. As one Church leader observed, '*We should be people of love. We instruct people to do this or that. But we have a problem of communicating this in love. You may have many good ideas, but you cannot accomplish anything without other people. So you must not offend them. One should be flexible to accomplish your goals.*'

Love is *the key* to winning the hearts of the people. One pastor was assigned to a struggling, divided Church; there were no Bible studies or prayer meetings. This pastor began to pray with the elders in his own house after Church. He went the extra mile and used his own money to buy bread and sugar. Then he began visiting the Church members in their homes and praying with them. After visiting them he began different prayer meetings and Bible studies in the different areas of his congregation. The Church began to grow so much because *they loved their pastor* in response to the *evident love of the pastor for them*. One family had bright children but no fees; the mother was a believer but the father a drunkard. So the pastor encouraged the members to help with fees. People gave and the children went to school. This pastor exhibited what *agape* love can do to unite a Church, promote good interpersonal relations and to build the kingdom of God.

We have already considered those attitudes which are antithetical to love. Jealousy focuses a leader on competition with people; anger repels a leader from people. Only love draws a leader toward the people. We have seen that people cannot love others if they do not have a healthy self-image. Above all, love for others is built on one's love for God. As one pastor observed, success in the ministry comes from a '*love for God and love for the people and the ministry. Without love, it is difficult to stay.*'

> The Christian leader's behavior toward other people is determined by what he is in himself. To put it another way, interpersonal relations on a horizontal plane are determined by interpersonal relations with God on a vertical plane. One of the reasons we get into so many human relations problems in the Church is that we have somehow confused ourselves into thinking that what we *do* for God is more important than what we *are* before God. A distinctly Christian life-style, with respect to shared ministries in a communal setting, requires the grace of mutual acceptance, a willingness to enter into mutual burden-bearing, and a generous dose of active love.[4]

Many practical suggestions will be given later for developing working relationships. But this chapter is a biblical study of the attributes of *agape* love. A successful Church leader is marked by *love* that reaches out to people and naturally produces harmonious interpersonal relationships. '*Love is the key to good relationships* and good relationships are indispensable to effective leadership [italics added].'[5]

The Characteristics of *Agape* Love

There are many different kinds of love so we are calling the love which was commanded by Christ, *agape* love. Why do we speak of *agape* love and not just *love*? *Love* is so distorted today as it was in ancient times, that we must emphasise the biblical concept of love, not the popular ones. We all know the natural affection that flows between parents and their children. Among the Greeks this was *storge.* Though noble in every way and marked by sacrifice, *storge* is narrow and very self-centred, being the love between parents and their children. *Eros* was the *erotic* passion between the sexes. The Greek philosophers called *eros* 'the most glorious gift from heaven for it puts an end to all self control and raises all senses to pitch of frenzy.'[6] But *eros* is self-centred with all the emphasis of what 'I' will get out of it. *Philia* is 'affection, fondness and liking' which arises out of friendship which affords one pleasure. Warfield describes *philia* as 'the glow of heart kindled by a perception of that in the object that affords us pleasure.'[7] Not bad, but once again, the emphasis is on the pleasure derived from friendship of those with mutual interests and likeable personalities.

Agape love stands out from all other loves. The classical Greek word, *agape,* was colorless and indefinite in meaning. The word may mean only to be content with something, or to welcome somebody with a courteous greeting.[8] It only had a slight trace of meaning 'to be well-disposed towards, to wish to benefit.'[9] The best feature of *agape* was that it was nobler than the other words with greater potential of expressing lofty ideas. Under divine inspiration, with the revelation of Jesus Christ, *agape* was transformed by the gospel into a word fit to express the divine attribute and also a fruit of the Holy Spirit. A leader who is motivated by *agape* love will minister to others even as Jesus did.

So what is *agape* love? Nowhere does the Bible 'define' *agape* love. Can it really be defined? One might say it is 'unmerited, self-giving love' to distinguish it from the other loves. However, the best way to define love is to describe *the attributes of love* as found in the 'Love Chapter' of the Bible.

Our principal biblical text will be 1 Corinthians 13. This 'Love Chapter' is sandwiched between those chapters dealing with spiritual gifts. Though the Christians in the Corinthian Church were highly gifted, they lacked *agape* love. The result was dissension and division between believers.

Paul begins the 'Love Chapter' by affirming that spiritual gifts are useless apart from *agape* love. Indeed, we may say that all of Christian ministry is useless apart from *agape* love. You may preach eloquently and powerfully, you may exercise great faith and achieve wonders, you may be generous in all you do for others, but without *agape love* you will 'be nothing' and 'achieve nothing.'[10] Paul then goes on to describe the attributes of love with echoes of the entire letter found therein. Here then is the description of love.

Love is patient

Agape love is 'patient about everything.'[11] According to *The Message*, 'Love never gives up.' Reflecting more the Greek, J.B. Phillips reads, 'Love is slow to lose patience.' The word means literally, *agape* 'suffers long.' The opposite of a 'short temper,' *agape* has a long fuse before it explodes. The early Church fathers described 'patience' as 'the greatness of the soul'; it is 'magnanimous.'[12] While some may be outwardly 'patient,' they are fuming and fussing inwardly. But *agape* triumphs over evil without becoming sour or bitter.

How important do you think patience is for Christian leaders? More leaders whom we interviewed attributed success in ministry to *patience* and *perseverance* than any other attribute. When dealing with people, one needs love that 'never gives up,' a love that is 'slow to lose patience.' Following are words of wisdom from others in the ministry.

'The pastor is handling different kinds of people and he needs patience. Be patient with people, hoping they will realise it is God's work and they should not fight.'

'In the ministry we have lots of problems. There is joy but things do come that disturb you and cause you to react. If you are not patient with these painful things, you can burst. Meetings become so hot.'

'Because of obstacles and problems you need patience. If you get discouraged easily, you can leave the ministry. Bear with people. Be patient in serving.'

'Don't push your ideas on the Church. Take your time. Don't push your goals too much because they will push you out of the Church. As people work with you they will trust you and will follow you.'

Love is kind

Patience is the negative side of love; *agape* bears up under oppression from people and does not strike back. However, one can be patient and yet selfish, neglecting the needs of others. But *agape* is *kind.* 'Love cares more for others than for self.'[13] Kindness is the positive side of love. *Patience* and *kindness* are the opposite sides of the coin and are used together in Paul's writings.[14]

To be *kind* 'denotes the disposition to put oneself at the service of others.'[15] 'It looks for a way of being constructive.'[16] *Agape* is not friendly by accident but by intention; that is her goal. *Agape* is liberal and out flowing. She foresees a need and extends her helping hand. *Agape* always acts in an amiable manner and is helpful in serving others.

Some leaders by nature are *task-oriented* while others are *people-oriented*; Church leaders do not come in the same mold. But leadership without reaching out to people and ministering to them will ultimately fail. 'People will never care how much you know until they know how much you care.'[17] A pastor may study hard and prepare marvelous sermons; but without *kindness* that ministers to the needs of others, the ministry will struggle. Love is *kind.*

Do you think someone should be *either* 'task-oriented' *or* 'people oriented'? Or should they be both? How can one be balanced? This is the great challenge.

Love is generous

Having stated the active and passive attributes of *agape* (patience and kindness), Paul enumerates the acts which *agape* does *not* manifest. Every negative is written with some condition of the Corinthian Church in mind. Every negative attribute has an implied positive attribute.

'Love does not envy,' or as *The Message* paraphrases it, 'Love doesn't want what it doesn't have.' We have studied *zelos* before from which our English words, *zeal* and *zealous,* are derived. To be zealous for the good is noble, but all too often this *zealous* attitude becomes a sinfully *jealous* or envious attitude toward others, wanting what the others have for self-centred reasons. The Corinthians were known for their *jealousy*; they were envious of those with more prominent gifts; they were striving after better gifts for selfish reasons, filling the Church with strife and divisions.[18]

Envy and jealousy cause uneasy feelings. A jealous person is discontent when seeing others more successful and enjoying a greater reputation. How much harm has been brought to the Church of Jesus Christ because of jealousy! Do you agree that jealousy is a major problem in the Church?

Agape love is *not* jealous. Instead, she is generous, giving thanks for the other and praising God for the successful brother or sister. *Agape* love is content with what God has entrusted to her. *Agape* is rejoicing while *zelos* (jealousy) is sad. *Agape* cements the union of the brothers while jealousy tears apart and divides.

Love is humble

'Love is never boastful.'[19] J.B. Phillips translates this, 'Love is not anxious to impress.' In classical Greek the word refers to 'bragging,' 'boasting' and 'showing off.'[20] The Corinthians were bragging and boasting of their superior gifts. The 'strong' felt superior to the 'weak.'[21] A weak leader who feels inferior not only becomes jealous of others; he boasts of his achievements to boost his pride and sense of worth. Division is inevitable.

Do you agree with this? What negative effects have you witnessed when Christian leaders boast about their achievements?

Agape love is humble and does not show off. As Proverbs teaches: 'Let another praise you, and not your own mouth.'[22] Boasting is not good. Paul did boast, but not in his achievements but in his weaknesses.[23] Why? Because his goal was to exalt Jesus Christ, *not* to exalt himself. God's power is manifest not in our strength but in our weakness.[24] That is the reason God may inflict his servants to teach them of their weakness so God alone is glorified.

Love is modest

'Love does not have inflated ideas of its own importance.'[25] 'Love is not arrogant.' 'Arrogant' means literally 'to blow up, puff up'; and figuratively, 'to make proud or arrogant.'[26] He inflates himself to appear bigger than he really is. The picture is of a bellows or a balloon blown up with air or a frog puffed up to appear bigger. Of the six times this Greek word is used in the New Testament, five times it appears in 1 Corinthians. The Corinthian believers were apparently arrogant and puffed up as they divided themselves up into different groups, some following Paul or Apollos or Peter or Christ[27]; the 'strong' felt bigger and better than the 'weak'[28]; they were even arrogant over the immorality in their midst.[29] The Corinthians made their fellow believers feel the weight of their superiority as they inflated their own self-importance.

In contrast, *agape* love is modest and does not parade her greatness. How amazing to see how success puffs up. If a young pastor becomes a good preacher, others appreciate this and he recognises it. Instead of giving thanks to God in humility, he becomes puffed up which leads to failure. A student earns his B.Th. and feels so highly trained. When he is assigned to a small, rural Church he complains, so the Church leaders reassign him to a town Church. There he struggles because he has not yet matured sufficiently with experience. Others later earn a Master's degree; some even achieve the ultimate of a Ph.D. Instead of modesty, the education leads to arrogance which only repulses people. People recognise 'greatness' when they see it; they also recognise arrogance and despise it. Arrogance is unbecoming and can only lead to a downfall.

What effects have you seen from Christian leaders being puffed up?

Love is courteous

'Love is not rude.' In other words, 'love has good manners.'[30] A jealous person is prone to boasting and arrogance; then jealousy becomes rude to others. The Corinthians acted with complete disregard for the feelings of others in their worship services which had no stated order. Noise, confusion and disorder prevailed.[31] Everyone wanted to contribute their gift. Many spoke with tongues and others prophesied all at the same time. No one was willing to defer to another. The heart of the problem was pride in spiritual gifts. Everyone considered their own contribution more important than the others. At the root of this behaviour was self-importance and pride.

In contrast, *agape* thinks of others and is sensitive to their feelings. *Agape* avoids every act which wounds. She is tactful and considerate. *Agape* acts delicately and sensitively, always mindful of the feelings of others. Though doing the right thing is good, doing it in a courteous manner is always best.

> Love is the most effective teacher of politeness and high courtesy. Love can never be rude. Love begets courtesy, and gentleness and consideration. A man possessing love will possess that fine courtesy which is the hall-mark of the true gentleman. For courtesy, after all, is not taught by rule. It is an emanation of the spirit.[32]

Love is unselfish

'Love does not *seek* its own.'[33] 'Love does not *insist on* its own way,' or as *The Message* paraphrases it, 'Love isn't always "me first."' An unselfish person does not demand his own way. *Agape* opposes every form of selfishness.

The same word is used in the context of Paul counseling the 'strong' and the 'weak.'[34] As the Corinthians divided between the 'strong' who felt they could eat food offered to idols, and the 'weak' who felt offended when any Christian did so, Paul urges the 'strong' not to be selfish in their pursuits. 'Let no one *seek* his own good, but the good of his neighbor.' Paul gives his own testimony: 'I try to please everyone in everything I do, not *seeking* my own advantage, but that of many, that they may be saved.' The difference between Paul and the self-seeking Corinthians is that Paul's goal was evangelism to please God; but the goal of the 'strong' was personal desire to please self.

Love is good tempered

'Love is not irritable,' or as J.B Phillips renders it, 'Love is not touchy.' The root meaning of the Greek word is 'sharp' and refers to a 'sharpening' of a knife.[35] Hence the Greek word means 'to provoke to wrath, irritate.'[36] Paul is not warning against *irritating* others but of *being irritated.* On the one hand, the 'strong' should not insist on their own way, nor boast or be arrogant. On the other hand, the 'weak' must learn not to be so *touchy* and *irritable*. Whereas some Corinthian Christians insisted on displaying their own gifts, the less gifted Christians felt annoyed and irritated at the more gifted. Paul does not condone rude behaviour which irritates. But here Paul strikes at a different problem – those who are so touchy and irritated. They too must seek God's grace to accept others as they are and learn some humility.

How many experiences one has in life that irritate and annoy as with a sharp knife! On the one hand, the more highly educated or more gifted must be sensitive to those who can easily be offended; they must never brag or boast or strut around in arrogance but conduct themselves with love and humility. On the other hand, those with lower education and fewer gifts of prominence must learn to be less *touchy*. *Agape* never angers or sours, never feels bitter toward her neighbour. When *agape* experiences annoyances and petty injustices, she remains sweet. She is not hasty or excited; instead, she remains calm and patient and *not irritated*. Irritation is an outward sign of pride and vanity.

Love is forgiving

'Love does not keep a record of when it has been wronged.'[37] Love does not hold grudges. The Greek word for 'keeping a record' was commonly used of numerical calculations recorded on wax tablets. It is so easy for one who feels irritated by injustices to store up in the memory a record of those wrongs. The memory is replayed over and over like a video. *Agape* does not; she erases the wax lines of writing which contain the record of evil done to her. 'Love doesn't enter in the account book wrongs, injuries and unkindnesses.'[38] In the words of the *ESV*, 'Love is not resentful.'

As we have seen, one of the necessary virtues in the ministry is to learn 'forgiveness.' No one can be successful in ministry when holding grudges. An unforgiving spirit will destroy the body and the soul of the minister and will destroy the ministry. As a pastor told me, '*I've learned to be big-hearted, to accommodate those who don't appreciate me. It is not easy to forgive and forget. Words are easy but action shows you have not forgiven.*'

Agape is both a fruit of the Spirit and a command to be obeyed. 'A new commandment I give to you, that you love one another; just as I have loved you, you also are to love one another. By this all people will know that you are my disciples, if you have love for one another.'[39] Evangelism with the lips is of no value when the life reflects an unforgiving spirit. *Agape* is forgiving.

Love is sincere

'Love does not rejoice at wrongdoing, but rejoices with the truth.' 'Love is never glad when others go wrong; love is gladdened by goodness.'[40] In the words of J.B. Phillips, 'Love does not gloat over the wickedness of other people. On the contrary, it is glad with all good men when truth prevails.' Possibly reference is here made to the Corinthian attitude toward the immorality in their midst. Either they were proud of the immorality or they merely congratulated themselves on their superiority over such temptations. This also strikes at the Corinthians who refused to rejoice with their brethren who possessed gifts they themselves did not have.

The worst evil we can do to someone is to rejoice over the wrongs they do or rejoice when they are struck with evil. *Agape* love is sincere; she feels sorrow when her enemies suffer. Church leaders need to manifest empathy towards others. They need to feel the way others feel and identify with the needs of others. To rejoice when others are hurt is perverse. Love is never glad about injustice. *Agape* is sincere.

The eight negatives in 1 Corinthians 13:4b-6 reflect the condition of the Corinthian Church. *Agape* love can alone bring the unity which they needed so badly. The final four attributes of *agape* should be understood in four successive steps. This a practical suggestion for dealing with unsavory reports that one may hear.

Love is gracious

The Greek word can mean 'to endure.'[41] Many translations follow this ('Love bears all things').[42] However, Spicq observes that this duplicates the fourth attribute (v 7c).[43] Hence he prefers one of the other lexical meanings, namely, 'to cover' or 'to protect.' Indeed, the verb, 'to cover,' is derived from the noun meaning, 'roof.' The Bauer Lexicon renders this passage, 'of love that throws a cloak of silence over what is displeasing in another person.'[44] That is, when *agape* hears of a fault in someone, instead of gossiping and spreading abroad rumours, she 'covers over,' 'roofs over' the evil of his neighbour.

This is no excuse to cover up a scandal. Rather, the thought is this. When you love someone, that means you trust that person. A report of wrong doing means that you do not participate in spreading rumours. You protect that person through responsible and honourable talk. *Agape* is gracious and not judgmental, protecting the individual until all the facts are known.

Love is confident

Agape displays a trusting spirit towards others. The mischief, which *agape* sees in the one loved, is kept secret. The deeds her neighbour does, she credits with good intentions. She is inclined to interpret all things as good. Love accords to her neighbour a favourable prejudgement. Instead of being suspicious, she displays a confidence in another. 'Love always believes all things.'

Though *agape* is hopeful and optimistic, she is nevertheless realistic. She does not deny the evil she sees, nor is she credulous. The faith she displays in another goes only so far until she discovers distinctly the opposite of the good she believed to find. But when concrete evidence of evil motives is lacking, *agape* is always prone to believe the best in another. Her constant attitude is to put the best construction on the motives of others, even if the conduct is difficult to understand.

Love is hopeful

Even when strong evidence is present for evil motives, *agape* continues to hope for the future. Where confidence is no longer possible, love continues to hope for the good. *Agape* never ceases to hope even when others fail to do so. 'When love has no evidence, it hopes for the best. And when hopes are repeatedly disappointed, it still courageously waits.'[45]

Love is enduring

Though the very hopes of *agape* love may be dashed upon the rocks of disappointment, she continues to hold out. *Agape* is magnanimous in her attitude towards others and, therefore, always continues to endure the trouble. Love is patient and endures to the end.

CONCLUSION

In this chapter we have repeatedly referred to *agape* love because the biblical concept of love is counter cultural – not what the culture sings about or thinks about love. *Agape* love is a heavenly love that is a fruit of the Spirit. And yet it is a command which Christians must learn to obey. We cannot love with *agape* love without the Spirit's enabling, but neither can we love by remaining passive and letting God fill us with love.

Agape love will transform the ministry of the Christian leader. People are drawn to a leader who loves them. If the leader does not lead with love, his followers will not work together in love. Love is the lubrication which makes the ministry move along smoothly.

Jesus Christ is the greatest leader in history in part because he led with love. Jesus is the supreme model of *agape* love. This is our study in the next chapter.

SEARCHING THE SCRIPTURE WITH APPLICATION

1. After studying the 'Love Chapter,' describe the characteristics of *agape* love so that we would know love when we see it.
2. Other attributes of *agape* apart from those listed in 1 Corinthians 13 are as follows. Study them and apply to your situation.

Love serves	Gal 5:13-15
Love is harmless	Ro 13:8-10
Love edifies	1 Co 8-10
Love is selfless	Php 2:1-4
Love unites	Col 2:2
Love is self-sacrificial	Eph 5:2, 25
Love is genuine	Ro 12:9
Love disciplines	2 Co 2:8
Love is generous	2 Co 8:24
Love esteems	1 Th 5:13

3. Discuss the reasons why *agape* love is important for Christian leaders?
4. What are the benefits for the leader when he leads with *agape* love?
5. What harm is done to the Church when leading is not done in love?
6. Reflect, consider and pray about the steps you will take to grow in *agape* love. Write these things down and hold yourself accountable.

Endnotes

1 1 Co 13:4f NLT
2 Osei-Mensah 1990:14
3 Stowell 1997:152
4 Gangel 1974: 36
5 Stowell 1997: 151
6 Kittel 1951: 25
7 Warfield 1918: 3
8 Kittel 1951: 28
9 Burton 1920: 515
10 1 Co 13:1-3
11 Bauer 1957: 489
12 Edwards 1903: 343
13 1 Co 13:4
The Message
14 2 Co 6:6; Gal 5:22
15 Godet n.d.: 244
16 1 Co 13:4
The New Testament
J.B. Phillips
17 Finzel 1994: 43
18 1 Co 3:3
19 1 Co 13:4 NEB
20 Vincent 1972: 264
21 1 Co 12:14-17; 21-26
22 Pr 27:2
23 2 Co 11:30; 12:5
24 2 Co 12:8
25 1 Co 13:4
The New Testament
J.B. Phillips
26 Bauer 1957
27 1 Co 1:10-4:21 esp. 4:6,18,19
28 1 Co 8:1
29 1 Co 5:2
30 *The New Testament*
J.B. Phillips
31 1 Co 11:2-16
32 Jones 1954: 113
33 1 Co 13:4c NASB
34 1 Co 10:24 and 33
35 Barnes 1949: 302
36 Bauer 1957: 634
37 1 Co 13:5c NLT
38 Jones 1954: 141
39 Jn 13:34,35
40 Barr 1950: 421
41 στοϱγη
42 NASB, ESV
43 Spicq 1959: 91
44 Bauer 1957: 773
45 Robertson & Plummer 1911: 295

20
THE SUPREME MODEL OF AGAPE LOVE

'But when the kindness and love of God our Savior appeared, he saved us, not because of righteous things we had done, but because of his mercy.'[1]

'The love of God is greater far than tongue or pen can ever tell;
'It goes beyond the highest star, and reaches to the lowest hell.
'Could we with ink the ocean fill, and were the skies of parchment made;
'Were every stalk on earth a quill, and every man a scribe by trade;
'To write the love of God above would drain the ocean dry;
'Nor could the scroll contain the whole, though stretched from sky to sky.'[2]

The best way of learning *agape* love is to see it modeled in someone.

But all efforts to imitate God's love are imperfect. Jesus Christ is the only perfect model of God-like love. In this chapter we will examine the life of Christ to learn how Christian leaders should lead with *agape* love.

The Love of Jesus

Jesus taught much about love,[3] but only a select number of references speak specifically of Christ's love for others. It seems fitting that most references to love in the Gospels are found in the Gospel written by John, the apostle whom Jesus loved.[4] Special reference is made of Jesus' love for Mary, Martha and Lazarus.[5] After Lazarus had died and was buried, Jesus stood by the tomb. When he saw Mary and the Jews weeping, he was 'deeply moved in his spirit and greatly troubled.' Then Jesus 'wept.'[6] When the Jews saw him weeping, they commented, 'See how he loved him.'

We are told that Jesus *loved* his disciples even to the end.[7] It is most touching to hear from Jesus, 'As the Father has loved me, so have I loved you.' That is awesome! The same love which the heavenly Father has for the Son, Jesus has for his disciples. Then he adds, 'Greater love has no one than this, that someone lay down his life for his friends. You are my friends...[8] The supreme example of Jesus' love was his sacrificial death on the cross for the salvation of lost men and women. That is real God-like love.

A study of *compassion* in the Gospels reveals the depths of Christ's love.

The Compassion of Jesus

The Gospel writers refer to the *compassion* of Christ twelve times.[1] The English word, *compassion,* means 'a feeling of deep sympathy and sorrow for another's suffering or misfortune accompanied by a desire to alleviate the pain or remove its cause."[9]

The Greek word in the Gospels, *splagchnizomai*, translated *compassion*, is derived from the root word meaning 'the inward parts, the entrails' which were thought to be the seat of emotions. So this word means literally, 'to be moved as to one's bowels.'[10] Every human being has experienced this gut feeling of deep inner emotions over some tragic event, illness or death of a loved one. *Splagchnizomai* is more than just 'feeling' sympathy for someone else; it touches the inner part of one's being with the churning of the bowels and the 'desire to alleviate the pain or remove the cause of suffering.' *Compassion* is a manifestation of love.

Jesus demonstrated a genuine identification with people in their deepest needs to the point of wanting to help them in their needs. His love was neither cool nor detached but a genuine *agape* love.

Matthew 9:35-37: In Jesus ministry he walked many kilometers on foot 'throughout all the cities and villages,' teaching, preaching and 'healing every disease and affliction.' Jesus knew his people up close, first hand. 'When he saw the crowds, *he had compassion for them,* because they were harassed and helpless, like sheep without a shepherd.'

Jesus looks upon them as 'sheep' needing a 'shepherd.' They needed someone who would teach them, correct them, guide them and protect them as a good shepherd. A loving compassion genuinely *feels* for the sheep with bowels churning with love. But *agape* moves beyond the feeling stage and takes steps to help. In this case Jesus observed the need for more workers. Changing the metaphor from shepherding to agriculture, Jesus said, 'The harvest is plentiful but the laborers are few; therefore pray earnestly to the Lord of the harvest to send out laborers into the harvest."

[1] The English word, *compassion,* is similar in meaning to the English word, *sympathy,* but the translators of the Authorized English Version never used *sympathy.* While *compassion* is derived from Latin, *sympathy* is derived from Greek. The root for both Latin and Greek words refers to the emotion and feeling of pain and suffering. With the prefix before *passion* (*com*passion) and *pathy* (*sym*pathy) the words denote 'to feel *with*' the feelings of another. There is 'harmony and agreement in feeling, as between persons or on the part of one person with respect to another.' Jesus entered into the feelings of others. He felt with them. He identified with them. He hurt with them.

How much time Jesus took to prepare his thoughts for teaching and preaching, we do not know. But Jesus was obviously concerned principally with *people*. He witnessed their condition of harassment and helplessness. He took steps to help the people in their need.

Matthew 14:13-21: According to 14:1-13 Jesus was informed about the death of John the Baptist. This was a deeply moving event. So when Jesus heard this, 'he withdrew from there in a boat to a desolate place by himself.' Can there be any doubt of Jesus' intention? He wanted solitude for thought and prayer. The death of Jesus' forerunner, John the Baptist, a friend and relative, had many implications even for Christ and his future. He desired to withdraw from ministry for a time of reflection with his disciples. Furthermore, the disciples had been on a preaching tour. Tired and dusty they needed some rest. According to Mark 6:31 Jesus told them, 'Come away by yourselves to a desolate place and rest awhile. For many were coming and going, and they had no leisure even to eat.'

But he no sooner landed on the other side of the Sea of Galilee in some 'desolate place' when the crowds came to him. He had tried to escape but the people had anticipated his destination and walked hurriedly by foot to meet him when he landed.

What would you do? I would surely be disturbed within me; dare I call it 'anger'? Can't a servant of the Lord ever find relief from the pressures of ministry? Must he continually be at the beck and call of those in need? What of his own need for rest and recuperation? Jesus did take time for rest and reprieve from the demands of ministry. But when people in need came to him, he was moved with *compassion*, not anger or frustration. The reason for his *compassion* in this context was the same as the one in Matthew 9:35-37. 'He had compassion on them because they were like sheep without a shepherd. And he began to teach them many things.' The people were spiritually hungry. They needed feeding with instruction.

Then a further problem arose. When he taught them a long time, the hour was getting late with the sun setting in the horizon. The disciples saw the need for the people to eat because it was a desolate place. They advised Jesus to send the crowd away into the villages to find food and lodging.[11] That was a very practical suggestion. Jesus must send them away before it became dark. The hour was late. But Jesus recognised the need and *felt* for the needs of the people. He anticipated the problem and therefore fed the 5,000.

Matthew 15:32-39: A similar situation arose when Jesus was teaching the crowds. 'I have *compassion* on the crowd because they have been with me now three days and have nothing to eat. And I am unwilling to send them away hungry, lest they faint on the way.' The disciples had no solution so Jesus stepped in and fed the 4,000 men besides women and children.

Do you get the picture? Jesus *deeply loved* the people whom he taught. His teaching, preaching and healing ministries were more than routine responsibilities faithfully carried out. He ministered to *people* and Jesus had *compassion* on people to the extent that he took steps to resolve the problem.

Matthew 20:29-34: In this text a crowd followed Jesus as he moved from Jericho in the Jordan Valley up to Jerusalem. As Jesus was leaving Jericho two blind men, sitting by the road, cried out to Jesus, 'Lord, have mercy on us, Son of David.' What was the reaction of the crowd? 'Be silent!' Shut up! The Teacher has more important things to do than to stop and listen to you! But Jesus did stop and asked what they wanted. When they said, 'Lord, let our eyes be opened,' Jesus *pitied* them and healed them. Jesus showed compassion, here translated *pity*.

Mark 1:40-45: On another occasion a leper came to him, 'imploring him, and kneeling said to him, "If you will, you can make me clean."' What was Jesus' reaction? *Splagchnizomai*! Jesus, the God-Man, found his bowels churning with deep feeling. He had compassion on the man who had an incurable disease. Leprosy did not confine one to a bed but isolated one from the community. He was a social outcast, a most pitiable condition.

The sick were all around. It is so easy to develop a ministry fatigue, becoming weary of helping. Jesus showed a remarkable love for others and seeing beyond his own situation; he showed a compassionate love.

Luke 7:11-17: One day Jesus and his disciples with a great crowd were walking through the town of Nain, when they saw a funeral procession for a young man who died, the only son of a widow. All grief upon the death of a loved one is real grief. But in this situation the grief was compounded. The widow's husband was gone and now her only son was departed. 'And when the Lord saw her, he had *compassion* on her and said to her, "Do not weep."' Jesus could see the deep anguish of the widow in her personal plight. He demonstrated love by being moved with compassion.

Luke 10:25-37: A lawyer inquired from Jesus how he might inherit eternal life. Jesus turned the question around and asked the lawyer what he understood from the law. To which the lawyer recalled the two greatest commandments, to love God with all your heart and to love your neighbor as yourself. Jesus replied, 'You have answered correctly; do this, and you will live.' But then he further asked, 'Who is my neighbour?' This was a very practical question, though he may have been insincere, for he was 'testing' Jesus. But it is practical. Should we treat *everyone* as our 'neighbour'? Even our enemies or apostates or those we don't even know? Jesus gave a very practical answer.

In the Parable of the Good Samaritan, a man journeyed from Jerusalem to Jericho. On the way he was beaten, stripped, robbed and left half-dead. A priest and a Levite separately passed that way and saw the man in a desperate condition. It is known that many priests lived in Jericho. When they journeyed to Jerusalem to serve there in the Temple, they often took the long route through Bethlehem in order to avoid the dangerous Jericho-Jerusalem road. The road from Jericho to Jerusalem was a steep ascent of 3,000 feet on seventeen miles of desolate country.

For some reason both the priest and Levite, traveling separately, found a need to journey to Jerusalem more speedily, so they passed the more dangerous route. Alas, both the priest and Levite were preoccupied with themselves. If either of them had gone over to the man to see if they could help, they would have defiled themselves ceremonially if he were actually dead. A ceremonially unclean priest or Levite could not serve in the Temple. Perhaps they were also concerned about safety, not knowing if the robbers were nearby.

Both were servants of the living God in the Temple; both were religious, devout Jews who kept the Ten Commandments. But at this time they feared for their lives from thieves and were concerned about ceremonial purity, so they avoided helping someone in need. Even though the injured man was a fellow human being and a Jewish brother; even though the priest and Levite were very religious, devout descendants of Abraham, they were more concerned for their own personal needs than the needs of this wounded brother.

Along the road came a Samaritan, someone who was despised by the Jews as an apostate half-Jew. If the Jewish man lying on the road had been in normal health, he would have rejected any offer of a cup of water from a Samaritan. That was the depth of the animosity between Jews and Samaritans. But instead of concern for self, we read that he had *compassion* on the man. When the Samaritan saw him, 'he had *compassion.*' He then dismounted the donkey, exposing himself to danger from robbers. He touched the man, risking ceremonial uncleanness. He poured oil and wine on the man's injuries, the customary remedies of the time. He even paid money for his care in the inn.

What a striking illustration of the kind of love a Christian leader must have if he is to lead men and women and show the love of God to others!

Luke 15:20: When the Pharisees saw the tax collectors and sinners drawing near to Jesus, they grumbled. Jesus should show greater concern for purity and not associate with sinners, so they thought. So Jesus told them three parables to illustrate the joy when the lost is found. In contrast to the elder brother who showed no compassion for the Prodigal Son returning home, the Father saw him returning home from a distance 'and *felt compassion*, and ran and embraced him and kissed him.' Even so our Heavenly Father feels *compassion*.

CONCLUSION

The love of Jesus, the Good Shepherd, leaves us breathless. Even so all his under-shepherds who care for the flock should be moved to demonstrate love. Leadership is all about people. Without genuine love and compassion no one can be an effective leader.

Not only should we imitate God in his love, we are also commanded to imitate God in his holiness. Holiness is another essential trait of every Christian leader. Holiness is the topic for *Part Five.*

SEARCHING THE SCRIPTURE WITH APPLICATION

1. How is the *compassion* of Christ a manifestation of his love?
2. What can we learn about Christ's love from our study of Christ's *compassion* to apply to our own lives?
3. Consider the difference or similarity between Christ's love and the normal, natural love which the unbeliever displays?
4. '*God is love*' (1 Jn 4:8). Jesus is the eternal *Word*, Incarnate, revealing that love. Therefore, we can justly say that the 'Love Chapter' speaks about Christ's love.

   Jesus is *patient* and *kind*; he *does not envy or boast*. Jesus *is not arrogant or rude*, *does not insist on his own way*. He is *not irritable or resentful*. Jesus *does not rejoice at wrongdoing*, but *rejoices with the truth*. Jesus *bears all things, believes all things, hopes all things, endures all things.*

   a. Reflect on the life of Christ and consider the times when these attributes of *agape* love were manifested in Jesus' life.

b. Reflect on your own life in the past few months and consider how closely you have manifested *agape* love even as Jesus did.
c. What steps should you take as a Christian leader to grow in your love?

5. *'Therefore be imitators of God, as beloved children. And walk in love, as Christ loved us and gave himself up for us, a fragrant offering and sacrifice to God'* (Eph 5:1-2). God's children are here commanded to imitate God.
   a. What in particular are God's children commanded to imitate?
   b. What particular demonstration of Christ's love is Paul here referring to in Eph 5:1-2?
   c. How did Christ's death on the cross demonstrate God's love?
   d. What lessons should we learn from this demonstration of *agape* love?
6. *We who are strong have an obligation to bear with the failings of the weak, and not to please ourselves. Let each of us please his neighbor for his good, to build him up. For Christ did not please himself...'*(Ro 14:1-23)
   How was Jesus the supreme model in not pleasing himself?

Endnotes

[1] Tit 3:4 NASB
[2] F. M. Lehman.
Copyright 1945,
Renewal Nazarene Pub House
[3] Mt 5:43-48; 19:19; 22:39; Jn 13:31-35; 15:12-17
[4] Jn 13:23; 20:2; 21:20
[5] Jn 11:5
[6] Jn 11:33f
[7] Jn 13:1,34; 15:9,12
[8] Jn 15:9, 13
[9] Random House College Dict., 1988
[10] Thayer 1983
[11] Lk 9:12

PART FIVE

HOLINESSS OF CHRISTIAN LEADERS

Without *humility*, Christian leaders in their pride usurp the glory of God, and thereby invite God's displeasure.

Without *agape love*, Christian leaders fall short of God's glorious love, and therefore, cannot serve as leaders with love.

Without *holiness*, Christian leaders fail to reflect the glory of God who declares, 'Be holy, for I am holy.'[1] Without a holy life no one can be a *Christian* leader. One may succeed as a *leader* without being holy, but no one can be a *Christian* leader without living a holy life!

In *Part Five* we first consider what it means to be *Holy to the Lord*. Essential for holiness is *integrity* of character. When a leader lives a holy life he is marked by *purity* and *honesty*. To live a holy life a Christian leader must maintain a pure heart. Therefore, *purity in heart* is our capstone for *Part Five*.

21 HOLY TO THE LORD

'You shall make [for the high priest] a plate of pure gold and engrave on it, like the engraving of signet, "Holy to the Lord."'[2]

The need is urgent today: Christian leaders **must be** '*holy to the Lord.*'

'The older I grow the more I am convinced that real practical holiness does not receive the attention it deserves, and that there is a painfully low standard of living among many high professors of religion in the land.' This was said by John Charles Ryle of England in 1879.[3] Nothing much has changed! Today the call to holy living among all Christians, especially Christian leaders, is urgent!

Why is holiness important?

Holiness is interwoven throughout the entire Holy Writings. The word, *holy*, in one form or another, is found over 600 times in the Bible. One whole book (*Leviticus*) is devoted to the subject. So why is holiness so important?

Because God is Holy: 'Holiness' in the Old Testament refers principally to the character of God. 'The LORD our God is holy!'[4] 'Holiness refers to [God's] essential nature; it is not so much an attribute of God as it is the very foundation of his being.'[5]

In the throne room of heaven where God is 'seated on a throne, high and exalted,' the seraphs call continually one to another: 'Holy, holy, holy is the LORD of hosts; the whole earth is full of his glory.'[6] Isaiah's response was holy fear and utter dismay.

The very first mention of the word 'holy' in the Bible occurs at the burning bush. When Moses drew near to observe this wonder, a bush that burned but did not burn up, God called to him from the burning bush, saying: 'Moses, Moses!...Do not come near; take your sandals off your feet, for the place on which you are standing is *holy ground*.'[7] Those who draw near to the presence of the holy God must respond with awe and reverence.

Moses cried out to Yahweh after the exodus from Egypt, 'Who is like you, O LORD, among the gods? Who is like you, *majestic in holiness*...?'[8] The majesty and splendour of the Holy One of Israel calls for reverential fear, wonder and awe. To worship, one must bow before his holy character.

Holiness is important for another reason.

Because God commands his people to be holy: Do you aspire to be a leader? You should never contemplate Christian leadership unless you commit yourself to being holy, living in full obedience to God's commandments. Essential for all of God's people, and especially for his chosen leaders, is a correspondence with God's righteous character. Yahweh had commanded his people: 'You shall be holy, for I the LORD your God am holy.'[9] Not only is this a command, God declares solemnly, 'without holiness no one will see the Lord.'[10] This moral emphasis is found throughout the New Testament.

'As obedient children do not be conformed to the passions of your former ignorance, but as he who called you is holy, you also ***be holy in all your conduct****, since it is written, "You shall be holy, for I am holy."'*[11]

Holiness is not a condition for salvation, but it is the fruit of salvation. No fruit – no salvation! The evidence of salvation is a changed life of holiness.[12] Although redemption is by grace through faith alone,[13] God's purpose in calling us to himself is that we might be 'holy and blameless before him.'[14] 'If there is not, then, at least a yearning in our hearts to live a holy life pleasing to God, we need to seriously question whether our faith in Christ is genuine.'[15]

Scripture goes even further.

> No one who abides in [Christ] keeps on sinning; no one who keeps on sinning has either seen him or known him. Little children, let no one deceive you. Whoever practices righteousness is righteous, as he is righteous. Whoever makes a practice of sinning is of the devil, for the devil has been sinning from the beginning...No one born of God makes a practice of sinning, for God's seed abides in him, and he cannot keep on sinning because he has been born of God.[16]

This is not sinless perfection but it is a holy lifestyle without which no one shall see the Lord. If holiness is incumbent upon all Christians, then Christian leaders are doubly responsible to strive for a holy life. We have seen before that the biblical standard for a Church leader is someone who is 'above reproach.'[17] Whenever a Christian leader fails to glorify God by visible obedience to the commands of God, he betrays his trust, dishonours God and creates a stumbling block for God's people.

What is holiness?

The concept of holiness, derived from the Hebrew Old Testament word, *qadash* (the primitive root of the word), contains two ideas:

Holiness is* 'apartness'** ***or 'separation.' God is holy in the sense that He is distinct from and separate from all creation. Expressing this thought, God says: '...I am God and not a man, the Holy One in your midst.'[18] Holiness in this sense refers to the very 'Godness' of God.[19] That which constitutes the very essential being of God is his being 'Wholly Other.' There are certain attributes of God's essential being that can never be communicated to others, qualities of his nature that forever distinguish him from his creatures, such as his omnipotence, omnipresence and omniscience. While God is infinite in all his Being, self-existent and eternal, his creatures are finite and utterly dependent upon God for their being. In this sense God is holy, eternally and fundamentally set apart from his creation.

This concept of separation is applied to people and things in the Old Testament that are set apart for divine worship. In the Hebrew worship everything that was devoted to worship was 'set apart,' made sacred, including the sacred furniture of the temple, the dishes, the animal sacrifices, the garments of the priests – everything associated with the worship of Yahweh was to be ceremonially cleansed and separated from the unclean to be sacred unto the Lord.

In this sense Christian leaders are set apart from ordinary work and consecrated unto the Lord for service to the living God. '*Holy to the Lord*' was engraved on the plate of gold worn on the turban of the high priest. This was a reminder that the high priest was set apart *unto* the Lord. There was both a physical separation *from* the mundane, common life of the people and a separation *unto* the Lord. The high priest was consecrated and devoted to the service of Yahweh.

To be called by God into Christian ministry is a high and holy privilege. To serve the King of the universe in the ministry of the Word is the noblest of professions. Every Christian leader must remember why he or she is in the ministry. Who called you to serve in ministry? Once your call is settled and you are assured in your heart that God has called you into the ministry, then you must understand that you are '*holy to the Lord*,' set apart from mundane work and consecrated to fulfill the ministry given by God.[1]

Holiness is righteous character: '*Holy to the Lord*' was more than religious separation with ritual and dietary implications. Holiness also signified separation from all that is morally unclean or evil. Holiness referred to the moral likeness of God – the righteous character of God. 'To be holy is to be morally blameless. It is to be separated from sin and, therefore, consecrated to God. The word signifies "separation to God, and the conduct befitting those so separated."'[20] The most prominent

[1] At this point we must clarify an important issue. *All* of God's people are 'holy to the Lord;' all are commanded to be holy. The vision of the Messianic era by Zechariah is that 'on that day' all distinction between sacred and secular shall cease (Zec 14:12). The bells of the horses shall be inscribed with, 'Holy to the LORD.' All vocations of God's people are holy and His people all have the privilege of serving the Holy God and building His kingdom.

Kenneth Baker sums up the teaching of Zechariah 14:12 by saying: 'There will be holiness in public life ("the bells of the horses," v. 20), in religious life ("the cooking pots in the LORD's house," v. 20), and in private life ("every pot in Jerusalem and Judah," v. 21). Even common things become holy when they are used for God's service. So it is with our lives' (Baker 1985:697).

However, this book is dealing with Christian leaders. Those who are called to minister the Word of God and proclaim the gospel of the kingdom have a noble privilege that has been granted to them by God. They are set apart and consecrated for the service of the living God with a calling that is not like any other. In Scripture the most severe punishment is reserved for leaders who become unholy. The greater the privilege of serving in the ministry of Christian leadership, the greater their responsibility to represent the holy God by living a holy life; and greater will be their judgement when they stumble and fall, despoiling the Holy Name of God.

emphasis in the Bible on holiness, especially in the New Testament, is the moral or ethical dimension of holiness.

When God commands his people, 'Be holy, for I am holy,' He is referring to his own moral character in whose image Adam and Eve were created. God will always retain his unique separation from all creatures; He will always remain God without sharing his glory with others. But rooted in his separation from the creature is his separation from all that is unclean. God is of 'purer eyes than to see evil and cannot look at wrong.'[21] His holiness is manifest in total righteousness and purity. This moral or ethical character of God is communicable. God commands his people to be like him in his moral likeness.

> *He chose us in him before the foundation of the world, that we* ***should be holy*** *and blameless before him.*[22]
>
> *You were taught, with regard to your former way of life, to put off your old self, which is being corrupted by its deceitful desires; to be made new in the attitude of your minds; and to put on the new self,* ***created to be like God in true righteousness and holiness.***[23]
>
> ***For this is the will of God, your holiness:*** *that you abstain from sexual immorality; that each one of you know how to* ***control his own body in holiness*** *and honor, not in the passion of lust like the Gentiles who do not know God…For God has not called us for impurity, but in* ***holiness.***[24]
>
> *Let us cleanse ourselves from every defilement of body and spirit,* ***bringing holiness to completion in the fear of God.***[25]

Christian leaders above all must strive to be holy lest they fall under God's judgement.

What is the standard for holiness?

The fundamental basis for the divine standard of holiness is the very character of God. The commandments in the Scriptures are not arbitrary 'do's' and 'don'ts.' All the divine commandments which bind Christians today are rooted in the very character and nature of God.

Sidlow Baxter states: 'Holiness is likeness to God, or, more precisely, likeness to the *moral character* of God…The Ten Commandments are simply an amplification of it in ten aspects: "Ye shall be holy, for I JEHOVAH YOUR GOD AM HOLY."'[26]

The biblical summary, then, of God's righteous standards is the Ten Commandments.

The first four commandments, the first table of the Decalogue, calls for God's covenant people to acknowledge the majestic and singular holiness of Yahweh, and to offer him absolute and total allegiance and worship *because* He in fact, is the only true and living God, the Creator of all things and the absolute potentate of the universe.

The sixth commandment, 'You shall not murder,' is grounded in Love as the sublime character of God.[27] Christ deepens this command by teaching that anyone who is angry with his neighbour and slanders him (or her) with ill will and ill feeling is guilty of breaking this commandment.[28]

Likewise, the eighth commandment, 'You shall not steal,' and the tenth commandment, 'You shall not covet,' are violating the loving character of God. Paul teaches that, 'The entire law is summed up in a single command: "Love your neighbor as yourself."'[29] By coveting what belongs to our neighbour or stealing (or misappropriating funds), we fail to demonstrate love and therefore violate the nature of God. Failure to reflect the glory of God is an offense to God because the human race was created to be God's image bearers; Christ died to redeem men and women to restore God's image in them.[30]

The ninth commandment, 'You shall not give false testimony against your neighbour,' is based on the truthfulness of God. Yahweh is 'the true God.'[31] He is genuine and no counterfeit. 'God is not a man, that he should lie.'[32] In fact, 'It is impossible for God to lie'[33] because God in his very nature is faithful, reliable and always true to his Word. God's people are therefore called upon to be truthful – faithful, honest and reliable in order to reflect God's character.

The seventh commandment, 'You shall not commit adultery,' is also grounded in God's character. God's love, truthfulness and purity are all violated when husbands and wives, pledged to marital fidelity, are unfaithful.

CONCLUSION

Our Lord Jesus made this astonishing statement: 'You therefore must be perfect, as your heavenly Father is perfect.'[34] Is this really possible? It is not only possible but an obligation for all Christians; and for those who are called to be Christian leaders, they must be 'above reproach.' By the empowering of the Holy Spirit and the spiritual disciplines of prayer and meditation on the Word of God, we as Christian leaders not only have the obligation but the privilege of growing daily in holiness, becoming more and more like our Father in heaven who is perfect.

The remainder of *Part Five, 'Holiness of Christian Leaders,'* is devoted to the exposition of these commandments and the tragic failure of many Christian leaders to live lives beyond reproach. Help will be given in Chapter 25 to grow in the likeness of our Heavenly Father.

SEARCHING THE SCRIPTURE WITH APPLICATION

1. Do a word study of 'holiness,' using dictionaries and other language tools you may have, in all languages you know (e.g. Greek, Hebrew, English, your mother tongue etc.). What does 'holiness' mean in these various languages?
2. Read Dt 7:1-11, especially 7:6: '*For you are a people holy to the LORD your God. The LORD your God has chosen you out of all the peoples on the face of the earth to be his people, his treasured possession.*' How should this truth work out practically in the lives of Christian leaders?
3. In Lev 20:26 Yahweh commanded: '*You shall be holy to me, for I the LORD am holy and have separated you from the peoples, that you should be mine.*' Now read carefully Lev 18:1-22:33. Note the many references to 'holiness' and the phrase, 'I am the LORD.' How does the concept of holiness help you understand the significance of these Old Testament regulations?
4. Compare Ex 19:5,6 and Dt 28:9 with 1 Pe 2:9,10. What is the significance of the children of Israel and the Church of Christ both being called 'a holy nation'? What is the meaning that we are 'a holy nation'?
5. What are the implications of the following passages on holiness (purity)?
   1 Co 3:16-17; 6:12-20; 2 Co 6:14-17; 7:1; Eph 2:21,22; 4:20-24; 5:1-10; Php 4:8; Col 3:5-15; 1 Th 4:3-7; 5:5,22-23; Heb 12:1,14-15; 2 Pe 3:11-14.

6. Why are Christian leaders judged more harshly than other Christians when they fall into sin and manifest an unholy life?

Endnotes

[1] 1 Pe 1:16
[2] Ex 28:36
[3] Ryle 1979: vi
[4] Ps 99:9
[5] Williams 2001:562
[6] Is 6:3
[7] Ex 3:5
[8] Ex 15:11
[9] Lev 19:2
[10] Heb 12:14 NIV
[11] 1 Pe 1:14-16
[12] 2 Co 5:17; 1 Jn 3:6ff
[13] Eph 2:4-9
[14] Eph 1:4
[15] Bridges 1985:38
[16] 1 Jn 3:4-8
[17] 1 Ti 3:2
[18] Hos 11:9
[19] Williams 2001:562
[20] Bridges 1985:19
[21] Hab 1:13
[22] Eph 1:4
[23] Eph 4:21-24 NIV
[24] 1 Th 4:3-7
[25] 2 Co 7:1
[26] Baxter 1973:107
[27] 1 Jn 4:8
[28] Mt 5:21-26
[29] Gal 5:13-15
[30] Eph 4:24
[31] Jer 10:10
[32] Jn 14:6
[33] Heb 7:18
[34] Mt 5:48

22
INTEGRITY

'Better is a poor person who walks in his integrity than one who is crooked in speech and is a fool.'[1]

Integrity is at the heart of what it means to be holy.

It is also essential for Christian leadership. To be a leader one must have followers. To have followers they must have confidence in their leader. To have confidence requires integrity of the leader.

So what is integrity?

What is integrity?

The meaning of integrity: Synonyms for integrity include: *honesty, truthfulness, veracity, reliability and uprightness*. The opposite of integrity is dishonesty. This is true and we will return to these meanings later, but we must go beyond the principle meaning of integrity today and seek to understand the root meaning of the word.

The English word, *integrity*, is the translation of the Hebrew word, *tom,* in the Old Testament. The Hebrew word has been translated in various ways: *integrity, completeness, simplicity, innocence, uprightness, and perfection.*[2] The basic meaning of *tom* is not unlike the root meaning of the English word.

In contemporary usage, *integrity* refers principally to *honesty* and *uprightness*, the 'steadfast adherence to a strict moral or ethical code.'[3] But its more basic meaning can be traced to the Latin, *integritas*, meaning *soundness, whole, complete, intact,* and *perfect* – perfect in the sense of being *pure, unmixed, unadulterated, complete, unblemished.* It is a quality or condition of being *whole* or *undivided*; *complete.*

To understand *integrity*, therefore, we must go beyond the common understanding of *honesty*. A person of integrity is one who is *whole* and *undivided, simple and complete.*

Opposites of integrity: Benjamin suggests that a consideration of the lapses or deficiencies of integrity will help us understand the meaning of integrity.[4]

The *moral chameleon* is anxious to accommodate others and not to offend. The *moral chameleon*, therefore, quickly changes or modifies itself to blend in with the crowd. In order not to offend, he placates others by adopting the popular view of the moment or of the people surrounding him. He has no moral centre, no moral convictions for which he will die. Instead, the *chameleon* compromises and changes colours to fit in. It can easily be seen that the *moral chameleon* is not undivided in his inner core; his beliefs and practices are not whole or complete. Therefore, he is not a person of integrity.

On the other hand, the *opportunist* is one whose primary concern in life is personal gain and getting ahead in life. The *opportunist* is willing to change with the circumstances if it to his own advantage. The *opportunist* takes every opportunity to achieve personal gain and advancement by changing and adapting to accommodate others for his own advantage. Self-centred ambition causes the *opportunist* not to be a person of integrity; his character is not *simple*, *undivided* or *intact* but marked by duplicity, seeking personal advantage. Therefore, he is not a person of integrity.

Neither is a *hypocrite* a person of integrity. A *hypocrite* pretends to live by certain standards but does not; he pretends to be one thing but his behaviour proves him otherwise. A hypocrite preaches one thing but practices another.[5] The elder invites everyone on Sunday to attend prayer meeting but does not attend himself. The pastor preaches against sin but then practices the very sin he preaches against. The layperson harshly criticises the elders for moral lapses but fails to keep the Ten Commandments himself. The problem with the hypocrite is that he is not *pure*, *unmixed*, *unadulterated*, *complete*, *unblemished.* The hypocrite is divided in his words and practice.

The *weak-willed* person may have a set of beliefs and convictions but is weak and unable to stand up for his convictions. He easily crumbles and collapses when the pressure is on. When a Church authority threatens him in ministry with a demotion, a transfer or suspension if he does not conform, the *weak-willed* surrenders his beliefs and gives in. The *weak-willed* are not people of integrity because their heart and will are not one, *whole* or *undivided.*

Those who do not think of themselves as dishonest may be *self-deceivers*. They are blind to the fact that they embrace conflicting and incompatible values and beliefs. They like to think of themselves as motivated by higher standards but in practice their conduct is motivated by something quite incompatible with their stated values. A married man develops an illicit affair with another woman. He deceives himself by rationalising that his wife has been unfair or unfaithful to him, or that this extra-marital affair is a fleeting moment while his marriage is of lasting value. Somehow, the *self-deceiver* compartmentalises his values which, in fact, are not harmonious or simple in nature. The *self-deceiver* is not marked with integrity of character.

In conclusion, what emerges from these portraits above is that *a person of integrity is someone whose whole being is simple, whole, undivided and perfect* in three dimensions: '(1) a reasonably coherent and relatively stable set of highly cherished values and principles; (2) verbal behavior expressing these values and principles; and (3) conduct embodying one's values and principles and consistent with what one says. These are the elements of integrity.'[6] This is what may be called, 'soundness of moral character – a sound, unimpaired, or perfect condition.'[7] Whatever he says or does reflects what is inside of him. There is nothing divided, contradictory or incompatible in the person.

Growing out of this basic, fundamental understanding of integrity are the attributes of integrity which are most familiar: *honesty, truthfulness, reliability, sincerity, uprightness.*

Why is integrity so important?

Christian leaders in recent years have suffered greatly from lapses in integrity. Engstrom suggests that contemporary society is suffering greatly from the AIDS pandemic – 'Acquired *Integrity* Deficiency Syndrome.[8] AIDS has wrecked havoc on those in ministry. So why is integrity so important?

Moral integrity is of extreme importance for several reasons:

1. God is perfect in his integrity: Holiness is likeness to God's moral character. One aspect of God's moral character is his integrity. Erickson clusters three divine attributes under God's integrity: genuineness (being true), veracity (telling the truth) and faithfulness (proving true).[9]

Genuineness: God is genuine in two ways: First, the God of Abraham, Isaac and Jacob is the only true (real) God.[10] Jeremiah ridicules the gods of the nations. 'Their idols are like scarecrows in a cucumber field, and they cannot speak; they have to be carried, for they cannot walk...They are both stupid and foolish; the instruction of idols is but wood...*But the LORD is the true God*; he is the living God and the everlasting King. At his wrath the earth quakes, and the nations cannot endure his indignation.'[11]

'God is real; he is not fabricated or constructed or imitation, as are all the other claimants to deity. In a world in which so much is artificial our God is real. He is what he appears to be.'[12]

Secondly, God is genuine in the sense of his consistency. What he says is what he does because there is no hypocrisy in God. He does not pretend to be something he is not. Smedes refers to 'an inner consistency, a congruency such that what you are outside is what you intend to be.'[13]

Veracity: Whatever God says is true; it accords with reality, what really is. 'The Glory of Israel will not lie...'[14] In fact, 'it is impossible for God to lie.'[15] Whereas Satan is 'a liar and the father of lies' who 'speaks out of his own character,'[16] it is contrary to God's nature to lie. Although God is almighty, he *cannot* lie. God cannot go contrary to his own nature.

Faithfulness: God keeps his promises; what he says, he will do. God is faithful to his Word. The faithfulness of God is prominent throughout Scripture. Moses says: 'Know therefore the LORD your God is God, the *faithful God* who keeps covenant and steadfast love with those who love him...'[17] Joshua reminded Israel: 'You know in your hearts...that not one word has failed of all the good things that the LORD your God promised...'[18] David sings: 'Your faithfulness extends to the clouds.'[19] The prophets proclaim: 'Great is your faithfulness.'[20]

Because of God's infinite perfection of wisdom and power, he would never promise something he could not fulfill; nor would he change his mind. As Balaam said to Balak, 'God is not man, that he should lie, or a son of man, that he should change his mind. Has he said, and will he not do it? Or has he spoken, and will he not fulfill it?'[21]

The second reason why integrity is so important for Christian leaders is:

2. God commands Christian leaders to have integrity: Christian leaders must continually grow into the likeness of their heavenly Father. They are commanded 'to put on the new self, created after the likeness of God in true righteousness and holiness.'[22] The aim of this process of sanctification is to become increasingly holy as we become more and more like God in his true righteousness and holiness. Holiness includes *integrity*.

Paul admonished a young Church leader: 'Show yourself in all respects to be a model of good works, and *in your teaching show integrity*, dignity, and sound speech that cannot be condemned…'[23] Some preachers are insincere in their preaching. They preach with ulterior motives. They seek personal gain and profit through their gospel of prosperity. They preach what they do not practice. It is incumbent for all Christian leaders to conduct themselves with absolute integrity. Always remember what David knew 3000 years ago: 'I know, my God, that you test the heart and are *pleased with integrity.'*[24]

Let us think of integrity for Christian leaders in the above mentioned three categories: genuineness (being true), veracity (telling the truth) and faithfulness (proving true).

<u>*Genuineness:*</u> Christian leaders need to be genuine in the sense of the root meaning of integrity: to be genuine, sincere, pure, unadulterated, complete, sound, intact, undivided, simple, and complete. This means that a Christian leader should not be a *moral chameleon*, an *opportunist*, a *hypocrite*, *weak-willed* or a *self-deceiver*. Instead, he should say what he thinks and believes, practice what he says and be a genuine and sincere in his profession of faith.

Being real is the key. No amount of talking will convince any one if you are not genuine in your profession. After some time people will know whether their pastor is genuine or not. Lay people may not be as well educated as their pastor, but they are quite capable of seeing through their pastor and knowing whether he is genuine or not.

The Greek word for true in the New Testament, (*alethes* and its cognates), all include this root meaning of the word: *to be real* and *genuine*. Before we ask the question, 'Are you truthful?' we must ask, 'Are you genuine, or are you a fraud?' When Peter was released from prison by an angel we read, 'He did not know that what was being done by the angel was *real*, but thought he was seeing a vision.'[25] To be real is to be in accord with reality. To be a genuine Christian leader you should always speak and do what in reality are your settled and cherished values and abiding principles in life. Be undivided and sincere. Don't be a hypocrite.

John's concluding concern in his first epistle is stark: 'Little children, keep yourselves from idols.'[26] This is preceded by reference to 'the *true* God.' Idols are simply imitation gods, not the true (real) God. To the Galatians Paul wrote that they were formerly 'enslaved to those that by nature are not gods.'[27] In contrast to these 'pretend' gods, John speaks of the *true* God, the One who is genuinely the real God. There is a vast difference between reality (what is) and what is imaginary. For the Christian leader to be real is a real challenge. Because he should not pretend, he must be united in his heart and mind in his love for God and commitment to his will reflected in his word so that whatever he says or does reflects what he truly is inside.

Joshua in his concluding address to the children of Israel, before his death, gives this challenge:

'Now therefore fear the LORD and serve him in *sincerity* and in faithfulness. Put away the gods that your fathers served…'[28] Let's face it! Many serve the Lord with lack of sincerity – they are not genuine with undivided love for God. Paul exhorts the Corinthians that their love should be genuine with demonstration of this love through generous giving to the saints in Jerusalem.[29] It is so easy to profess but fail to practice.

Veracity: Integrity of character means telling the truth; never lying. The primary idea conveyed by the word, 'integrity,' is *honesty, truthfulness, veracity, reliability and uprightness.*

'Like father, like son.' Adam and Eve, initially created in the perfect image of God, were a perfect reflection of their heavenly Father. Since God is full of integrity, so Adam and Eve were truthful. But having fallen in temptation through the lies of Satan, the human race has taken on the same character of Satan who is marked by deceit, duplicity, and unfaithfulness. The promises of human beings are unreliable. They say one thing and do another.

The ninth commandment attacks this major problem in the Church today; it was obviously a problem in Israel as well. '*You shall not bear false witness against your neighbor.*'[30] Swearing to tell the truth before the Judge in a law court was intended to guarantee truth telling. To bear false witness in court is roundly condemned in this ninth commandment. As Proverbs say, 'A faithful witness does not lie, but a false witness breathes out lies.'[31] 'Whoever speaks the truth gives honest evidence, but a false witness utters deceit.'[32]

Jewish rabbis, however, distinguished between swearing in Yahweh's name and swearing by something lesser. As a result, conversation became cluttered with oaths without using the name of the Lord for two reasons: swearing was intended to give the impression of truthfulness; but since the oaths were not in the name of Yahweh, the oaths were not binding. Jesus cut through this and said flatly: 'Do not swear at all…Simply let your "yes" be "yes," and your "no," "no"; anything beyond this comes from the evil one.'[33]

The application of this ninth commandment is broad. God forbids lying of any kind because God is a God of truth. Paul admonishes: 'Each of you must put off falsehood and speak truthfully to his neighbor…'[34] Lying is an abomination to the Lord[35] who pronounces judgement on all those who lie.[36] In fact, lying is listed among the most heinous crimes – 'all liars, their portion will be in the lake that burns with fire and sulfur, which is the second death.'[37]

Anyone who announces a contribution at some *harambee* (a Kenyan tradition of community fundraising) but fails to fulfill his promise is like 'clouds and wind without rain.'[38] Words do not conform to reality. A promise is broken. A lie is spoken. In contrast, 'The righteous hates falsehood.'[39]

Words may be intended to hide the intent of the heart. How many speak smooth words of flattery while concealing hatred! 'The one who conceals hatred has lying lips, and whoever utters slander is a fool.'[40]

Christians slander and malign the character of others for personal gain or enmity. Paul says explicitly, 'Get rid of all…slander…'[41] Slander is uttering false and malicious statements which destroy another. Slandering is sinful for two reasons. Not only is slander dishonesty – a distortion and misrepresentation of another person's character – slander also defames another and destroys his reputation. Slander is thus the breaking of the command to love.

Whenever truth is spoken, it must be spoken in love.[42] The goal of every Christian leader must be to represent his Head who is Truth and Love, and to build up the Body of Christ. Truth is concerned with veracity, but love is concerned with relationships. Truth must never be sacrificed because of a desire to maintain loving relationships; but neither should love in a leader be sacrificed when seeking to tell the truth. This takes great wisdom and humility but the Bible is clear: both truth and love are attributes of Deity. In the Person of God there is never a conflict between the two.

We must observe, however, that people are not obligated to reveal everything.[43] Concealing the truth is not necessarily telling a lie. You can refuse to answer. Compare the practice of the Hebrew midwives[44] who were honoured by God; and the concealment of Samuel which was ordered by God.[45] Disinformation in warfare or censorship is not reprehensible lying. In military conflict one is not obligated to divulge military plans.[46] Mistakes are not lies.

Faithfulness: God expects his servants to be faithful, even as He is faithful; proving to be true to their word, fulfilling their responsibilities and living up to their commitments. 'It is required that those who have been given a trust must prove *faithful*.'[47] Faithfulness is the one requirement for Christian service. Worldly success measured in position, power, prestige will never be rewarded by God. What He rewards is *faithfulness*. Jesus emphasised this many times. To those who are faithful in the use of their God-given gifts, He will reward and commend: 'Well done, good and *faithful* servant. You have been *faithful* over a little; I will set you over much. Enter into the joy of your master.'[48]

A Christian leader marked by integrity is someone who keeps his word. Making promises is easy; keeping them is not. Therefore, wise Christian leaders are slow to make promises that cannot be fulfilled. Be forthright and straightforward. If you are not sure whether you will be able to attend a function, or fulfill someone's request, just say so. Obviously, Christian leaders are not Godlike in their knowledge and power. Because of unexpected events, people are not always able to do what they had promised. But when this becomes a life-style, something that happens repeatedly, then the Christian leader demonstrates a characteristic of unfaithfulness. This must be avoided at all costs. When people loose confidence in their leader, serious consequences result. When you speak, be sure to be faithful to your word.

A third reason why is integrity is so important is this:

(3) Integrity makes Christian leadership possible: Christian leaders must live the truth and tell the truth because that is the only way to develop a community and ensure confidence in your leadership. 'When we can no longer depend on one another to do what we said we would do, the future becomes an undefined nightmare.'[49]

> Community is held together by truth. Imagine a community – just imagine! – a community in which everybody expects leaders to lie wherever a lie serves them, when teachers are expected to pretend to know what they don't know, when religious leaders are expected to be hypocritical, when the media is expected to distort the truth, when sales persons are expected to misrepresent their products, when spouses are expected to cheat. In such an environment, no community is possible.[50]

CONCLUSION

We conclude that integrity is in the interest of everyone. No one can escape the reality. God is genuine, truthful and faithful; and he commands his servants to reflect his likeness. In the end, the integrity is to the advantage of everyone.

So why do so many leaders fail to live with integrity? This may be due in part because those who serve in public positions often develop a 'performance-oriented piety' that 'cares more about what things look like than what is true.' In public we try to win approval from people rather than from God.

Roberta Hestenes, minister-at-large for World Vision, who made that observation stated above, says that she has found three simple 'habits of the heart' that help strengthen her desire and ability to maintain inner integrity while engaged in public ministry. First, is to commit herself to a 'small covenant group that practices prayer and accountability.' Second, she has learned the discipline of secret service and secret giving. The third secret is to memorise 1 Corinthians 13 and 'pray it into mind, heart and life regularly.'[51]

Integrity is part of holy living but holiness is much more. Holiness includes purity. A holy person is 'pure in heart.' *Purity* is the next topic in the following chapter.

SEARCHING THE SCRIPTURE WITH APPLICATION

1. Read Ge 20:1-18. (The Hebrew word, *tom*, in v 5 is translated 'integrity' in the *AV* and 'clear conscience' in *NIV*). Discuss the consequences of Abraham's lack of 'integrity' before this Gentile (Philistine) who acted with integrity. What are the effects of Christian leaders without integrity today?
2. Discuss the characteristics of a moral chameleon, an opportunist, a hypocrite, a weak-willed person and a self-deceiver.
   How do these negative examples of integrity help you understand the meaning of 'integrity'?
3. Do a Bible study on God's integrity. Why should God's integrity affect our own behaviour as Christian leaders?
4. Study the following Proverbs on lying (6:17; 10:18; 12:19,22; 13:5; 17:7; 21:6; 26:28). How does each proverb help you understand God's attitude toward lying?
5. Discuss the ways in which Christian leaders should manifest integrity (being genuine, truthful and faithful).
   In what ways do they sometimes fail in being genuine, truthful and faithful?
6. Read Eph 4:17-32. What practical steps should a Christian leader take to develop greater integrity, based on the teaching of this passage and from your own observations in life?

Endnotes

[1] Pr 19:1
[2] Brown 1983;
Wigram 1980
[3] American Heritage Dictionary: 2000
[4] Benjamin 1990:47ff
[5] Mt 23:1-3
[6] Benjamin 1990:51
[7] Random House College Dict., 1988
[8] Engstrom 1987:7
[9] Erickson 2002:316f
[10] Jn 17:3
[11] Jer 10:5-10
[12] Erickson 2002:316
[13] Smedes 1991:5
[14] Jer 15:29
[15] Heb 6:18
[16] Jn 8:44
[17] Dt 7:9
[18] Jos 23:14
[19] Ps 36:5
[20] La 3:23
[21] Nu 23:19
[22] Eph 4:24
[23] Tit 2:7
[24] 1 Ch 29:17
[25] Ac 12:9
[26] 1 Jn 5:21
[27] Gal 4:8
[28] Jos 24:14
[29] 2 Co 8:8
[30] Ex 20:16
[31] Pr 14:5
[32] Pr 12:17
[33] Mt 5:34,37 NIV
[34] Eph 4:25 NIV
[35] Pr 12:22
[36] Pr 19:5
[37] Rev 21:8
[38] Pr 25:14 AV
[39] Pr 13:5
[40] Pr 10:18
[41] Eph 4:31
[42] Eph 4:15
[43] 1 Co 2:11
[44] Ex 1:19-20
[45] 1 Sa 16:1,2
[46] 2 Ki 6:14-20
[47] 1 Co 4:2
[48] Mt 25:23
[49] Engstrom 1987:2
[50] Smedes 1991: 11
[51] Hestenes 2001:41

23 PURITY

'Keep yourself pure.'[1]

One of the three greatest reasons for failing in ministry is impurity.[1]

In order to avoid crashing in ministry, Paul advised Timothy, 'Keep yourself pure.' Every Christian leader who is 'holy to the Lord' must take concrete steps to keep pure in order to please the holy God and to be effective in ministry. Young leaders, fresh out of training, are often faced with rejection by the elders because of their youth and lack of experience. Paul had good advice for 'young' Timothy: 'Let no one despise you for your youth, but set the believers an example in speech, in conduct, in love, in faith, and *in purity*.'[2] So the question arises, what is purity?

Purity

The word, *purity,* is closely associated with *holiness* and *integrity*, which we have studied previously. The elements of purity[3] include:

1. Freedom from an alien element: That which is pure is not mixed with an alien substance. Pure milk is not mixed with water; pure petrol is not mixed with kerosene. The new Jerusalem will have streets of 'pure gold' and a river flowing with 'pure water.' In this sense purity is closely linked with the root meaning of integrity as we have seen. It is genuine and real, pure through and through.

2. Cleanness; freedom from dirt or foulness: That is, something that is not dirty, foul, filthy, unclean or impure. Food that is clean is pure because it is free from dirt and contamination. Pure air is clean and free from pollution of smoke or gaseous fumes.

[1]After years of observation and reflection, I have concluded that the three basic reasons why people fail in ministry are: **lust of the flesh** (immorality, impurity), **lust of the eyes** (greed, stealing and misappropriation of funds), and the **pride of life** (pride – struggles for power, position and prestige).

3. Freedom from guilt or the defilement of sin: Whereas the above two elements of purity pertain to substances of this world, this third element is religious or spiritual. Purity in this sense means innocence, chastity, and purity of life. Impurity is therefore to be unchaste, obscene, unclean, lewd and impure in ideas, language or conduct. To be pure is to be free from the defilement of sin. A spiritually pure person is holy.

The word for purity in the Greek (*hagneia*) is clearly related to the word for holy (*hagios*). The root for both words is *hag.* Holiness, as we have seen, refers to that which is set apart from the world and unto God; hence, a holy person is separate from the world's defilements and shares God's holiness.

The concept of *purity* (to be *clean*) in the Old Testament often refers to ceremonial purity with rites and ceremonies intended to make things and people externally pure (clean).[4] These Levitical ceremonies were shadows and types, intended to teach people the importance of spiritual purity.

When referring to purity in the highest sense, the Bible usually refers to separation from fleshly sins which defile both the body and spirit.[5] Young women are told to 'love their husbands and children, to be self-controlled and *pure*...,'[6] clearly referring to sexual purity.

Joseph is a pristine example of a *holy person* who kept himself *pure.* When Potiphar's wife tempted Joseph to lie with her, he responded, 'How then can I do this great wickedness and *sin against God*?'[7] As a true son of Abraham, Joseph was separate from unholy fellowship and devoted to the Lord. Since God had laid down strict laws concerning the sanctity of the marriage bond, Joseph would not defile himself by becoming impure.

Impurity

The seventh commandment is terse: 'You shall not commit adultery.'[8]

Broad sense of this commandment: Broadly speaking, God forbids in this commandment any impure sexual relationship, including fornication and homosexuality.[9]

Fornication is generally understood as voluntary sexual intercourse between an *unmarried* man and woman, though the English word is broad and can include all kinds of sexual immorality. In the Old Testament this was represented by the Hebrew word, *zanah,* and most often used of harlots and prostitutes.[10] It also was used metaphorically of Israel 'playing the harlot' when she went a whoring after other gods.[11]

In the New Testament, sexual intercourse between two unmarried people is clearly forbidden. The Greek word, *porneia*, refers to 'every kind of unlawful sexual intercourse,' including prostitution, unchastity, and fornication.[12] Thayer vigorously asserts that *porneia* must be understood as 'sexual immorality' in general in many New Testament passages.[13] 1 Corinthians 6:12f must be understood in the light of the Greek culture which regarded sexual immorality lightly; 'the heathen' frequently indulged in it. Hence, Christian converts tended to be lenient toward this sin as well. Paul clearly distinguishes between adultery and fornication.[14] The New Testament stands against this impurity of fornication.[15]

> But sexual immorality and all impurity or covetousness must not even be named among you, as is proper among saints.[16]

> Put to death therefore what is earthly in you: sexual immorality, impurity, passion, evil desire, and covetousness, which is idolatry. On account of these the wrath of God is coming.[17]

> For this is the will of God, your sanctification: that you abstain from sexual immorality, that each one of you know how to control his own body in holiness and honor, not in the passion of lust like the Gentiles who do not know God…[18]

Narrow sense of this commandment: Although sexual purity in general is commanded in Scripture, the focus of the seventh commandment and most of the Old Testament is on adultery, the sexual intercourse of a man with another man's wife.[19]

The reason for this emphasis is the sanctity of marriage. God is the designer and planner of marriage.[20] Genesis 2:24,25 relates the sexual union of man and woman in marriage to God's directive will. The physical union of husband and wife is for the specific purpose of procreation of the human race,[21] though the Bible does not restrict the purpose to the birth of children. Marital faithfulness is obligatory and any infidelity brought divine judgement.[22] This judgement includes the emotional pain, fighting and inner stress that accompanies the breaking of this intimate union. 'He who commits adultery lacks sense; he who does it destroys himself.'[23]

This is such an important issue because marriage and the family are foundational in society. The integrity of the marriage must be guarded with total commitment. Whenever and wherever marriage breaks down throughout a society with adultery and divorce, that society will begin to crumble.

So sacred is the marriage relationship that God compares his relationship with his people in terms of the bonds of holy matrimony. Both Old Testament[24] and New Testament[25] describe the unfaithfulness of God's people in idolatry to harlotry.

Deeper sense of this commandment: Our Lord deepened the spiritual meaning of the Ten Commandments in his Sermon on the Mount. He went beyond the literal letter of the Law and filled it with deeper, spiritual meaning. 'You have heard it was said, "You shall not commit adultery." But I say to you that everyone who looks at a woman with lustful intent has already committed adultery with her in his heart.'[26] Needless to say, these words apply to wives as well as husbands.

The Message makes this graphic paraphrase:

> 'You know the next commandment pretty well, too: "Don't go to bed with another's spouse." But don't think you've preserved your virtue simply by staying out of bed. Your heart can be corrupted by lust even quicker than your body. Those leering looks you think nobody notices – they also corrupt.'

Hendriksen expresses it well. This man is 'looking, gazing, staring at a woman in order to lust after her, to possess and dominate her completely, to use her for his own pleasure.'[27] As Christian leaders we dare not limit the seventh commandment to its literal meaning – committing adultery physically with another person. A lustful desiring of the heart is sinful and dangerous.

We should also understand this positively from Christ's perspective. God demands of his people that they be absolutely faithful in their marital covenant. That extends to the thought life, not merely the physical sexual act.

Entertaining lustful thoughts and then acting on those thoughts reduces human beings to mere animals. Holy matrimony for men and women, who are made in the image of God, far surpasses animal drives. Chickens and rabbits don't need marriage to procreate. Jeremiah describes the animal drives in his day when he said: 'When I fed them to the full, they committed adultery and trooped to the houses of whores. They were well-fed, lusty stallions, each neighing for his neighbor's wife. Shall I not punish them for these things?'[28]

A distinction must be made between temptation and sin. Temptation is the entrance of the thought in one's mind; sin is the entertainment and enjoyment of the thought. As Martin Luther observed, 'You cannot prevent a bird from landing on your head; but you can prevent it from building a nest.'[29] Living in a toxic society where sensuality is on TV, in advertisements, and on people's tongues, one may experience thoughts and ideas rushing into the mind. The question is, 'What do you do with those thoughts?'

'God's Word still calls to us, insisting that for those who are his people there can be but one standard for marriage – absolute fidelity. The one word that sums up the Seventh Commandment is PURITY – purity of thought and of deed in sexual relations.'[30]

Sexual Addiction

Some actually become addicted to lust. *Lust* for a woman (or man) is a relentless sensual desire for someone who is not your spouse. If not confronted and dealt with, that lust will ultimately lead to sexual addiction. Lust becomes attached to fantasies which at first can be managed, but if left uncontrolled, those fantasies become obsessions which are addictions. Beware!

How does sexual addiction develop?

Laaser uses the metaphor of a building to describe the process which leads to sexual addiction. Following are the building blocks for sexual addiction.

Sexual fantasy: This is the cornerstone of the building. Sexual stimulation is in the eye, both the natural and the mental seeing. The person is stimulated by looking at certain types of people or body parts – their appearance, age, dress, gender or personality. As the addict fantasizes, the desirable person becomes 'all-caring, all-attractive, perfectly nurturing, and perfectly sexual.'

> Many dangers accompany the entertainment of fantasies. A world of fantasy becomes more powerful and more compelling than reality. Lustful fantasy makes reality drab and uneventful by comparison…Lust is damaging to a marriage because the partner is less perfect than the fantasy. Minor faults or defects are magnified by comparison. The lust-prone spouse is easily angered and is dissatisfied because neither self nor others can sustain in reality the standard portrayed in the fantasies.[31]

Pornography: Magazines, videos, TV, movies and in these days, the Internet, are avenues for viewing pornography. Nudity and sexual acts stimulate the mind with unhealthy, immoral and sinful desires.

Masturbation: For the sexual addict, masturbation is a preoccupation done repetitively, some doing this as many as twenty times in a day. Of course, masturbation is always accompanied by sexual fantasies.

These buildings blocks form a cycle. 'Pornography stimulates fantasy. Fantasy needs to be expressed. Masturbation allows a "release" of that need.'[32]

Sexual addiction usually moves beyond self-absorption of fantasy and masturbation. Sexual fantasies *may* lead to sex with consenting partners or with prostitutes. Sexual addiction *always will.* However, you can be sure of one thing. Whenever someone falls into this sin of fornication or adultery, this has been preceded by unconfessed and uncontrolled fantasy and lustful desires. The act follows the desire.

Do Christian leaders fantasize with lustful desires?

Speaking of the American scene, Laaser says that sexual addiction among pastors is 'a widespread problem.' In a survey of pastors by the *Leadership* magazine, they found that among the 300 pastors who responded, 23% said they had done something sexually inappropriate with someone other than their spouse. Of those pastors 12% had engaged in sexual intercourse with people other than their spouse. Prominent televangelists, such as Jim Bakker and Jimmy Swaggart, have been disgraced and removed from public ministry because of sexual immorality.[33]

How widespread is this problem among your Churches or in your area? No doubt many are struggling who have not yet fallen before the public eye. Friends of the pastor, who may be struggling with this hidden sin, may need to be observant in order to help through prayer, counseling or otherwise. Laaser suggests several warning signs that indicate a Christian leader may be struggling with sexual addiction.[34]

- *Trouble in the pastor's marriage:* The spouse may seem depressed or angry. Rumours of unhappiness may float around.
- *Counseling at strange times and places:* Whenever the person counsels someone of another gender at night or behind closed doors, or makes frequent house visits – that may signal a problem.
- *The pastor spends lots of time alone:* He may seem distant and withdrawn because of guilt, shame or fear of getting caught.
- *Mood swings:* The person fluctuates wildly in his moods; being depressed at times and then becoming excited and giddy; sometimes doing lots of work and other times doing little.
- *Use of sexual humour:* A person preoccupied with sexual fantasies will often tease or joke with sexual overtones.
- *The pastor visits questionable places:* A sexual addict may be seen frequenting places where pornography is available or spending inordinate amount of time on the Internet.

A Christian leader may not yet be preoccupied with sexual fantasies. But anyone who entertains sensual thoughts needs to follow Jesus' advice.

Importance of Purity

Why is purity so important?

The reasons are similar to the reasons why integrity is so important.

God is pure (holy), separated from the defilement of his fallen, rebellious creatures. Habakkuk prays to God: 'You are of *purer eyes* than to see evil and cannot look at wrong.'[35] Because God is pure, all his words are pure.[36]

Therefore, God commands his people to be pure. Without total purity no one can see the Lord. 'Blessed are the *pure in heart*, for they shall see God.'[37] Fellowship and intimacy with God are impossible without purity. David asks, 'Who shall ascend the hill of the LORD? And who shall stand in his holy place? He who has clean hands and a *pure heart*...'[38] 'Nothing unclean'[39] will be permitted in the New Jerusalem. Speaking of Christ's return, John says: 'Everyone who thus hopes in him *purifies himself as he is pure*.'[40]

Christian leaders must engage in the personal discipline of growing in purity. If we desire to be an effective leader in our shamelessly impure societies, we must learn to live with a pure conscience. 'Fewer things distort, distract, and disarrange a well-ordered ministry like an impure heart. It leaves us feeling defeated when we have to continue to look victorious to those around us. Our hearts scream the charge, "Hypocrite!" at our soul...Impurity breeds fear and focuses a shepherd's attention on self-protection.'[41]

Every Bible student, however, knows full well that no one can be pure in God's presence on the basis of his own purity because our human best is impure before God – mixed with impure motives and imperfections. Isaiah comments, 'We have all become like one who is unclean, and all our righteous deeds are like a polluted garment.'[42] As a result, 'None is righteous [in themselves], no, not one.'[43] Only by grace through faith is one declared righteous when the person is clothed with the righteousness of Christ.[44]

Nevertheless, we must say: unless there is evidence of purity in one's life, there is no evidence of the new birth. Unless the Christian leader is growing in his hatred of the impure and thirsting after righteousness, the stage is being set for a serious fall in ministry. Mark my word!! The purpose of this book is to help you know the secret of 'the making of a Christian leader.' It is an ongoing process which takes commitment. So many leaders have fallen into immorality that we can say with confidence: if you do not take this issue seriously and address the areas of impurity in your life, you are preparing for failure.

What advice can be given to avoid falling into sexual immorality?

When Jesus spoke of sexual immorality, he prescribed a harsh treatment. 'If your right eye causes you to sin, tear it out and throw it away. For it is better that you lose one of your members than that your whole body be thrown into hell.'[45] Jesus of course did not mean this to be taken literally. A blind person is perfectly capable of sexual fantasy. What Jesus is saying is: 'Take this problem seriously or it will lead you to hell!' Indeed, if anyone entertains sexual lusts with accompanying fantasies and falls into a habit of sexual preoccupation, the warning lights should flash and major steps taken to deal with the problem!

What steps should be taken?

1. *Be honest with yourself.* Admit your problem. Don't deny it. Unless you can be honest with yourself, there is no hope.[46]

2. *Recognise that you are in a spiritual battle and prepare for warfare.*[47] Your old, carnal nature is drawn to sensual pleasure that is contrary to God.

3. *Repent, confess and draw near to God through prayer and the meditation on God's Word.* Nothing strengthens the inner man to resist sin like the Word of God with the empowering of the Holy Spirit.[48]

4. *Stop fantasizing!* This may not be easy. Even as a drug addict experiences struggles and withdrawal symptoms, someone who has conditioned himself to respond with sexual fantasies when aroused by certain sights, times or smells, will struggle. In the name of Jesus and by the power of the Holy Spirit *you must* and *you can* 'take captive every thought to make it obedient to Christ.'[49]

5. *Stop feeding those fantasies.* Starve your lustful desires; don't feed them. Stop listening to music with suggestive lyrics – that may include most pop songs on the radio. Stop watching TV programmes with sexual innuendos. Stop it completely! Satan is invading people's minds through TV in ways that are unbelievable. Harvard University did a study of TV and found that 70% of all allusions to intercourse on TV in America involve unmarried couples or prostitutes. The homosexual agenda is infiltrating TV. Violence is pervasive. If you think that TV cannot adversely affect your mind, you are out of your mind!

6. *Seek a prayer partner* with whom you can share and to whom you will be accountable. If necessary, seek professional counseling. Do *everything* necessary to defeat this demon or it will defeat you.

CONCLUSION

Without purity, no one can be holy. But holiness includes more than integrity and purity. It includes honesty – keeping the eighth commandment. Chapter 24 focuses on the necessity of Christian leaders being honest.

SEARCHING THE SCRIPTURE WITH APPLICATION

1. Discuss the meaning of *purity* and why purity is so important for Christian leaders.
2. Do a word study of *fornication* and *adultery* with their meanings in as many languages as you can. Are there clear distinctions in your mother tongue between *fornication* and *adultery*?
3. Read the following Scriptures and write down the various things you learn about God's attitude toward sexual immorality: Gal 5:16-21; Eph 5:3-7; Col 3:1-11; 1 Th 4:3-8.
4. What is the connection between 'lust' and 'sexual immorality'? See Jas 1:14, 15.
5. From your observations, how serious is this problem of impurity among Christian leaders, including those in the local congregation?
6. Discuss those elements in the culture and society which contribute toward sexual impurity?
7. What elements in the lifestyle and worldview of a Christian leader need to be addressed in order to eliminate sexual immorality?
8. What practical steps should be taken to follow Jesus' advice to 'gouge out the eye' and 'cut off the hand' to deal with adultery in the heart?
9. What steps will you personally take to become 'pure in heart'?

Endnotes

[1] 1 Ti 5:22
[2] 1 Ti 4:12
[3] Webster's Dictionary Unabridged: 1959
[4] cf. Lev 13-15
[5] 1 Co 6:18-20
[6] Tit 3:5
[7] Ge 39:9
[8] Ex 20:15
[9] Jude 7
[10] Ge 38:24
[11] Ex 34:15f
[12] Bauer 1957
[13] Thayer 1983:533
[14] Gal 5:19
[15] Ro 1:29; 1 Co 5:1; 6:13,18; 7:2
[16] Eph 5:3
[17] Col 3:5
[18] 1 Th 4:3f
[19] Dt 5:18; Lev 20:10
[20] Ge 2:18ff
[21] Ge 1:28
[22] Lev 20:10
[23] Pr 6:32
[24] Hos 4:9-19
[25] Rev 17:1-6
[26] Mt 5:27-28
[27] Hendriksen 1973:302
[28] Jer 5:7b-9
[29] Known by common knowledge.
[30] Honeycutt 1966:90
[31] Walters 1985:87,88
[32] Laaser 1992:29
[33] Laaser 1992:63f
[34] Laaser 1992:56f, 75
[35] Hab 1:13
[36] Ps 12:6
[37] Mt 5:8
[38] Ps 24:3,4
[39] Re 21:27
[40] 1 Jn 3:3
[41] Stowell 1997:190
[42] Isa 64:6
[43] Ro 3:10b
[44] Ro 3:21-26; Gal 3:6-14
[45] Mt 5:29
[46] Ps 32:1-5
[47] Eph 6:10-18
[48] Ps 119:9-11
[49] 2 Co 10:5

24
HONESTY

'You shall not steal.'[1]

One of the three greatest temptations for Christian leaders is dishonesty.[1]

Christian leaders are particularly vulnerable to dishonesty for several reasons. *First,* the pastors and elders handle the money contributed by the Church. They may collude and share some of the contributions for personal needs. Excuses are many: pastors are not paid well and they only intend to borrow the money and pay it back later. *Secondly,* there is lack of transparency and accountability with safeguards. Counting money and paying bills are done behind closed doors with no proper report of expenditures and income ever provided for the people. Neither is there an external audit. *Thirdly,* some Christian leaders mix their own personal money with the money belonging to the Christian organization and confusion results. While the initial purpose is innocent, because of the absence of accountability, the waters become murky.

The Hebrews had their own problems with dishonesty as well, because we all share in Adam's fallen nature. In the Old Testament a common form of dishonesty was using false balances in dishonest business deals.[2]

> You shall not have in your bag two kinds of weights, a large and a small. You shall not have in your house two kinds of measures, a large and a small. A full and fair weight you shall have, a full and fair measure you shall have, that your days may be long in the land that the LORD your God is giving you. For all who do such things, all who act dishonestly, are an abomination to the LORD your God.[3]

Honesty is grounded in the very nature of a holy God. To be holy, we must be honest in every aspect of our lives. God demands honesty!

---

[1]See footnote on page 175.

Dishonesty

What does the Bible teach concerning dishonesty?

The eighth commandment is brief: 'You shall not steal.'

Dishonesty includes lying, cheating and stealing. Stealing is taking anything that belongs to another and appropriating it to yourself.[4] In contrast, *honesty* includes integrity, sincerity and truthfulness. An honest person has a *good reputation* because he is *upright* and *sincere*. He is free from *deceit* or *fraud*. Thus an honest person does not tell lies and does not steal. He does not use deceit or trickery for unfair and dishonest gain.

Implicit in this command for 'not stealing' is the right of private property. Nowhere in Scripture do we read of communal ownership where everyone owns their share of everything. Not even the kings in Israel with kingly authority had the right to take what did not belong to them. See the example of Ahab taking the vineyard of Naboth.[5] Though king Ahab was willing to pay a good price, Naboth refused to sell his land because it had family significance. So 'the little man' in Israel refused the king's desire to take what belonged to him.

The ultimate owner of the land was not the individual Israelite; the owner was God.[6] The Israelites only held the land in trust. The land belonged to the Lord[7] because God had conquered the land and had given it to the children of Israel.[8] Even the cattle and wild life belong to God.[9] 'Wealth belongs to God. The starting point of this ethic is the fact that wealth belongs to God.'[10] It is God's decision to give or withhold.

Therefore, the land is sacred, even holy, because it belongs to God. 'Personal property assumed a degree of sanctity, although on the human level, it was set aside for the use of a particular person. That which was absolutely holy because it belonged to God came to share characteristics of holiness as men served as stewards of that property.'[11]

These truths on the ownership of land and private property gave rise to penalties on those who took what was not rightfully theirs. Since all property is essentially God's possession, God is the only one who has the right to give to individuals. But no one has the right to steal. To steal from people not only breaks the second greatest commandment (loving your neighbour as yourself) but breaks the first and greatest commandment (loving God with all one's heart). Stealing from others is taking what God has given to another and this is a violation of one's supreme devotion to God.

All sins seem to grow in poisoned clusters. No doubt anyone who steals has first coveted those things. To cover over the stealing, there is lying and deceit. To steal is to break the law of loving your neighbour as yourself. You cannot break one commandment without breaking a number of them together.

Just as the practice of lying and sexual immorality will keep one out of heaven; so no one who practices stealing will inherit the kingdom of God.[12]

How is dishonesty practiced today?

Dishonesty is practiced in many ways by Christian leaders, some very explicit, others more subtle and less noticed.

Obvious examples of stealing are the handling of God's money and putting some in the pocket for personal use. Oh yes, there are excuses. 'I need this for transportation in ministry.' 'The Church has not paid my salary for the past two months.' 'I have the urgent need of finding fees for my daughter in school.' The excuses go on and on. No doubt these are genuine needs. But when money is taken without proper accounting or proper reporting, that is stealing.

Some leaders may 'borrow' money, intending to repay it. But over time they either forget or find difficulty in paying it back. The sin is not in borrowing the money but in borrowing it without official permission and proper accountability. Without transparency any handling of money is open to abuse.

A less obvious form of stealing is laziness. When someone is employed as a secretary, the employer expects a full return of labour. Coming to work late, leaving early, and taking extra long tea breaks, reading the paper instead of working, becoming busy only when the supervisor is present is plain stealing by cheating. The pastor has no supervisor, no clock to punch, no boss to report to – his honesty depends entirely on his personal integrity. To cheat by not giving a full day's labour is stealing.

Shoplifting by taking little things from the shop or market is done in America. Do Christian leaders ever do that in Africa? Cheating on paying taxes by not reporting all the income is a form of stealing. Being careless with something that is borrowed and returning it damaged or spoiled, or never returning it, is dishonesty. Jumping the queue (line) in the post office or government office is depriving someone else of his or her rightful place. By trying to 'save' time for yourself, you are actually stealing from others who will 'loose' time. There are scores of ways to cheat and take from others what does not rightfully belong to you.

One major form of stealing is the most serious – stealing from God by not giving him what is rightfully his. Malachi pronounces a curse on those who do not give their tithes and offerings to the Lord.[13] This is shocking, isn't it? But it is biblical. We need to be honest with our fellow mankind and also with God.

A Biblical View of Wealth

Old Testament view of wealth: It is true that the Old Testament generally sees wealth as a blessing; it is given by God.[14] But even before Christ the prophets warned of the dangers of wealth. Moses warned that when the children of Israel would enter the Promised Land and become rich, they would become proud, self-reliant and turn away from the Lord.[15] Indeed, we find the same true today. Few powerful and rich truly love the Lord with all their hearts.[16] Riches are two sided – a blessing but also a temptation. Righteous living is to be preferred to riches. '*Riches do not profit in the day of wrath, but righteousness delivers from death.*'[17] '*Better is a little with the fear of the LORD than great treasure and trouble with it.*'[18]

Many warnings were given in the Old Testament about the dangers of wealth. There is vanity in seeking riches for it can disappear as quickly as it comes. '*Do not toil to acquire wealth... When your eyes light on it, it is gone, for suddenly it sprouts wings, flying like an eagle toward heaven.*'[19] '*He who loves money will not be satisfied with money, nor he who loves wealth with his income; this also is vanity.*'[20]

Perhaps the wisest prayer on money was offered by Solomon. "*Give me neither poverty nor riches; feed me with the food that is needful for me, lest I be full and deny you and say, 'Who is the LORD?' or lest I be poor and steal and profane the name of my God.*"[21] Tragically, Solomon did not follow his own advice. In his wealth he forgot the LORD who gave his wealth in the first place. The consequences for his offspring and his country were disastrous.

New Testament view of wealth: Jesus spoke a great deal about riches and always negatively. Ellul surprises us with this claim: 'Incontestably, in the New Testament wealth is condemned. To my knowledge there is not one text that justifies it.'[22] While it is true, as the Old Testament recognised, that riches may be a gift from God and a blessing to those enriched thereby; more often, however, wealth lures God's children away from their devotion to the Lord.[23]

A pivotal teaching on wealth is found in the Sermon on the Mount.[24] The Authorized Version renders 6:24 with the familiar words: '*You cannot serve God and mammon.*' *Mammon* is an Aramaic word which means 'money' or 'wealth.' Jesus personifies 'money' in this text and treats it as something of a god. *The Message* translates this, '*You can't worship two gods at once. Loving one god, you'll end up hating the other. Adoration of one feeds contempt for the other. <u>You can't worship God and Money both</u>.*'[25]

Money has an enticing power that acts like a god. People want money because of what money offers them, but to their disillusionment, they never can get enough wealth. As Solomon learned centuries ago, '*He who loves money will not be satisfied with money.*' Somehow those with some money always find that they need just a little more because wealth cannot satisfy the human heart. Yet *Money* is like a god that entices people to seek more and in the process lures them away from trust and primary allegiance to God. So Jesus warns, '*Take care, and be on your guard against all covetousness, for one's life does not consist in the abundance of his possessions.*'[26]

Jesus taught and experience has demonstrated that, '*Where your treasure is, there your heart will be also.*'[27] Therefore, as Christian leaders and servants of our Lord Jesus, we must face this challenge head on. What treasures are we seeking? What riches are we saving? Is our preoccupation on earthly wealth or on eternal riches? Jesus advises his disciples that they should not be preoccupied with money, riches and wealth for that is what people without God do. '*But seek first the kingdom of God and his righteousness, and all these things will be added to you.*'[28]

Practical Advice for Christian Leaders

This is a very practical problem for those in ministry. On the one hand, God has given us bodies that need feeding, clothing and housing; children who need medical care and education; and a ministry which requires transport, books and supplies. Poverty is a real curse which can make people feel helpless and lack self-esteem. While Christian leaders may recognise the vanity of chasing money, the plain truth remains: Christian leaders need money to live on.

On the other hand, money has been a problem to Christian leaders from the beginning of the Church. Paul's counsel to Timothy and the Churches he shepherded stands for all time. '*There is great gain in godliness with contentment, for we brought nothing into the world, and we cannot take anything out of the world. But if we have food and clothing, with these we will be content. But those who desire to be rich fall into temptation, into a snare, into many senseless and harmful desires that plunge people into ruin and destruction. For the love of money is a root of all kinds of evils. It is through this craving that some have wandered away from the faith and pierced themselves with many things*'[29] [and we may add: some Christian leaders have become preoccupied with material wealth, left the ministry or fallen into dishonesty, bringing reproach on the Lord and on themselves.].

Following is some advice to which you may add additional insight.

Develop a spirit of contentment:[30] This is biblical and practical! Life lived with dissatisfaction and discontent is not worth living. Focus on God, wife and children, blessings and promises of God. Don't compare yourself with others. Say 'no' to covetousness. Be who you are and what God has made you to be.

Grow in your relationship with God: Find your joy in him. Learn to trust him. Paul learned contentment in all circumstances – and he learned he could trust God for all his needs.[31]

Distinguish between needs and wants: Needs include food and clothing; wants are certain kinds of food and clothing for which you long. Needs include an education for your children; wants are the kind of school or its location. God promises to provide our needs.[32] He encourages us to pray for our desires – and God often does provide but not always.[33]

Be transparent and accountable: Always handle money with transparency and accountability. Whatever your situation may be, never, ever allow yourself to get into a situation where people can accuse you of mishandling money. Never handle money alone. Be fully transparent and public.

Seek God's will in the ministry: Learn to discern the will of God in ministry. Quitting the Lord's work is not an option; forsaking your call can never be acceptable. But a Christian leader must care for his family and it may just be possible that your present ministry does not afford you this opportunity. Be in prayer. Distinguish between covetousness and concern to meet needs. Perhaps you need to do some 'tent making.' But never take what is not yours.

CONCLUSION

To be holy, a Christian leader must be truthful, pure and honest; even more important, leaders must be *pure in heart*. Holiness manifested outwardly is always generated by inward purity. *Purity in Heart* is our next topic.

SEARCHING THE SCRIPTURE WITH APPLICATION

1. Do you ever become envious of the rich? Read Ps 73:1-21. Why should we not be envious of the rich, according to this Psalm?
2. According to Ecc 5:10, what is another reason why riches are not rewarding? Discuss examples of this that you have seen.
3. Why do riches gained through dishonesty not have lasting value? Read Jer 17:11. Share some observations or experiences related to this.
4. The Hebrews used various dishonest means to become rich. Read Neh 5:1-13; Jer 22:13-19; Pr 21:6-7; 28:8. Discuss the various ways in which people in your community become rich through dishonesty.
5. 'Better is the little that the righteous has than the abundance of many wicked' (Ps 37:16).

Discuss the ways in which this is true.

6. Study 1 Ti 6:6-10. Discuss the various ideas in this paragraph that should help a Christian leader develop a holy attitude toward money.
7. Read Jas 5:1-6. Discuss the reasons why the wealth of these rich people will vanish.
8. Study Mt 6:19-24. Where does Jesus advise us to store our treasure? How does one lay up treasures in heaven?
9. Money is a medium of exchange that is neutral in value, just as food and possessions are used for bartering. Riches are not evil in themselves. Why then does the Bible take such a negative view towards wealth?
10. What lessons should the Christian leader learn from all of this?
11. The Balanda of Sudan say, 'God is a great eye. He sees everything in the world.' How should this truth affect our attitude toward dishonesty?
12. Reflect on your own life as to what changes should be made.

Endnotes

1 Ex 20:15
2 Lev 19:35-37; Pr 11:1; 16:11
3 Dt 25:13-16
4 Random House College Dict., 1988
5 1 Ki 21:1ff
6 Isa 8:8
7 Hos 9:3
8 Jos 23:3,10; 24:11-13
9 Ps 50:10-12
10 Ellul 1984:43
11 Honeycutt 1966:98
12 1 Co 6:9,10
13 Mal 3:8,9
14 1 Ch 29:6-17; Pr 3: 9f: 10:15; Ecc 10:19
15 Dt 6:10-12; 8:10-18
16 1 Co 1:26-31
17 Pr 11:4
18 Pr 15:16
19 Pr 23:4,5
20 Ecc 5:10
21 Pr 30:7-9
22 Ellul 1984:35
23 Mk 4:19
24 Mt 6:19-34
25 Mt 6:24 *The Message*
26 Lk 12:15
27 Mt 6:21
28 Mt 6:33
29 1Ti 6:4-10
30 Heb 13:5
31 Php 4:11-13
32 Php 4:19
33 Ps 37:4

25
THE PURE IN HEART

'Blessed are the pure in heart
for they shall see God.'[1]

Nothing is more important in life than your *heart*.

The heart is where everything begins. I will never forget my first real shock as a small boy. The father of a good friend of mine, a pastor in the same denomination where my father served as pastor, suddenly requested his 'bishop' permission to divorce his wife and marry a married woman in his congregation. Such an idea was bizarre. Anyone in his right mind would know that the 'bishop' would never permit such a thing; furthermore, a pastor divorcing his wife and marrying a woman in his own congregation? Nothing but crazy! He was out of his mind.

Indeed! The whole bizarre incident came straight from the fantasies and delusions of his mind. He was not thinking straight, let alone thinking God's thoughts. He was in another world of his own making – the world of his mind.

This taught me an important lesson in life. Whenever you discover shocking behaviour of someone, whether it is sexual immorality or theft or any other moral deficiency, always remember this: it was preceded by thoughts and desires entertained and nurtured by the heart.

The Heart

An insightful African proverb states, 'As the wound inflames the finger, so a thought can inflame the mind.' Careful attention must be given to the care of the mind lest a thought inflames the mind, to the point that the thought life is out of touch with reality and disobedient to the Word of God.

This is the meaning of James' words: '*What causes quarrels and what causes fights among you? Is it not this, that your passions are at war within you? You desire and do not have, so you murder. You covet and cannot obtain, so you fight and quarrel.*'[2] There you have it. The fights, quarrels, and murders all begin from within the person with his thoughts, emotions and desires, all springing from the inner heart.

What does the Bible mean by the *heart*?

In the Old Testament *heart* (*leb*) is used most of the time in a figurative sense of 'the innermost part of a man.'[3] This is the 'inner man' as opposed to the 'outer.'[4] The heart is the seat of the mind, the will and the emotions. The *mind* (heart) remembers, considers, thinks and reflects; the *emotions* and passions (heart) feel joy and gladness, sorrow and vexation; the *will* (heart) resolves, decides and inclines to do things.[5] The heart may also refer to the conscience or the moral character of a person.

The New Testament use of heart (*kardia*) reflects the Old Testament use and not the classical Greek understanding. It is the centre of the inner life of man and the source of all functions of the soul and spirit. 'Even more strongly than the Septuagint [the Greek translation of the Hebrew Old Testament], *kardia* concentrates on the heart as the main organ of psychic and spiritual life, the place in man at which God bears witness to Himself.'[6] The *heart* is the central place where God meets a person and where our faith and obedience to God have their roots. The heart determines our conduct.

Like the Old Testament, the heart (*kardia*) in the New Testament is the seat or source of understanding, thought and reflection (the *mind*); the seat of feelings and emotions, such as joy, pain, sorrow and love (the *emotions*); and the seat of the will which decides and resolves (the *will*).[7] Thus the heart is the centre of our personality which includes the mind, will and emotions. Somewhere I read that A.T. Robertson had analysed the use of *kardia* in the New Testament and concluded it was used about equally to refer to the mind, emotions and will; and also to the inner life in general.

Why is the *purity of the heart* so important?

The purity of the external actions and behaviour are not as important as the purity of the inner heart. Why is this true?

Because all sin comes from the heart: Jesus explains this in his teaching in Mark 7:1-23. The Jews were most concerned about external purity – the washing of hands, cups, pots, copper vessels and dining couches. Jews were concerned with ceremonial cleansing. This, of course, was taught by Moses.[8] But the purpose of the Levitical laws on ceremonial cleansing was to teach them to live holy lives. 'Be holy for I am holy.' When Jerusalem was destroyed and the Jews were carried into Babylonian captivity because of idolatry, the Jewish leaders became aware of the importance of keeping the Law. So they added their own traditions in order to build a fence around the Law, taking every measure to prevent people from disobeying the Law of Moses. Jewish rabbis made meticulous rules and regulations governing daily life of the people – laws pertaining to agriculture, feasts, marriage and purification.

Jesus confronted this Jewish concern for the external while neglecting internal purity. He declared that nothing that goes into a person defiles a man because it does not go into the heart, but only that which comes out of a person can defile him. '*What comes out of a person is what defiles him. For from within, out of the heart of man, come evil thoughts, sexual immorality, theft, murder, adultery, coveting, wickedness, deceit, sensuality, envy, slander, pride, foolishness. All these things come from within, and they defile a person.*'[9]

Examine the list of sins mentioned above by Jesus. They include *everything* that we have been discussing in this book on developing a godly character. The primary way to deal with evil thoughts, sexual immorality, dishonesty, hatred, adultery, covetousness, deceit, sensuality, envy, slander and pride is to deal with the heart. For that reason we will spend twice as much time in this chapter as we have spent on many of the previous chapters. Because the key to character that is beyond reproach is dealing with the heart – especially the mind which influences the emotions which influence the will.

In some Christian traditions there is great emphasis on correct externals – dress, cosmetics, jewelry, and hairstyles. Mind you, when the heart is pure there will be a change in the externals. Women will not dress scantily and expose themselves to the world. Men and women will seek to dress modestly, which is becoming to a godly person.[10] But the Bible puts the emphasis on the purity of the heart. Another reason why purity of the heart is so basic is:

Because worldliness comes from the heart: John clearly states that 'worldliness' is not primarily something that is external but internal. '*Do not love the world nor the things in the world,*' John says. '*If anyone loves the world, the love of the Father is not in him.*' So we ask, 'Is this "world" the external world or the internal?' John continues, '*For all that is in the world, the lust of the flesh and the lust of the eyes and the boastful pride of life, is not from the Father, but is from the world. The world is passing away, and also its lusts; but the one who does the will of God lives forever.*'[11] The Christian is destined for eternity with God. But the world with its lusts is 'passing away.' Only the one who does the will of God lives forever. So it is most essential that the Christian leader deal with the spirit of worldliness that is within him.

Virtually all the sins that emanate from the heart, which are mentioned above in Mark 7, are related to the three aspects of worldliness that John speaks of, namely, *lust of the flesh*, *lust of the eyes*, and *the boastful pride of life*.

Lust of the flesh: Lust is a 'passionate or overmastering desire,' usually 'a sexual desire that is uncontrolled and unlawful.' Therefore, the 'lusts of the flesh' mentioned in Mark 7:21,22 include: *evil thoughts*, *sexual immorality*, *adultery* and *sensuality* (lewdness – obscene and indecent language). However, if *lust* is understood as 'unlawful desires,' then we may include any such desires that come from 'the flesh' (the bodily appetites) including *gluttony* (desiring more food than is healthy), *laziness* (desiring more rest than is needed) and *drunkenness* (desiring drinks that are not wholesome).

Lust of the eyes: This includes any unlawful desire that enters the mind through the eyes.[12] 'The lust of the eyes' includes *envy*, *coveting* and *theft* taken from Mark 7:21, 22.

Pride of life: This is the basic sin problem of human beings. The attitudes and actions spring from pride that are mentioned in Mark 7:21, 22 would include *pride* (feeling superior), *slander*, *deceit*, *malice* (wickedness – desiring to inflict injury on others), and *murder*.

We see then that worldliness is an issue of the heart.

Is there any other reason why purity of the heart is so important?

Because whatever is stored in the heart is revealed outwardly: Jesus taught that only 'good trees' can produce 'good fruit,' while 'bad trees' bear 'bad fruit.' The kind of tree is recognised by the kind of fruit it bears.[13] He then speaks of the importance of the heart. '*The good person out of the good treasure* *of his heart produces good, and the evil person out of his evil treasure produces evil, for out of the abundance of the heart his mouth speaks.*'[14]

The mouth with its tongue 'is a fire, a world of unrighteousness' – 'no human being can tame the tongue. It is a restless evil, full of deadly poison.'[15] No human being can tame the tongue but God can, but only as his children store up good thoughts in their hearts.

Jesus speaks of storing up good treasure or evil treasure in the heart. The main avenue of storing thoughts is through the eye and ear gates. Through the eyes and ears we build up treasures in the heart that will become manifest through the mouth for speaking and the hands and feet for doing. Out of the abundance of what one stores in the heart, the person speaks and acts.

On the one hand, the heart is 'deceitful above all things, and desperately sick.'[16] Unbelievers are 'futile in their thinking and their foolish hearts are darkened.'[17] That is the condition before conversion. On the other hand, when one is regenerated, the heart is circumcised and the impurities are removed;[18] the heart is sprinkled clean with the blood of Christ,[19] Christ comes to dwell in the heart,[20] and the Spirit is given in the heart as a guarantee of ownership.[21]

Every Christian leader must recognise that there is a spiritual battle within, between 'the old self' and 'the new person' in Christ.[22] Paul states that 'the sinful mind is hostile to God' and leads to death, but 'the mind controlled by the Spirit' leads to life.[23] It is therefore so important that one feeds the mind with that which edifies, and starves the mind of those ideas and desires which are hostile to God so that the Spirit of God can lead the Christian from within.

The words spoken by Christians reflect what has been stored up in the heart (mind). Joking and jesting can be unkind, rude, suggestive or conceited. Comments can reflect deceitfulness, an uncaring attitude, or an unforgiving spirit. Afterwards the person may say, 'I'm only kidding. Can't you take a joke?' But words don't lie. The fruit of the lips reveals the kind of tree that we are. Much more will be said later about how we should store up good treasures.

'Above all else,
Guard your heart
For it is the wellspring of life.'[24]

Because only the pure in heart shall see God: The final reason why purity in the heart is so important is because Jesus said that only they will see God.[25]

Seeing God 'face to face' is the joyful hope of all believers.[26] But no one who is impure in heart shall ever abide with the holy God. 'Can two walk together, except they be agreed?'[27] Only 'the pure in heart' shall see God. The '*pure*' refers to the *sincerity* and *integrity* of believers, but much more. It refers to those who are holy and clean – those who are morally like God. Personal fellowship with God requires the reflection of God's holy character.

Therefore, we conclude that the major ambition of every Christian leader must be to become like God – to be pure in heart.

Covetousness of the Heart

What is the one *sin of the heart* forbidden by the Ten Commandments?

All the Ten Commandments we have considered so far seemingly refer to external acts – committing adultery, murder, lying and stealing. Jesus made clear that these commandments should be understood spiritually, commencing with the heart. Sin is not limited to external acts of committing adultery and murdering, but includes lustful thoughts and hateful attitudes.

But the tenth commandment deals with the inner thoughts and intentions of the heart: '*You shall not covet…*'[28] Unlike the other commandments which deal with outward actions, the tenth commandment focuses on motivation and inner desires. Coveting is 'the mother sin' because coveting money is 'the root of all evil.[29] Coveting underlies the motive for adultery and stealing; and often for lying and murder for a cover up. Covetousness in Jewish thinking is the beginning of every sin. Because covetousness is the source of many grievous sins, Christian tradition has named covetousness one of the Seven Deadly Sins.

It seems significant that when Jesus named the Ten Commandments which should be kept for the Rich Young Man to receive eternal life, Jesus mentioned six commandments but omitted the tenth commandment, not to covet. Many people have not stolen or committed adultery physically, but everyone has been guilty of coveting, having a strong desire for some forbidden thing.

Covet (*chamad*) basically means *desire* and can be used in a positive sense. 'More to be *desired* are they [the precepts of God] than gold, even much fine gold.'[30] More often, however, *chamad* refers to the 'inordinate desire, selfish desire.'[31] *The Good News Bible* therefore paraphrases the tenth commandment: 'Do not *desire* another man's house.' In keeping with the negative sense, *The Message* reads, 'No lusting after your neighbor's house…' Solomon warned his son about the adulteress, 'Do not desire [lust] her beauty in your heart.'[32]

Covetousness is such a major sin against God because it strikes at the core of his lordship. 'The earth is the LORD's and the fullness thereof.'[33] Since God is the owner of all things and the Lord of all, he in his sovereignty is the one to give or withhold. For the creature to desire what has not been given by the Creator is nothing less than idolatry. The Bible says so. Paul admonishes the Colossians, '*Put to death therefore what is earthly in you: sexual immorality, impurity, passion, evil desire, and covetousness, which is idolatry*.'[34] Covetousness is idolatry because it usurps the authority of God by desiring something contrary to the will of God. Many people make material possessions and wealth their priority in life, giving absolute devotion to things, while neglecting true devotion to God. Covetousness is not limited to people with wealth. Poor people are just as capable of covetousness. When the desire for material things becomes the controlling drive in one's life; when worship and service of God are sacrificed at the altar of material gain, that person is guilty of idolatry. 'Things' become gods and rule in their lives. This is a real temptation for Christian leaders.

'Sin represents man's refusal to accept his role as a created person by seeking to usurp the prerogatives of God and attempting to play the role in his own life which only God can play. Thus pride… lies at the heart of man's sinful rebellion.'[35] This is a powerful insight. Human beings exalt themselves over others when they feel their desires and needs are superior to the needs of others. Covetousness is pride, lifting up one's own desires above the needs of others; covetousness is also idolatry, usurping the right of God to grant his resources to people.

This sin of covetousness is what has thrown the human race into the present fallen, sinful condition. Satan, in the form of a serpent,[36] tempted Eve in the Garden of Eden to eat of the forbidden fruit. God had graciously provided a garden full of 'trees that were pleasing to the eye and good for food' for them to enjoy and eat,[37] but made one restriction. '*You are free to eat from any tree in the garden; but you must not eat from the tree of the knowledge of good and evil, for when you eat of it you will surely die.*'[38] The emphasis is on the generosity of God who provided a garden full of beautiful fruit-bearing trees for the welfare of Adam and Eve. But Satan raised doubts about God's intention when God restricted them from eating one particular tree. This was God's test. Will they obey the LORD God, their Creator? Will they honour and glorify him by loving God's will? Or will they rebel against God's revealed will?

How then did they fall into disobedience? '*So when the woman <u>saw that the tree</u> was good for food, and that it was a delight to the eyes, and that the <u>tree was to be desired</u> to make one wise, she <u>took of its fruit and ate</u>, and she also gave some to her husband who was with her, and he ate.*'[39] Here we find the significant sequence. Eve first *saw with her eyes* that the fruit was delightful and desirable; she then *desired (coveted) this fruit* because it would make her wise; that covetousness then led to the *taking and eating*. This is the anatomy of sin which begins with the *eye (or ear)* to see something that is forbidden by God. This seeing then arouses a *wrongful desire* in us. The end result is that we actually *do* that which is forbidden.

The example of Achan illustrates again the whole wicked process of *seeing*, *desiring* and then *stealing*. After the great victory over Jericho, Joshua led Israel in the attack of Ai, a very small town. They were defeated because of the sin of Achan. God had commanded that *everything* in Jericho should be 'devoted to destruction'[40] but Achan had disobeyed. When Achan was discovered by lot, this was his testimony. 'Truly I have sinned against the LORD God of Israel, and this is what I did: when *I saw* among the spoil a beautiful cloak from Shinar, and 200 shekels of silver, and a bar of gold weighing 50 shekels, then *I coveted* them and *took* them.'[41]

Taking what was forbidden was neither the first nor basic sin. First, he *desired* (*coveted*) it after he *saw* it. The most elementary way of not stealing (or committing adultery) is not to see. Achan no doubt was looking and searching for what was forbidden because it was actually hidden in the earth. Why should he dig in the earth for something that was devoted to destruction? If per chance inadvertently one sees something that is forbidden, then one must immediately stop the seeing and desiring. Once your heart settles on coveting something, sooner or later there will be open theft.

Likewise, the first sin in the primitive Christian Church was the covetousness and theft of Ananias and Sapphira.[42] No surprise! Covetousness remains a dominant temptation for Christian leaders today. Whole cultures manifest a dominant theme of placing value on possession of things. Jesus warned against this very thing. 'Take care,' Jesus said, 'and be on the *guard against all covetousness*, for one's life does not consist in the abundance of his possessions.'[43] And yet that is what our cultures today emphasise. A person's value is determined by his wealth.

Coveting material gain is a major reason today why servants of the Lord fall into sin and fail in ministry. Several Kenyans told me: '*There is too much* ***materialism*** *among church leaders – wanting more, not being satisfied, striving for control over the church money. Love of money causes many pastors to fall. Pastors feel their church salary is very little, so they move from one place to another. It leads to their removal.*' '*Major temptations in the ministry are wealth and greed; this is very common. One of our weaknesses as Africans is* ***greed****. It causes most of the poverty in Africa. Leaders gather wealth at the expense of the people.*'

Coveting is not restricted to possessions (things) that may be stolen; coveting applies to sensual lust. Hear the tenth commandment in full: '*You shall not covet your neighbor's house; you shall not covet your neighbor's wife, or his male servant, or his female servant, or his ox, or his donkey, or anything that is your neighbor's.*' When the illicit object of *desiring* is a woman, this becomes *sensual lusting*.

Covetousness, though subtle and unseen, is listed by Jesus among the most heinous sins of theft, murder, adultery, pride and slander.[44] Covetousness is listed among those sins committed by men who do not know God.[45] Jesus is very blunt: '*You can't worship two gods at once. Loving one god, you'll end up hating the other. Adoration of one feeds contempt for the other. You can't worship God and money both.*'[46] Far from being tolerated, Paul said there 'must not be even a hint' of greed among the saints.[47] James asks the question: '*What causes quarrels and what causes fights among you? Is it not this, that your passions are at war within you? You desire and do not have, so you murder.* ***You covet and cannot*** *obtain, so you fight and quarrel.*'[48]

Covetousness is the opposite of contentment. The contented person does not struggle and strive for more; nor does he covet what others have.

What is the difference between healthy desiring and covetousness?

Clearly, the Bible warns against covetousness – excessive, selfish desire. But what of desiring to improve and do one's best? Like improving skills for ministry through more education, or building a larger and more permanent house, or providing the best education for one's children, or ensuring the family is dressed well? If everyone would be totally 'content' and passive, accepting whatever lot came his way, how could anyone advance or improve? How can we tell when something is covetousness or a healthy desiring?

Covetousness must be distinguished from an appreciation or admiration of something; it is also different from a mere *desire* for something. Passing through life we observe many things – anything ranging from clothing that people wear to houses and its furnishings where people live; from land acquisition to the source of livelihood from that land. To admire, appreciate and desire to imitate or learn from that person is not covetousness in itself. People learn from one another. Moreover, an earnest desire for something is noble when accompanied by honourable motives. Paul admonished, '*covet earnestly* the best gifts.'[49] Newer translations avoid the word, 'covet,' and say instead, '*earnestly desire* the greater gifts.'[50] Such earnest desires are noble when motivated by godly ambitions – to glorify God and advance his Kingdom.

Sinful covetousness is an excessive desire, an insatiable appetite, an unlawful craving for something forbidden. It is an 'acquisitive desire beyond reason; it is greediness.' A greedy person is characterised by an eager and often selfish desire.[51] 'There is no limit to the amount of possessions, particularly money, that a person can seek to amass. Possessions can become a goal sought for themselves, for the power and status they bring, or as a sign, for example, of God's favor or predestination unto salvation.'[52]

Wealth and possessions bring power and prestige in society so people strive after wealth to become 'great' and 'significant.' This drive can be found in the church and can take a religious twist by making wealth a sign that one is truly blessed by God – a total perversion of biblical teaching. You 'name it and claim it' and contribute 'seed money' so that you can acquire God's blessing in wealth. One church leader told me:

> We have seen in the 'Prosperity Gospel' that is coming into this country how people associate success with prosperity and money, instead of what God does in their lives. When they don't get the positions they think they ought to have then they go off and start something else so they become successful. The message these days is that when you don't have success, you are a sinner. You cannot be a Christian without success, so the leader becomes proud. Pride and wealth begin to lead them because success is associated only with gold. But Christ had no place to sleep. So the 'Prosperity Gospel' is misleading for us who live among the poor. It may succeed for those who work in factories and sleep in the streets, but it is a partial truth. Of course God will give success to his people. But there are many wealthy people who live sinful lives. Wealth has nothing to do with a measure of our success or godliness. We may be poor in earthly wealth but rich in spiritual things. Those are the best riches we can ever want. The 'Prosperity Gospel' is not only the message of the Pentecostals; this is the message of the televangelists. 'Give out your money. Try Him. That is why you are poor. That is why you cannot make ends meet because you don't trust enough.' The 'Prosperity Gospel' is on the air every day. There is no more gospel of repentance but only healing and wealth. 'What do you have? Give it.'

Thomas Watson gives some helpful suggestions[53] to determine whether our desires are healthy and wholesome or whether they are covetous. A covetous spirit is evident when:

(1) ***One's thoughts are wholly taken up with gaining material goods.*** A good man's thoughts are devoted to Christ and his will, in seeking to love God with all one's heart and to please God in all things. But the covetous person is preoccupied with the things of this world, how to get ahead and to improve one's lot in life.

(2) ***One takes 'more pains for getting earth than for getting heaven.'*** This is one of balance and priority. A covetous person will relish the world, pursue it and never cease till he gets it, all the while he neglects spiritual things.

(3) ***One is so set on getting earthly gain that he will sacrifice heavenly wealth in order to gain the things of this world.*** Like the rich young ruler who came to Jesus, wanting to know how to have eternal life. He 'went away sorrowful,' preferring to hold on to his material wealth rather than to give up his wealth for the kingdom of God. When it comes to a decision, whether to attend Bible study and prayer meeting, or whether to work and labour for earthly gain, if you choose earthly gain over spiritual things, this is a good indicator of covetousness.

(4) ***One talks all about the things of this world and how to gain wealth.*** The speech of a covetous person betrays him for the covetous are always speaking of secular things while the godly are speaking of the heavenly values.

(5) ***One overloads himself with worldly business.*** He has many irons in the fire and has so much business that he cannot find time to serve God. He scarce has time enough to eat but never to pray.

(6) ***One is so eager to get the things of this world that he does not care what means must be used.*** Whether means are legal or honest, whether they hurt others or cheat them is not his great concern.

Overcoming Covetousness and Impurity of the Heart

Make no mistake about this. The thought life is so important that every Christian leader must take radical steps to bring the thought life into captivity to Jesus Christ. We are what we think. If a Christian leader is to fulfill his calling before God and achieve the goals laid out before him, *he must* learn to master his thought life. If your eye leads to impure thoughts, Jesus says: 'tear it out and throw it away.'[54] This means that one must take drastic action to deal with impure thoughts. Character formation begins with the thought life. As a well known verse goes:

Sow a thought, reap an act; Sow an act, reap a habit; Sow a habit, reap a character.

Following are three pithy recommendations for becoming pure in heart.

(1) ***Become militant in dealing with your thoughts.*** Paul says, 'take every thought captive to obey Christ.'[55] This is in the context of spiritual warfare. We are in a spiritual battle between the truth and the error, between the wisdom of God and the wisdom of this world. It all centres in the mind. The realm of the mind is treated as a fort or citadel which must be torn down so that the thoughts might be made captive to obey Christ.

In societies where the laws of God are devalued and replaced with godless values, it is inevitable that the mind will be bombarded with lustful thoughts. But you can deal ruthlessly with those thoughts; you can refuse to allow Satan to build into your mind nests of covetousness. You must take every thought 'captive' and make it obedient to Christ. It is a matter of life and death.

'Discipline is the secret of godliness...Discipline means *work*; it means *sustained daily effort.*'[56] Jesus said, 'Take up your cross *daily.*' Though we were born in sin, it has taken practice to develop our particular style of sinning. Militant discipline is required to deny self of the old practices and habit patterns. Purity in heart comes only through disciplined living.

(2) ***Close the eye and ear gates to lustful ideas.*** This is a challenge! What kind of music do you listen to? What kind of TV do you watch? To what unsavory influence do you subject yourself? 'One of the primary ways we program our mind is through the eye-gate: visual input. Powerful things can happen in just seconds when we see something sexually explicit.'[57] The place to start controlling the cravings of the flesh is to reduce exposure to temptation.

Lust is all over the place: in popular songs, in advertisements, in movies and videos, in books and magazines, in the dress and clothes people wear. The testimony of those who attended the sexually explicit dances of Congolese and Zairean bands was this: 'We love these dances because they create a hot atmosphere. We move and sweat to the rhythm of the dancers' waists and this transports us to an ecstasy I can't describe. It's simply fantastic.'

Decisions must be made all the time what to watch and what to listen to. How do you decide? Here are several questions to consider:

- Is it helpful – does it build me up spiritually, mentally or physically?[58]
- Does it bring me under its power – am I becoming enslaved to it?[59]
- Does it hurt others – cause others to stumble and be a poor example?[60]
- Is God glorified by this – what would Jesus do? Would he listen to this, watch this, go here, do that?[61] This is a major issue.

By watching TV, attending movies and gulping in all the garbage in our degenerate age, Christians lose their sensitivity to the spiritual standards of sex. Like frogs in a kettle of water, the Christian conscience is destroyed without knowing that the water in the kettle has reached the boiling point. Spiritual sensitivity is numbed. When watching 'soap operas' on TV, Christians cheer for one couple which is having an illicit affair. Instead of hating the very smell of immorality, we enjoy it. We find entertainment in the very things God hates.

Moreover, in our consumer age where the latest in technology or style of dress are promoted and advertised, the Christian becomes discontented. Desires for more and the best and the latest are stirred up. Coveting follows the seeing.

Learn to be honest with yourself. Recognise what captures the desires of your lower nature. Above all else, learn to love God with your mind. Utterly refuse to subject yourself to the enticements in the world. If you had a dangerous animal in your house, would you feed it or kill it? When you open your eye and ear gate to lustful ideas you are feeding the animal, not starving it.

(3) ***Be transformed by the renewing of the mind.***[62] The only way to develop godly character is to renew the mind to become pure and holy. Jerry Bridges, a staff member with Navigators, comments: 'Obedience is the pathway to holiness, but it is only as we *have* His commands that we can obey them. God's Word must be so strongly fixed in our minds that it becomes the dominant influence in our thoughts, our attitudes and our actions.'[63] In keeping with Navigator's emphasis on disciplined discipleship, Bridges asserts: 'One of the most effective ways of influencing our minds is through memorizing Scripture.'

For the renewing of the mind, which is more important: prayer or meditating on Scripture? Strictly speaking, you cannot practice one effectively without the other. But the most basic ingredient for the renewal of the mind is the Scriptures – but always the Scriptures being prayed over.

CONCLUSION

This chapter is twice as long as others because it is twice as important. The mind is where everything begins. Only those with a pure heart will 'see' God. Only those with a pure heart can please God with worship and service.

The first half of this book has been on the *character* of the leader. Character begins with the mind. Without a godly character, a Christian leader will fail.

The remainder of the book is now devoted to the *skills* of leadership.

SEARCHING THE SCRIPTURE WITH APPLICATION

1. Study 2 Co 3:1-4:6.
   a. What does Paul mean when he says, 'the god of this age has blinded the minds of unbelievers so they cannot see the light of the gospel' (4:3, 4)?
   b. What happens to the heart when people are converted to Christ? (4:6)
   c. How is the believer transformed to become more like Christ? (3:18)
   d. How is one transformed by 'beholding' (*AV* and *ESV*) Christ?
   e. How does a believer 'behold' Christ? Discuss the means used.
2. Discuss the many reasons why a 'renewal' of the mind (Ro 12:2) is so crucial for the believer?
3. Why is 'renewal' of the mind especially important for the Christian leader? What happens to the leader when the mind is not renewed?
4. Study Ro 6:19.
   a. How does one offer the body with the mind to impurity?
   b. How does one offer the body with the mind to holiness?
5. What should be done to help Christian leaders become 'pure in heart'?

Endnotes

[1] Mt 5:8
[2] Jas 4:1-2
[3] Behm 1965:606
[4] Ps 84:2
[5] Brown 1983:524f
[6] Behm 1965:611
[7] Behm 1965:611ff
[8] Lev 11:1-47; 13:1-15:33
[9] Mk 7:20-23
[10] 1 Ti 2:9
[11] 1 Jn 2:15-17 *NASB*
[12] Mt 5:27-32
[13] Mt 12:33
[14] Lk 6:45
[15] Pr 18:21; Jas 3:6,8
[16] Jer 17:9
[17] Ro 1:21
[18] Ro 2:29
[19] Heb 10:22
[20] Eph 3:17
[21] 2 Co 1:22
[22] Ro 7:7-25
[23] Ro 8:6-8
[24] Pr 4:23
[25] Mt 5:8
[26] 1 Co 13:12
[27] Am 3:3 *AV*
[28] Ex 20:17

[29] 1 Ti 6:10
[30] Ps 19:10
[31] Brown 1983:326
[32] Pr 6:25
[33] Ps 24:1
[34] Col 3:5
[35] Honeycutt 1966:115
[36] Rev 12:9
[37] Ge 1:29-30; 2:9
[38] Ge 2:16,17
[39] Ge 3:6
[40] Jos 7:11f
[41] Jos 7:20,21
[42] Ac 5
[43] Lk 12:15
[44] Mk 7:23f
[45] Ro 7:8
[46] Mt 6:24
The Message
[47] Eph 5:3 *NIV*
[48] Jas 4:1,2
[49] 1 Co 12:31 *KJ*
[50] 1 Co 12:31 *NIV*
[51] *Webster'sDictionary Unabridged*: 1959
[52] Hunter 1990: 64
[53] Watson 1965:23f
[54] Mt 5:29
[55] 2 Co 10:5
[56] Adams 1972:4,5
[57] Anderson 1994:160
[58] 1 Co 6:12
[59] 1 Co 6:12
[60] 1 Co 8:13
[61] 1 Co 10:31
[62] Ro 12:2
[63] Bridges 1985:88

PART SIX

ATTRIBUTES OF CHRISTIAN LEADERS

Not only should a Christian leader have *character* that is 'beyond reproach;' he should have *competence* in the field of leadership. While Christian leaders often fail because of faulty character, many godly Christian leaders fail to live up to their potential because they do not know the principles of good management.

The latter part of this book is devoted to *competence* of leaders in order to help godly men and women develop more fully the skills of leadership needed in order to be capable leaders of God's people.

In *Part Six* we shall lay the foundation for the leadership skills, dealing with *the nature of Christian leadership, the marks of an effective leader, mistakes of Christian leaders, the leader as a change-agent, and Nehemiah as a model leader.*

26
THE NATURE OF CHRISTIAN LEADERSHIP

'Having gifts that differ according to the grace given to us, let us use them:...the one who leads, with zeal.'[1]

If you want to lead, you need to know the nature of Christian leadership.

The topic of *leadership* can be confusing because there are so many different definitions. Finzel has counted 'more than 350 definitions.'[2]

Who can be called *a leader*?

Are you a leader because you have a *position* of leadership in the Church or in an organisation? Position does not make a leader, though position can enhance the influence of a leader. Position gives people opportunity to lead. But many people occupy seats of authority without displaying the characteristics of true leadership.

Are you a leader because you have *followers*? This is more on target. If you have no followers, you surely are no leader. Leadership is relational in nature. Oswald Sanders in his classic, *Spiritual Leadership*, says this: '*Leadership is influence, the ability to influence others.*'[3] Along that same line John Gardner says: '*Leadership is the process of persuasion or example by which an individual (or leadership team) induces a group to pursue objectives held by the leader or shared by the leader and his or her followers.*'[4] A public figure has said leadership is '*the capacity to move, inspire, and mobilize masses of people.*'[5] Finzel comments that, '*A leader takes people where they would never go on their own.*'[6] Now that is influence of leadership. Is your influence due to the sheer force of your personality, or your ability to inspire and motivate?

Or are you a leader because of *what you can do*? Ted Engstrom says that leadership is '*the ability to make things happen.*'[7] Indeed, your many followers will cease following you if you are unable to 'make things happen.' This is key.

The fact is that the nature of leadership is not self-evident. Many experts have concluded that leadership is not an exact science; 'it's an inexact art.'[8] What constitutes leadership is neither self-evident nor predictable; it is neither orderly nor neat. Leaders come in all sorts of strips and colours. The most unlikely of people become leaders and those who seem like 'natural leaders' may fail. Many leaders throughout history felt unable to lead before they were chosen; in their opinion they lacked the qualities of leadership. Yet they succeeded in remarkable ways.

In summary we may say that the nature of leadership is variable, different for each leader. But no one is a leader without followers who believe in him and are influenced by him. Every leader inspires and motivates his followers to do things together to accomplish great things and achieve significant goals. A leader makes things happen.

What is the difference between a leader and a *Christian* leader?

A Christian leader shares many of the qualities of a natural leader. A leader is a visionary leading the way; he is inspirational and motivational with followers, and effective as a change agent. The essential distinction between an natural leader and a Christian leader is his or her relationship with God in Christ. A Christian leader sees himself as an *under*-shepherd, serving under the direction of Christ and doing God's will. A Christian leader is a *servant* leader, serving God preeminently and others – not himself. Oswald Chambers contrasts natural leadership with spiritual leadership.[9]

Natural Leaders	**Spiritual Leaders**
Self-confident	Confident in God
Knows men	*also*, knows God
Makes own decisions	Seeks to find God's will
Ambitious	Self-effacing
Originates own methods	Finds and follows God's methods.
Motivated by personal considerations	Motivated by love for God and man

In brief, natural leaders are led by their own natures – egotistical and proud. Whereas, spiritual leaders are led by the Spirit – all for the glory of God!

> Ted Engstrom defines *Christian* leadership as that which is motivated by love and given over to service. It is leadership that has been subjected to the control of Christ and his example. The best Christian leaders exemplify to the utmost all those attributes of selfless dedication, courage, decisiveness, compassion, and persuasiveness that mark the great leader.[10]

The Christian leader should not 'unilaterally decide what others should do and then try to get followers to do it.' The Christian leader is not the boss, making others do his bidding. Rather, 'the emphasis is upon service to the group, not control over the group.'[11] The best form of Christian leadership does not treat people as subjects or herd them like cattle. Rather, the leader serves. A Christian leader is 'one whom others will follow willingly and voluntarily. That rules out tyrants, bullies, autocrats, and all others who use coercive power to impose their wills on others.'[12]

Israel's shepherd-leaders all too often followed the pattern of the world. Instead of feeding the sheep, the shepherds made personal profit at the expense of the sheep. Through Ezekiel the prophet, God condemned them for not behaving as good shepherds.[13] Good shepherds should feed the sheep, strengthen the weak, heal the sick, bind up the injured, look for the lost sheep which went astray and bring them back to the fold. In the same way Christian leaders should be serving others in their need – being people oriented and doing God's will.

The fascinating thing is that over the past one hundred years, management theory in the western business world has moved away from a top-down authoritarian leadership to more of a sensitive, people-centred leadership. In the early 1900s the concern was to develop the most efficient means of producing a product. So people were placed under great stress to produce more and more goods. But over the years leaders began to realise that when workers were placed under great stress, they became less efficient as workers. Gradually, moral issues were raised as to the ethics of manipulating people as objects and mere means of production. By the end of the 20th century there was a consensus that the best way of encouraging efficient work among the workers is to care for their needs. People do matter.

> In summary, prior to 1900 managers of an enterprise generally saw no compelling reason to be concerned about the personal needs of workers. Since 1900, however, personal needs have loomed larger as a management concern. On the theoretical level there is the moral obligation to serve the highest good of the worker. On a very practical level there is the fact that a demonstrated concern for the needs of workers tends to enhance their performance. For the good of the enterprise, managers need to care about what is happening to their employees.[14]

In conclusion we may exclaim: God's ways are the best ways! The Bible teaches that all leadership should be God-centred; it further teaches that caring for the needs of people is both right and beneficial to the building of God's kingdom. Management theory concurs that the leader can only ignore or abuse the workers to his own detriment. Whenever the Christian leader shows personal concern for his teammates and involves them in decision making, the team will pull together with greater unity and efficiency. When the leader serves God and is truly concerned for the people, his leadership is most effective.

Are leaders *born* or *made*?

Over the years there has been much debate on whether a leader is born to be a leader with innate gifts, or whether an individual learns to be a leader through training.

As in most debates, there is truth on both sides. Surely, leadership is a *gift* endowed by God. The Bible says so! Among the thirty different gifts mentioned in four epistles, leadership is one.[15] Engstrom comments that 'leadership qualities are part of the basic makeup of the individual.'[16]

But that truth can be misrepresented as when Peter Drucker wrote in 1954, '...[L]eadership cannot be created or promoted. It cannot be learned.'[17] This is a partial truth. If you are not gifted for leadership, you cannot learn to be a leader. But a 'born leader' can grow as a leader through training and learning through experience. All people with gifts of leadership can learn better how to lead effectively. Individuals may not give any indication of leadership skills; but when thrust into the responsibility, they thrive as leaders. They grow by learning leadership skills both through theory and in practice. But the gift of leadership was received by God at conception and activated by God's calling.

Therefore, when the invitation is given to assume some leadership position, no one should shy away. The gift hidden away in your life can spring forth with training. Read books, attend seminars and take courses. In-service training can enhance the leader's ability. However, some things cannot be learned apart from experience. Experience is the best teacher of leadership when coupled with training.

What is the leader's relationship with his followers?

Building on what has been said about the nature of Christian leadership, the leader should look upon his followers or constituencies as a *team.* No one is a leader without the team uniting together and sharing both responsibilities and recognition.

This book is intended to cover a wide range of leadership roles: Church overseers who shepherd pastors; pastors who care for the local flock; school heads who lead teachers; ministry organisational heads with their employees. For reasons that will become evident, we will call all these workers, employees, pastors or followers of the leader *team members.* We shall look upon the leader as part of a ministry team that works together to accomplish goals. So in our thinking the denomination, the local congregation, the school or para-Church organisation are all viewed as teams working together with their leader to accomplish something for God's glory and the building of his kingdom.

Rush defines a team as 'two or more people moving along a path of interaction toward a common goal.'[18] This implies that a team involves interaction between several members all united with a common goal. A football team is a prime example. A team can do so much more than one individual, but the one prerequisite is that unity prevails with one goal. When Jesus chose twelve disciples he formed a team. Great things are accomplished with teams.

The leader should view himself as a *team leader* who is blessed to have members with differing gifts. We should all recognise that no one, not even the leader, has all the gifts; no one is strong in every area. Instead of disparaging a member because of some weakness, the leader should help the member discover his or her gift to contribute to the work of the team. Everyone is needed.

The attitude of the team members is crucial. 'Me-ism'[19] is a self-centred attitude that is more concerned with personal goals and desires than the success of the team. More often the leader is guilty of 'me-ism.' His reputation and personal benefits are his priorities. Instead, he must model and encourage a spirit of 'we-ism.' The leader should consciously identify with the team and promote team unity.

Building the *team spirit* is the responsibility of the leader. Essential for the leader is a positive attitude. No pessimist can unite a team to do great exploits. By developing personal relationships with every team member and affirming each one, the leader will enhance the possibility of achieving the goals. Welding a team together so that they are enthusiastic, motivated and energised toward achieving a common goal is the leader's great challenge.

But some may ask, 'Must all leaders be *team* members?' Must they all relate to their workers in the way mentioned above?

What part does culture play in shaping leadership?

The description of a leader in this unit as a *team leader* doesn't fit the cultural traditions of all African peoples. We have seen that in Chapter 13. It is true that there were differences among the peoples. Some communities were more participative and less authoritarian in their leadership. If a leader behaved like a Big-Man in those communities, the people would not respect him. Christian leaders from those communities do not see the present tendency for authoritarian leadership as a carry over from African culture. But most Christian leaders we spoke to do believe there is a link with the past.

The Big-Man mentality, common among leaders today both in government and the Church, was prevalent in the past among many communities. The leader was the final authority. It is true that the chief worked with the Council. He consulted with many deliberations. He would surely consult with all the elders. But in the end his decision was personal. Though his decisions were formed by his consultations, his decision was not necessarily the will of the majority. When he made his decision, no one dared to challenge him. Traditionally, when the head of a family said, 'Today we will leave here and do this…,' no one questioned him. The Big-Man spoke and everyone obeyed. The voice of the Big-Man became the voice of the people.

Alan Bukusi observes: '…the big-man has straddled and strolled the continent [of Africa] like a colossus for most of fifty years.'[20] Did he 'slip into Africa,' as Bukusi suggests, evolving from the colonially instituted 'chiefs'? Or is he the result of corruption of cultural systems by external forces? Or did the Big-Man evolve from the way the colonialist leaders treated their subjects? Or did he grow out of the fertile soil of African culture? The origins of the Big-Man leader may be debated.

We do believe that this authoritarian way of leadership is inherent within human sinful nature. We have all observed that before being chosen as a church leader, many are people of integrity. But after election some become corrupt and assert their privileged position. As one person said to me, 'It is in all of us. Consciously or unconsciously we become the bullies we have hated. In campaigns they point to the failures of others but after winning the election they become like the ones they condemned.'

The reality is that the Big-Man culture persists today and influences society. There are different definitions of a *leader* but in the end, a leader in Africa is the Big-Man. He is like a traditional chief, or if not, then like the medicine- man. People feel he is above the average; he has something beyond human ability. He has super powers, almost like a demigod.

Today, older students bully Form 1 students, forcing them to wash floors or their socks. The older students treat the younger ones as subservient until the younger ones become senior students and they do the same. Church leaders call younger pastors, 'boy;' both an insult and an assertion of their superiority.

In many communities leadership was associated with supernatural powers. People became leaders either through inheritance or through the call of the spirits. Leadership was determined supernaturally. So when that person proved to be an effective leader, his word was law. They could bully people to bring gifts, donate land, and give daughters for wives of the chief. He was more than a public figure; he was treated as a supernaturally superior person to be obeyed.

Bukusi describes the Credo of the Big-Man in the following ways: He is the leader who knows everything, is superhuman who can do no wrong, is permanent and indispensable. Nothing can run without the Big-Man. All power and authority emanate from the Big-Man. To challenge him is sin – anathema, treason. The Big-Man is feared rather than respected.[21]

Education has undermined the Big-Man's authority, though it persists, especially away from urban centres. In rural areas people more readily submit to the word of the Big-Man. 'When an African Church leader travels in rural parishes, he is often overwhelmed by the receptions and kindnesses of these uneducated Christians in the villages.'[22] African traditional leadership still has tremendous influence there where great loyalty and respect is given to leaders. But in urban centres people question and challenge. Today older leaders do consult with the younger educated people, something unheard of in the past.

Should the Christian Church wait until education takes its course to create a better kind of a leader? Or should the Church take a lead in studying the Scripture and searching the kind of leader that should characterise the Church? David Gitari observes that, 'In the world the great man is the one who controls others; the man who is master; the man to whose word of command must be obeyed, and whose presence will make the ruled to be filled with fear and trepidation.' But he goes on to observe that in the Christian assessment, 'service alone is the badge of greatness.'[23]

According to the Bible, the natural leaders of this world are led by their own natures. They are full of themselves. But the spiritual leaders should be led by the Spirit and seek to serve Jesus Christ. "If traditional African leadership is to be compatible with Church leadership, or to influence it in any way," Payne asserts, 'then *complete loyalty to the "Chief" of the Church, Jesus Christ, must be paramount.*'[24] The Church should be the salt and light of this world instead of being molded into the pattern of this world.

For thirty-five years John Stott has traveled to many countries and observed Church leadership. He laments that too many lead 'in defiance of the teaching of Jesus and his apostles.' 'Our model of leadership,' Stott claims, 'is often shaped more by culture than by Christ. Yet many cultural models of leadership are incompatible with the servant imagery taught and exhibited by the Lord Jesus.'[25] Our challenge is to follow our Lord Jesus who came to serve.

Is there a difference between leadership and management?

For several decades experts have taught that a clear distinction exists between leadership and management. Following are the contrasts:

- A *leader* is a visionary with long-term vision who seeks to bring change in the organisation; *managers* are practical technocrats and bureaucrats who achieve organisational goals.
- A *leader* is a change-agent who upsets the status quo; *managers* are predictable who produce orderly results.[26]
- A *leader* is transformational, wanting to transform the present organization to make it work

better; *managers* maintain the organizational structure and are concerned with stability.[27]

- A *leader* is a risk-taker; *managers* are adverse to risk.
- A *leader* is concerned with getting things done right, wanting to improve the way of doing things; *managers* are concerned with getting things done through the organisational structure.

But today many recognise that there is an overlap of leadership and management skills. 'A good leader must have some good management skills, and good managers usually have some leadership qualities.'[28] Gangel argues that in Christian ministries, 'It is nearly impossible to be an effective leader in a ministry organization without carrying out high-quality administrative work. Likewise, it is difficult to be an administrator without having some leadership responsibilities.'[29]

The approach taken in this book is that a leader must lead with vision, enthusiasm, motivation and care for those following him. But he is also a manager who leads his team in planning, goal setting, organising, delegating, motivating and guiding everyone to the achievement of the goals.

CONCLUSION

The Christian leader must think through his relationship with those whom he leads. What part does African culture play in determining the role of the Christian leader over his followers? And what teaching of Christ and his apostles should shape the role of a Christian leader?

The nature of Christian leadership is very different from the nature of African traditional leadership or contemporary western models of leadership. Christian leaders must *learn how to lead in a Christian manner*.

What then are the marks of an effective Christian leader? The following chapter will explore that topic.

SEARCHING THE SCRIPTURE WITH APPLICATION

1. Think of several leaders whom you know and admire. What sets them apart from their followers? Why are they leaders and the others followers?
2. Define leadership as you understand it and from insights gained from this chapter. What are the implications for Christian leaders from these definitions?
3. Discuss what should be the difference between the nature of non-Christian leaders and Christian leaders.
4. Peter was the accepted leader of the Twelve Apostles. What can we learn about the nature of leadership from the example of Peter?
5. Peter grew as a spiritual leader. In what way was Peter different, as reflected in 1 Pe 5:1-4 from Peter as a leader in the Gospels?
6. Do you believe leaders are born or made? Discuss what you believe.
7. What can be done to provide more leadership training for those who are or will become leaders?
8. How do most Christian leaders today relate to their followers? Are they authoritarian

top-down leaders who give directions or are they team leaders who seek the contributions of their team members?

9. Contrast the authoritarian top-down leader with the team leader. Discuss the advantages and disadvantages of both.
10. Which is more in keeping with the New Testament concept of leadership, the authoritarian top-down leader or the team leader? Discuss.
11. Do your people manifest a Big-Man kind of leadership? Explain.
12. You can find examples of authoritarian top-down leaders in the Old Testament. But Jesus Christ changed everything. Read the Gospel of Mark and consider the nature of Jesus' leadership.
13. Is there any New Testament support for the authoritarian top-down Big-Man type leader for the Christian Church today?

Endnotes

1 Ro 12:6,8
2 Finzel 1994:16
3 Sanders 1980:31
4 Gardner 1990:1
5 Habecker 1987:17
6 Finzel 1994:16
7 Engstrom 1979:20
8 Habecker 1987:18
9 Sanders 1980:35
10 Engstrom 1976:27
11 Means 1989:58f
12 Means 1989:60
13 Eze 34:1-4
14 Richards 1980:166
15 Ro 12; 1 Pe 4; Eph 4; 1 Co 12
16 Engstrom 1976:24
17 Peter Drucker as found in Engstrom 1976
18 Rush 1983:48
19 Perkins 2000:128
20 Bukusi 2004: 72
21 Bukusi 2004:73
22 Payne 1968:72
23 Gitari 2005: 4f
24 Payne 1968:74
25 Stott 2002:113
26 Haas 1992:56
27 Rima 2000:28
28 Means 1989:61
29 Gangel 1997:106

27
THE MARKS OF AN EFFECTIVE LEADER

'The mark of a good leader is loyal followers; leadership is nothing without a following.'[1]

The Bible says, 'The mark of a good leader is loyal followers.' So agree the experts in management today. But what is there in a leader that causes the followers to be so loyal?

Marks of a Leader in African Tradition

What were the African marks of a leader? Following is a composite of the marks of a traditional African leader taken from many communities:

Age: Traditionally, wisdom was learned in the University of Experience. The older one was, the wiser he was. This could only mean that the youth lacked sufficient wisdom to lead. Younger age-mates consulted with the elders. Young people could never imagine doing anything without first seeking advice from the elders. 'Same age-mates will not help each other to cross the river,' says a Kikamba proverb. Because they would joke while crossing, they would be swept away. So the advice of the elders was valued.

This meant that elders were held with deep respect and fear. Leaders kept their distance even though the younger consulted them. When approaching the elders, no one would just pop in. Instead, they stood at a distance to be seen by the elders, waiting to be called for a talk.

However, in other communities, such as the Samburu, the elders were expected to be in touch with the people, spending time with them. The Samburu leader was not supposed to be aloof from people but near them.

Wisdom: Wisdom in various forms was required for leaders. He should understand people and their situations and know how to handle them, how to tackle problems without causing confusion. The leader was expected to know their culture and customs, the traditional beliefs and practices of the community. He needed to be informed with knowledge of what was happening around him.

It was not simply old age that brought you respect but your wisdom and knowledge and what you have been able to do to prove yourself. When the elders gave you errands to run, the way you handled yourself proved your wisdom and competence. As time progressed in the colonial era, people expected their leader to be educated so he could represent them in the country.

Wealth: Traditionally, wealth gave power to elders. A leader arose from among the wealthy elders. He owned many cattle, goats and had many possessions all of which were cared for by the many wives and children. A leader was expected to work hard and not be lazy so that he could accumulate cattle and goats and become wealthy.

Generosity: Wealth caused people to respect you because you were able to provide food for the hungry and give a cow for the council of elders to eat. People recognised you as a good and capable person who was able to care for them. If you could not help them, you were not liked.

In a sense, 'You bought your way to the top of leadership.' When you attended meetings you were supposed to provide goats and sheep to feed the elders. By the age of 50 you had given so many goats and sheep. So it was not simply age that brought respect and leadership but generosity from your wealth.

Many Wives and Children: The more wives and children, the greater respect an elder received, because he was able to multiply his possessions and care for them with many workers. Polygamy was a status symbol.

Courageous: Leaders did not fear anything. They proved always to be on the top, like a cock crowing as the top bird. A leader could never be weak but showed himself to be fearless. When he coughed, the people ran. The leader was strong to fight, showing himself to be the leader.

Particularly among the communities that engaged in cattle raids, courage was essential. Leaders needed to fight courageously and retrieve stolen cattle. The leader needed courage to handle problems. In colonial times they needed courage to approach government authorities about community concerns. When a rumour surfaced, a leader would stand up and say, 'Let's do this.' He was decisive and took action.

Articulate Communicator: The leader was an articulate speaker at public gatherings. He could put his ideas across forcefully. Being able to think on his feet, he could speak with courage and challenge others verbally. Opening the mouth was very important. His voice was always ringing through the community.

The leader was the 'Chairman' of the council. He guided, controlled and concluded the discussion. He always invited the members to express their thoughts and ideas. Among the Gikuyu, even the women could offer their advice while the leader listened. But in the end, the leader concluded by giving his decision. He would pick the ideas he chose and conclude. Once he spoke, no one challenged him. But if the elders were evenly divided, the issue was left pending and left for more talking. Or the witchdoctor was consulted for superior advice.

Supernatural Powers: In some communities the people recognised a potential leader because he was untouchable with protection from witchcraft. He was known as a 'mysterious man,' such as a rainmaker, a prophet or someone with mystical powers. Because he had supernatural powers as a magician, no one dared challenge him; but his powers needed to be tested. If someone did challenge him because of his own special powers, it was a power contest. This mystical power enhanced the authority of the leader.

An Exemplary Life: In every day life the leader was expected to be an example that others could follow. His family life was also to be exemplary.

Uniting the Community: The leader was capable of handling all kinds of disputes, such as family struggles and inter-clan conflicts. Because a divided community could not stand up against its enemies, the leader needed to pour water on the fires of conflict.

In conclusion we may say from all the above statements that the basic quality that set the leader apart from all others was that he was most highly respected. This respectability came from his age and wisdom, his wealth and generosity, his family and success in life. He was even-tempered, predictable and reliable, and was proven over time.

A leader never appeared suddenly from nowhere; he did not spring up quickly. Rather, he began from the bottom and proved himself. He had to show that he could care for himself and his family. A person climbed the ladder from the bottom to the top of leadership.

Today many young people feel that if they go to a higher level of school, they should be automatically recognised, respected and given top leadership positions. But even today you must prove yourself before you can be accepted as a leader, even as in the former years.

Many of these traditional marks of community leaders have carried over to present times, both in Church and in civil society. Especially in rural areas and among certain communities, the elder must be advanced in age with long experience; he must have witnessed many things and, therefore, knows everything by experience. When the older leader speaks, he does not want anyone to challenge him. He desires to make the final decision. The Luo leader commanded things to take place. No one dared to challenge him. If someone does challenge a Luo leader's authority in many Churches today, he breaks away and forms an Independent African Church.

When a very senior elder stands up to speak in a council, everyone keeps silent out of respect. Even an elder with tainted character is esteemed because of his age. Instead of choosing a person of character for Church leadership, the people choose someone well known with wealth and who is worldly-wise. This has created many problems.

The traditional respect for the wealthy carries over into politics today. People ask, 'What have you done for us?' Early pastors trained by the missionaries did not receive a large salary. But they worked in their *shamba* so that they could help people. The people used to come to missionaries for clothes and food; so people also desired their pastor to be like the missionaries and their traditional tribal leaders.

Western education is the greatest reason why traditional African culture has been turned upside-down. Culture has changed; things are not what they used to be. It is no longer the aged who are the most knowledgeable but the younger who have gone to school. Today the older consult the younger;

and yet the young need the wisdom that comes from experienced maturity. Likewise in contemporary society, the old need the young and the young need the old.

Marks of an Effective Christian Leader

The singular mark of an effective leader is 'a loyal following.' But why are the followers loyal? We have examined the marks of traditional African leaders. What are the marks of an effective *Christian* leader today? Following are the responses of Christian leaders we interviewed. These marks are rooted in biblical teaching and strengthened by traditional values whenever they do not conflict with biblical values. We have divided the comments into two categories: Personality Characteristics and Moral Character. These do tend to overlap, but the distinction is useful. Since the moral character has been dealt with extensively elsewhere, these are only mentioned briefly.

Personality Characteristics

1. A People-Person: Since leadership is relational with followers, being a people person is foundational to all effective leadership. The effective leader is not a lone-ranger but someone who leads others, involving the whole team in leadership who share the vision together. A loner who moves forward all alone can have no followers; hence, he cannot be a leader.

The leader loves his team members, shows personal interest in them and cares for them. He is a father figure who defends and supports those under his care. The team members feel comfortable with him.

The leader is approachable and teachable. Team members find it easy to approach him; he associates with them freely. The leader does not repel you or instill fear in you. You can approach him under any circumstance with confidence that your relationship with him will not be damaged because of any mistakes done. You can share your dreams without feeling embarrassed. You are confident that he will accept you.

The leader understands and accepts his need for wisdom and counsel from others. Leaders fail when they force their own ideas on the people. When others give their advice, he picks up good ideas from them in order to encourage them, even when nonsense has been spoken. He is truly thankful for their contribution. The leader proposes and then asks, 'How do you see that?'

A people person is sensitive to the thoughts, desires and needs of his teammates. Not everyone will readily agree with the leader. Not everyone will desire to follow his thoughts. An effective leader will listen and learn from the team members. Perhaps their ideas are better. A wise leader will learn. If their ideas are not better, the effective leader will be patient and talk with them in such a way that they will all accept the consensus of the team. A people-person keeps in touch with the people so that the whole team moves forward together.

When a particular congregation, on one occasion, was building their worship centre, the church held many *harambees* for contributions but with little response. When the elders met to discuss their fruitless contributions they realised that they were going in different directions. As a result, the pastors met with the leaders of the small groups to involve them. In one month they came together and raised over one million shillings ($15,000). When the leader is in touch with the people, he can take the people along together with him.

2. Visionary: A true leader, above all else, must see ahead and have a vision where he wants to lead the people. While a manager sees the details within the confines of the organisation, the leader has the big picture in mind that encompasses many relationships. He is drawn into the future.

Because the leader sees ahead, he is able to anticipate danger if certain decisions are made. He must then have wisdom to know how to circumvent those dangers.

Being short-sighted, having a parochial mindset, being narrow minded, is death to leadership. Instead of a soaring vision of the future that captures the imagination of the team, a narrow minded leader leads with ignorance and short sightedness.

Once the leader and his team have a vision with goals for the future, the leader must maintain the focus of the group. Priorities must be followed. Sidetracks and detours will never lead to the vision. It is up to the leader to remain focused so that the ministry team will achieve its goals.

On the one hand, a leader is quiet and content with God's present blessing and favour. On the other hand, an effective leader is restless, wanting to see things move forward. Though he experiences contentment, he is yet dissatisfied with things as they are and wants to change and move forward. The driving vision for improvement, greater effectiveness or a new direction motivates him.

3. Commands Respect: People desire a *strong* leader. Traditionally, this entailed many attributes that brought both admiration and fear. A Christian leader in Africa today also needs to command respect as a person with authority. Such a person is fully assured and confident; he is knowledgeable and a step ahead of others. He is known for courage.

This need to command respect, partially drawn from African culture, can lead many astray from a biblical model of servant leadership; but it need not. Money and property in the past lifted a leader above the average. His lifestyle was above the common person. So the African Independent Churches and the charismatics tap into these cultural roots with their authoritarian leadership style and emphasis on wealth.

As we have seen, however, a biblical leader, who follows in the footsteps of Christ, should be a servant leader. Various examples have been given of African Christian leaders who do not use their position, knowledge or accumulated wealth to feel superior over others; instead they serve. A *strong* leader can also have a *servant* heart, for the leader uses his strength and respect to *serve* God and his people. Instead of serving himself, he serves others; instead of enriching and empowering himself, he enriches the Body of Christ and empowers others to serve and use their gifts for God's glory. If a strong leader uses his strength to resist corruption, he will truly serve God faithfully.

There is a delicate balance between being highly respected and being a people person. A leader should socialise with his people, but when he is in the office or exercising his ministry, he should behave as a leader. Socialising informally is part of being a people person in order to know the people. He must come down and be with the people. But in the office or in his ministry he must act officially and with dignity.

An effective leader is also respected as a family man. Because he is able to lead his family and clan well, he is recognised and respected as a leader.

4. Strength with Flexibility: An effective leader is marked by courage and strength to face challenges. No one can be a leader who finds difficulty making decisions. While decisions must be made carefully and wisely, vacillation, hesitation, or ambivalence do not mark an effective leader.

Vacillating in decision making is not leadership. Elijah asked the people, 'How long will you waver between two opinions?' Wavering leaders are indecisive and therefore ineffective leaders. You must be decisive. Yes, the leader takes time to investigate and consult; he must think and pray about the alternatives. But at the end of the day, the leader must make a decision. Once the decision is made, the leader needs strength of character to hold to that decision. Decision making by arm twisting will lead to confusion.

Courage in leadership is essential when some reject the decision made by consensus. Leaders may feel cowered. Compromise may seem like the only way to make peace. Some members may be furious or oppose some decision made, or demand a pay raise or seek to impose their views. Someone has said, 'You are never a good leader until you are rejected.' Remember Moses? An effective leader must stand firm.

But an effective leader will also show great flexibility and be able to change with the times. Of course he will not change in his doctrinal beliefs or compromise the moral standards due to pressure; a faithful servant of God does not accommodate behaviour and beliefs that contradict the Scripture. But within those basic parameters of the faith, the effective leader must be flexible.

Rigid building structures are more likely to break because they cannot sway with the wind. Therefore, tall skyscrapers and bridges are built to bend so that they will survive the hurricane force winds. In the same way leaders must learn to be flexible so that they are not rigid when facing situations An effective leader will be able to adjust his expectations or plans to suit the realities before him. Inflexible people are rigid and insist on their way of thinking. Inflexible leaders find great difficulty in coping with different personalities or traditions.

Some day, the young pastors will become old and so the same truth applies to both young and old. The older one grows the more he tends to be rigid, holding to the traditions of the forefathers. It takes great wisdom and strength of character to be strong and resistant on the fundamentals but flexible on the non-essentials.

*5. **Dispensable:*** An effective leader recognises that his leadership is not unending, that he really is dispensable in God's timing. This means that a leader's priority is to identify younger people with potential for leadership and develop their leadership skills. The leader must prepare his successor and spend time training the person. An effective leader should develop an exit strategy for leaving, because he knows that sooner or later he will leave office. No leader is successful without preparing a successor.

One problem that discourages leaders from training others to be leaders is a perfectionist mentality. Leaders often want to duplicate themselves in their successors. But this will never work. Each person is different – an original. Successors will have weaknesses that the present leader does not have and vice versa. Remember, if someone tries but does not succeed, he is not a failure. A failure is someone who does not try. The responsibility of the leader is to discover what gifts and talents people have and then develop their gifts. Out of a rich supply of potential leaders, the true successor will be found.

6. Wisdom and Knowledge: In leadership many decisions need to be made. Decision-making requires discernment. This implies maturity of years, years of experience and a constant quest for sufficient information to make an informed decision. Decision-making can never be made out of impulse. Stirred emotions do not form a basis for decision making. Wisdom is also needed to lead different kinds of personalities. An effective leader will learn how to lead them wisely so that in the end they will be satisfied with his leadership.

Both wisdom *and* knowledge are needed in leadership. *Knowledge* is 'acquaintance with facts, truths or principles as from study or investigation.' A leader needs sufficient education with the know-how and skills to lead. Knowledge is expressed by competence which must be seen and accepted. *Wisdom* is a step above knowledge that combines good understanding with good judgement. An educated person has acquired knowledge of facts and truths, but a wise person exercises prudence and judgement in making decisions and in working with people.

7. Persuasive Speaker: A leader must master communication skills. He must know how to organise a speech and be able to persuade. But if a leader is to persuade, he needs more than skills; he must know whereof he is speaking. Persuasion comes in part from content. He must be knowledgeable. The leader must be able to formulate his vision with confidence so that people will believe that he knows what he is doing.

8. Ever Learning: Someone who knows it all and feels no need to learn further will be a disaster as a leader. A leader must know that he has much to learn. By reading, attending seminars and even taking courses of study, the leader will continue to grow intellectually and in skills.

Moral Character

1. A Model to Follow: In every dimension of life, an effective Christian leader must be a model. With a life of transparency he reveals who he really is. He should be a spiritual leader who walks with the Lord daily and is sensitive to whatever God speaks to him through the Scripture. People do look up to their spiritual leaders and expect much from them. The leader must be above reproach. He should not be taking people's things or living an immoral life. A spiritual leader must be growing in his walk with the Lord. No leader can lead his team further than he has gone.

Furthermore, you cannot ask your team members to do what you yourself are unwilling to do. You cannot say, 'Do this' and not do it yourself. Leaders must lead by example. As one person said, 'A leader is a signpost: he knows the way, shows the way and goes the way.'

On one occasion, when a need arose to build a road for a Church, the Church leaders showed the way by doing the work and then asking others to work with them. The leader must be steps ahead of his followers. He sets the pace and does the work so that others will follow. If they don't follow, the leader should not wait but move ahead. Eventually, they will follow.

Moral integrity is a big one. Leaders must model a high standard of morality to be respected. They need to be trustworthy. When they speak today, you should be able to count on them doing the same thing in the days to come. If the leader asks the people to be diligent, he must be diligent. If he wants them to be on time in a meeting, he must be on time. Expecting honesty in handling money of the Church means he also must be trustworthy.

The leader's family should be a model with the wife and children showing respect to him and following God's way. A neglected wife or family will bring reproach on the pastor when they are out of control. If the wife or children have a poor standing in the community and Church, this reflects badly on the leader.

2. Humble: In humility he accepts and admits mistakes when confronted. He is willing to say, 'I'm sorry,' and he repents. He is willing to change his ways and adopt a new life when admonished by others. Village elders often have pride that leads to domination; they lord it over others. The foreman shouts and calls names. His authority is seen. Politicians can be unbending, always blaming others instead of accepting blame. Human nature likes to be the boss, with people carrying your brief case, cleaning your mess and always looking for mistakes. But a Christian leader is humble. He admits mistakes.

3. Patient: Because stones are thrown at him from every corner – rumours, false accusations and petty fault finding – the leader needs patience. Many people throw up their hands and quit, but the leader must persevere.

4. Fair Minded: Prejudice or unfair treatment of his team members will spell the death knoll of effective leadership. The leader can never favour one member over the other. The leader must unite the people through his impartiality, not divide them with favouritism.

5. Self Sacrificial: A genuine leader is willing to sacrifice himself for the good of the people. Since he is not in leadership for himself, he will spend his life giving to the people, not desiring to receive.

6. Grateful: A leader must learn to appreciate anything good received from people. Some leaders don't remember to thank team members for work well done. Anyone who does good to you should be thanked. This thankful attitude toward the team members will motivate them to serve better. Don't withhold comments of praise. Be generous by telling them what they have done well. Offer them compliments when they do well because your positive attitude toward them will enable them better to receive some correction when needed.

7. Humorous: Because he deals with people, the leader must have a sense of humour. He must not take himself too seriously. He should be able to laugh at himself, be jovial and encouraging, showing the joy of the Lord.

8. Loyal: The leader is like a father to his people. They look up to him with respect and trust. He must reciprocate by relating to them in a fatherly manner – defending and protecting his people and making them feel secure from attack. Leaders must be 'mature Christians who run on petrol and not on diesel,' as one leader told me. Mature Christian leaders do not leave behind them diesel fumes that hurt the eyes of his team members. In contrast, immature leaders speak unwisely and foolishly, emitting a lot of smoke that disturbs people and creates misunderstanding and division.

9. Faithful: Faithfulness is required of leaders to carry out responsibilities and to protect the resources. In the secular world, faithfulness is expected by 'the gods of the organisation.' For the Christian leader, however, faithfulness is based on the fear of God and obedience to him.

CONCLUSION

These are the marks of effective Christian leaders as presented to me personally by various Christian leaders in many African countries. For characteristics of Christian leaders described in books, check the bibliography.[2]

Why then do leaders fail? The following chapter discusses mistakes of leaders.

SEARCHING THE SCRIPTURE WITH APPLICATION

1. Discuss the marks of the traditional leaders among your own peoples.
2. In what ways are they similar to the composite marks of African leaders given above, and in what ways are they different?
3. To what extent have cultural concepts of leadership become part of the concept of leadership in Christian circles?
4. Which traditional marks of an effective leader should be valued and appropriated today by Christian leaders? Which marks should be avoided?
5. Compare the African traditional marks of a leader with the marks of a Christian leader stated above. How are they similar and how are they different?
6. Think through the accounts of various biblical leaders, like Abraham, Moses, and David. How do their characteristics of leadership compare with the African traditional marks of leadership?
7. Contrast the marks of Jesus' leadership style as found in the Gospels with the African traditional marks of a leader. How are they similar or dissimilar?
8. We have shared with you above what Christian leaders said should be the marks that characterise leaders today – both personality characteristics and moral character. Evaluate their opinion. Have they missed some important marks or can some marks stated above be further elaborated in your opinion?
9. What caused people to respect leaders in traditional African culture?
10. What causes people to respect Christian leaders today?
11. Why does a leader need to show strength in leadership and yet be flexible?
12. Discuss the difference between knowledge and wisdom? How do you obtain knowledge and how do you gain wisdom?
13. Many younger leaders have gained much knowledge through schooling so that they 'know more' than their elders. Why doesn't that automatically qualify them to become leaders?
14. What can younger leaders learn from older ones? And what can older leaders learn from younger ones?
15. Evaluate this statement: 'The character of a person is the most important mark of a leader, both in African traditional culture and also in biblical teaching.'

Endnotes

1 Pr 14:28 The Message

2 Sanders 1980:71f; Gardner 1990; Myra 1987; Engstrom 1976; 1979; Beasley-Murray 1990; Kouzes 1993.

28
MISTAKES OF CHRISTIAN LEADERS

'Observe the people who always talk before they think – even simpletons are better off than they are.'[1]

Lessons are learned not only from effective leaders but from their mistakes.

Following are comments derived both from African Christian leaders who shared their wealth of experience and observation and also from other Christian leaders who have written about them. These comments will be short and pithy for they have been developed elsewhere in this book. But bringing them together in this pointed way will drive home certain important pointers.

1. Spiritual Insensitivity: Due to busyness or delinquency, the leader lapses in his spiritual disciplines. He no longer prays as he should; nor does he spend time with God in his Word. He ceases to be sensitive to the leading of the Holy Spirit and relies on self rather than God. His lifestyle does not glorify God nor reflect a love for God and dependence on his leading. Decisions are no longer made according to biblical principles. Elders are chosen on the basis of clan and not according to biblical standards. Above all else, the leader must give God preeminence in all things. Out of this failure flow many other failures.

2. Pride: The greatest mistake is formed in the mind. People think they are leaders because they are the only ones who can lead. They feel they know it all; they will not listen to others because they think, 'I know it because I am the leader.' A wise leader will recognise his own limitations and seek counsel, guidance and advice from others. An effective leader has wise assistants and discerning advisors.

Another form of pride is the assumption that everyone will agree with you; that everyone should respect you as leader and follow your ideas. This is a big mistake. An effective leader must recognise that opposition is inevitable and that the opposition may be correct. The leader may be wrong. In humility you should accept this.

3. Living in Sin: Some leaders live in sin and feel comfortable with it. They follow their evil ways while hiding it from people. They keep doing evil but stay in the ministry. One leader told me: *'Hiding sin has killed the Church in Africa today.'* In African culture the leader is always right; he never makes mistakes. So this tradition follows in the Christian Church today.

4. Nepotism: Appointing people to positions for which they do not qualify simply because they are from your own family, clan, tribe or circle of friends. The leader must resist enormous pressure to do the right thing. To be effective, leaders must choose the best qualified personnel who can move the ministry toward accomplishing the goals if they want to be effective.

5. Favouritism: The leader will naturally appreciate some team members more than others, either because of their personality, contribution or some relationship. Leaders make divisive mistakes whenever they favour one person over the other. Tribalism and clanism are deadly mistakes. The leader must avoid all cliques and never favour certain ones over others. Such attitudes will be noticed and will be destructive in one's leadership.

Favouritism can take another form: the leader works with only a few of the elders instead of all the elders and the whole congregation. All the others are kept in the dark. The end result is division, mistrust and quarrels. The effective leader will be transparent and fair minded, working with all the people.

6. Over-Commitment: A leader who becomes overly busy because he has accepted too many responsibilities will not be able to anything well. You must determine before the Lord what your focus should be – that goal which you desire under God to fulfill and do well.

7. Indecisive: A weak leader finds difficulty making decisions and acting upon those decisions. He listens to different viewpoints and vacillates. He is swayed one way and then the other. Leaders must consult and they must be wise in all decision making. But after investigation, thought and prayer, a decision must be made which the leader will stand by.

8. Inadequate Training: Education is no substitute for gifts. But gifted leadership without adequate training will leave you bereft and unable to fulfill your potential. Some Church leaders do not value education. 'Education is not something that is needed,' they say. But they are wrong! A solid basic education is foundational. Reading books, attending seminars, and taking courses will help the leader keep growing and remain up-to-date.

9. Failure to plan: Because of lack of training and understanding, many leaders just deal with things as they come. They fail to plan for future growth and development. Hence the Church fails to grow and prosper. Leaders must learn how to plan.

10. An Unprepared Successor: Assuming that you are the president, bishop, chairman, or principal for life is the sign of a failed leader. No leader can be considered successful if he does not prepare a successor. Observe from the first day who is capable. Prepare several people to replace you so that you don't end with panic. Training others, developing the gifts in others and growing a pool of trained team members will drive every effective leader.

11. Failure to Delegate: Many leaders fall into the pitfall of trying to do everything themselves;

they fail to delegate. For various reasons this failed leader is common. 'I know some leaders,' said one person, 'if they died today, no one would know what to do. He keeps all the files and records to himself. No one else has access to them.'

12. Neglect of Teaching: Many pastors fail to provide systematic teaching from the Scriptures. They jump from one topic to another topic each Sunday. There is no plan to teach the whole counsel of the Word of God. As a result, people are not grounded in the Scriptures.

Teaching the Scriptures requires study. Many leaders are lazy and fail to prepare their sermons. Many, many do not have higher education. Those who have basic Bible training are content with rehashing whatever they learned in Bible School without digging deeper. Laziness leads to shallow preaching, which leads to superficial understanding of the Christian faith, which leads to immaturity and sin in the Church.

Because of a desire for numerical growth with large and impressive buildings and financial prosperity, many Church leaders loose their focus. As a result, the people are not taught the Word of God. This leads to Christians who are shallow in their faith and understanding.

13. Slandering others: Gossiping about the failures of others, or slandering other members on your ministry team can only bring division and dissension. An effective leader knows how to control his tongue – ever being positive, never being pessimistic about the future or being negative towards others.

14. Breaking confidentiality: Nothing destroys confidence in the leader more than the breaking of confidentiality. Your team members must be assured that whatever they confide with you as the leader will remain confidential. This must be one of the laws of the Medes and of the Persians – *never* to be broken.

15. Unwise discipline: Leaders create all kinds of problems when they exercise discipline on team members without adequate research and with an unbalanced understanding of the situation. Even when a leader has a proper view of things, he can create chaos if he is unwise in his approach or is judgemental in his words.

16. Hasty actions: The unwise leader will rush and hurry into decisions without patience and wise counsel. He will push ahead without the consensus or support of the elders and the people. When he hears a report, he rushes to a hasty conclusion without proper investigation. The consequences are a major mess when the leader is proved wrong.

CONCLUSION

The book of experience is rich in wisdom in knowing how to be an effective leader and how to avoid common mistakes made by leaders. These experienced Christian leaders we have consulted offer wise counsel for those eager to learn.

One of the most important aspects of leadership, and yet one that is potentially divisive, is bringing about change. No one is a leader who is not a change-agent but this requires great wisdom. Chapter 29 explores this topic.

SEARCHING THE SCRIPTURE WITH APPLICATION

The Book of Proverbs is a gem to learn what mistakes a leader should avoid in order to be effective. Study the following Proverbs and apply to leadership.

Laziness

'How long will you lie there, you sluggard? When will you get up from your sleep? A little sleep, a little slumber, a little folding of the hands to rest, and poverty will come upon you like a robber; and want like an armed man' (5:10,11). [poverty connected with laziness in 10:4,5; 13:4; 15:19; 18:9; 19:15,24; 20:4,13; 21:25; 22:13; 24:30-34; 26:13-17; 28:19; hard work is the antidote to poverty in 12:11; 14:23; 28:19]

Lack of knowledge and wisdom

'It is not good to have zeal without knowledge' (19:2). [c.f. 1:7]

Disregarding advice

'The way of a fool seems right to him, but a wise man listens to advice' (12:15). 'Do you see a man wise in his own eyes? There is more hope for a fool than for him' (26:12). 'Plans fail for lack of counsel, but with many advisers they succeed' (15:22).

Speaking rashly

'He who guards his lips guards his life, but he who speaks rashly will come to ruin' (13:30). 'A patient man has great understanding, but a quick-tempered man displays folly' (14:29). 'A gentle answer turns away wrath, but a harsh word stirs up anger' (15:1). 'A hot-tempered man stirs up dissension, but a patient man calms a quarrel' (15:18). [c.f. 12:18,23; 13:3; 16:32; 22:24; 29:11,20]

Slander and gossip

'A gossip betrays confidence, but a trustworthy man keeps a secret' (11:13). 'A perverse man stirs up dissension and a gossip separates close friends' (16:28). [c.f. 6:12-19; 10:18; 16:28; 17:9; 18:8; 20:19; 27:20-26]

Loose talk

'It is to a man's honor to avoid strife, but every fool is quick to quarrel' (20:3) [c.f. 10:8,10,14,19; 11:9,11,20; 12:13,14,22; 15:2,4,28; 17:14,19; 18:6,7; 18:21; 19:28; 29:22; contrast in 17:27,28; 21:23]

Lack of self-control

'Like a city whose walls are broken down is a man who lacks self-control' (25:28).

Partiality – 'To show partiality is not good…' (28:21). [c.f. 24:23-25]

Gullible – 'A simple man believes anything …' (14:15).

Giving-up – 'If you falter in times of trouble, how small is your strength' (24:10).

Being stingy – 'A stingy man is eager to get rich and is unaware that poverty awaits him' (28:22). [c.f. 11:26; 23:6,7]

Endnotes

[1] Pr 29:20 *The Message*

29
THE LEADER AS A CHANGE-AGENT

"Then I saw a new heaven and a new earth, for the first heaven and the first earth had passed away… He who was seated on the throne said, 'I am making everything new.'"[1]

Anyone worthy of being called a 'leader' is a *change-agent*.

In this world everything becomes old or dirty and needs to be changed – made new. Filthy clothes need to be changed.[2] Old laws need to be changed.[3] Even the present heavens and earth will wear out like a garment and need to be changed.[4] God, as the Sovereign Leader, is supreme in bringing about change and making things new.

Christian leaders, who serve as God's under-shepherds, must facilitate change for God's glory and the building of his kingdom. No one is a leader unless he is an agent for change. Any growth or new development is change: adding a new course of study in a Bible School, building a new worship centre, changing the constitution.

Resistance to Change

Most people are very conservative; they resist change. Jesus observed that new wine poured into old, inflexible wineskins that could not change their shape will cause the wineskins to break.[5] Change is difficult but if a Church or ministry organisation does not change over time, it becomes stagnant and begins the process of dying. Change is difficult but inevitable. As Heraclitus, the ancient Greek philosopher, once said, 'Nothing endures but change.' This has been quoted many times and is a truism that rings true through the ages. The effective Christian leader is the key to help bring about desirable change.

Finzel observes that all organisations tend to go through cycles: birth, infancy, childhood, adolescence, adulthood, middle age, graying years, old age and death. In the earlier stages there is life, vitality and development of an organisation with new and exciting ideas. In adulthood the organisation reaches its prime. But as age sets in, the zest and zeal of earlier years are lost. Gradually new ideas are rejected and the chief goal is to maintain the organisation. Nothing of importance happens.[6]

The sign of old age and the beginning of the death process is rejection of new ideas. Innovative leaders are put in their place by such comments as: 'That's impossible.' 'We don't do things that way around here.' 'We tried something like that before and it didn't work.' 'I wish it were that easy.' 'It's against our policy to do it that way.' 'When you've been around a little longer, you'll understand.' 'Who gave you permission to change the rules?' 'How dare you suggest that what we are doing is wrong?'[7]

For many reasons people resist change: they favour tradition and feel comfortable with the old ways of doing things, they lack ownership of the change because they never participated in the decision making process, change is being forced on them, they feel threatened with the loss of something precious or they feel burdened with the heavy cost of the new project. Whatever the reason for resistance, the leader is faced with the challenge of leading into the future.

Qualities of a Change-Agent

The leader as change-agent needs three characteristics: *creativity* to explore what changes are needed, *courage* to bring about change, and *wisdom* to know how to lead in change.

Creativity: Creativity and innovation are needed to bring about change. 'Creativity is the generation of new ideas, and innovation is putting them into practice. Creativity and innovation are essential in a changing world.'[8] But where do creative and innovative ideas originate?

Surely, the leader must lead into the future. He sees a problem and imagines the solution. Finding fault and criticising shortcomings are not indications of genius; but finding new ways of doing things in order to avoid the difficulties does require a creative genius.

Oft times, however, the best ideas for change spring from the grass roots. The role of the leader is to stimulate his team members to think beyond the status quo; his role is not only to be creative but to create an environment for the team members to think creatively. 'The milieu required for the stimulation of hearts and minds is one in which people are free to express themselves. An atmosphere restricted by fear of ridicule, traditionalism, legalism, or a "holier than thou" attitude stifles thought and interchange. Creativity also requires appropriate places and times for thought and prayer.'[9]

Change for change sake is futile. But change to improve and grow is a sign of youthful vigour. Keep reading the Scriptures prayerfully with reflective and thoughtful observations. How can your Church, institution or ministry organisation become more faithful and pleasing to God? Keep your ear to the ground, listening to your people. What new problems or conditions are arising? What changes would help you minister better in these changing conditions? Keep your eye on developments in your community, nation or sphere of influence. What changes out there impinge on your ministry which requires thoughtful and prayerful change? Think and imagine creatively!

Courage: Fearful leaders are afraid of the negative consequences of change; they fear making decisions because of the fallout from bad decisions. But fearful leaders cannot lead.

For the Christian leader, courage in ministry is found in one's trust in the living God and his Word. Moses feared an inability to speak eloquently before Pharaoh, and he feared rejection by the people. God assured Moses, 'I will be with you.'[10] When Joshua succeeded Moses, God admonished him to be 'strong and courageous.' Success was promised to Joshua if he meditated on the Book of the Law day and night to carefully observe God's commandments.[11] This idea is repeated over and over in Scripture: 'The LORD is with me; I will not be afraid. What can man do to me?'[12]

'Courage is not the absence of fear; it's the ability to face our fears and lead effectively in spite of them.'[13] Admit your fears before God in prayer but do not collapse under your fears. Keep your focus on your calling and the goals before you. 'Fear is dispelled when you focus on your purpose.'[14]

Leaders fear failure due to poor judgement in decision making. Keeping the status quo is the most secure in the short run. For the near term, sticking to the old ways is the easiest; eventually, however, the status quo may lead to deep problems. The leader does well to remember that good judgement comes from experience, and experience comes by learning from mistakes of poor judgement. Mistakes are not the end of the world. Every leader makes mistakes in judgement. Only through such experience does the leader learn how to make good judgement decisions.

Wisdom: A Kenyan proverb says, 'Wisdom outweighs strength.' Indeed, great wisdom is needed to be strong and avoid unnecessary or foolish mistakes. Mistakes will be made but the wise leader takes care to avoid as many mistaken decisions for change as possible. Following are some basic principles that should help the Christian leader be wise as an effective agent for change.

1. Go slowly: 'A professor once told his class that he would place on the board the most important principle relative to the process of change. Thereupon he turned and spent the next fifteen minutes etching out two words: GO SLOWLY. Good leaders know and consistently practice this crucial axiom.'[15]

No principle is more African than this one. Many African proverbs speak to this issue. The Swahili say, '*Hurry, hurry brings no blessing.*' The Akamba say, '*Slowly, slowly is the way to go.*' '*Hurry, hurry does not give me time to take a good look*' goes another proverb. Real understanding of a situation takes time and therefore one must bring about change slowly. The Kuria say, '*Slowly, slowly the porridge goes into the gourd.*' Another proverb says, '*Chew slowly and eventually you can swallow.*' Patience will bring success, not hasty actions.

No principle is more important than this. *Never* make or suggest changes during the first year of ministry. People will watch closely a new and aggressive leader who comes with a bag full of new ideas. Trust must be earned first before venturing into the potentially difficult task of innovation. When considerable resistance prevails, it is best and wisest to delay. It is more important to change people's attitudes and values than to change policies or practices. Change will come in its proper time. Don't rush it. Unity is to be valued above all else.

2. Engage in prayer, reflection and sharing: If the leader and people recognise that Jesus Christ is the Lord of the Church, then his people must be in thoughtful prayer and reflection to determine God's will. This is not a formal two minute prayer before a discussion; neither is it two days of fasting and prayer, though it may include that. A spirit of prayer and dependence on God must pervade the whole exercise. Instead of someone forcing his will on the people, the leader and his team seek to know God's will for their ministry. And this all takes time.

*3. **Enlist team members in decisions:*** Change comes more easily when the group has participated in the decision making process. Resistance arises from surprise announcements; resentment boils up because of lack of participation. 'Involvement in the planning process tends to generate the necessary force for change itself. Facts personally researched are better understood, more emotionally acceptable, and more likely to be utilised than those passed down by someone else. Participation in analysis and planning helps overcome resistance, which arises from proceeding too rapidly or too slowly.'[16]

Some African Christian leaders may not feel a need to consult. 'In my culture the leader does not need to seek the opinion of his people in order to make decisions,' said one person. That may have been valid in his community in the past but never within a Christian community. 'That approach is very dangerous,' observed another leader. 'Traditionally, that approach was correct but in the Christian Church it can only lead to a dangerous split.' Christian leaders must not be authoritative and overbearing. Leaders must seek the opinion of others and listen to them. 'I would say,' said one leader, '*it is very important to seek consensus. If a leader makes a decision without consulting, if the project fails, he is considered a failure. But if the decision is made by consensus, leaders are not considered failures.*'

One strong pastoral leader said that he would describe the problem to the Church committee. He would then ask, 'What should we do?' They would all discuss it. Then at the appropriate time he would join in the discussion and suggest his ideas. They would often agree. At other times he would make his proposed solution at the beginning and ask, 'What do you think?' They would all discuss it and eventually make a decision, usually agreeing with the pastor. For many years after his departure people still look back on this man as a wise leader who united the people. Kamau refers to this approach to decision making in these words, 'The group develops a sense of ownership and are highly motivated to contribute toward the implementations of the decisions made. The leader's role is one of service and assistance to the building and maintaining of a productive group.'[17]

A strong and persuasive leader may succeed in pushing his will through. Progress may be quick and impressive. But if the team does not truly support the change, it will all collapse when the leader departs. One pastor made the following observation to me:

The only decisions I make personally are my messages. People must have a voice in decision making. I speak to the people and say, 'We have finished this. Now what do you want?' The Church replied, 'We want a Church hall.' I asked them, 'Will you contribute to this?' 'Yes,' they agreed. You cannot dictate to the people. If you impose your will on the people, it will collapse when you leave.

*4. **Provide motivation for change:*** Although the team should partner together in making decisions for change, the burden of bringing about change rests with the leader. In order to motivate people for change the following principles should be followed:[18]

- Inspire with a vision and a dream of what could be accomplished through this contemplated change. Make it goal oriented change.
- Talk of the rewards and benefits that will flow from the change.

- Communicate freely, frequently and effectively so that everyone is brought together with the excitement of the future prospect.
- Be transparent and accountable to your team members so that they will gain trust in you as the leader. Be sincere and genuine; be humble and readily acknowledge faults and failures, weaknesses and limitations.
- Gain credibility by showing confidence and knowledge concerning the plans for change.
- Provide compelling reasons for achieving the goals through change.
- Help people see how their problems will be resolved through change.
- Receive, assimilate and utilise suggestions coming from the people.

CONCLUSION

Deciding to change takes wisdom. But,

> ...once a decision is made, don't look back or second-guess yourself. Expect and demand commitment to the decision on your part and on the part of those who are going to be working on it. Don't seek popularity in decision making. Leadership can be a lonely business. Be consistent in applying the consequences of your decision. Don't vacillate.[19]

But if things do go wrong and you fail to achieve the intended goals, don't blame and find fault. Get proper feedback. Was it the planning or organising or implementation that went wrong? Perhaps the wrong individuals were improperly assigned the task? If over time you decide a better alternative is needed, go through the decision making process again to make changes.

We can learn much from a model leader in Scripture who has written a diary of his leadership experiences. Our next chapter will be on Nehemiah.

SEARCHING THE SCRIPTURE WITH APPLICATION

1. What changes have been attempted within the last five years in your Church or place of ministry?
2. What was the response of the people to this change or attempted change?
3. If the change was made successfully, what were the reasons for the successful making of the change?
4. If the change was not made successfully, what might have been done differently?
5. Josiah, King of Judah, made dramatic changes in Israel during his reign (2 Ki 22:1-23:30; c.f. 2 Ch 34:1-35:26). Read and consider what elements contributed to the change Josiah was able to make?
6. The apostles made a significant change in the administrative arrangements of the early Church (Ac 6:1-7). Read and consider what elements contributed to this successful change?
7. The one element in the above two cases, that is not true in most Christian contexts today, is the absolute authority of the King in Judah and the Apostles in the early Church. In light of the more democratic character of administration today, what principles should guide a leader in seeking to make change?

8. Following are some of the possible objections to change. For each objection, devise a plan how to deal with that.
    a. The older elders and former leaders object to changes from past practices that have been followed for many years.
    b. People fear the cost and the loss that would arise from the changes.
    c. Key individuals do not see the value or importance of the change.
9. What should a wise leader do if considerable resistance continues after he has taken much effort to persuade people with answers to their objections?
10. Change for the sake of change has no value. Discuss the possible circumstances which should cause a leader to explore possibilities of change?

End Notes

[1] Rev 21:1,5
[2] Zec 3:3,4 AV
[3] Heb 7:12
[4] Ps 102:26
[5] Mt 9:17
[6] Finzel 1994:67f
[7] Finzel 1994:71
[8] Wofford 1999:142
[9] Wofford 1999:155
[10] Ex 3:12
[11] Jos 1:6,8
[12] Ps 118:6 NIV
[13] Perkins 2000:46
[14] Perkins 2000:48
[15] Gangel 1997:205
[16] Gangel 1997:208
[17] Kamau 1996:48
[18] Barna 1997:191f
[19] Engstrom 1976:154

30
NEHEMIAH:
A MODEL LEADER

'They all plotted together to come and fight against Jerusalem…
But we prayed to our God
and posted a guard day and night to meet this threat.'[1]

The Christian leader relies on God totally but accepts full responsibility.

In Nehemiah's memoirs of his Jerusalem venture we find a model leader who embraces God's sovereign rule while accepting full responsibility for his work. Faced with a threat, what did he do? He prayed. No book in the Bible contains more evidence of a person who was consciously dependent on God. And yet Nehemiah's diary account reveals a brilliant leader-manager who practices the ageless principles of management.

The events of Nehemiah occurred after the destruction of Jerusalem in 587 B.C. when Nebuchadnezzar took thousands of Jews into captivity. After the seventy-year captivity, Cyrus, the Persian king, issued an edict permitting the return of the Jews to their home country. Ezra records the first return of 49,897 under Zerubbabel in 538 B.C. The exiles rebuilt the altar and offered sacrifices. Under the prophetic ministry of Haggai and Zechariah the temple was completed in 515 B.C. A further number of exiles returned in 458 B.C. under Ezra's leadership.

Nehemiah's account begins in 445 B.C. when he learns of the frightful conditions of the Jewish exiles who had returned to Jerusalem. Without a wall built around the city of Jerusalem, the people were under continual harassment by their enemies. The account of Nehemiah's response to this dismal report from Jerusalem displays a model of leadership from which every Christian leader should learn.

Notice the following attributes of leadership in the life of Nehemiah drawn from his memoirs.[1]

1. Nehemiah manifested an unselfish concern for God's people.

Nehemiah served in the elevated and comfortable position, albeit a potentially dangerous one, as cupbearer to King Artaxerxes I of Persia (465-424 B.C.). As a royal butler, Nehemiah was a trusted friend of the king who would first taste the drinks before offering them to the king, to ensure that the king would not be poisoned. Because of his relationship with Artaxerxes, he was no doubt a confident and advisor to the king in the royal palace.

In the latter part of 445 B.C., Hanani, Nehemiah's brother, came from Jerusalem to the royal portion of Shushan (or Susa) where Nehemiah was serving the king. He had come with a very discouraging report. The remnant of Jews in Jerusalem was 'in great trouble and shame. The wall of Jerusalem is broken down, and its gates are destroyed by fire.'[2] Upon hearing this Nehemiah 'sat down and wept and mourned for days,' fasting and praying.[3]

Why should Nehemiah be so concerned? He was not even born in Israel and lived a long journey of eleven hundred miles from Jerusalem. Following the Fertile Crescent, Ezra had taken four months to travel the road by foot thirteen years before in 458 B.C.[4] The road was treacherous because of thieves. Nehemiah was far from their difficulties and he was comfortably situated.

But Nehemiah was concerned for God's people, as all Christian leaders should be. Unselfishness in wanting to help others is the trait of a godly leader. Peter admonished the bishop-elders in Asia Minor, 'Be shepherds of God's flock that is under your care, serving as overseers – not because you must, but because you are willing, as God wants you to be; not greedy for money, but eager to serve… '[5] Danger is real that leaders will use their position for greedy gain and selfish interests. Not so for the God fearing leader.

2. Nehemiah identified with his people.

No effective leader looks down on his followers or distances himself from them. Rather he follows Nehemiah's example by identifying with them.

When Nehemiah confessed the sins of Israel he prayed, 'I confess the sins *we* Israelites, including myself and my father's house, have committed against you. *We* have acted wickedly… *We* have not obeyed the commands…'[6]

Did Nehemiah actually participate in the sins which led to the exile? He was not even alive at that time! But instead of condemning and distancing himself from them he identifies himself with them.

An effective leader thinks 'we'; not 'me' and 'you.' We are in this together. If the people fail, 'I' have failed in my failure to communicate adequately; in my failure to mentor and train; in my failure to guide and instruct. In a similar manner, Daniel identified with his people in prayer.[7]

[1] Numerous volumes have been written on Nehemiah as a leader, including: *From Rubble to Rejoicing: A Study in Effective Christian Leadership based on Nehemiah* by Donald R. Jacobs; *Nehemiah and the Dynamics of Effective Leadership* by Cyril Barber; *Excellence in Leadership* (drawn from a study of Nehemiah) by John White; *Hand Me Another Brick: Principles of Effective Leadership* by Charles Swindoll; *Victorious Christian Service: Studies in the Book of Nehemiah* by Alan Redpath.

3. Nehemiah was a student of God's Word and taught it to the people.

When Nehemiah prayed, he recalled the instructions given by Moses in the Pentateuch.[8] All prayer is strengthened when one can quote the promises of God and praise Him through the words of Scripture. This careful knowledge of the Word of God is evident throughout Nehemiah's memoirs.

On October 8, 445 B.C. soon after Nehemiah had returned to Jerusalem, all the people assembled in Jerusalem to mark the beginning of the civil year. This was also celebrated as the Feast of Trumpets when all labor ceased.[9] Led by Ezra the priest and scribe, and Nehemiah the Governor, they read the Law of Moses, explained its meaning and taught them.[10] For five to six hours the people stood to hear the Word of God read and taught. This continued every day for the whole week of the Feast. Not only did Ezra the priest teach, but also Nehemiah, the civil leader, 'instructed the people.'

This emphasis upon the Word of God continued sixteen days later when the people gathered in sackcloth and ashes in penance in the spirit of the Day of Atonement.[11] For three hours the people stood to hear the Word of God.

No one can be an effective Christian leader unless he or she is saturated with the Word of God. Nehemiah was not the religious leader but the civil leader. But Nehemiah stood beside Ezra to give support in this exercise. Ezra 'devoted himself to *the study* and *observance* of the Law of the LORD, and to *teaching* its decrees and laws in Israel.'[12] What an example: studying the Bible, obeying the precepts of the Bible and teaching the Bible to the people. This is foundational to all effective Christian leadership.

4. Nehemiah depended on God in prayer.

Nehemiah was a man of prayer. Nine prayers are recorded in his memoirs. As soon as he heard the discouraging report, he went to God in prayer.[13] He not only prayed but he humbled himself before God by fasting and praying 'for some days.' Every Christian leader must know where he must turn when confronted with challenges that are inevitable in leadership. How many leaders confirm that they find great consolation and strength through prayer!

The character of Nehemiah's prayer in chapter one exemplifies a man well conversant with communicating with the eternal God. Notice the reverence and respect he shows toward God[14] and the humility in confession of sins.[15] On the basis of the promises in Scripture, he intercedes on behalf of God's people.[16] It is not until the very end of the prayer that Nehemiah actually prays his petition that concerned him at the moment: 'Give your servant success today by granting him favor in the presence of this man [King Artaxerxes].'[17]

Prayer in most languages means 'to ask' or 'to beg.' At its core, prayer is the language of someone in need. Self-reliant and self-sufficient leaders do not pray. They have no need to pray because they are all-sufficient. However, they are not *Christian* leaders but leaders that reflect the bravado of this world. An effective Christian leader is proficient, professional, competent, and fully capable. But he recognises that he is utterly dependent on God.

The lifestyle of prayer manifested in the life of Nehemiah is fascinating. He is a prime example of one who 'prays without ceasing.' Scattered throughout his memoirs, Nehemiah refers to his prayer life.

Standing before the king he breathes a quiet, fleeting prayer to God.[18] When confronted by mocking enemies he breathes a word of prayer for help.[19] When recalling his great personal sacrifice in not accepting a salary through taxation of the people; and furthermore, when he remembered his generosity in feeding the people instead of demanding the food allotment for the governor, he then prayed to God, 'Remember me with favor, O my God, for all I have done for these people.'[20] It is good to remember that when we serve God faithfully, he does reward us. Nehemiah prayed this not for selfish reasons but because he knew that God does reward those faithful to him. Throughout Nehemiah's ministry he was breathing prayer as naturally as a human being breathes air.[21]

5. Nehemiah had a personal relationship with God.

This is evident in his prayer life and in his understanding of God.[22] A personal relationship with God includes a deep theological understanding of who God is: his majesty and splendour, his righteousness and holiness; his mercy and grace, his unfailing love and redemption, and his faithfulness – all found in this simple prayer.

But a relationship with God includes more than a cognitive knowledge of God's attributes; it includes a personal relationship with God. To *know* God is deep and personal that binds the inner soul with the Eternal Spirit.

Prayer can be formal and nominal. Theologians and pastors can pray beautiful phrases because they have trained in Bible Colleges and because they have much experience in Churchly affairs. But an effective Christian leader knows what it is to 'walk' with God as Enoch did and enjoy his fellowship.

6. Nehemiah had courageous faith.

Four months elapsed between the time Nehemiah heard of the troubles in Jerusalem[23] and the time he approached King Artaxerxes.[24] What was he doing? Clearly, he was not rushing into this without much prayer and forethought. The memoirs of Nehemiah reveal a mature leader who thought and prayed before he acted.

He had every reason to hesitate. What Nehemiah was attempting was a major undertaking that could even cost his life. Nehemiah's master, King Artaxerxes I, was the very reason why the Jews were in such despair. After Ezra had led a second contingency of Jews back to Jerusalem thirteen years earlier, the Jewish enemies opposed the continued building of Jerusalem. So in response to the complaint by the Jewish enemies, after some research, Artaxerxes wrote a letter saying that Jerusalem did indeed have a 'long history of revolt against kings.' Therefore, he issued an order to stop all the work on the city so that it would not be rebuilt.[25]

Though we have no record of Nehemiah's thoughts, he faced a daunting situation like Esther. Queen Esther of Ahasuerus (Xerxes I) who immediately preceded Artaxerxes I, took courage and placed her life in jeopardy when she approached the king in order to save the Jews from extinction. With the fatalistic words she said, 'If I perish, I perish.' Like Esther, Nehemiah was now taking his life into his hands.

The cupbearer must never be sad in the presence of a king with absolute power. Who wants a moody, sad-faced, discouraged cupbearer to serve you? Sadness could even mean dissatisfaction which eventually would lead to the assassination of the king. A sad countenance could lead to instant death. But Nehemiah had the courage to show a sad face before the king because of his deep concerns.[26] What Nehemiah did was both selfless and courageous.

Later in Jerusalem Nehemiah learned of the plight of the poor Jews who were being exploited by wealthy Jews.[27] Nehemiah's approach is exemplary. He erupted in righteous indignation *against* the wealthy who exploited their poor brothers. But he did not rush into a decision; he was not rash with thoughtless words and actions. Though he was angry, he 'pondered' in his mind what to do.[28] The *NASB* says he 'consulted with himself.' It was only after thinking it over that he reached a conclusion which was both just and courageous. He addressed the wealthy class and told them that their actions were wrong. He communicated well and they agreed to stop their abuse of power.

No leader can succeed unless he or she has courage that grows out of a relationship with God in prayer, deep reflection and thought. Stephen Wise comments somewhere, 'Success is not the reverse of failure; it is the scorn of failure. Always dare to fail; never fail to dare.' An effective leader has courage to decide to do the right thing even when confronting the powerful and wealthy.

7. Nehemiah planned with foresight.

Every effective leader must think ahead and plan his course of action. Nehemiah repeatedly shows himself to be a planner; he did not lead simply by reacting to events as they arose.

When King Artaxerxes asked Nehemiah why he was sad, Nehemiah with a quick prayer to God gave a specific answer, showing that he had done previous thought and laid out specific plans in his mind.[29] The extraordinary detail of his proposal shows that Nehemiah was well prepared in his thinking. He knew what he wanted to do.

8. Nehemiah understood God's gracious favour on him.

Repeatedly, throughout his memoirs, Nehemiah acknowledges that all the successful turn of events were due to God's gracious hand of favour. When some leaders experience success, they are filled with vain conceit and pride, failing to recognise and acknowledge that success comes from God. Leaders are responsible to plan, seeking the mind of God as they plan. But at best, leaders only 'know in part.' When success comes, it comes only from God's hand. As the Bible teaches, 'Many are the plans in the mind of a man, but it is the purpose of the LORD that will stand.'[30]

Notice the frequent references to God's gracious hand. Nehemiah prayed for God's favour whenever he would speak to the king.[31] When the king granted his request, Nehemiah did not assume that this was due to his clever planning or eloquent speaking. Nehemiah responds, 'And the king granted me what I asked for the good hand of God was upon me.'[32] When Nehemiah talked with the Jews in Jerusalem, he testified again to God's gracious hand on his efforts.[33] The enemies of the Jews heard of Nehemiah's confidence in God.[34] When the wall was completed in just fifty-two days, their enemies 'were afraid and lost their self-confidence because they realized that his work had been done with the help of our God.'[35] When the wall of Jerusalem was dedicated they worshipped and gave thanks to God for enabling them to do this.[36]

Nehemiah was a God-centred leader, not a self-centred one. Instead of pumping up his chest and boasting of success, he led the people to understand that all the work accomplished was due to God's favour. Yes, every work of God requires diligence and faithfulness on the part of people. But success only comes from God and the leader recognises it, testifies and praises God for it.

9. Nehemiah did extensive research.

When Nehemiah first heard of the difficult situation in Jerusalem from eye witnesses, he questioned them to understand the situation better.[37]

When king Artaxerxes sent Nehemiah on this mission to Jerusalem, he sent Nehemiah with army officers and a cavalry because Nehemiah was being sent as the Governor. Sanballat, probably a Moabite and the Governor of Samaria, and Tobiah, an Ammonite who was probably the Governor of Transjordan, were the enemies of the Jews. Nehemiah's arrival in Jerusalem was not welcomed by these two descendants of Lot who were the sworn enemies of descendants of Abraham. With these realities in mind, Nehemiah displayed wisdom and discretion. He did not flaunt his power and position. He did not arouse premature suspicion and opposition.

Without telling anyone of his dreams, 'what my God had put in my heart to do for Jerusalem,' he inspected the walls under the cover of darkness with only 'a few men' with him. Rebuilding the wall required technical knowledge as well as people to do the work. A survey of the wall was necessary to know the extent of the damage and what was needed.

Research in leadership is crucial. Prayer is not enough. Leaders are irresponsible if they assume the Holy Spirit will lead them without fulfilling their human responsibility to research. Too many leaders make hasty decisions without proper information. They assume too much and assumptions can lead to disastrous consequences. Nehemiah was a model for all good managers for he was a man of extensive research.

No responsible Christian leader should plan without research; and no leader should leave all research and investigation to others; he should become involved personally. Leadership and management must be based on facts on the ground. So we read that when he arrived in Jerusalem, after three days of rest and recuperation, he did personal research of the walls at night to avoid notice from Sanballat and Tobiah.[38] By the light of the moon he inspected the whole wall to assess the need for repair.

10. Nehemiah displayed a decisive will and call to action.

A leader not only must think and pray, plan and research; he must be decisive and act like a leader. Courageous decisions must be made. An ambivalent or vacillating person does not make an effective leader.

After much thinking, praying, planning and research, Nehemiah steps forward to communicate the plan of action to deal with the trouble in Jerusalem. 'Come, let us build the wall of Jerusalem,' Nehemiah urged, 'that we may no longer suffer derision.' He communicated this effectively, testifying of God's gracious hand upon him. This motivated the Jews to work and 'strengthened their hands.'[39]

11. Nehemiah was a leader with followers.

No one is going to follow someone who does not know or is unsure of himself. A decisive and confident leader draws followers. A leader by definition is someone with followers. If you don't have followers, you are not a leader.

Nehemiah had followers. He stepped forward, communicated his recommendation to the men and they followed his directives. Every leader needs the gift of motivational speaking. Nehemiah's speech in 2:17,18 contains important elements of motivation: (1) Identification with the people: 'You see the trouble *we* are in.' (2) The problem: 'Jerusalem lies in ruins and its gates have been burned by fire.' (3) Call to action: 'Let us rebuild the wall.' (4) Purpose of rebuilding: 'that we will no longer be in disgrace.' (5) Assurance of God's favour: 'And I told them about the gracious hand of God upon me.'

Nehemiah was appointed Governor by King Artaxerxes I, but he needed to command respect. This was done through prudent and decisive leadership by someone who was confident and comfortable with his role. Throughout the memoirs we read that Nehemiah did indeed have followers.

When Nehemiah called the men to work, they responded, 'Let us start building.' They *owned* the vision. So they began 'this good work.'[40] Chapter 3 records where all the men worked. They continued working, despite the insults of Sanballat and Tobiah, 'till all of it reached half its height, for the people worked with all their heart.'[41] They followed Nehemiah their leader and paid no attention to the ridicule of their enemies. When Nehemiah later rebuked the Jews for their unjust treatment of the poor in their midst, they agreed to do all that Nehemiah demanded of them.[42]

They followed Nehemiah in part because he *led* them; he did not merely direct them. Nehemiah was not used to manual labour for he was a cupbearer in a royal palace. Nevertheless, he laboured with sweat. He not only challenged the men, 'Let *us* rebuild'[43]; he joined the men. Nehemiah worked 'from the first light of dawn til the stars came out.'[44] Neither did he take off his clothes at night, but with all the other men he remained ready to protect the city from attack.[45] 'Spirituality is no substitute for sweat.'

Position often does give a measure of credibility and authority to a person. But credibility must also be earned. Leaders may have reluctant followers but Nehemiah commanded their respect and they willingly followed his lead. People follow inspirational leaders, not cold, written objectives.

12. Nehemiah was a capable organiser of people.

Planning can be ethereal and abstract – a dream for the future. But a true leader-manager is one who can then take those plans and make them concrete by organising resources and personnel. Organising to rebuild the wall was an enormous task. Nehemiah was a master organiser.

The description of the builders in chapter 3 indicates that Nehemiah assigned 39 different groups. All classes of people participated in the building: priests,[46] goldsmiths and perfumers,[47] rulers and the womenfolk,[48] and merchants.[49] Nehemiah wisely organised them so that they built the wall next to their own dwelling places.[50] Directed labour to help others is surely a sign of charity and goodwill. But when the leader can organise people to work on projects that affect them personally, this can generate greater enthusiasm. Nehemiah gave out very specific assignments, designating where each party should work. Organising around natural groupings, such as youth, women, elders, labourers and teachers, is another way of developing a natural grouping of workers. Nehemiah was a master manager.

Organising personnel includes delegation and appointments. The values, which are reflected in his choice of workers, make Nehemiah a model leader. When the wall was rebuilt and the gates were in place, Nehemiah appointed gatekeepers, singers and 'the commander of the citadel.'[51] Just north of the temple, this 'citadel' was the place where the royal garrison was located under the commander appointed by the Persian king. Nehemiah did not appoint someone to oversee the security of Jerusalem on the basis of military expertise, bravery or political connections. Nehemiah chose Hanani 'because he was a man of integrity and feared God more than most men do.'[52]

How many appointments are made and how many people are elected on the basis of human criteria. Saul appealed to the Jews because he had the appearance of a king – tall and impressive. When Saul failed, God chose David whose heart was right before God. When the apostles chose deacons to oversee the distribution of the food for widows they specifically chose men who were 'full of the Spirit and wisdom.'[53] Leaders are successful when they seek out those who are people of integrity, faithful and devoted to God.

13. Nehemiah overcame hindrances.

No leader can expect to serve without experiencing opposition from within and from outside. Successful Christian leaders are assaulted with slander, gossip and unjust treatment. The real test of a leader is his response. Knowing how to overcome hindrances is the difference between success and failure.

When Nehemiah faced opposition he displayed a single minded purpose, ever focused on the goal of rebuilding the wall. Children can be distracted from what they are doing, but an effective leader is focused on the goals and will not allow distractions to divert attention to anything else.

First, the builders of the wall in Jerusalem were faced with the challenging task of removing all the rubbish of the previous century which covered up the large stones needed in the wall building effort. Secondly, Sanballat and Tobiah ridiculed the Jews, disparaging their efforts in building the wall. Third, when that failed, they 'plotted together to come and fight against Jerusalem.'[54]

How did Nehemiah overcome their plots? He and his people '*prayed*' and '*posted guard* day and night to meet the threat.'[55] Nehemiah was both devout and practical. He relied on God's help and urged his workers to trust in God's great power.[56] He also did all he could humanly speaking ('posting a guard'). While half of the men worked to rebuild the wall, the other half stood guard with swords, spears and bows. Even those who worked carried a weapon in one hand while working with the other. They all stayed in the city so that men could guard the city by night and work on the wall during the day.[57] Read it! It is an amazing example of Nehemiah's organising skills and determination to overcome hindrances. He organised the men in such a way that the work went forward even while they protected themselves against possible attack.

When Sanballat, Tobiah and Geshem the Arab used subtle deception, Nehemiah used spiritual discernment to see through their false reports.[58] God gave him wisdom to avoid falling into a plot.

14. Nehemiah demonstrated humility by attributing all praise to God.

The Lord has declared, 'I will not give my glory to another.' When a leader falls into pride, conceit and boasting for success in his leadership, he places himself under the direct judgement of the Lord. For God will not share his glory with his servants. Nehemiah repeatedly attributes his success to the gracious hand of God.[59] When a Christian leader humbles himself before God and attributes all success to God's gracious hand, the Lord will lift him up.[60]

CONCLUSION

Spirituality is fundamental but it is no substitute for management skills. Nehemiah provides us a model that combines extraordinary faith in God with extraordinary practical management skills.

Part Seven details the management skills needed as leader.

SEARCHING THE SCRIPTURE WITH APPLICATION

1. Nehemiah was a man of prayer; he was also a man of action.
   a. Reflect on how prayer and action (of leadership) should compliment each other or how they can compete with each other.
   b. Are prayer and action in separate compartments (now we pray, then we work), or do they interconnect with each other? How does a leader 'pray without ceasing'?
   c. How does prayer impact action? And how does action impact prayer?
   d. Consider your own practice of leadership. How do prayer and action (of leadership) compliment each other in your experience? What changes should you undertake to make prayer and action more effective?
2. Nehemiah was an efficient manager who was able to build the wall in Jerusalem within 52 days, a feat that had not been accomplished in nearly 100 years since Zerubbabel returned to Jerusalem. John White defines efficiency as 'achieving goals with the smallest waste of resources.'
   a. Should all Christian leaders seek to be efficient managers? Why?
   b. Read Nehemiah 1-6 and note the different steps of action Nehemiah took to build the wall and why he was so efficient in accomplishing the task so soon?
   c. What things could have gone wrong to make the work take longer?
   d. What steps can you take to become more efficient in your leadership, 'to achieve oals with the smallest waste of resources'?

Endnotes

1 Ne 4:8f
2 Ne 1:3
3 Ne 1:4
4 Ezr 7:8f
5 1 Pe 5:2
6 Ne 1:6,7
7 Da 9:5,6
8 Ne 1:8,9
9 Nu 29
10 Ne 8:1-9
11 Ne 9:1-3
12 Ezr 7:10
13 Ne 1:4
14 Ne 1:5
15 Ne 1:6f
16 Ne 1:8
17 Ne 1:11
18 Ne 2:4
19 Ne 4:4,5
20 Ne 5:14-19
21 Ne 6:9,14; 13:14-31
22 Ne 1:5-11
23 Ne 1:1
24 Ne 2:1
25 Ezr 4:17-23
26 Ne 2:1-4
27 Ne 5:1-13
28 Ne 5:7
29 Ne 2:4-8
30 Pr 19:21
31 Ne 1:11
32 Ne 2:8b
33 Ne 2:18
34 Ne 2:20
35 Ne 6:16
36 Ne12:27-40
37 Ne 1:2,3
38 Ne 2:11-16
39 Ne 2:17,18
40 Ne 2:18
41 Ne 4:6
42 Ne 5:12,13
43 Ne 2:17
44 Ne 4:21
45 Ne 4:23
46 Ne 3:1
47 Ne 3:8
48 Ne 3:12
49 Ne 3:32
50 Ne 3:30
51 Ne 7:1,2
52 Ne 7:2
53 Ac 6:3
54 Ne 4:1-8
55 Ne 4:9
56 Ne 4:14
57 Ne 4:13-23
58 Ne 6:1-14
59 Ne 5:15f; 6:16; 7:5; 12:27-40
60 Jas 4:10

PART SEVEN

MANAGEMENT SKILLS OF CHRISTIAN LEADERS

Leadership skills include the ability to manage. Unless a Christian leader knows how to manage, he cannot succeed. Management is all about vision, setting goals, organising resources, setting schedules, directing and controlling so that goals are accomplished. Without management skills a leader will lead aimlessly.

Part Seven focuses on the four ingredients of management:

(1) *Developing personal relationships.*
(2) *Planning* with a vision and goals for future development.
(3) *Organising* the workers by staffing and delegating.
(4) *Shepherding* the workers by supervising, motivating and correcting so that the goals will be achieved.

31
DEVELOPING RELATIONSHIPS

"Love one another with brotherly affection.
Outdo one another in showing honor…
Live in harmony with one another.
Do not be haughty, but associate with the lowly."[1]

Developing relationships is foundational for all management.

Management is all about vision, setting goals, organising resources, setting schedules, directing and controlling so that the goals are accomplished. But how does a leader achieve this? The leader cannot do it alone; he needs a team of people to share the vision and carry the load. People are the greatest resource to achieve goals. Nothing can be accomplished unless the leader's team pulls together to accomplish the goals mutually agreed upon.

Many African proverbs teach the importance of team work, a whole community pulling together to achieve a goal. As one African proverb says, '*You cannot play a drum with one finger.*' The Yoruba and Igbo of Nigeria say, '*It takes a whole village to raise a child.*' Rearing children is a community effort. The Akamba say, '*One finger can't kill a flea.*' The Kuria of Kenya say, '*One person is thin porridge; two or three people are a handful of ugali* (stiff cooked meal).' The thin porridge is for the sick or light food taken at breakfast. But *ugali* is firm with heavy consistency, signifying strength. As the Bible says, '*Two are better than one…A threefold cord is not quickly broken.*'[2]

Relationships are essential when working with people. Learning the skills of management in classroom or through experience in the ministry is useless unless the leader first learns how to develop good relationships with those whom he is leading. Hence, developing relationships with your team-members is foundational for all management skills.

Many gifted leaders fail in this area. They are visionary, energetic, intelligent, self-disciplined and well trained. But they do not know how to work with people. No leader can succeed who has not learned how to develop wholesome relationships with those he leads.

> *Leadership* is not so much a function of status or authority as it is of the quality of relationship, the interaction that takes place between the leader and his followers. *It is not a matter of having power over subordinates; it is a matter of having influence with them* (italics added).[3]

Leadership is all about leading people; if one has not learned how to work with people, all leadership is finished. Productivity goes down whenever people are not happy. Relationships are all important in Africa. Nothing can be achieved without harmonious working relationships. Furthermore, developing good relationships is biblical.

A mutual sharing of life between two people goes to the very heart of who people are. Made in the image of God, men and women are intended to reflect the eternal, loving interpersonal relationship of God the Father, God the Son and God the Holy Spirit. Since the fall of Adam and Eve, most of mankind's problems are interpersonal relationships, whether marital or family, vocational or societal, racial or tribal, domestic or international. Because of broken relationships, society breaks down; and leaders have difficulty leading.

Learning how to cultivate wholesome and positive relationships is a challenge but it can be done with God's grace. It takes love and humility. Just read the Bible and learn the kind of character every Christian should have. You may begin with Romans 12:9-21. If anyone follows the precepts outlined in that one passage, that person will go a long way in learning how to develop relationships so basic to leadership. Just read the first part of this book on the character of a Christian leader – the humility, love, purity and integrity of a leader – and you will know exactly what is needed.

However, in this chapter we will summarise the recommendations made by African Christian leaders who have learned these lessons in ministry. From their experience we learn that a leader in Africa *can* lead his people towards the achievement of goals while at the same time valuing relationships and putting people before the work.

Developing Relationships

How do you develop relationships?

1. Respect everyone, even your opponents. It is good to esteem others better than yourself; excel in showing honour to them. To honour someone is to recognise the other person's worth or value. When you honour your team-members, you enrich yourself because you surround yourself with people of worth. But when you dishonour your team-members, you impoverish yourself because you are surrounded with team-members of little value.

At the most basic level, everyone has intrinsic value because they are made in the image of God.

> The most inept, the most degraded, the most incapable or the most handicapped person alive still has intrinsic worth and value as a person. It is not that the person has value *for* society or for any other end…They have a dignity that belongs to their personhood as eternal beings made in God's image…[4]

Leaders should also value and respect their team-members because of their performance and achievement. In public and private give them expressions of praise, esteem, appreciation, affirmation, approval and commendation. Be generous, never stingy. Show them honour through non-verbal means such as the tone of voice, the look of the eyes and the expression of the face, all reflecting a sincerity and genuineness in your communication. A touch can express honour by touching their hand, putting an arm around the shoulder or giving them a warm-hearted hug. Be genuinely concerned for their best interests. Be present with them on their important occasions.

Respect them, be a friend to them and humble yourself before them. Respect for others is shown through kindness. Acknowledge their status in life, their gender or position in society. Respect is shown by not interfering with their plans or property. Cooperate with them and whenever deemed wise, respond to their requests positively. Don't kick back against those who are not friendly toward you. Attend to their needs even if they manifest a negative attitude toward you.

2. Show love and kindness to your team-members. Love is basic when developing personal relationships. This includes care and compassion for those in need. Friendship and kindness are expressions of love. No one can truly develop a positive relationship with others apart from love. See chapters 16-20.

The love of friends assumes a certain mutuality with each person making a contribution. Friendship cannot be one sided only. 'A friend in need is a friend indeed.' Friendship implies a helping hand. In times of grief or anxiety, be present to console and comfort. In times of joy or celebration, be there to congratulate or encourage. In times of sickness, visit them. During times of financial stress from accident, sickness or death, heavy burdens can be felt; when the leader offers some form of help, this bonds the team together with gratitude. Sensitivity to people in their needs will go a long way in cementing a relationship of trust and gratitude.

3. Learn to know your team-members. Down deep inside, every person has a desire to be known. When someone does understand us, we feel accepted and loved. Yet the compelling desire to be known is not matched by the desire to know others, all because of our incurable selfishness. Self is more important than others; our own person and ministry are more significant than others. Saint Francis of Assisi prayed, *'Let me not seek to be understood but to understand.'* That should be the prayer of every leader. Leaders must devote their lives to the unselfish task of knowing and understanding those whom they lead. 'The truth is that you cannot lead people, you cannot serve people and you cannot manage people unless, to some considerable extent, you take the trouble to know them and to understand them.'[3]

A leader cannot develop relationships without knowing the person. That means the leader must draw near to that person by visiting in their homes. From the beginning it is important for the leader to understand that the development of relationships takes a lot of time. Informal settings are required for building relationships so that people can relax and socialise. Sponsor retreats where the team-members can eat together and socialise informally. Do not restrict relationships to places of work. Be friendly with them; share food and fellowship together. Laugh and cry together. Participate with them in the events of life, such as weddings and funerals. This means the leader must be where the people are in order to know them. What problems do they face at home or at work? What challenges do they experience in their family? The leader must be active in cultivating a personal relationship by being close to the people and becoming part of their lives in times of need and in times of joy. Friendship is essential. People need to *desire* to be together; otherwise, relationships are plastic. You cannot detach emotions from relationships, and relationships are essential for successful ministry.

4. Accept people as they are. A leader must recognise the quirks, wrinkles and idiosyncrasies of each person. We are all different in our personalities with strengths and weaknesses which attract or repel. A leader must learn to accept people as they are and not be turned off by their defects or deficiencies. Try as they may, leaders cannot refashion people into their own likeness. By accepting them as they are, a leader can help them grow into the person that will increasingly glorify God and contribute to the building of his Church.

5. Show a personal interest in team-members. People are not merely workers who contribute toward the goals of the institution; people are not merely personal assets who are more precious than material assets. They are *people* and people need a personal touch. Greet them; inquire of their well-being. Show a personal interest in them. Be engaged with them in personal ways. Healthy relationships can only be developed when the leader helps to meet people's needs – their emotional, spiritual, material and work needs. Treat people as human beings by meeting their felt needs, and they will value their leader. When the leader shows personal interest in his people, they will reciprocate by respecting the leader and cooperating with his efforts to lead.

6. Cultivate a trusting relationship. If leaders are to succeed, they must be able to trust their team-members, and the team-members must be able to trust their leader. This means that both team-members and leaders must know one another. The greatest burden, however, is on the leader to demonstrate that he is indeed trustworthy.

The two essential qualities of a successful Christian leader are character and competency. If either one is lacking, the team-members will loose faith in their leader. Character is crucial. Integrity of the leader, his honesty and truthfulness, his purity and holiness of character must be beyond reproach. Competency is second in importance. Team-members must know that their leader knows what he is doing; that he knows the way and how to get there.

If people are to trust their leader, there must be transparency. Self-disclosure is essential for any meaningful relationship to develop. Be open and candid. They need to know who their leader really is, and what their leader is thinking or wanting. If a leader is reserved, people will not know or trust him. People should see and know their leader. This of course makes the leader vulnerable. People will soon learn that their leader is not a 'superman' but someone with flesh and blood like other people; someone with foibles and limitations. But when the leader in all humility and honesty shares of himself, people will respect and trust him.

Tom Marshall in his excellent book on relationships says this:

- You will never understand the other person unless they reveal themselves to you.
- They will never reveal themselves to you unless they trust you.
- They will never trust you unless they know you.
- They will never know you unless you reveal yourself to them.[5]

The burden therefore rests on the leader. For team-members to trust their leader, he must make himself vulnerable through open and honest transparency. Despite the risks, the rewards are immeasurable.

Some team-members feel insecure and are easily threatened. A skillful and wise leader will learn how to develop and maintain good relationships with difficult people. People need to know there is no hidden agenda; no one is seeking their positions. Helping them to feel secure is important in relationships. Therefore, the leader must be humble and patient in order to reassure everyone that they are on the same team together. Working together is important to succeed so everyone needs to be in it together. The team brainstorms together and develops the vision and goals together. The team is consulted from time to time. When success is achieved, everyone is recognised. This kind of trusting relationship builds a firm foundation for success.

7. Share your vision with your team-members. A leader must rally the team-members to the one compelling vision embraced by the team. In the process of accepting the vision and goals, not everyone may be on the same page. Some may be reluctant but consenting; others may be accepting but unclear about the vision. Still others may vacillate and change their minds. So the leader must continually refresh the fire that kindled the acceptance of that vision. By sharing the vision enthusiastically with people individually and collectively, the leader is able to generate support by those who will help implement that vision.

8. Work together with the team. Nothing brings a leader closer to the people than standing shoulder to shoulder and working together with them. Whenever a leader assigns work and directs the team-members in their work assignment without joining them, the leader speaks loud and clear: 'I direct and give orders but do not share the burden of work with you. I am not one of you but above you.' This attitude does not build relationships. But an incredible impression is made upon the team-members when their leader joins hands with them in accomplishing some task together with them.

When team members fail to do their job well, it is easy to damage relationships when correcting them. If you criticise them with a stern correction, they will become unhappy and will not perform their duty well. A wise leader will be a servant leader by demonstrating how to do it; he will come down to their level. The leader will show them practically how to do it.

9. Never embarrass people. It is one thing for the leader to correct in private the way someone is doing his work; it is another thing to make the person loose face in front of others. 'I don't mind my work being criticised,' said one person, 'but I do not want to loose face before others.' It is important *never* to embarrass a person. *How* a leader corrects another is most crucial. *Never* correct someone in front of others. *Never* make someone look bad.

Always avoid public confrontations. When a controversial issue arises in a meeting with disagreements, it is best to suspend the agenda. Lead the team in a time of corporate prayer. Give them time to think and pray over the matter individually. Consult the persons concerned privately to discuss the controversial issue. For a leader to push the issue in a group will only deepen the resistance and create misunderstanding. In a shame-culture, everything must be done to avoid making someone look bad. Help save his face through patience, prayer and private diplomacy.

10. Use a personal touch in directing people. Issuing instructions through the impersonal touch of paper or electronic communication falls short of the personal word. A faceless instruction is less compelling than a face-to-face encounter. Meeting face-to-face will no doubt take more time, but it is worth far more than an impersonal one. A meeting may be scheduled two months in advance and noted in the diary. But a sudden person-to-person encounter is more compelling and will easily override plans made months earlier.

11. Provide an environment where people feel valued. There is nothing so satisfying as working in an environment where one is appreciated and valued. A leader is wise when he seeks opportunity to commend a person's work and express sincere and genuine appreciation for the work done. Be generous in offering sincere and personal words of commendation for work well done. Recognise the achievements of a worker through a written note or a little award at the end of the year. Conduct annual meetings of recognition to express public and sincere appreciation of the contribution which the workers have made. Even when the leader must correct the team-members, if it can be done in the context of appreciation for the good things done, it will help the team-members to accept the correction better.

12. Be gracious in leadership. While the leader should plan in the normal way, people almost always fall short of expectations. For the sake of maintaining harmonious relationships it is important to move forward together with the people. Time schedules must give way so that people can continue being part of the team which keeps moving in the right direction.

13. Assist the team-members to develop their gifts. Everyone likes to grow and develop to reach their God given potential. Whenever a leader shows a personal interest in them by sending them on field trips or to seminars, people will be grateful. A training course to enhance the skills needed in the workplace, whether long or short, will ingratiate the team-members so that they will appreciate the leader more. Such training not only improves productivity but also encourages the team-members to do their best.

14. Be fair to everyone. Favouritism does not breed unity; nor does it motivate. Every worker should have a sense that justice and equality prevails. Whenever the leader displays favoured treatment toward some and negligence of others, ill-will is generated, relationships are damaged and work productivity suffers. Favouritism can spring from many sources: race, tribe, clan, family relationships, class, education, personality or personal interests. But a leader must be fair.

CONCLUSION

A Christian leader must be skilled both as a manager and as a builder of relationships. A leader is expected to be firm in decision making and courageous in leadership to achieve the mutually agreed upon goals. However, this must not be at the expense of maintaining good relationships; in fact, achieving goals and developing relationships are not exclusive.

Much care must be given to avoid the breakdown of relationships. At all costs a leader should avoid the following:

- Failing to show love by being unkind to the team-members.
- Disliking certain team-members.
- Using people as a means to an end instead of valuing them as people.

- Criticising or faultfinding so that people loose face before others.
- Being insensitive to their needs by not listening to them with empathy.
- Showing favouritism or prejudice.
- Loosing people's trust by falling short of godly character.
- Failing to admit mistakes.
- Deceiving team-members instead of being transparent.
- Being unreliable, untrustworthy, inconsistent, thoughtless or careless.
- Embarrassing or humiliating team-members.
- Correcting or confronting without love, humility, patience and grace.
- Ignoring or disregarding team-members.
- Failing to show gratitude and appreciation for work well done.

When the leader has developed a trusting relationship with the team-members, the next important step in management is to *develop a vision* of what should be accomplished. The next chapter will show you *how to plan.*

SEARCHING THE SCRIPTURE WITH APPLICATION

1. Read 'the works of the flesh' in Gal 5:19-21.
    a. Which 'works of the flesh' deal with broken relationships?
    b. What are the main reasons for these broken relationships?
2. Leadership often fails because of broken relationships.
    a. Which 'works of the flesh' often lead to failed leadership? Explain.
    b. Why do these 'works of the flesh' often lead to failed leadership?
3. Read 'the fruit of the Spirit' in Gal 5:22-23.
    a. Which 'fruit of the Spirit' would contribute to good relationships?
    b. Explain how the fruit strengthens personal relationships?
    c. What should leaders do to eliminate 'the works of the flesh' and manifest 'the fruit of the Spirit' to be a Christian leader?
4. The Church is 'The Body of Christ' (Ro 12:4f; 1 Co12).
    a. What does this metaphor teach concerning our relationships with one another?
    b. How do church leaders and members often fail in relationships?
    c. How can leaders build up the Body of Christ?
5. Paul refers to relationships when he speaks of 'one another.' Examine the following examples of 'one another' and tell how the teaching of each 'one another' would strengthen a person's leadership?
    Ro 12:10; 13:8, 16; Gal 5:13; 6:2; Eph 4:2, 32
    Col 3:13, 16; 1 Th 4:9, 18; 5:11
6. Healthy leadership requires a *trusting relationship*.
    a. What evidence might suggest that a leader is not trustworthy?
    b. What steps should a leader take to strengthen trust in himself?

7. Healthy leadership requires a *loving relationship*.
    a. What evidence might suggest that the love of a leader is lacking?
    b. What steps should be taken to strengthen a leader's love for people?
8. Healthy leadership requires a leader to *respect* his followers.
    a. What evidence might suggest the leader fails to respect others?
    b. What should a leader do to show more respect for others?

Endnotes

[1] Ro 12:10-16
[2] Ecc 4:9,12
[3] Cribbin 1972:8
[4] Marshall 1989:45
[5] Marshall 1989:64

32
PLANNING

Commit to the LORD whatever you do,
and your plans will succeed.'[1]
'Many are the plans in the mind of a man,
but it is the purpose of the LORD that will stand.[2]

Leaders plan to fail whenever they fail to plan.

Once a Christian leader establishes strong personal relationships with his teammates (and not until then!), the most basic principle of management is to plan. If you don't care where you are going, any road will take you there. But if your destination is important, then planning is essential.

Planning never takes place for many leaders. Their approach to leadership is to deal with crises whenever they arise. Failed leaders are forever dealing with problems. Instead of planning how to develop a flourishing forest, they keep fighting grass fires that threaten what they already possess. 'A fire fighting strategy' for leadership can only lead to the failure of a leader. Yet, the Bible reminds us that the plans of men often fail but God's purposes will stand.

Importance of Planning

We cannot overstate the importance of planning. Any leader who succeeds does so in part because of planning. Effective leadership *requires* that the leader learn how to plan.

Learning to plan is not alien to African tradition. Some people believe that long-term planning was not done by Africans traditionally.[3] Certainly, long- term planning with goals, as outlined in this chapter, was unknown; but the people did plan for their distant future.[4] Blessings were pronounced by old men on their family with the distant future in mind. Plans for marriage were made by fathers of children not yet born. Men planned for large families and rich estates in their quest for creating an influential clan in the future.

Some Christians today reject planning with objectives because they believe this replaces the guidance of the Holy Spirit. To plan is to ignore the leading of the Spirit, they think. They wrongly believe that when the Spirit guides, he does so with spontaneity and without any forethought by Christians. The biblical truth is that planning should always be under the guidance of the Holy Spirit and normally with forethought.

The Bible clearly commends the virtue of planning. Jesus commends the planning of builders and warriors to determine whether they will succeed or not.[5] He denounces foolish people who fail to think ahead and realise that a house built on sand will collapse during a flood.[6] Paul challenges Christians to emulate the athlete who plans and organises for winning an athletic contest. Paul himself says, 'I do not run like a man running aimlessly.' Paul runs the Christian race to win.[7] Advice is given by Solomon how to plan.[8] Scripture indicates that even God plans, though his plans are from eternity past. God says, 'What I have planned, that will I do."[9] So planning is divinely sanctioned.

Not only is it biblical to plan, it is necessary for progress to be made.

Not to plan is a plan itself, for planning is basically nothing more than attempting to decide in advance what we will or will not do in the next minutes, hours, days, months or years. For the Christian leader, planning asks the question as to whether we will affect the future at random or with purpose.[10]

Elements of Planning

Different scholars and schools of thought approach management with differing terminology. For our purposes in this chapter we divide planning into two stages with two labels: *vision* and *goals*.

The philosophy of management for the Christian leader should begin by thinking of the overall *vision* of what the ministry organisation is called to do; it then reduces that broad, overarching vision into a series of prioritised *goals* which can be measured and accomplished within a given timeframe.[11]

Planning therefore has two essential elements:

1. Discerning a vision of God's will for the future: This vision is stated broadly and in general terms which cannot be measured.

This first stage of planning centres on the big picture, the broad vision that calls one to the future. This we choose to call, *a vision*, emphasising the compelling picture of future possibilities that motivates people to do great exploits for God.[1] The *vision* is the ultimate purpose for which you and your ministry organisation are called by God to do.

2. Developing specific goals with detailed steps how to fulfill that vision: The objectives are specific and achievable in a definite time period.

This second stage of planning grows out of the vision. This stage of planning is detailed and

[1] What we are calling *vision*, Gangel calls *mission* (1997:276) and Engstrom calls *purpose* (1976:85f). A *vision* or *mission* or *purpose* describes in general terms what the ministry organisation is called to do – its purpose in the Kingdom of God.

specific. It entails the writing of a specific and detailed plan with measurable goals and a strategy how to achieve this within a definite time frame. This we choose to call *goals*.[2] Most teachers of management embrace this two-stage approach to planning but use different terminology.

Planning Begins with a Vision

Planning does not begin with specific, detailed ideas of what should be done in the future. Planning begins with a big, broad picture of what God is calling you and your team to achieve in the future. Although the whole team should be involved in the formulation of this vision, the leader plays a central role.

In fact, the major distinction between a leader and a manager is that the leader has the vision which inspires the team to move in a particular direction; whereas, the manager manages the organisation according to the preset goals. A leader without a vision is an oxymoron, that is, a self-contradiction. No one is a leader without a vision. 'Vision is the very stuff of leadership – the ability to see in a way that compels others to pay attention.'[12]

What is a *vision*?

The English word, *vision*, comes from the Latin word meaning '*a seeing*.' A leader sees afar. Vision distinguishes him from the masses who are not leaders. Whereas the tortoise cannot see beyond the grass, let alone the trees, the giraffe sees far beyond. The tortoise can never be a leader of a giraffe because the giraffe sees further than the tortoise. Yet many of our Christian leaders are tortoises who cannot envision a future that is any different from the present. A leader is a forward-looking visionary with a future orientation.

Vision has been defined in various ways:

- 'A vision is *an image – a picture of what could be*.'[13]
- A vision is '*a mental picture of the completed plan*...which stimulates action, innovation and, creativity.'[14]
- A vision is '*seeing the invisible and making it visible*.'
- A vision is '*sanctified dreams*.'
- A vision is '*foresight with insight based on hindsight*.'[15]
- Several characteristics of a vision are:

1. A vision is God-imparted. A Christian leader with his team can only be *Christian* if they submit to the lordship of Christ. Since Christ is the Head of the Church, only he can impart the vision that glorifies God. This means that both the leader and the team spend much time in prayer and reflection on God's will as revealed in the Word of God and God's will for their lives.

2. A vision is change-oriented. A vision means that one is dissatisfied with things as they are at present; change is desired. Those, who are satisfied with tradition and complacent with things as they are, will not be excited about developing any vision of future change.

3. A vision is action-oriented. A vision statement is useless unless acted upon and achieved. 'A vision without action is just a dream; action without vision is merely a passing of time; but a vision

[2] What we are calling *goals* have also been called *objectives* (Engstrom 1976) or *vision* (Gangel 1997).

with action can change the world.'[16] Therefore, a vision must be followed by the setting of specific goals and a strategy to achieve them in a measurable period of time.

4. A vision is both faith-based and realistic. A vision implies a faith that sees beyond the present status quo; achieving the vision will require faith. But the vision is also realistic. Vision is not dreaming the impossible but dreaming what is possible with God's help. The fearful and lazy will not be enthusiastic about faith-based vision.

Why is *vision* important?

A vision statement is only part of the process of planning but it is very essential. Why is a vision so important?

1. A vision points to the future and gives direction. Instead of going around in circles and repeating the same activities, a vision shows the way to advance and break new ground. A vision is essential for living a life worth living. Helen Keller was blind and deaf. When asked, 'What could be worse than being born without sight?' Her response was, 'Being born with sight and no vision.'[17] Vision is essential for a productive life and ministry.

2. A vision gives a reason to live with exuberance. The life which God has entrusted to us in this world is exceedingly short – at best, 70 or 80 years. It should be lived with purpose and meaning; it should be devoted to the service of our great God who has saved us and called us to ministry. A vision for life shows the way forward and gives us a reason to live with enthusiasm. As Martin Luther King, Jr. observed, 'If a man hasn't found something he is willing to die for, he isn't fit to live.'[18]

3. A vision creates passion and enthusiasm. Maintaining the status quo is boring and monotonous. Doing the same things over and over again without any sense of accomplishment or achievement is unfulfilling. But a vision for some divinely appointed mission or some new development or enterprise that glorifies God and builds the Kingdom of God is captivating; it is energizing.

4. A vision that is all-consuming is contagious. Everyone desires to be part of a ministry that is on the move. When a leader is passionately committed to a vision, this generates an impact that is contagious. Others will follow and share that vision. But a visionless leader cannot lead anyone.

5. A vision creates unity and reduces conflict. When every team member within a ministry organisation or Church is agreed upon the big picture, what God wants them to do in life, this will generate unity of purpose. Disagreement of course may arise by different perceptions of how to fulfill that vision, but the mutually agreed upon vision should reduce team conflict.

6. Developing a vision is where planning all begins. Planning specific objectives always follows a vision; they do not precede a vision. 'People do not follow programs, but leaders who inspire them. They act when a vision stirs in them a reckless hope of something greater than themselves, hope of fulfillment they had never before dared to aspire to.'[19] Vision becomes a motivating force, a compelling reason to join the team and give one's life to fulfilling that vision.

How do you develop *Vision*?

Leith Anderson summarises his thoughts on how a vision statement is written: 'Most visions come from a lengthy process of learning, praying, observing, brainstorming with others, trial and error, rough drafts, trial balloons, false starts, refinement, partial agreement, eventual adoption, and incremental implementation.'[20] Development of a vision statement therefore must involve the following:

1. The leader with his team must look to God for that vision since a vision for God's will in the future is God-imparted. What is it that God desires you to accomplish for his glory alone? Much time should be devoted to prayer, seeking God's wisdom and learning his vision for planning. Ask God for special wisdom.[21] Commit your future into his care.[22] Write down thoughts from Scripture that impress you as you meditate on the Word of God. Even during on-going discussions with the team it is valuable to pause for prayer for divine guidance when a need for divine help becomes evident.

2. Gather information from everywhere. Read what God is doing elsewhere; visit a variety of ministries to see what God is doing among others. Expose yourself to the vision which God has imparted to other servants of the Lord. Never try to duplicate or copy others. God has made you and your team unique. He has a unique vision for you. But the process of learning from others will broaden your understanding of what God is doing elsewhere and quicken your thoughts.

3. Always think prayerfully in the presence of God, seeking his guidance. That is what it means 'to pray without ceasing.' Allow time to pass. Don't rush into making a decision of a future vision. God often works in the sub-conscious. When time elapses an idea pops into the mind from 'nowhere.' That may be God who is working through your sub consciousness.

4. Brainstorm with your team. Interaction with team-members not only enables them to own the vision but will create a better vision statement. Many minds are better than one. Insight and inspiration are generated when several people interact together. Make the team an integral part of the process of developing a vision statement. A Kamba proverb says, '*A fool does not ask for counsel.*' Another says, '*One mouth can't determine whether the food is well cooked.*' As you brainstorm, is a picture forming in your mind of exactly what God's will for your future ministry looks like? Do you begin to understand what direction God is taking you in the future? What changes he is leading you to adopt?

5. The most essential part of the vision statement answers the why question. Why do you exist? What is the purpose or the reason for your own existence and the existence of your ministry?

6. Write down the vision statement on paper. Following are the characteristics of an effective vision statement:

- It is a phrase or sentence (not longer) which uses 'words that are active, compelling and appealing. The tone should be upbeat. The task must seem reasonable.'[23]
- It can be easily explained and understood by people.
- It can be memorised within two or three minutes. If it is so long and complex that it requires more effort to memorise, the vision statement is neither memorable nor effective.
- It is owned by the leader and team-members.

Planning Requires Goal Setting

Arising out of the God-given vision for future ministry, the leader with his team must develop specific goals. Vision statements must be made concrete by team-members. Specifically, what do you seek to accomplish in order to accomplish your vision and fulfill God's purpose for your life and ministry?

How do you develop *goals*?

The process of developing goals is similar to the process of developing a vision statement. The whole process must be saturated with prayer from beginning to end. Since no one can do everything at once to fulfill their vision, goals must be made that are based on priorities. In this process differences of opinion will inevitably arise. This means that the team-members, who develop goals, must be in a spirit of prayer continually.

What Leith Anderson said about the process of developing a vision statement may be also said about goal setting. Goal setting comes 'from a lengthy process of learning, praying, observing, brainstorming with others, trial and error...'[24]

What are the characteristics of *goals*?

1. Goals are stated in terms of end results. For example, 'By the end of this year I will have finished reading the Bible through from Genesis to Revelation.' A goal should never say, 'I am going to read the Bible through by the end of the year.' Goals are not written in terms of process or activities but in terms of end results.

2. Goals are achievable in a definite time period. That is, goals must have an ending date. Goals cannot be ongoing and unending. An example of an effective goal is this: 'Within a decade from this decision, our Church will have erected a worship centre accommodating one-thousand people.' One should never say, 'Our goal is to erect a worship centre in the foreseeable future.' That is imprecise and open ended. What is 'the foreseeable future'?

3. Goals are definite as to what is expected. For example, 'By the end of this course, the students will have read the following three books in their entirety: (name the book titles and authors).' To say, 'The goal of this course is for students to read several books on management,' breaks all the above stated principles: (1) Goals should be stated in terms of end results, not in terms of process or activities; (2) Goals should be achievable in a definite time period, and this 'goal' says nothing about when the books should be read; (3) This 'goal' is imprecise – what books should be read, and by what date?

4. Goals are practical and realistic. This is a balancing act – not too easy and not too hard. If we only plan what will happen without much effort, then planning has not accomplished much. We should make sure our goals are beyond what we can do in our own strength in order that God will receive the praise. But if we plan by presumption some unrealistic feat, we only confuse presumption for faith. The Akamba say: 'Water runs in the stream; it does not flow along the crest of the hill.' Beware of goals impossible to achieve.

5. Goals should be written in simplicity. Goals should be limited to one goal per goal statement. Keep the sentence simple, not compound with an 'and' connecting two components of the sentence. State the goal precisely in terms of dates, numbers and items included.

How do you achieve your *goals*?

1. Arrange a programme of steps to achieve your goals. Having an end goal in mind is not sufficient. The intermediate steps, that are required to achieve the goal, are essential. What personnel are needed and what activities need to take place? Arranging a programme of activities and personnel needed to achieve the goal requires meticulous and careful thought. Concrete goals are useless unless concrete programmes are planned.

2. Arrange a schedule of when the different activities of the programme will be accomplished. Be practical! Leaving uncertain the time when each activity is accomplished is impractical. Nothing will be accomplished. Even if the schedule must be adjusted, at least everyone knows the time goal toward which everyone is working.

3. Arrange a budget to cater for the needs of the programme of action. A budget includes not only finance but personnel and other resources needed. Budget and goal setting go hand-in-hand. A goal should never be set which is impossible to achieve because of cost. Therefore, a careful accounting must be made, first, to ascertain whether the goal is feasible; and second, to keep track of the ongoing cost of the project.

CONCLUSION

Though planning is basic, in many ways it is the easiest part of management. As the Akamba say, '*Seeing a bow is not having meat.*' Owning a bow is not sufficient; you must hunt, and that takes work. Disciplined work is necessary to bring reality to the dreams and visions of the team-members.

Organising the workers and shepherding them toward meeting of the goals are the subjects for the following chapters.

SEARCHING THE SCRIPTURE WITH APPLICATION

1. Is *planning* biblical or does planning usurp the leading of the Holy Spirit? How do the following Scriptures help answer the question? Mt 7:24-27; Lk 14:28-33; 1 Co 9:24-27; Pr 15:22; 16:3; 20:18; Isa 46:11.
2. What steps should be taken to invite and allow the Holy Spirit to guide in the process of planning?
3. What is the difference between a *vision* and a *goal*?
4. If you have a *vision*, why is it necessary to set goals as well? Why is it important to have both a *vision* and *goals*?
5. Which of the following are *vision* statements and which are *goals*?

    'Our Church seeks to nurture and train fathers.'

    'By next year this time we will have constructed the Church office.'

    'The development of a Master's degree programme is our next project.'

    'We will train the fathers in our Church in a six day seminar in August this year through the use of materials from Navigators on how to relate well with their children.'

    'Our Church shall be evangelistically minded to bring people to Christ.'

    'During each Saturday in January next year we will conduct seminars in our Church, using Life Ministry materials, to learn how to witness and share the gospel.'
6. How do you develop a *vision*?
7. Develop a *vision* statement for your ministry organisation.
8. Develop *goals* for achieving some aspect of the vision for your ministry.

9. Some leaders are brilliant in dreaming and expressing a vision. But they are poor managers in bringing that vision to reality. What must a leader do to ensure that his vision does not remain abstract and theoretical and without any practical achievement to show for his leadership?
10. Some people are practical and hands-on but without a captivating vision for the future growth and development. What will happen to their style of leadership?

Endnotes

[1] Pr 16:3 NIV
[2] Pr 19:21 ESV
[3] Mbiti 1971:26f
[4] Gehman 1987: 66-71
[5] Lk 14:28-33
[6] Mt 7:24-27
[7] 1 Co 9:24-27
[8] Pr 15:22; 16:3; 20:18
[9] Isa 46:11
[10] Engstrom 1976:45
[11] Engstrom 1976:85f
[12] Ford 1991:99
[13] Wofford 1999:51f
[14] Rush 1983:84
[15] Barna 1992:28
[16] Source unknown to author
[17] Helen Keller as found in Barna 2002:70
[18] Martin Luther King Jr., as found in Barna 2002:71
[19] Habecker 1987 121
[20] Anderson 1999:196
[21] Jas 1:5
[22] Pr 16:3
[23] Barna 1992:139
[24] Anderson 1999:196

33
ORGANISING

'But all things should be done decently and in order…
For God is not a God of confusion but of peace.'[1]

The task of organising people in a structure must follow planning.

Without people, you have no team; without a team, your plans fail. A vision is an empty dream unless the leader can mobilise people in a workable structure so that everyone pulls together to accomplish the goals. Organising people is essential to achieve whatever is planned. As a Swahili proverb says, '*If birds travel without coordination, they beat each others' wings.*' Energy is wasted whenever the birds are not organised to fly in formation.

Organising

What is *organising*?

Organising is the process of assigning team-members a particular ministry to contribute toward achieving certain goals by arranging them in *an orderly structure*.[1] Organising means several things:

1. Team-members relate to one another according to an official, pre-arranged order which is indicated by the 'Organisational Structure.'
2. The Organisational Structure indicates who you are responsible to and who is responsible to you. This is laid out in the 'flow chart' (i.e. the 'Organisational Structure') showing the 'command structure.'

---

[1] *Ministry of Management* by S. Douglas, B. Cook and H. Hendricks is a helpful book which is used extensively in this chapter.

3. Just like a tall building has a steel skeleton which holds the building together, so the Organisational Structure holds the team-members together in an orderly, organised manner, with members knowing how to relate to one another. It shows how official communication flows naturally from one to another.

Why is *organising* important?

Can you imagine the chaos that would occur if everyone did whatever interested them? Could any leader achieve goals without organising?

1. Many tasks would be overlooked because people would find certain ministries uninspiring or unimportant, and they would fail to do them.
2. Team-members would duplicate the work of others because no one would be concerned about complimenting others or meeting needs.
3. Conflicts would arise between team-members because different teammates would desire to do similar roles.

Organising is essential to enhance any spiritual ministry. John Wesley, the 18th century English revivalist, not only preached powerfully; he organised the converts so well that they became known as *Methodists*. John Wesley was a *methodical* organiser. He divided each religious society into 'classes' of twelve which met weekly under a 'class leader.' Thus did the Methodist Church grow!

Dwight L. Moody was a 19th century American evangelist who preached to millions of people on both sides of the Atlantic Ocean. Not only was God's Spirit on him to declare the gospel of Jesus Christ; God had gifted him to organise and prepare for each evangelistic campaign. Before he ever preached, Moody would set up workshops to train lay workers to do essential work behind the scenes: to conduct prayer meetings, to reach those not attending church, to nurture new converts, and teach methods of follow-up.

If a leader does not have the spiritual gift of organising, he would show great wisdom if he would enlist someone with such a gift and delegate that responsibility. Leadership without ability to organise is flawed.

How do you *organise*?

The probability is that whenever a person is chosen to be a leader in the Church, a theological institution or a ministry organisation, an Organisational Structure is already in place. The wise leader will first serve within that structure and develop relationships with the team-members. Only after some time and experience should he think of improving, adapting or changing the Organisational Structure. It may be that a project arises which needs volunteers to join together to accomplish a task. Following are some principles to follow in developing an Organisational Structure (i.e. Organisational Chart):

1. Clarify the vision and goals of the organisation before the Organisational Structure is developed or modified. Strategy comes before the structure. What are you seeking to accomplish? Be focused; be specific. Only when you know precisely what God wants you to do can you then develop a structure that will serve your purpose.

2. Organise with natural groupings in mind. Think of the different categories which represent your team-members – ages, genders, education, occupations, gifts, home locations. Divide up your team-members in appropriate categories which reflect these natural groupings.

3. Be specific when assigning ministries. Job Descriptions should specify identifiable work assignments which can be examined and evaluated. If the grounds-man is expected to care for the compound outside the place of worship or the institution, for example, specify exactly what this person is supposed to do, so that the grounds-man is clear about his responsibilities and the leader is in the right when he observes weaknesses in the person's performance.

4. Draw an Organisational Chart on paper, using rectangular blocks to represent groups or persons functioning in certain capacities. Be clear on the qualifications for each position outlined. Draw vertical lines showing who is subordinate to another and who is responsible to whom. If the Organisational Chart is flat, that is, if there are too many people reporting to the leader, then the leader is worn out by being responsible to oversee too many people. If the Organisational Chart is too deep, with too many subordinates overseeing people, then the leader is too far removed from the team-members on the ground and he becomes isolated from the actual work on the ground.

5. Write on paper all the names of the available personnel. Briefly describe their strengths, weaknesses and previous experience. People have unique personalities, interests and abilities. A wise leader recognises that individual team-members can do some things well and other things not so well. To build up the team-members and the organisation, every person must be placed where they can serve best.

6. Place the names of the qualified persons in the Organisational Chart, beginning from the top. Always match the person's strengths and proven experience with the needed qualifications for each position on the Organisational Chart; and always consult with the person for his consent.

7. *Write a job description for each person on the chart.*

8. Remember, all organising is a **process**. This means that no organisational structure is permanent or unchangeable. As the organisation grows or changes, it will be necessary to grow and change the structure. A leader must continually re-evaluate to see if any changes need to be made in the structure. Organising the structure is not done once and for all.

Job Descriptions

An essential part of organising is the writing of Job Descriptions.

Why are *Job Descriptions* important?

Job Descriptions are unknown in many places; they seem alien and impractical. Why then are Job Descriptions so important?

1. Job Descriptions help the team-members know exactly what their responsibilities are.
2. Job Descriptions help the leader to remember what was agreed upon.
3. Job Descriptions will avoid misunderstanding and conflict.

True, there are situational differences. Job Descriptions are absolutely essential for employees within institutions, ministry organisations and urban Churches. However, when dealing with volunteers within a local Church setting, this becomes more complex. Volunteers within urban Churches with better educated people are more understanding of such formalities. Job Descriptions are less familiar in rural Churches, certainly among the illiterate.

However, a written job description is strongly recommended even for volunteers within the local Church, at least for the personal use of the leader. Memories fail. Conflict may arise due to different recollections. Exactly, what was agreed upon will be forgotten unless written down. If the leader is to oversee the team-members, he must supervise with fairness, confidence – and authority. A written document helps. If someone is employed by a local Church, then a written job description is essential. If the pastor is overseeing Church members who serve as volunteers, such as elders, deacons, Sunday School teachers, then the pastor should use personal discretion. Nevertheless, a total neglect of a written job description for use by the pastor can lead to problems.

How do you write a *Job Description*?

A Job Description is something like a contract that is mutually agreed upon by the workers and the administration. In the drafting of this Job Description it is helpful if the workers actually contribute to the composition of the document so that they are committed to what it says. The leader should present a draft of the Job Description to the workers and let them interact with it by asking clarification, making certain requests, or offering alternative suggestions. By so doing the worker becomes committed to his work.

This working document answers the following questions:

1. *What are my responsibilities?* (What is my job?)
2. *What authority do I have?* (What am I authorised to do?)
3. *To whom do I look for directions?* (Who is my boss?)
4. *Who looks to me for direction?* (Who reports to me?).

Every person in the organisation has *responsibilities* to carry out, is given *authority* to carry out them out, and is *accountable* to someone for what he or she does. All of this is indicated in the Job Description.

Just as organising is a process, so the writing of a job description is a process – changes are frequently made. The leader should review the job description with the workers once every year. This gives opportunity for the leader to review the agreement while reinforcing the memories of the workers about their responsibilities.

Every Job Description has the following elements:

1. *Title* – the title of the position.
2. *Purpose* – the purpose of the position.
3. *Scope* – the extent of responsibility, whether in the local Church, a group of the local Church, within a region or nationwide.
4. *Areas of Responsibility and Authority* – list the specific responsibilities and the authority entrusted to carry out those responsibilities, and the times when the work is to be done.
5. *Working Relationships* – the person you report to, the persons who report to you and those you work closely together with should all be indicated.

Delegation

Delegation is essential if the leader desires to be successful. 'To be a good leader and a poor delegator is a contradiction in terms.'[2] D.L. Moody once said, 'I'd rather get ten men to do the job than to do the job of ten men.' When any leader does the job of ten men, he will burn out, like Moses who failed to delegate.[3] Too many leaders have this 'Moses Syndrome' of not knowing that they should delegate, or how to delegate; they may be unwilling to delegate.

One of the most common complaints about Church leaders in Kenya was their failure to delegate. Hans Finzel mentions deplorable delegation as one of the ten top mistakes of leaders in America.[4] Leaders *must* learn to delegate if they are to become effective leaders.

What is *delegation*?

Delegation is the assigning of certain tasks, and authority to carry out those tasks, to some other team member within the organisation. These tasks are in addition to their assigned responsibilities outlined in their job description. The leader takes one or more of his own responsibilities and delegates someone else to assume those responsibilities with authority to perform them.

What are the advantages in *delegating*?

Delegation offers rich dividends for the leader.

1. The leader lightens his own work load so he avoids burnout. 'Many hands make the work light.'
2. By delegating, the leader frees himself of burdensome details so that he can devote all his effort to the major goals before him.
3. The leader ensures more work will be done when he enlists others to join hands in the task. Without delegation the work suffers.
4. The leader is wise when he recognises his own limitations. He excels when he delegates tasks to those more competent than he.
5. Delegation is a great way to train future leaders. A leader without a successor is a failure, but successors without training will fail. Delegation is a great way of preparing future leaders by training.

   [Delegation] is the best process for personal development because it gives people the opportunity to learn by doing, to take risks, and to become comfortable with the consequences of their own performance.[5]
6. The leader will motivate team-members with increased confidence and ability when he delegates in a proper manner.

Why don't leaders want to *delegate?*

If leaders can benefit so much from delegation, why don't they delegate?

1. Leaders fear giving up their authority.
2. Leaders fear that others will do the work better than they can and thus be a threat to their own positions.

3. Leaders fear that others may not do the job as well as they want.
4. Leaders are unwilling to invest the time needed to train others.

Because of human selfishness, leaders prefer to do everything themselves rather than to delegate the authority together with the praise that comes when others succeed and do well.

How do you *delegate*?

Describing the benefits of delegation is easy. But the actual process of delegation takes wisdom and skill. If done poorly, the end result will not be pleasing. Team-members may be unhappy because they are coerced to do a job they do not want. The leader will be unhappy because he finds the work not done well. Following are the principles that should guide one in delegation:[6]

1. Decide what should be delegated. The key aspects of the leader's job description should never be delegated. Do not delegate powers to decide policy issues. But routine details that divert the leader from his chief responsibilities may be delegated. If the leader does not have needed expertise for some task, that task should definitely be delegated to someone who is better able to perform well. The leader may also delegate the highly technical details of a project that bog the leader down and keep him from devoting himself to focusing on the goals for which they are striving.

2. Choose the right person for the task. Not everyone is suitable. Those who lack competency or confidence should not be chosen. Those who are unhappy to take on the assignment should not be coerced. Avoid all favouritism that engenders jealousy by always delegating to the few who are experienced and willing. Choose the person who desires additional responsibility or shows potential. The leader may even choose someone whose potential is not known in order to learn whether he is capable of greater responsibilities in the future.

3. Transfer the work. Meet with the team member chosen. When transferring the work, make sure the team member fully accepts the delegated assignment. Provide a full explanation of the instructions, requirements and other factors associated with the delegation. Once the leader gives the explanation, request the person to explain in his own words what needs to be done to be sure there is clear understanding. Offer training where needed.

4. Transfer the authority for doing the work. Above all, transfer the authority necessary to do the work. The team member must know what decision-making authority he has in doing the work and what resources are available. Once the delegation has been made, do not interfere with or make decisions for the person. Do not convey distrust or suspicion by excessive observation. Theodore Roosevelt once said, 'The best executive is the one who has the sense enough to pick good men to do what he wants done and self-restraint enough to keep meddling with them while they do it.'[7]

5. Follow up with encouragement and assistance when asked. The leader remains accountable for the work that was delegated; he also is committed to the success of the team member. So the leader should not abandon or neglect the person. Always remember: it is not what you *expect* that will be done, but what you *inspect* that will be done. Delegating responsibility means you never let them go but you persist in mentoring them and *inspecting* their work, not just *expecting* it to be done.

But there is a fine line between follow-up and a bothersome interference. The leader is interested in the progress and needs of the person without usurping authority. Make yourself available to the person so that he feels free to consult and ask advice. But once the leader delegates, the work is delegated and entrusted to the team member. The work and responsibility is his. But the leader should not neglect the team member. Instead, he should wisely and prudently follow up with encouragement and help when needed.

Why does *delegating* sometimes fail?

Leaders fail when

- They fail to give full authority to do the work. Frustration arises.
- They fail to define what authority they do not have. Conflict arises.
- They fail to define their job description clearly. Confusion develops.
- They fail to invest the time and effort required to observe, teach, listen, and follow-up, all which are necessary for successful delegation.
- They take back the work assigned because they are perfectionists and feel the work was not done satisfactorily.

CONCLUSION

Management skills for effective Christian leaders must begin with relationship building. Without trust and respect, no leader can manage his team. Together they plan by developing a vision of what God has for them. Growing out of the vision are the measurable goals they desire to accomplish.

But goals will remain unachieved unless the leader can organise his team-members so that that all members contribute their gifts and skills to achieve the goals. An organisational structure is necessary with a clear chain of command. Each team member must know his responsibilities and what authority he can exercise. He must know to whom he reports and who reports to him.

But much more needs to be done. The leader must shepherd and guide the team-members toward achieving the goals. How does the leader direct, guide and control the process so that goals are achieved? That is our next topic.

SEARCHING THE SCRIPTURE WITH APPLICATION

1. Define what we mean by 'organising.'
2. Is organising appropriate for the Church and Christian ministries? Why?
3. This chapter is about organising people in a team to accomplish goals. But we also organise programmes of education and worship. Read 1 Co 14:26-40. Although this 'order' of worship was more fluid than many worship services today, it was not pure spontaneity. List all the guidelines and directions which Paul gave to the Corinthians.
4. What happens in a worship service without order?
5. What happens in society when there is no organisation?
6. Review the principles of 'how to organise' and the writing of 'Job Descriptions.' With those in mind, develop a Flow-Chart (an Organisational Structure) of your own Organisation or Church, showing how each person fits in the chart – who reports to whom and how each person relates to the other.

7. Imagine you are a teacher in the institution where you are currently studying or where you have studied. Write a job description for the teacher, following the guidelines mentioned above in this unit.
8. What is meant by 'delegation' and why is 'delegation' so important for Christian leaders?
9. Why do so few Christian leaders actually delegate? Discuss.
10. Delegation can fail. Why does delegation often fail?
11. Discuss all the details that make delegation successful?
12. Evaluate your Church or ministry organisation in the following areas:
    a. Is there an Organisational Chart (i.e. Flow-Chart) that shows how each person relates to one another, tracing the levels of authority and who is responsible to whom?
    b. Does each person have a proper Job Description that indicates: (1) the purpose of their position, (2) the extent and limitations of their responsibility, (3) a specific list of responsibilities, and (4) their working relationships (who reports to them and to whom they report)?
    c. Draw up a Job Description for officers in your Church or organisation.
    d. Discuss what problems arise because of any lack in these areas and what can be done to improve the Organisational Structure.

Endnotes

1. 1 Co 14:40, 33
2. DePree 1992:154
3. Ex 18
4. Finzel 1994:23f
5. DePree 1992:154
6. Engstrom 1979:162ff
7. Theodore Roosevelt as found in Engstrom 1979:172

34
SHEPHERDING
PART ONE

'Woe to the shepherds of Israel who only take care of themselves! Should not shepherds take care of the flock?'[1]

The leader must *shepherd* the team-members to accomplish the goals, once the planning and organising are done.

Purpose of Shepherding

Why speak of *shepherding* for management?

Traditionally, this phase of management is referred to as *directing* and *controlling*, a process of ensuring that the performance of the workers is according to the plan. The manager supervises and controls the work so that the goals will be achieved. But *directing* and *controlling* are authoritarian terms that frequently entail confrontation – not an appropriate concept for the context of Africa.

For this reason, instead of *controlling*, we have chosen the term, *shepherding*,[2] because it is more biblical and more pastoral – less authoritarian and confrontational, though both ideas are embedded in *shepherding*. The oriental shepherd did not drive the sheep as they do in Africa, but he led the sheep. Even so the leader achieves his goals not by driving his team-members but by leading them and modeling for his followers what should be done. The priority of the good shepherd is to take care of the sheep first of all, not to take care of his own personal interests.[3] Severe judgement was pronounced by God on Israel's shepherds who selfishly looked after their own interests to the neglect of the sheep.

A shepherd first of all meets the needs of his sheep by providing green pasture and quiet running water; he protects them from external threats. He carries with him a rod as his instrument of authority. With his rod he protects from the attacking lion and disciplines the straying sheep. When the shepherd cares for the sheep, they cooperate with him; he leads them in the paths of his choosing to achieve the goals laid out to reach the planned destination.

Is goal-oriented planning possible in a people-oriented culture?

In Africa the cultures are more people-oriented, less goal-oriented. So do we have a conflict between western ideas and African values? The Christian leaders we consulted all admitted that *directing* and *controlling* (or what we would call, *shepherding*) are indeed a challenge but it is still possible and desirable. In fact, planning and time orientation were found in the people-oriented cultures of traditional Africa. The father in the home kept an office in front of the house where he counseled and settled disputes. He always had time for everyone and did not allow a few people to take all of his time. Goals were set and met.

But in life, including Africa, *the ideal* of planning often proves to be different from *the practical* implementation of the planning. Long term planning is strategic but the short term planning of a few months is more practical for the thinking of the team-members. The urgent need of the moment with a face-to-face encounter has greater priority than a written notation in a diary that was planned five months earlier. So shepherding is a challenge, but it is both possible and necessary. It just takes great wisdom.

Shepherding is possible when the following conditions are met:

(1) *The team-members are involved in every stage of the planning.* When they participate in the planning and organising, then they are more willing to be led in the shepherding stage.

(2) *The team-members own the project.* If the project is *yours* as the leader, they will not embrace it. But if the project is *theirs*, because they have participated in laying the foundation for the project in planning and organising, then they will embrace it and support it. As an ancient Chinese proverb says, 'Of a good leader, when his work is done with the aim fulfilled, the people will say, "We did this ourselves."'

(3) *The team-members are guided and not commanded.* Relationships are all important. The leader can and must shepherd his people but this requires people-skills in knowing how to guide and correct.

Shepherding by Motivation

Motivating the team-members must be a priority for the leader. If leaders are to *lead* their team-members, not drive them, they must be motivated. Some leaders are by nature outgoing and interested in their people. Motivating others is second nature for them. But some leaders are more reserved; or at least, they do not give priority to the important task of motivating others. They assume that their team-members are doing fine without really knowing.

What is *motivation*?

A *motive* is 'something that prompts a person to act in a certain way'; it is a *reason* for doing something.[4] *Motivation* can be external and negative (a threat of consequences if work is not done well) or internal and positive (a reward if work is done well). The Christian leader should instill internal motivation by providing an inducement, an incentive, inspiration or enthusiasm for work.

Why is *motivation* so important?

Engstrom observes that 'since the function of leadership is to lead, getting people to follow is of primary importance.'[5] Motivation is essential to 'getting people to follow' the leader's direction.

My experience in life shows me that *everyone* needs to be motivated in their work. When Christians are perfected in glory, they will not need anyone to encourage them to serve and glorify God. But short of entire sanctification, people are in need of continual motivation from their leader because they lack enthusiasm for the work, they fail to understand the importance of the work, they lack confidence that they can do the work, or they lack commitment to the work. A wise leader will make motivation a priority in his daily agenda.

How does a leader *motivate*?

Myron Rush says, 'There is no set formula for motivation.'[6] Some may be motivated with a word of encouragement while others are spurred on with material incentives. To be motivated by the Word of God and a desire to please him with zealous labour is noble indeed. A wise leader will find effective ways to inspire his team-members to do their best.

Engstrom says that, 'A leader's success as a motivator is directly related to his sincerity in showing concern for his subordinates.'[7] The sincerity is shown in all his relationships with his team-members. They will quickly know if your interest in them is selfishly motivated or whether you are genuine.

The key in all elements of management, and particularly in motivation, is the leader.

> The leader's own self-esteem is the key to his ability to help others improve their sense of security. A leader with a high degree of self-esteem exhibits confidence. He can think about the needs of others because he does not have to compete with them to meet his own needs.[8]

Affirm team-members: There are four ways of building a climate of affirmation where the team-members feel respected and affirmed:[9] (1) Acceptance, (2) Trust, (3) Reward, and (4) Support.

(1) *Acceptance* is a deeply felt need for everyone. To be accepted means one is respected as a person of worth. Respect is shown by appreciation and acceptance by others. If one is accepted he is included within the Team as one of 'us.' He feels included because of being connected and related to the whole team. The leader must find ways of giving each team member a sense of belonging and being included in the team. Give personal attention to each one; never play favourites. Never give reason to make anyone feel excluded.

(2) *Trust* in someone conveys the idea of self-worth. When the leader neglects or overlooks someone by not entrusting him with responsibility, he demoralises the person. This will affect his work performance. For some people, there is no greater incentive to work hard than to be trusted

with new responsibility. 'Unfortunately, leaders often are more effective in communicating low expectations than high. What leaders say matters less than what they do. Expectations are communicated more frequently by nonverbal signals.'[10]

(3) *Reward* is recognition of work well done. The reward may be in terms of praise, a certificate of recognition, or in some material gift.

(4) *Support* is another way of affirming someone's worth. It is important to provide support that is commensurate with his actual needs; and where that is not possible, to take steps to supplement the salary with other kinds of support. Team-members need to know that their leader cares and is concerned for them.

Communicate verbally: By far the simplest and most effective way of motivation is through verbal affirmation. 'A study has revealed that only 25% of what motivates people to perform well is through activities like goal setting. But 75% of the influence which motivates and inspires and approves performance is verbal affirmation.'[11] Perkins says, 'If you want to maximize the effect of your words, catch people doing things right – and immediately praise them.'[12]

Effective Christian leaders in Africa have shared the following advice in this section of what they have done to motivate those with whom they work.

(1) *Congratulate them both publicly and privately for work well done.* Recognising people in public as trustworthy workers is a way of giving them credit and they appreciate it. Praising people in the presence of others is a real motivation. Public affirmation is good.

(2) *Compliment people whenever they do well.* 'Tell them, "That is very good work. I appreciate that." Human beings like to be told when they do well. Purposely go to the site of their work and express your appreciation for their good work. "That was a wise decision. It helped me a lot."'

(3) *Pray with them.* Tell them, 'I realise you have a big responsibility and I want to pray with you.'

(4) *Encourage those who are discouraged.* 'I keep telling my people, "A failure is someone who gives up. Those who try are not failures."' When people are discouraged, share with them your own experiences and read the Scripture to them. They brighten up when they hear this.

(5) *Be aware of people who are able to improve more.* The gifts of people differ. The leader needs to identify those who have reached the maximum of their gifts and those who could do more with some encouragement. Assure them privately that you are convinced they can do better because they have untapped gifts and potential to do well.

(6) *Remind them of the goals and encourage them to keep focused.* When team-members have participated in setting goals and are committed to them, they need to be encouraged to achieve them through diligent work.

Provide tangible gestures of appreciation: Expressions of appreciation may be accompanied by gifts, certificates, food and fellowship. Following are some of the things that have been done:

(1) 'On one Sunday each year we assemble the congregation with all the leaders of our various children's and youth's programmes. We congratulate them, and give them small gifts.'

(2) At the end of the year, one church provides a meal with fellowship; then they give presents or certificates of accomplishment in recognition of service well done. In another church the Council

determines who the faithful leaders were and who were lazy. They show appreciation to the faithful ones with gift tokens.

(3) Written notes of appreciation are sent to encourage people.

4. One Bible School Principal calls all his staff together for a dinner twice each term. Both teachers and support staff meet at the same time to avoid hurt feelings. They talk, express thanks and pray together.

(5) Leaders are taken away for a retreat where they can relax and open up in discussion and sharing.

Share yourself and offer yourself as a model: When a leader is transparent before his team-members and shares with them his own life, his relationship with God, his struggles and secret of success, they are motivated by the leader's example. In the words of the Christian leaders:

(1) 'I give younger pastors my history and tell them all about my past; I share concerning the little salary I received as a younger pastor. This greatly encourages them. To show the road you traveled encourages them.'

(2) 'As the Overseer, I don't complain whatever I am given. The Lord has given me contentment. I never ask for more salary or another church. I never complain. Whatever is given, I am satisfied. So this shames the pastors and motivates them to be content.'

(3) 'For many years I served in the largest church in our church region. When I was elected as the Chairman, I requested to be assigned a smaller church. Now I leave at 4:30 A.M. to walk two hours to the church for the 7:00 A.M. prayer meeting.' The life of this servant-leader models a humble servant of God and motivates the pastors under him to do the same.

Visit team-members in their homes: An ultimate way of showing personal interest and concern for team-members is to visit them in their homes. One gifted administrator said that when he takes tea in the home of a team member, he opens up by sharing and inviting the person to offer his ideas and suggestions. 'I welcome their ideas and advice accordingly. If something cannot be done, I say so because of A., B., and C.' Another conscientious pastor visits his Sunday School teachers to show his interest in them and find out their needs.

Provide material and financial assistance: When it is possible, material and financial assistance may be given to show personal concern for their well- being. This motivates team-members to be faithful and work harder.

(1) In one church the Sunday School teachers came early without eating. So the church decided to buy them tea after teaching. This encouraged them so much that the teachers grew in number from two to seven.

(2) To encourage the Bible School teachers in an expensive urban setting, the Council decided to pay half of their medical bills.

(3) At the end of the year, one Church Council gives to the pastors a financial supplement on top of the usual salary as an expression of thanks to them. This encourages the pastors.

(4) Provide the fees for courses which improve the skills of team-members. People desire to improve their skills. Help given will motivate them.

What are some motivation killers?

If a leader takes a real interest in his team-members and expresses that concern with the various suggestions given above, he will surely motivate the members – *unless* he actually kills motivation by some foolish acts. A psychologist and personnel consultant observes that the following actions on the part of the leader will actually *kill* all motivation, no matter what else the leader does.[13] The leader should *never, never, ever* do the following:

- Belittle a subordinate.
- Criticise a subordinate in front of others.
- Fail to give subordinates your undivided attention.
- Seem to be preoccupied with your own interests.
- Play favourites.
- Be insensitive to small things.
- Embarrass weak employees.

Shepherding by Communicating

One of the primary reasons for leadership failure is a breakdown in communication. Research among leaders has demonstrated that 'poor communication was their number one leadership and management problem.'[14] When the leader fails to communicate, motivation suffers.

Unity within the community is impossible without effective communication. How do you feel when things happen around you without your knowledge? Suddenly, the ground is broken and the foundation of a building is laid! What is happening? You feel left out of the loop of communication. Even more serious is failure by the leader to communicate your responsibilities. You feel demoralised and become critical and negative when blamed for failure of not doing the work. Confusion arises when people do not know what is expected of them, or have not participated in the decision concerning their ministry. Why have certain decisions been made? When the leader fails to communicate clearly the goals of the institution, members loose their focus and commitment.

Why does communication break down?

Leaders do not understand the importance of adequate communication: Many times leaders fail to realise that the smooth running of the organisation breaks down without proper communication. Confusion and conflicts arise without proper understanding. If the leader does not maintain a close relationship with his team-members, he will never know the criticism and frustration that arises with a breakdown of communication. Morale declines and the team-members loose incentive to give their best. Productivity declines and people become idle because they do not know what to do.

Leaders are lazy and make no effort to communicate: It takes work to communicate well. Effective communication is more than a simple announcement. Distractions or misunderstandings easily confuse and distort the message. The communication must be repeated on numerous occasions and in different forms so that everyone has heard and understood. Communication breaks down when team-members have a different understanding of something from the leader. It takes effort to ensure that your communication is properly understood.

Leaders assume that everyone knows: 'Never assume that anyone knows anything. This is a core leadership principle. We can never communicate enough in our organisation. Like the pulsing red cells rushing through our veins keeping our bodies alive, communication systems are the lifeblood of organisations.'[15] If any team member does not know what is on the minds of those in leadership, he may feel insecure, frustrated and uncommitted.

Leaders do not take time to listen: Listening is an essential part of effective communication. A Kenyan proverb says, '*Talking is loving one another.*' Love is reciprocal and requires listening. Conversely, the Akamba proverb says, '*He who doesn't listen is awakened with an axe head.*' If you don't pay attention to what people tell you, the results could be devastating.

Leaders often confuse *information* with *communication*. 'Information is *giving out*; communication is *getting through*.'[16] The leader cannot simply utter pronouncements (give out information) and assume that people understand. Communication breaks down when the leader has a different understanding of something from the people. Leaders assume the people know. Leaders answer the questions of people without understanding the real intent of the questioner. They try to communicate without understanding the people in their situation and hence miscommunication occurs.

Leaders are not transparent: If a leader has something to hide, he is not open and honest with the people. Transactions or decisions may have been made that the leader desires to hide. Effective communication requires walking in the light and being accountable. At times it may be necessary to go public and admit failures. To acknowledge a mistaken judgement or decision will bring respect and trust. To hide the mistake and cover it up will only lead to loss of confidence. A leader who does not want to be accountable to others will fail in effective communication. He is basically a hypocrite.

Leaders protect their power through secrecy: Knowledge is power. To know more than the people sets the leader apart. If people know as much as the leader knows, his power is diminished, so he thinks. Traditionally, information was restricted. Information was withheld by leaders from the people. This traditional secrecy is carried over today.

Of course, wisdom must be used in communicating information. Leaders should only share information that is suitable for the team-members. People's confidence must be respected. Never break confidentiality. Not everything is suitable information for everyone.

But times have changed. The people who are being led today are also educated. They think for themselves. They understand the corruption that takes place with absolute power. Leaders must be accountable and transparent. People need to know. If information, which people should know or will know in time, is withheld from the people, the leader himself is in trouble.

How do we communicate well?

Communication has been defined as '*the process we go through to convey understanding from one person or group to another.* Unless understanding occurs, we have not communicated. Therefore, when people complain about poor communication, they are actually complaining about the lack of understanding and not about the lack of conversation, discussions, memos, or correspondence.'[17] How can we ensure that others understand what we say?

First, we must understand sound communication theory: Communicating is more complex than simply transferring ideas from one mind to another. Note the different elements of effective communication.[18]

- SOURCE: The source of the idea is in the mind of the communicator. But the idea must be spoken if people are to understand.
- ENCODING: The idea must be encoded. This includes not only words but also body language such as gestures, facial expressions and tone of voice. Without encoding, the idea will not be communicated.
- DECODING: Misunderstanding arises when the Receiver decodes the message wrongly. How often we say, 'I didn't mean to say that.' The Source was misunderstood.
- RECEIVER: The receiver is the one who hears the message. When the Receiver is close to the Source, their mutual background ensures a greater understanding. Yet even husbands and wives misunderstand each other. The different histories and backgrounds of the Source and Receiver lends to greater misunderstanding.
- FEEDBACK: The Source needs to hear feedback to be sure the Receiver truly comprehended the message.

Secondly, the leader should observe the following principles:

(1) *Develop strong personal relationships with all your team-members.* The better they know you, the better they will understand you – and vice versa. Demonstrate love for them. Be friendly, polite, considerate and personally concerned for each one.

(2) *Face-to-face communication is best,* though sometimes written communication and telephone conversation are needful. Misunderstanding often occurs in the absence of body language. The extra effort made to be with a person pays big dividends. Experts estimate that only 7% of understanding comes from words. Another 38% depends on the tone of voice; and 55% on other non-verbal aspects, such as body language. Thus 93% of meaning is transmitted through tone of voice and non-verbal actions or expressions.[19]

(3) *Communicate with people informally* – at their places of work and in their homes. The good manager wanders among his people and shares a word with them on a person to person basis.

(4) *Prepare carefully when speaking to large audiences.* Know the audience. Speaking to smaller groups is better because there is opportunity for feed-back.

(5) *Desire feedback.* Listen carefully to feedback. Ask questions. Ask them to repeat in their own words what you have told them. This will enable the leader to know whether his communication has been understood.

(6) *Always be sincere.* 'Genuine sincerity can cover and atone for a multitude of technical errors. Often this depends on the love a team leader brings to the group.'[20]

(7) *Be generous when communicating with team-members.* Freely give them information on plans, developments and challenges. Don't be stingy with information. Don't allow members to be caught by surprises, seeing things develop of which they were unaware. Don't expect them to hear from others what you yourself should be telling them. Be in charge of sharing with the team everything they should know and everything that they will end up knowing. Make them feel part of an exciting

and developing ministry. Regular times of reporting and information can build rapport, confidence and good will.

(8) *Always be transparent and close to your people.* Staying at a distance can only create suspicion and misunderstanding. Rumors and gossip abound in the absence of communication.

CONCLUSION

The Christian leader would do well to master the skills of motivation and communication. Without inspirational motivation and effective communication, shepherding will break down. But there is much more to shepherding. The next chapter continues the subject of *shepherding*.

SEARCHING THE SCRIPTURE WITH APPLICATION

1. Discuss your culture, whether it is goal-oriented or people-oriented? In your culture, which would come first in priorities, reaching a goal or maintaining personal relationships?
2. Which is more biblical, goal orientation or people orientation? Why do you say so?
3. In your opinion, are goal-orientation and people-orientation incompatible? Must you choose one or the other? Discuss your reasons.
4. Share examples of how leaders can kill motivation.
5. For each motivation killer you mention, think of some biblical teaching that either supports the motivation killer or opposes it. In the final analysis, are motivational killers biblical or unbiblical?
6. Will the saints in heaven ever need motivational leaders? Why?
7. Why do the saints in this world need motivational leaders? Why?
8. How have motivational leaders helped you by inspiring you and encouraging you to be more diligent and committed to your ministry?
9. What words have you said or actions taken that have demoralised those who worked for you? How did those motivational killers affect the quality of their work and of your relationships?
10. Why is communication important to maintain unity and motivation?
11. From your own observation, tell of communication breakdown and how this affected the motivation and productivity of workers.
12. Why do you think leaders fail to communicate effectively and adequately?
13. In your own words, explain the communication theory outlined above.
14. What lessons in communication are derived from that theory?
15. How will the leader gain if he communicates to everyone effectively?
16. How will the leader loose if he fails to communicate with everyone sufficiently and effectively?

Endnotes

1 Eze 34:2 NIV
2 Compare Ps 23
3 Compare Eze 34
4 Random House College Dict., 1988
5 Engstrom 1979:127
6 Rush 1987:110
7 Engstrom 1979:127
8 McDonough 1979:112
9 McDonough 1979:112-124
10 McDonough 1979:116
11 Zig Ziglar, Top Performance, p 47f; as found in Perkins 2000:182
12 Perkins 2000:182
13 Engstrom 1979:128
14 Rush 1983:115
15 Finzel 1994: 115
16 Finzel 1994:118
17 Rush 1983:115
18 Gangel 1997:405ff
19 Rush 1983:125
20 Gangel 1997:414

35
SHEPHERDING
PART TWO

'But you were straying like sheep,
but have now returned to the Shepherd
and Overseer of your souls.'[1]

'Management by objectives' doesn't just happen. It takes work.

As the Akamba say, '*Fatty meat doesn't chew itself.*' Achieving goals doesn't just happen. It takes focused discipline and great wisdom. For the Christian leader to shepherd his team so that they will work together and accomplish goals, this not only requires motivational and communication skills but also an ability to correct those who need correction.

Shepherding by Correcting

Painful times will come when the leader must correct the errant sheep. Motivating the workers and communicating with them may not be sufficient.

The work of the shepherd in feeding and guiding the sheep is enjoyable. But even the shepherd carries a club which he finds necessary to use in correcting the errant sheep. It is one thing for an animal shepherd to correct a sheep; but for the pastor (shepherd) to correct someone in his congregation, that is another dimension in life. The goal of the leader is to ensure that goals are achieved and this requires, from time to time, that the shepherd *correct* a team member.

This is a problem everywhere but especially in cultures that are shame- oriented and people-centred. One leader even told me that it an 'African problem' because of the cultural pressures that cause most leaders to avoid confrontation. Confronting and correcting are so difficult that many leaders ignore a problem even when it is a sin issue. How to strike the balance of maintaining good relationships and achieving goals is a challenge. But after talking with leaders in Kenya, we have concluded that with wisdom correcting *can* be done; and it *must* be done.

How does one exercise *control* in management?

Following are some thoughts on how shepherd-leaders may correct those who are not fulfilling their responsibilities well. Because they are failing to carry their load, achievement of the goals is in danger. Therefore, the leader, who desires to ensure that the performance of the workers is according to plan, will need to correct erring team-members. Everyone needs to make his contribution towards reaching the goal according to his gifts and calling.

But you will note the care and wisdom that the leader needs to exercise. The accent in this book is on the positive. Many of the ideas suggested below do not seem to be related to *correcting*. Through a wise and positive approach, the actual process of correcting need not be common. Correcting is only a small part of the bigger picture of shepherding people to accomplish the goals. Some of the ideas below may be repetitious, but they are repeated for a reason. There is a way to manage affairs in Africa to achieve goals; but this can only be done within a context of a wise, loving and strong shepherd-leader.

1. Develop strong, personal relationships with every team member. When each person respects and trusts their leader – and likes their leader – they will be open to correction that is given in a positive and affirming manner. Remember, the Receiver who Decodes the message given by the Source may interpret and understand the message differently. If a person's attitude toward the leader is negative, he may very well interpret the message in a negative manner. We cannot emphasise too strongly that a strong, personal relationship between the leader and his team-members is the foundation for all correction.

This means that the leader must be a *people-person*. That is, the team-members must feel comfortable with him. He is approachable under all circumstances. He understands them and appreciates them. Friendship between leaders and followers is essential because emotions cannot be detached from ministry. The leader and his team-members must enjoy each others' company.

One youth pastor has developed a very close relationship with his youth. When one of the ladies developed an unhealthy relationship with a man, he had to confront her. She was sorrowful and made things right. Because of a good relationship with her, the leader was able to counsel her successfully.

One bishop advised on the need to meet with the team-members regularly, sit with them and eat with them. 'Find out how they are doing. When they feel free, they will tell you where they hurt and what their needs are. You must win their support so that they can support you. Befriend them, get closer to them. When you are near the people, they will respect you and not fear you.'

2. Include all the team-members in the process of setting goals. If the members participate in the process of setting goals, they will be more committed to doing their part in fulfilling the goals. For the leader to impose his own goals on a people and then expect them to contribute toward achieving the goals is total futility. Rather, the leader must find ways of motivating the team-members so that they will want to work hard. By including them in the process of setting goals, they will be motivated. The goals should be people centred so that they can see and experience the benefits of those goals.

This process may take time. The members may not see a need like the pastor does. But in some things of leadership there can be no hurry. Make sure you take time before you start a project. Moses thought he was ready to deliver Israel from injustice, but he was not ready. He needed to mature.

In one case, the pastor and elders agreed that the Church needed a women's fellowship. But the people could not see the value. So the elders thought they should move ahead anyway. The pastor cautioned patience and took six months to visit the women to learn why they were not interested in it. After six months the women agreed and the women's fellowship was started successfully. The women needed time to mature in their thinking and understanding of the idea.

There are times when the pastor fails to convince the elders and people of the need to do this or that. Eventually, time may prove the pastor to be right but the time is too late. The desirable project failed. However, for the pastor to push through his idea without the support of the people, the project will fail.

3. Include all the team-members in drawing up a programme to achieve those goals. It may be easier and quicker for the leader to do all the planning, but the implementation will be more difficult. When members agree to the ways of achieving the goals because of their participation, the leader will have less difficulty in shepherding the members in fulfilling those goals.

4. Train the team-members so they know how to do their work. The leader must be a servant and come down to the level of his team-members, in order to show them what to do. Be a servant! Demonstrate practically how to do it. Come along side of the people and be willing to do yourself what is required of them. The team-members will grow in confidence when their leader helps them to do their work well. As a result of training, not only will they do their work better but they will love their leader because he has helped them. When the leader has trained the person, the leader has greater freedom to talk with them and make any corrections that need to be made.

5. Help the team-members enjoy their work. They not only need to know that their leader is happy with them; they need to know that God is pleased with them. And they should feel proud of their work that they are doing because they know that they are serving God. Continually remind them of the purpose and goals for the ministry. Remind them that above all they are serving God who will reward them. Their work rendered unto God will be remembered and rewarded.

6. Use the Word of God when instructing them. The Christian leader is wise to teach them the Scriptures in such a way that they will understand their responsibility toward God. 'They will always respond when they understand the Scriptures,' is the experience of one leader. The Bible is rich with instruction on the importance of diligent work. Read the Proverbs[2] and check the following New Testament teaching:

> Servants, do what you're told by your earthly masters. And don't just do the minimum that will get you by. Do your best. Work from the heart for your real Master, for God, confident that you'll get paid in full when you come into your inheritance. Keep in mind always that the ultimate Master you're serving is Christ. The sullen servant who does shoddy work will be held responsible. Being Christian doesn't cover up bad work.'[3]

7. Stay close to those delegated with work. A major mistake which leaders make is to abandon their team-members once a work assignment has been entrusted to them. Stay close to them, ask how they are doing and help them whenever necessary. One Principal commented, 'I never wait until the end but keep close to them to observe their work. In the past two years I have had no failure or disappointment with any of them.'

Be willing to come down and work with the person, showing him once again how to do it properly. Patience with humility and love will go a long way to help the person be successful in his work. The Akamba say, 'The one who voluntarily helps his grandmother will not fail to get secret gifts.' Kindness does go a long way in bringing rewards. Help him and you will be rewarded as the shepherd-leader.

8. Leaders must be consumed with the vision to complete the task. The leader is the key. He must stay on top of things. He must keep people moving forward by instilling the vision of accomplishing the goals, by inspiring them to work with words of encouragement and by helping them overcome some difficulty they are having. If the leader is not consumed with the passion of completing the goals, he cannot expect his team-members to do the same.

9. The actual task of correcting requires interpersonal skills. The actual task of correcting is the most difficult part of being a leader. Many leaders have a difficult time of correcting effectively. Perhaps they don't know how or they are afraid of hurting a relationship. Correcting is possible but only with social skills of knowing how to work with people. Some leaders have this gift naturally. Those who don't must learn – and learn quickly. A leader can win the argument but loose a friend. Skills are needed to communicate in such a way that the team member is both corrected and remains a friend.

10. Begin correcting by speaking to the whole team in general terms. Though the leader may know who in particular needs correction, by speaking to the whole group in general he avoids embarrassing the individual. When the pastor desires some changed behaviour in the congregation, he can make a general rebuke once or twice. The leader thus avoids personal confrontation. If the persons are good people who desire to serve God and do their best, they will learn from the public admonition.

11. Begin talking to individuals personally by asking questions. Never begin from a judgemental attitude. Don't assume you know that the person is wrong. Find out what made him do what he did. 'Did you know what to do? Did you understand? Did you have the means to do it?' If the person has a reasonable excuse, the leader should forgive him.

12. Be wise and respectful when correcting. The language of correction must be laced with wisdom and respect. 'Respect means to have a "we" attitude. We are in this together. Each of us has something to contribute to the relationship and the work.'[4] Respect for those falling short means that the leader sees value in that person and desires to help him reach his potential.

If a person is older, recognise his age; give him due respect whenever mentioning his wrong doing. This is not easy to do. If the wrong doer is an elder or a retired distinguished official with grey hair, it can be difficult. A younger person can use an older man to confront a powerful man. The use of intermediaries can be helpful. Effort must be made to win agreement by both parties on the nature of the wrong doing. Otherwise, the elder may curse the youth.

Always remember the wisdom of the African sages. A Kamba proverb says, '*Water once spilt cannot be collected again.*' You may and must apologize for thoughtless and cutting words spoken in anger but you can never recover those words. The words were spoken and can never be collected again. '*The arrow shot in the dark comes back the same way it went,*' say the Akamba. Great care must be taken in how you correct someone because careless words may come back to haunt you. Again they say, '*The trapper that sets the trap badly will get caught and not be able to release himself.*' If you are not careful in what you say, you may become a prisoner of your own making.

13. Never embarrass a team member before others. Never correct him or criticise him in front of others. One leader said to me, 'I don't mind my work being criticised but I don't want to loose face or be embarrassed. It is important never to embarrass a person.' The leader praises his people both publicly and privately but he only corrects them in private. With love and wisdom, talk with the person privately and work it out.

14. Always correct the person privately and in love. A leader could make a short cut and simply use his authority to order, rebuke or correct. But the end would be disastrous both for the leader and for the project. But if the relationship is good between the leader and his team, there is no difficulty in correcting. If you love a person, he will know that your correction is for his good. Therefore, it is acceptable. All correction *must* be done with loving concern for the welfare of the person. The manner of correcting is in love.

When the leader precedes his personal discussion with several public announcements or rebukes, then the leader can single out the erring one and talk with him to work out the problem. Keeping good personal relationships is so important in achieving goals because friends can learn from each other and go forward together to achieve goals together.

15. Never erupt in anger or rage. Never rebuke with an emotional outburst. The leader must master his feelings. He may have a genuine basis for being upset, but showing anger is counterproductive. 'Slowness to anger makes for deep understanding; a quick-tempered person stockpiles stupidity.'[5] Remember that most of communication is in the tone of voice and body language. Any hint of an emotion of annoyance, rejection or anger in the face or voice will destroy all hope of effective communication.

16. Always speak the truth in love; be sensitive, loving – and yet firm. Truth is divine, for 'God is truth.'[6] The leader must never compromise with truth. But speaking the truth should also be done in a loving manner, for 'God is love.'[7] Whenever you correct, you do it friend to friend. The manner of correcting is always in love.

Can you give an *example* of the controlling process?

One pastor and Overseer said that the first thing is to explain the goals, discuss them and let the members suggest how they might achieve them. Thus the team-members are involved in setting goals and arranging for their implementation. There is discussion in each step.

For example, the pastor gathered the members together to discuss the serious HIV/AIDS pandemic in their area. They discussed what could be done. The pastor gave some ideas. They decided to do some research, so the teachers identified how many orphans were in the area; the youth counted the population. Research was made into how many die within a given month.

Once the goals were discussed, then the pastor asked for volunteers. Each one *volunteered* to do this or achieve that. Once they, volunteered the pastor went around checking on how they were doing, to help them and give advice. They also asked one another for help.

Periodically, the group met to review the progress and see how well they were doing. Therefore, no team member makes a big mistake before it is discovered and corrected.

Because of the wise and caring shepherding process, there is seldom any need to confront or correct. Whatever correcting is needed is done in a culturally sensitive manner so that no one is embarrassed and the leader is not coming on the errant person in any abusive or offensive manner.

In conclusion, we may say that several leaders have mentioned that they have had no trouble when correcting because of taking the steps given above. Yet difficulties are not uncommon. Some members are not truly *team-members* in their hearts. They are not supportive of the leader. Those who are defiant and difficult have their own problems. They may have unmet needs and want attention. If the leader recognises them and rewards them for achievement, they may come around. But when some are corrected they may become sullen and unfriendly toward the leader. Others just leave the Church and go elsewhere.

Correcting is tricky business and must be done with great care and wisdom. But unless the leader has the strength and courage to deal with those who fall short, his leadership is deficient because goals will not be achieved.

Flexibility in timing is necessary when striving toward a goal. The important issue is not accomplishing the goal on time as planned but moving toward the goal and accomplishing it as the team-members are able. Therefore, the leader must keep his eye on the goal and not fret over deadlines.

Shepherding Towards the Goal

The work of a shepherd is to lead the sheep out to pasture and then to lead them back home. The work of the shepherd-leader is to lead his team-members through the challenge of life toward meeting certain agreed upon goals. The way is not straight or even. Many unexpected and unhappy events occur that make the journey a challenge. But the responsibility rests upon the shepherd – to keep the goal in mind and keep leading the sheep towards that goal, arriving home before nightfall.

The shepherd-leader always remembers that God is in control, no matter what disappointments come. Although people plan, the outcome may be somewhat different. The Akamba say, '*The trap is set for a leopard but it catches a hyena.*' The best laid plans can fail. Always remember, '*As weather shapes mountains, so problems make leaders.*' Disappointments, frustrations and problems are part of the shepherd's lot. They are God's means of developing character within the leader. Centuries ago Augustine reportedly commented: 'God had one Son without sin; he has no sons without suffering.' Suffering is a way of life in this fallen world. God uses those disappointments to teach patience, perseverance, love, and a forgiving spirit – and drive us into a closer and more trusting relationship with God. The Chagga say, '*Suffering is prior to attaining success or perfection.*' The Dagbani of Ghana say, '*If God breaks your leg, He will teach you how to limp.*' If you fail to achieve your goals, God is in that too, and will show you how to deal with it.

The effective shepherd, however, knows where he is going, and has faith and courage to press on; he will succeed by God's grace to reach the desired destination, accomplishing the goals in God's timing and will. If the shepherd is undisciplined or lazy, he may loose his way and the goals will remain illusive. But if he keeps his eyes on the goal, and remains convinced that God has led in the planning process, the sheep will reach the goal.

The burden of leadership has been entrusted to you by God. With his help, you can succeed. As the Akamba say, '*An elephant is not overcome to carry its trunk.*' Neither is a mature Christian leader overcome by disappointments or setbacks. By God's grace, you will succeed in accomplishing the will of God.

CONCLUSION

Always remember that, 'The chief is like a rubbish heap; everything comes to him.' Leading a people to accomplish agreed upon goals is not easy – he becomes the recipient of much criticism and misunderstanding. But it is not the calling of the Christian leader to look back but to keep looking to the future.

A few more issues on leadership remain to be considered.

SEARCHING THE SCRIPTURE WITH APPLICATION

1. Correcting a worker is not always easy. How have you corrected someone in the past and tried to help them perform their responsibilities better? How have they responded to your correction?
2. From your experience, what are the best suggestions for correcting someone that are found in this chapter?
3. Which suggestions do you believe will not work?
4. Why is a strong personal relationship with team-members *the key* to correcting someone?
5. What mistake do many leaders make when they try to correct someone?
6. Why do people become upset or defensive when they are corrected?
7. What does that tell you about the proper way to correct?
8. Which is more important: the words you use in speaking or the your body language when speaking (the tone of voice, the look in the eye, the attitude, emotion or temper conveyed)?
9. How can your manner of speaking (your body language and tone of voice) convey to the person the meaning you actually felt in your heart, even when you do not accurately communicate the meaning by your words?
10. Why should we bother trying to correct others if it so often creates misunderstanding, hurt feelings or broken relationships?
11. Why would anyone be offended by what you say, if you as the leader have a cordial and trusting relationship with a team member, and if you speak with love and humility, and if you approach the subject with a positive, helpful attitude? Discuss.
12. Leadership is all about vision and leading people to achieve that vision. The only way a leader will perform well over the long-term is if he or she fully comprehends the end goal. Why is it essential for the leader to be focused on long-term vision with its goals, if they are ever to be accomplished?

13. An African proverb says, 'You cannot blow your nose and whistle at the same time.' No one can do two things at the same time. How can this piece of wisdom be applied to shepherding the team successfully to the completion of the goals?

Endnotes

[1] 1 Pe 2:25
[2] Pr 10:4f; 12:11,24,27; 13:4; 14:4; 20:13; 22:29; 27:23; 28:19; 30:25f.
[3] Col 3:24-25 *The Message*
[4] McDonough 1979:113
[5] Pr 14:29 *The Message*
[6] Jn 14:6; 17:17
[7] 1 Jn 4:16

PART EIGHT

ISSUES FOR CHRISTIAN LEADERS

Life with its responsibilities of leadership is not a short sprint but a life-long marathon. Certain issues must be mastered by the Christian leader in order to remain effective over the long haul. The issues discussed in this chapter which need to be mastered include:

(1) *A Balanced Life-Style,*
(2) *Self-Discipline,*
(3) *Maintaining Unity,*
(4) *Growing as a Leader in Character,* and
(5) *Growing as a Leader in Competence.*

36
A BALANCED LIFE STYLE

'And Jesus grew in wisdom and stature,
and in favor with God and men.'[1]

An imbalanced lifestyle will lead eventually to a failure in leadership.

Nothing is more important for the leader than to understand that he is not 'the almighty'; he cannot do everything. God has granted every person twenty-four hours in a day. No one has more time and no one has less. God has granted a unique calling and particular gifts to each person. Only a fool pretends to be what he is not. The leader is responsible to use those gifts and live those twenty-four hours in a balanced way so that no part of his life suffers and every part is sufficiently nourished. Anything short of a balanced lifestyle will lead to personal disaster.

Jesus, the God-Man, *grew* intellectually and physically, spiritually and socially as we read in Luke 2:52. At every stage in his life, Jesus was perfect in his intellect/wisdom, his physical development, his spiritual relationship with the Father and in his social relationships with people. His life was perfectly balanced throughout, and yet *he continued to grow* throughout his life.

He grew in *wisdom.* Wisdom goes beyond the intellect but it includes cognitive knowledge. Jesus grew in his intellectual understanding and beyond that, in that spiritual dimension of applying truth to life so that he was perfectly wise in his approach to people and life situations.

Jesus grew in *stature.* That is, he grew physically in stature and in age. Jesus had a physical body that needed care and attention.

Our Lord also grew in *favour with God.* Jesus' relationship with his Father in heaven was vital. It was nourished through prayer, meditation and retreats into the presence of God. Jesus thus grew spiritually.

He also grew in *favour with man*. That is, he grew socially. As he interacted with people, they increasingly responded with goodwill and favour.

Every leader must learn to grow in each of these dimensions of life. This chapter focuses on ways to grow healthy as a person with a balanced way of life.

Philosophy of a Balanced Lifestyle

Balancing a lifestyle must grow out of basic premises. Included are these:

1. Balancing your lifestyle is a life-long challenge. Every leader I spoke with admitted that maintaining a balanced lifestyle is 'very hard,' 'difficult,' a 'challenge,' and 'a great problem.' The reason for this is twofold:

First, a balanced lifestyle is not choosing between good and evil; it is choosing between equally important and valuable responsibilities in life. Which is of less value in the kingdom of God? Caring for your body? Nourishing your relationship with God? Loving your wife and children? Being faithful in ministry? Being a Christian testimony in your community? Evangelising the lost? Shepherding your flock?

Balancing your lifestyle is an issue of priorities. As Howard says, 'Doing good is imperative. Doing everything is impossible.'[2] This needs to be shouted from the house tops. Life is full of many demands. For the Christian leader, all these demands are worthy of your attention. But '*doing everything is impossible*.' Therefore, priorities must be set. How much time will be devoted to each? Which receives your first commitment?

Secondly, balancing your lifestyle is a challenge because situations change continually, calling for your attention. Your child becomes sick. A major misunderstanding arises in your ministry organisation. The building project consumes more time than expected. Whenever life moves along smoothly, you can learn how to balance your priorities. But when an unexpected crisis erupts, the pressing problem alters the equilibrium you had established.

So the first thing a leader must understand is that you will never outlive the need to struggle in maintaining a balanced lifestyle.

2. Balancing your lifestyle, though a challenge, is essential. If you desire to be effective, you have no alternative. You *must* achieve balance in meeting the demands of life. Let us consider what happens when you fail.

Your body, the only one which God has given you, will deteriorate if you neglect it. Through failure of an imbalanced diet, lack of proper rest and sleep, and failure to exercise, you will become overweight and be susceptible to diabetes and heart disease. Your immune system will not function well so that you will get sick from viruses that a healthy person can normally suppress.

Your relationship with God, the most important relationship any child of God has, will grow lukewarm. When your spiritual senses become dull you yield to temptation and fall into sin – first, the little sins of the mind unnoticed by people, then more visible sins that become obvious to your family and close friends. Finally, a fall from grace will destroy your life and your ministry.

Your family will suffer. How many children of pastors have gone astray from God because their father was too busy with ministry? He failed to father them, teach them, befriend them and guide them. The wife may suffer in silence and because of greater maturity may persevere. But a loveless marriage without a husband attending to the needs of the wife cannot bode well.

A leader who neglects his ministry responsibilities may be able to keep things going but without the prosperity and blessing that could be experienced if the leader would have been faithful. Remember, God does not require superb preaching or charismatic leadership if God has not gifted you with five talents.[3] But God does require faithfulness – doing your best because you love him.

A Christian leader who tries to do everything will eventually burn-out. When you light a candle on both ends, it burns out quickly. When you disregard your need for sleep, fail to eat properly, neglect your family, become unfaithful in your ministry responsibilities and above all, neglect your relationship with God, your candle will burn out.

3. Balancing your lifestyle requires biblical priorities. The first and greatest commandment is to love God supremely.[4] Maintaining a trusting and obedient relationship with God is of first priority. The second greatest command is: 'Love your neighbor as yourself.'[5] Howard writes:

> You cannot love your neighbour 'as yourself' unless you love yourself. 'That makes me highly important.' 'That means I must assign top priority to my life, my growth, my relationships, my responsibilities. That means everything about me becomes significant – my thoughts, my feelings, my decisions, my body, my attitudes, my sexuality, my words, my reactions.'[6]

Howard concludes that it is not biblical to put self at the bottom of the list of priorities. If we think that the list of priorities should include God, family, Church, work, government and the world; it is dead wrong to put *self* at the end of the list. Taking care of yourself is essential.

There are different ways of looking at life but we suggest that every Christian leader must carefully consider his or her following responsibilities toward God in order to please Him:

- Cultivating a relationship with *God*;
- Attending the needs of *the body* and *mind*;
- Loving and caring for *wife, children and extended family*;
- Faithfully serving God in the *place of ministry*;
- Relating to the *community, society and government* as salt and light.

Can you think of any other area of responsibility that needs your attention?

These responsibilities are not prioritised in the above list. In fact, you cannot make a prioritised list. Loving your family or being faithful in ministry is not less important than cultivating your relationship with God, or is it?

Because of our biblical priorities of loving God with all our hearts, and loving our neighbours as ourselves, this means that God must be at the very centre of life. Our personal relationship with God is unending. All of life centres on Him – loving him, obeying him and serving him. Each Christian leader, given his circumstances, calling and gifts, must decide before God how he will fulfill all his responsibilities.

Essentials of a Balanced Lifestyle

Given the limitations of time, physical strength and material resources, every Christian leader must consider how best to fulfill those responsibilities each day, each week and each month and year.

Many of these responsibilities will compete for your attention. It is not an issue of choosing between the good and the best. It is choosing between all that is important. Always remember – '*Doing good is imperative. Doing everything is impossible.*' God does not expect you to do all that people might demand of you. But it is your responsibility before God to consider prayerfully and thoughtfully how best to care for each of those responsibilities. Following are some suggestions.

Cultivating a relationship with *God*

One young leader acknowledged, 'I have not really balanced my lifestyle. Balancing is very hard. The ministry is overwhelming the spiritual side. This is very hard. I need more self-discipline. Ministry takes most of my time.' Indeed, his ministry is prospering. But unless this dear brother deals with this imbalance, he is headed for barrenness, professionalism and spiritual failure. A leader's relationship with God cannot be neglected without consequences. Worship of God both privately and corporately with the Body of Christ assembled together in the house of God glorifies God and nourishes the soul.

Because this subject is so very important, we have already discussed the topic in chapter 7, 'The Spiritual Disciplines' of a Christian leader. You are urged to review that unit again.

Attending the needs of the *body* and the *mind*

Through the years of living in Africa, the author has made this curious observation. Many of the diseases which have devastated the African peoples have been eliminated in western countries; such as, malaria, typhoid, bilharziasis, amoeba, and debilitating dysentery. These illnesses come from polluted water, contaminated foods and the prevalence of anopheles mosquitoes. In contrast, westerners have suffered from illnesses caused by their lifestyle and diet; namely, diabetes, hyper-tension, heart disease and cancer.

Today much has changed but not for the better. Medical knowledge and medicines are reducing the sicknesses that were endemic throughout Africa in the past. But the western lifestyle and diet has penetrated Africa so that peoples are becoming sick with 'western diseases.' Because of a sedentary lifestyle, many no longer walk or work in the gardens. Instead, they sit in offices, stand in classrooms and ride in cars. When they eat in restaurants and hotels, they eat fried fish and fried chips, and drink soda (with nine spoons of sugar). At home they eat white bread and drink tea (with several spoons of sugar). The result? We see a dramatic increase of obesity with accompanying diabetes, hyper-tension, heart disease, and cancer. While Africa is rushing down this road of modernity, western countries, alarmed by the growing obesity of their population, are seeking ways to reverse the trend. Africa needs to do the same.

For the Christian leader to care for his body, he must attend to exercise and proper diet. Ironically, the traditional lifestyle in Africa of walking to your destination and doing manual labour was healthier than it is today. The diet of maize and beans, *ugali* made from maize meal, and vegetables with meat limited to special occasions was far much healthier than the diet is today.

Physical exercise:[7] For the Christian leader who uses his two legs for transportation and walks three or four miles in a day, he may be in good physical shape. But for the leader who is more sedentary and dependent on vehicular transportation, he must find other opportunities for exercise. Physical exercise not only strengthens the body's resistance to disease, it also helps to maintain a healthy weight. A waist that is larger than forty inches is a health- disaster waiting to happen. Anything under a thirty-five inch waist is best.

Physical exercise should include three areas ideally: (1) aerobic exercise, meaning oxygen-using exercise which raises the heart rate, such as jogging or walking; (2) resistance exercise which strengthens the body and tone of the muscles, such as weight lifting; (3) flexibility training which stretches the muscles and tendons, especially important as one grows older.

If you live in a town or city, you may find gyms specially designed to provide paying customers all kinds of machines to achieve what was normally accomplished through normal, routine daily living. Why pay money when you can do the same through self-discipline in daily living? Playing sports or active games can be both enjoyable and healthy. Walking or running for three or four miles daily is excellent and can be combined with memorising of Scripture and contemplative prayer. Working in the garden, bicycling, doing manual labour around the house are all helpful.

However, you must remember two things: (1) You must exercise long enough to be effective, preferably, forty to sixty minutes. Exercise until you perspire; exercise until your heart rate is elevated for a period of time. Both the duration and intensity of your exercise should increase over time. (2) You must exercise often enough each week to be effective, at least five days each week. Aim for six days to allow for that unexpected interruption in your schedule.

Caring for your body is your physical life. For further help, seek guidance.

Balanced diet:[8] One-hundred years ago Americans did not have a balanced diet. This led to various minor illnesses including stunted growth. Because of affluence today, their diet has become richer, full of calories and fat. This has led to obesity with its attendant illnesses. The same has been true in Africa. A healthy diet is balanced with sufficient proteins, carbohydrates, fiber, fat, vitamins, minerals and water.

Protein is needed for growth and repair of body tissues. Foods that provide protein include fruits, vegetables, nuts, beans, meat, eggs and cheese. Although animal products are a good source of protein, they are also more expensive. You can derive all your protein needs from beans, fruit and vegetables without the expense of meat.

Carbohydrates provide the fuel which the body needs to give you energy. Complex carbohydrates are found in nuts, vegetables, whole grains and legumes (beans). Simple carbohydrates are sugars and fruits. The refined sugars found in candy and cakes and the sugar used in tea are not the healthiest. You would be wise to limit your consumption of such sugars. Wild honey is better than highly refined honey in stores; course, dirty looking sugar is less refined and, therefore, healthier than the highly refined white sugar. Bread made from whole grains is healthier than white bread which is highly refined with most nutrients removed.

Fiber plays an important role in proper digestion without increasing calorie intake. It can prevent colon cancer. Fiber is derived from the cell walls of plants, such as whole grains, vegetables, legumes (beans), and certain fruit. Since the peoples in developing countries consume five or six times as much fiber as Americans, Africans rarely suffer from constipation and other digestive disorders.

Vitamins and minerals are essential. They are mostly derived from vegetables and fruit. Vitamins B and C are water soluble and cannot be stored in the body. Therefore, they must be derived from food daily.

A certain amount of fat is needed in the diet; but too much fat, especially the wrong kind of fat, will lead to heart disease and obesity. Fried foods in saturated fat like coconut oil, palm oil, corn oil and cottonseed oil are health- risks. Margarine with its hydrogenated oil is also unhealthy. Meats, dairy products and butter all contain saturated fat which will accumulate as plaque in the arteries and will eventually lead to heart attacks. Western type diets heavy with fat leads to all kinds of illnesses. The best advice is use fats, oils and sweets sparingly.

Water is the most essential part of one's diet. A person can live for weeks without food but will die in a few days without water. Tea is no substitute. Water is needed to regulate body temperature, assist in digestion and the elimination of food and maintain the immune system. Water also keeps the brain adequately hydrated.

The problem with water is that when it is contaminated people become deathly sick. In fact, polluted water is one of the greatest sources of illness in Africa. The World Health Organization says filthy drinking water and mosquitoes in stagnant water kill 13 million people a year throughout the world. The old system of purifying drinking water was to boil it for twenty minutes. Medical doctors have now concluded that water in clear glass or plastic bottles, without paper wrappings, setting in the full sun light for six hours or more will become purified from the ultra violet rays of the sun. This discovery now makes the purification of water cheaper and more accessible. Since tea is boiled, the water in the tea is usually purified. Abstaining from all water that has not been properly purified will reduce disease considerably.

Developing the mind: Woe to that leader who thinks that Bible School or College has provided all the learning needed in life! Too many think this way. Others feel the solution is to go on for further education. They become professional students. The purpose of an education is to teach you how to teach yourself in the future, to learn and grow on your own. An educated person does not need endless degrees to function well. The leader simply needs to learn how to learn and how to grow on his own.

There are many steps that the leader should take to develop the mind:

Learn of the current events in your community, nation, Africa and the world. A Christian leader should keep abreast of world events. Local radio stations, BBC world news, newspapers and news magazines are good sources. The preacher should have the Bible in his right hand and the newspaper in his left so he can be relevant in his preaching.

- Learn of developments among missionaries; write to the missionaries, welcome them to your Church to preach and report; learn of their cultures, challenges in evangelising and planting Churches. Keep your people up-to-date on the missionary developments in the world.
- Also learn of Christian news in Africa and African Christian thinking by reading African books and journals, such as the *Africa Journal of Evangelical Theology*. Look for and invite speakers for your church who can enlarge your horizons. Every African Christian leader should be growing in his knowledge of Christianity in Africa.

- Study and prepare for preaching as if the President of your country were attending. Read the biblical text, the context, commentaries, and other resource books so you can *teach* your people. Certainly, if you are a teacher, never grow stale by teaching old notes, but update continually by reading and research.
- Attend seminars on relevant topics. Arrange for seminars among your Churches on special topics by inviting experts in different fields.
- Pick a topic of special interest on some aspect of traditional culture and religion. Often a young leader is quite ignorant or naïve on these issues. Young leaders will commend themselves to their elders when they show interest in African tradition. Do field research by inquiring from the older people on particular topics. Use this information for illustrations in sermons and application of biblical teaching.
- Develop an inquisitive mind. Ask questions, gain information, understand the thinking and presuppositions of people.
- Never neglect books. Though books are expensive you may be able to find ways of borrowing books or exchanging books with friends so that you can keep growing.
- In the pressure of ministry, arrange for occasional days off for retreats to get away from everyone for Bible study and prayer. Don't neglect Bible study. Out of a deeper knowledge of God's Word, you will grow.

Loving and caring for your *spouse, children and extended family*

The leader's family is basic to any success in ministry. A chaplain in Kenya said, 'It is important to take care of your family. Develop your family. When you are in trouble, your family provides the cushion. Love your wife, be good to her, and develop real fellowship with her and your children. When all people reject you, your family is your refuge. Get them involved in ministry.'

One pastor said, 'You must keep fellowship with your family first, then your Church second. You need to help your family grow in the Lord. When you are right with the family, you do well in the Church. Create an atmosphere in the home that is good so that you can do well in the Church.' Another pastor said, 'Our relationship with our family determines our effectiveness in ministry. Take seriously family relationships.'

A Bible College teacher said, 'Approach the ministry holistically – balance your family, ministry and life. Face the ministry as a human being and not as a spirit. Some people pretend they came from heaven.' There is no getting around this major point. If the leader neglects his spouse and children, that leader will suffer serious loss as a person and as a servant of the Lord.

We urge each reader to purchase the TAG publication, *A Biblical Approach to Marriage and Family in Africa* from Scott Theological College in Kenya. This 220 page book contains everything that should be said in this book and much more than space allows here. If your family does not recognise you as their spiritual leader, who else can?

Faithfully serving God in the *place of ministry*

Perhaps less needs to be said of serving in ministry because so many Christian leaders tend to concentrate their efforts in ministry and neglect all the other aspects of the Christian lifestyle mentioned above.

Two things must be said: (1) Always remember, you are serving God first and foremost, not people who can be demanding and unappreciative. What God requires of you is faithfulness to him. When you feel like shirking your responsibilities in ministry, remember, you are failing God to whom you must give an account. (2) Devote your life to training others, discipling others and equipping others so you can delegate the work to others. Don't do the work of ten people when you should be training ten people to do the work. If you are overcome with work, perhaps you need to organise and delegate to others.

Relating to the *community, society* and *government* as salt and light

Each leader must determine what his role is in the community. The role of the pastor is different from a bishop and a bishop's role is different from a Bible School teacher or principal. Whatever your position, the Christian leader must find his place in the community. Become acquainted with your community leaders, be of service and thus become salt and light in the world.

Scheduling a Balanced Lifestyle

Scheduling your day is simply planning what you should do to fulfill all your responsibilities. Of course, we all recognise that interruptions will occur. Wisdom is needed in handling those interruptions, so that interruptions can become divine appointments for ministry and not mere interruptions.

Nevertheless, a life that is not planned is a life not worth living because of little fruit that results. Remember, all your responsibilities are important. It is just as important for a Christian leader to eat as it is to witness. Family responsibilities are just as important as Church responsibilities. When God is central in life, then all these responsibilities have their proper place. Write on paper, in order of priorities, what you believe God would have you do the following day, beginning with the most important to the least. Howard states:

The main issues on the subject of priorities are first, which things in life are really important, and second, in what order should they be placed. The Scriptures make it clear that the things that are really important are God, self, and significant others (Church, work, government, world and family). Life is too complex and time is too short for us to be vague on these matters.[9]

A time schedule that grows out of a biblical philosophy of a lifestyle will help the Christian leader to discharge his responsibilities in a responsible way.

The approach of one productive Church leader is this: he awakes very early in the morning, around 5:30 A.M., prays with his wife and studies the Word. By 6:30 A.M. he is praying with his children. When his wife and children leave the house, he takes another thirty minutes to pray and read the Bible.

Then he goes to ministry. By 4:00 P.M. he returns back home so that when the family returns to the house he is there to welcome them. This occurs every day unless he is on a safari. However, in the rural area people come to his home any time and he must welcome them and meet their needs. Obviously, this leader has established his priorities in his mind.

A Bible College administrator finds balancing a lifestyle to be difficult but he makes this attempt. 'I have set times for prayer and Bible study. Every evening I meet with my family. We have set times to be together, to pray and eat together. On my day off we are together. Office hours are scheduled. I visit people in their places of work. If your priority is money, you sacrifice family, ministry and relationship with God for acquiring things. If you give yourself to the Lord, then God is your priority and you devote yourself to God's calling.'

CONCLUSION

We conclude that balancing your lifestyle is difficult without self-discipline. Excuses may abound why a balanced lifestyle is impossible. We can all become defensive on this issue. But those who succeed in ministry do so because they have learned self-discipline which is necessary to maintain a balanced lifestyle.

Self-discipline is the topic of the following chapter to help you balance life.

SEARCHING THE SCRIPTURE WITH APPLICATION

1. Describe what you understand to be a balanced lifestyle.
2. Compare Lk 2:52 with 1 Sa 2:26. Why is it important for each person to develop each aspect of life as mentioned in these verses?
3. What happens to someone if -
    a. The body is taken care of but the relationship with God is not?
    b. One's relationship with the Lord is cared for but the body is neglected?
    c. The ministry is adequately cared for but not one's family?
4. What biblical values and priorities should guide a leader in knowing how to spend his time during the week? Discuss.
5. Why does it become so difficult to balance one's responsibilities if the Bible is so clear what our priorities should be? Discuss.
6. What should you do to care better for your relationship with God?
7. What should you do to care better for the needs of your body?
8. What should you do to develop your mind and understanding?
9. What should you do to be more faithful to your wife and family?
10. What should you do to be more faithful in the ministry?
11. What should you do to have a better influence on your community, society and government than you now have?
12. In view of your past struggles for a balanced lifestyle and in view of your obligations according to the Scripture, what practical steps must you take to change and care better for all your responsibilities in life?
13. Paul admonishes Timothy, his young disciple, '*Watch your life and doctrine closely. Persevere in them, because if you do, you will save both yourself and your hearers*' (1 Ti 4:16). The leader's first

responsibility is to care for himself – then also his teaching. The order is significant. The verb is present imperative: '*Keep on paying attention to your self.*' Some leaders are careless about caring for their personal lives. The implications of failure are important – '*because if you do, you will save both yourself and your hearers.*' Discuss the implications of this apostolic advice for leaders today. What happens if a leader is devoted primarily to ministry and neglects the required care of his own self and family?

Endnotes

1 Lk 2:52 NIV
2 Howard 1983:16
3 Mt 25:16ff
4 Mt 22:37,38
5 Mt 22:39
6 Howard 1983:45
7 See Klag 1999:33-51
8 See Klag 1999:5-29
9 Howard 1983:159

37
SELF-DISCIPLINE

'Everyone who competes in the games exercises self-control in all things... I discipline my body and make it my slave...'[1]

Every winner is self-disciplined.

What is self-discipline?

Self-discipline is self-policing, self-management and self-control. Children need adults to oversee them to ensure their proper conduct. Lazy workers need supervisors so that they will fulfill their work responsibilities. But a self-disciplined leader is one who governs himself to do what should be done. 'The true spirit of leadership cultivates a self-control that regulates one's focus and orders one's life. The disciplined lifestyle distinguishes leaders from followers.'[2]

Many Christian leaders, particularly pastors, serve without any immediate supervision. Unlike civil servants, businessmen or teachers, pastors can sleep late in the morning; they can occupy themselves with personal projects and cheat on their preparation time for sermons.

Not so an athlete! If someone desires to win, the athlete must exercise self -control, discipline his body and focus on the goal of winning. Nothing counts but winning; trying does not count, nor do good intentions. Because only one person receives a prize, even though all compete in the race, Paul admonishes: 'run that you may obtain it.'[3] The self-disciplined leader, like a self-disciplined athlete, is focused on doing his best for the Master.

'The spirit of discipline is rooted in self-control, which is a fruit of the Spirit. Leaders live with the understanding that:

- He who cannot control his thoughts will never control himself.
- He who cannot rule himself will never control life.
- He who cannot rule himself will never rule a nation.
- He who cannot control himself will be controlled by others.'[4]

No one can lead others until he has learned to lead himself. No one can balance his lifestyle unless he has learned to discipline himself. Although self-discipline is here discussed near the end of the book, it is of first importance for any success in leadership – self-discipline in every dimension of life.

What should be the *motive* for self-discipline?

Athletes deprive themselves of rich food, drive their bodies and endure bone-weary fatigue in order 'to receive a perishable wreath.' The treasured prize for the early Olympic heroes was a crown of leaves from an olive tree – highly treasured and extremely perishable.

What is the motive for a Christian leader? Unfortunately, all too many leaders think of temporal rewards – promotions, position, power and pay. These too will all perish. For the leader who is focused on pleasing Christ, such reward is unworthy of human sacrifice. Paul reminds us, 'They do it to receive a perishable wreath, but we an imperishable.'

Our Lord God does promise to reward his servants, not for the size of their Church, the number of converts, their status or fame in this life. He promises to reward them for their *faithfulness* in serving. Jesus told a parable of a wealthy businessman who went on a journey and entrusted 'talents' to his servants so that they could invest the money and earn a profit. When he returned, he asked his servants for an accounting. When the two reported their efforts he replied: 'Well done, good and *faithful* servant. You have been *faithful over a little*; I will set you over much. Enter into the joy of your master.'[5] The lazy leader was unfaithful in fulfilling his responsibilities; his reward was rebuke and loss of reward.

Paul states that 'it is *required* that those who have been given a trust *must prove faithful*.'[6] Every master *demands* that his steward be faithful. How much more does the eternal sovereign God demand faithfulness of his servants.

A faithful leader goes beyond the call of duty. He sees what needs to be done and takes on additional work. A faithful leader is trustworthy, always looking after the welfare of the Church and the glory of the Saviour, and not the selfish gains of self-centred leaders. A faithless leader limits his work to the minimal expectations of others; he refuses to serve beyond the minimal obligations unless he receives extra payment of money. A faithful leader pours himself into his calling without consideration of pay or reward, for his eyes are on eternal rewards.

Faithfulness to earn an eternal reward, of course, can also be self-centred. The true motive for a self-disciplined life of faithfulness in our ministry is *love for the Lord.* Nothing else is adequate. When we truly understand what the Lord Jesus has done for us, can we do anything less than to serve him faithfully, with all our hearts and with self-abandonment?

The motive of faithfulness grows out of the *vision* that drives the leader – the vision of Christ, loving and serving him because of his sacrificial death. No vision of temporal gain will ever suffice.

Munroe observes: 'Vision is the source of discipline and the mother of leadership…the man or woman with a clear vision lives a very focused life that requires strong self-discipline. This makes life very simple…[7] The kind of vision you have (whether Christ-centred or self-centred) will determine your priorities, the use of your time, your reading material, the use of your energy, your diet, and your attitude towards the future. In brief, your vision determines your life. What is your vision?

After Peter's fateful denial of Jesus on that dark night, he had an encounter with his Lord on the Sea of Galilee. Peter had decided to go back to his first love, a love for fishing. But after a whole night of fishing, he and several other disciples caught nothing. When Jesus had fed them breakfast with fish that he had provided, Jesus posed a serious question to Peter. 'Do you love me more than these?' Peter was troubled. When Jesus had predicted his denial, Peter protested firmly, 'Though they all fall away because of you, I will never fall away.'[8] And yet, Peter was the one disciple to openly betray his Lord. Jesus wanted to know, 'Do you love me *more than these*?'

What is Jesus referring to? 'Do you love me *more than these*?' Many believe this refers to the other disciples. 'Do you love me more than *these other disciples*?' Peter boasted that though the other disciples might deny Christ, he would never. Peter was full of himself. Even as Peter denied Jesus three times, so Christ asks the question three times, 'Do you love me?'

However, '*more than these*' could also refer to the fish, the fishing, and the occupation which Peter loved before his call to follow Jesus. Peter had left following Jesus and returned to his prior love of fishing for fish before Jesus had called him to fish for men. Jesus asks, 'Do you love me *more than these*?' Grammatically and contextually this understanding is possible.

This is a challenge to all Christian leaders. Jesus asks each of us, 'Do you love me more than fame, position, salary, benefits or power?' Motive is everything. If you love the Lord Jesus and desire to be faithful to him, this will strengthen your resolve to be self-disciplined. You will want to make every moment of every day count for the Lord who loved you and gave himself for you. Life is fleeting. Time lost cannot be recovered. If you desire to be faithful to Christ, then you must exercise self-discipline. What is your vision?

How does a self-disciplined leader manage his time?

Whole books have been written on this vital subject.[9] What helpful advice can be offered in a few paragraphs? Many live under the tyranny of the urgent. Needs arise that demand immediate attention. Leaders become stressed out because of the pressure of obligations. When leaders take on excessive work, they put their whole lives under strain – their relationship with God, family, health, friends and ministry. Then there is the tyranny of meetings. 'It has been calculated that about 400 million people – approximately one-tenth of all humanity – get to a meeting every day of the year.'[10] How much time could be saved if we canceled all committee meetings!

What every Christian leader must consider is that time is a gift from our heavenly Father – an opportunity to serve him. God has granted life and strength, and opportunities for each day. For some, God grants long life; others are snatched away prematurely. Some exhibit vast sums of energy; others are more limited in health and stamina. Some have prominent opportunities of service; others serve in concealed corners of the vineyard, away from the public eye. But the gift of time is equally distributed – just twenty-four hours in every day, no more and no less. The big question is this: How will you use the time allotted to you?

Engstrom slips a little gem into his text without elaboration: '*Time as measured is the enemy of the time as lived*.'[11] When we live under the pressure of the watch, we loose the joy of living. Squeezing as much activity as we can into each hour is a western concept that is concerned with productivity and material gain. Have you ever watched the matatu (taxi) drivers? They become stressed out because they are measuring everything by the clock – in order to earn more money.

Instead, the Christian leader must see himself as a responsible steward of God-given time. Time must not be squandered but neither should we be enslaved by it. The successful leader learns how to manage time.

Engstrom asks the question, 'Is TIME the problem… or are YOU the problem?'[12] Time cannot be the problem since it is only the measurement of one dimension of our existence. The problem is our failure to manage time. When we say, 'There isn't enough time in a day,' what we really mean is that we try to do too much in the day. Or we have not properly planned our day. Leaders live under stress when they try to do too much without planning – and when they live under the tyranny of the urgent.

How then should Christian leaders manage their time? Before the beginning of each day the leader must lay out what should be done – a list of things that need to be accomplished.

- *Begin by setting your goals and priorities*! What *must* be done and what can wait for another day if need be?
- *Prioritise your activities*! Make sure that the most important things are done first. Frequently ask yourself this question, 'What would happen if this were not done at all?' Be clearheaded! Understand that not everything that comes your way is of the same importance.
- *Be flexible*! Don't be obsessed with time. Scheduling appointments is important. But expect interruptions and changes.
- *Learn to delegate*! The overstressed leader must always ask, 'Which of the matters that calls for my attention could be done by someone else?' The solution to overwork is delegation of work and better planning.
- *Avoid distractions*! Time wasters include: prolonged socialising, lost focus on the goals, failing to communicate properly, procrastination, lack of discipline, excessive use of the cell phone, too much talking, and loosing focus. Learn to redeem the time.
- *Fight stress*! Chalke advises: slow down, be realistic, learn to say no, take time to reflect, enjoy yourself, take care of yourself, get a balance with quieter times to allow the body to revitalize.[13]

From time to time the Christian leader must step back and evaluate how well he is exercising self-discipline in managing his time. Let's face it. No one manages time perfectly. We are frequently thrown off balance by emergencies and the unexpected. However, because the effective Christian leader values a balanced lifestyle, he will continually evaluate how well he is doing in managing his time. He will then take steps to correct the imbalance. This is a sign of self-discipline.

How does a self-disciplined leader manage a balanced lifestyle?

Tied together in one bundle are self-discipline, time management and a balanced lifestyle. No one can lead a balanced lifestyle unless he exercises self-discipline in his time management. In the previous chapter we discussed the need for a balanced life lifestyle.

How does self-discipline help in cultivating a relationship with God? To meet God early in the morning, you must discipline yourself to go to bed in sufficient time so that you are rested and ready to pray and meditate on Scripture in the morning. Having a faithful walk with God requires discipline.

Attending to the need of the body and mind requires discipline. Most people are lazy by nature. To exercise or to eliminate fattening food goes against natural human desire. Sitting before a TV is hypnotic. It takes strong will-power to push away from the 'idiot box.' A true leader knows how to rule his bodily desires. If he does not, how can he rule others?

Family is often shortchanged – the wife and children are neglected all in the name of 'ministry.' When the leader recognises the importance of his family, he will ensure that they are central in his concerns. Time will be scheduled and held sacrosanct to be with the wife and children.

Ministry is not exactly of second importance. But since ministry could consume a person's life many times over, the Christian leader must learn to cut the job down to size so that every other part of his precious life is well cared for. Delegate, add personnel, become more efficient, plan better or learn how to say 'no' when necessary. 'Burn out' is the other alternative.

CONCLUSION

Do you know of an effective Christian leader who leads a balanced life-style? You can be sure that he has learned the secret of self-discipline. Without discipline, time is squandered and responsibilities are neglected – either the family or the ministry or the personal life. A moderately gifted person will excel in ministry when self-discipline is exercised; but a brilliantly gifted person will fail by squandering his natural abilities through lack of self-discipline.

Another major issue in leadership is *conflict resolution*, or put more positively, maintaining unity. It takes wisdom and leadership skills to maintain unity. Without unity nothing can be accomplished. Unity is our next topic.

SEARCHING THE SCRIPTURE WITH APPLICATION

The Greek word for 'child' is *paidion*. Related to that word is the verb (*paideuo*) meaning to 'train,' 'instruct,' 'correct' or 'discipline by chastening.' That verb meaning, 'to instruct,' is found in 2 Ti 2:25; 3:16; Tit 2:12. That verb meaning, 'to discipline by chastening,' is found in Heb 12:6,7,10. So the background of 'discipline' is the training of children.

The English word, *discipline*, is not found in the Authorized Version of the Bible (King James). *Chastise* was the word used in A.D. 1611. The English word, *discipline*, is obviously related to *disciple*. A *disciple* of Jesus is a *learner* and hence a *follower* of Jesus. The English word, *discipline*, means 'training,' 'instruction' or 'punishment inflicted by way of correction and training.' So the English word, *discipline*, has the same meaning as the Greek word, *paideia* (meaning 'the whole training and education of children'), but without the connotation of training of a 'child.'

With this understanding in mind, discuss the following questions:

1. How do you *train* a child with words, example and correction? (Eph 6:4 'Fathers, do not provoke your children to anger, but bring them up in the discipline [*paideia*] and instruction of the Lord' [*ESV*]. The *NIV* translates *paideia,* 'training.')
2. How does the boss *train* an adult who has become employed in a job?
3. Why is it necessary to exercise *discipline* over students in school?
4. What is the purpose of discipline (in the sense of 'punishment inflicted by way of correction and training')? Read 1 Co 11:27-32; 'we are being disciplined so that we will not be condemned with the world' (11:32).
5. Why is it necessary to maintain *discipline* in a place of employment?
6. Which is better, to exercise *discipline* over employees or for the employees to exercise *self-discipline*? Why?
7. How does one learn self-discipline?
8. What happens to a *disciple* of Christ who fails to learn *self-discipline*? (c.f. Heb 12:7-11 in the *NIV* or *ESV*).
9. What happens to a Christian leader if he or she does not exercise self-discipline? Discuss.

Endnotes

1 1 Co 9:25, 27 *The Message*
2 Munroe 2005:267
3 1 Co 9:24
4 Munroe 2005:268
5 Mt 25:21
6 1 Co 4:2 NIV
7 Munroe 2005:269
8 Mt 26:33
9 Engstrom 1977
10 Perry 1983:110
11 Engstrom 1977:22
12 Engstrom 1977:25
13 Chalke 1998

38
MAINTAINING UNITY

'Be diligent to preserve the unity of the Spirit in the bond of peace.'[1]

A challenge for the effective Christian leader is maintaining unity.

The hallmark of Christianity is love marked with unity; this unity starts with the leader. An effective leader must know how to resolve conflict.

Most Christian leaders are not trained to resolve conflict; they would prefer to sweep the problems away into some hidden corner. But disunity, if left unresolved, will simmer into a major crisis God cannot be glorified and his kingdom cannot be built wherever conflict prevails. The Christian community does not need more leaders with academic degrees or charismatic personalities; what it needs is Christian leaders filled with love and humility, and gifted with relational skills to bring factions together.

Importance of Unity

Unity grows out of love and love is the fruit of the Holy Spirit. Yet love is more than a fruit; it is a command. When Jesus prayed in the Garden before his crucifixion, he prayed specifically for the Church today. After praying for himself and for the eleven apostles,[2] he prayed specifically for those who would believe thereafter.[3] He was burdened to pray just one prayer: *'I pray...that all of them may be one, Father, just as you are in me and I am in you...that they may be one as we are one...May they be brought to complete unity to let the world know that you sent me and have loved them even as you have loved me.'*[4]

Jesus did not pray that they might have great power to preach and heal; he did not pray that they would be successful in their evangelism and in the planting of many Churches. But he prayed for unity.

Jesus knew what was in the human heart.[5] He saw his own disciples clash with each other. Peter was impulsive and self-assertive. James was ambitious, short tempered and judgemental. Thomas was a pessimistic doubter. Philip was a doubter and a questioner. Matthew was a tough, dishonest man with a bad reputation before his conversion. Judas was greedy and treacherous. So who leads the Church in the centuries to come? People just like his Twelve.

These interpersonal disputes were between a homogeneous group, all Jews from Galilee, except for Judas Iscariot. What would happen with cross cultural missions? When the Gentiles were brought into the Church there was room for even more conflict.[6] Favoritism, ethnic insensitivity, suspicion and all the array of human emotions formed fertile ground for conflict.

So Jesus prayed for *unity* among those who would believe in the days to come – including you and me and our Churches today. This is not primarily an organisational union with an outward display of unity. It is a spiritual unity, a unity that grows out of love.[7] It is unity that is found in the Godhead between the Father, Son and Holy Spirit.

Unity is of supreme importance for two reasons. *First,* love and unity draw people to Christ. The world is full of conflict. If the Church is no different from the world, why should others believe in Christ? But the people of God should be different because they are indwelled by the Holy Spirit, united with Christ and instructed by the Word of God.

Secondly, a Christian leader needs a united people if he is to lead them to do great exploits for Christ. Satan divides in order to conquer. A house divided against itself cannot stand.[8] When the energies of a group are focused on conflict and conflict resolution, there is no time, energy or resource left to move forward. It is therefore incumbent upon the leader to resolve conflict.

But unity must not be understood as the absence of different opinions. Conflict in the sense of people seeing things differently can be healthy if the leader handles it well. Through creative thinking and discussion, with each one seeking to understand the other and each one willing to submit to the consensus as it emerges, difference of opinion can be constructive. When people do not listen to one another with respect and do not submit to the wisdom of the group, then destructive conflict arises.

Inevitability of Conflict

Jesus' prayer for unity can be fulfilled. The Church has all the resources necessary to maintain unity. Through the faithful teaching of the Word of God, the power of the inner working of the Holy Spirit, the skillful leadership of the pastors, the humble and loving dialogue of believers, and united prayer, there is no fundamental reason why unity should not prevail – except that Christians fail to appropriate all that is available for them. But the tragic reality is this: leaders should embrace the inevitability of conflict.

> Jesus, the greatest leader of all time, experienced conflict among his disciples, between the disciples and himself and between the religious and political leaders and himself. As long as your team is growing and maturing, there will be conflict. If you refuse to see conflict as an inevitable part of life, you are likely to view it as an unnecessary interruption of the flow – and you will respond to conflict with frustration, anger and intolerance.[9]

There are many different kinds of conflict. Most conflicts are over *personal issues.* Personality differences lead to clashes, insecurity leads to defensiveness and sensitivity; selfish ambition leads to power struggles, lack of recognition leads to hurt feelings. Other conflicts are *material in nature.* Struggles develop over property rights and garden disputes; unhappiness arises over salary, fringe benefits and housing. Still other conflicts are *ideological or theological in nature.* Conflicts arise over theology, spiritual gifts, eschatology, liturgy of worship on Sundays, the singing of hymns or choruses. Many conflicts arise over *change.* No worthy leader can lead without focusing on the future and finding a need to change. In fact, Barna says that, 'Leaders create conflict simply by pushing people to focus on God's vision.'[10] Most people resist change. So if the leader seeks to bring about change, resistance is inevitable.

Principles of Conflict Resolution

Following are some biblical and contextually appropriate principles which Christian leaders may use to help resolve conflict whenever it arises.

1. Seek reconciliation quickly. The common practice of letting misunderstandings continue without resolution is not healthy. Anger should not simmer over night.[11] Jesus admonishes, 'Settle matters quickly...'[12] Many small, simple problems become complex and tangled when left to grow and simmer over time. The leader is wise to seek reconciliation speedily.

2. Use loving, humble and gentle words. The Bible is clear! 'A soft answer turns away wrath, but a harsh word stirs up anger.'[13] Many times one person is clearly in the wrong. But the 'victim' responds with harsh, unkind, judgemental words that complicate everything. No one can bring reconciliation if harsh and angry words are used. As Solomon wrote, 'A soft tongue will break a bone.'[14]

3. Reconciliation efforts begin with the two offended. Conflict can best be resolved when done immediately by the two in conflict.[15] This requires kindness and a gentle tongue, as well as honesty and humility in admitting wrong doing. Both should seek to understand the other rather than being self-defensive. Look at the situation from their point of view. Understanding helps bring reconciliation. Often the problem is a thoughtless or unintentional word or action. If the person who caused the offense would humble himself and apologize, the matter could be resolved. If he is stubborn and refuses to admit wrong doing, the other person can easily feel hurt, raise his voice and speak harsh words. Both parties must seek to avoid these unfortunate turn of events.

4. If reconciliation fails, make another attempt; this time with other companions. Both parties should be in a spirit of prayer. When departing after the first attempt, avoid all acrimony or heated words. Speak peaceably and humbly, neither being judgemental nor harsh. But if the first attempt does not succeed, seek out wise, mature persons to accompany you for reconciliation.[16] Who may be invited to accompany the person depends on the situation. Through a network of family and friends, one may find family members, friends or elders to act as mediators between the two.

5. Take steps for personal, private reconciliation. Depending on the nature of the conflict, the offended party may need to take the mature, Christian approach by 'forgiving' that person unilaterally. If the other person cannot admit wrongdoing, the offended person should not allow himself to become victimized where he harbors resentment and bitterness towards the other person. Such an attitude does not contribute toward resolution of the misunderstanding. It only destroys the person who harbors bitter feelings. Depending on the nature of the offense, it is best to become reconciled to that person unilaterally by forgiving that person and demonstrating love for him.

These first five principles assume that the individuals concerned are mature in their Christian faith and well taught. The Christian leader should teach these principles from the Word of God so that individual Christians can solve their own conflicts without taking extra ordinary measures.

6. The Christian leader has a particular responsibility in conflict resolution. Many times the Christian leader must step in with extra-ordinary measures beyond those which are mentioned above. Seeking to resolve conflict is not easy. By entering into the fray the leader becomes vulnerable to misunderstanding and attack. It is easier to keep away from involvement. However, avoidance of conflict resolution is shirking responsibility as a leader.

How else will disagreements be resolved? Efforts can be made through violence or through litigation in the courts – this happens even in Churches! Or the whole disagreement can be ignored and avoided, hoping it will go away. But neither of these approaches is helpful. The only successful way is through mediation and the Christian leader has a responsibility to become involved. Perkins observes, 'If you're going to manage conflicts, it's essential for you to forgive wrongs committed against you and to expect the same effort from the rest of your team.'[17] Whenever the leader seeks to reconcile factions he may become the object of attack and therefore must be prepared to forgive.

7. A mediator should be found who is acceptable to both factions. The best mediators are usually found within the group. They are insiders and know all the cultural nuances of the problem. The role of the mediator is to make communication easier between the factions in the conflict. Choosing the right mediator takes great wisdom.

Skilled leaders know how to manage conflict. However, leaders are not all gifted in the same way and it may be that one leader may not be skillful as a mediator; yet he is the leader. A wise leader will recognise his strengths and weaknesses. If weak in the area of mediation himself, he should connect with those whose strength is in reconciling warring parties. As the Akamba say, 'Can I pay for a corpse smart enough to look into the future?' The wise person knows what is beyond his own ability and therefore enlists others to help. Even in this case, however, the Christian leader is responsible to ensure that effective efforts are made to resolve conflicts within his sphere of leadership. The leader will fail if the conflict is not resolved amicably.

The mediator should be a mature Christian who is prayerful, knowledgeable of the Scripture and accepted by both parties as a fair minded person. He should be an authority figure who commands respect because of his age or position in the community. He should be loving, humble and prudent in his choice of words; he should not be given to anger. Since the Word of God is authoritative and commands respect by all believers, the mediator should be able to use Scripture to bring reconciliation.

8. The aim of the mediation should be reconciliation and restoration. John Mungania observes that the traditional method used by Africans for conflict resolution was mediation, illustrated by the group consensus in decision making. 'No other process can favour consensus as a means of decision making except mediation where there is no loser or winner.'[18]

If sin has occurred, then confession and repentance is required. If the sin is of a serious nature, such as adultery by a Church elder or pastor, then obviously discipline must be administered. But if the conflict is merely over a misunderstanding or difference in opinion, then the mediator should aim to bring the parties together through discussion until a consensus is reached, so that 'there is no loser or winner.'

William Zartman concurs with Mungania quoted above when he says, 'Many of the practices associated with traditional African conflict management are classical mediation, or negotiation with a third-party catalyst, within a particularly strong integrative spirit.'[19] He goes on to say that 'the distinguishing African characteristic' is the focus on reconciling the interests of all contestants. The emphasis is on 'recuperation and reinsertion of the errant member back into its place in society.' In other words, unlike the western approach which seeks to punish the guilty with abandonment, the African approach is to reintegrate the errant parties.

9. The mediator should normally act through the council of elders. Though the mediator should be an authority figure, it is best for him to work through a council of elders.

10. The mediator should be well informed. The better he understands the problem, the better he is able to help reconcile. He must know the subject well and get all the facts. Bad mistakes can be made when he rushes to judgement in wanting to reach a conclusion.

CONCLUSION

Books can help in learning to mediate.[20] But skills of mediation are best learned through experience. Hence the mediator should be a mature, experienced, highly respected person who is proven. Blessed is the Christian leader who can oversee mediation to maintain harmony within the group.

Christian leaders must keep growing until they retire. No one has ever learned it all. The next chapters point to ways of growing in leadership skills.

SEARCHING THE SCRIPTURE WITH APPLICATION

1. Discuss the various kinds of problems that often lead to conflict?
2. How are these conflicts handled usually?
3. What problems arise when leaders neglect to resolve the conflicts?
4. Why does the leader often fail to deal with the conflict?
5. Why is unity so important?
6. Unity does not mean unanimity of opinion. Why do some leaders become upset when ideas that are suggested by people are different from the ones promoted by the leader?
7. How can the leader be the cause of conflict when he rejects out of hand a different idea?
8. Conflicts often arise because of proposed changes. How should the Christian leader introduce or promote change to avoid unnecessary conflict?
9. Why is it urgent for the leader to deal with conflict as soon as it arises?
10. When conflicts evolve into complex and divisive divisions between two factions within the community, how should the leader go about resolving the conflict?
11. What approaches have you seen to be effective?

12. From your observation what approaches have failed?
13. What additional principles of conflict resolution would you add to the ones found in this chapter?
14. Mt 18:15-17 provides the most explicit teaching in Scripture on conflict resolution.
    a. Do a study of this Scripture.
    b. Wherein have leaders succeeded or failed when applying any of these principles in conflict resolution? Discuss and evaluate.
15. Discuss what other biblical principles can help in maintaining unity or in resolving conflict?

Endnotes

1 Eph 4:3 NASB
2 Jn 17:1-19
3 Jn 17:20-26
4 Jn 17:21ff
5 Jn 2:24f
6 Ac 6:1
7 Ro 12:9-21; Jn 13:34; 15:12,17
8 Mk 3:24,25
9 Perkins 2000:145
10 Barna 2002:139
11 Eph 4:26,27
12 Mt 5:25
13 Prov 15:1
14 Prov 25:15
15 Mt 18:15
16 Mt 18:16f
17 Perkins 2000:157
18 Mungania 1994:46
19 Zartman 2000:220
20 See *Conflict Management* by Mbogori

39
GROWING AS A LEADER IN CHARACTER

'We are to grow up in all aspects into Him who is the head, even Christ.'[1]

No worthy leader stops learning! We must all keep growing.

Over these years I have followed with keen interest those whom Florence and I had the privilege of mentoring and helping to prepare for Christian ministry. After some time a few have dropped by the wayside, stumbling on issues of character. Others have continued on in ministry, faithfully serving but plateaued in their skills of ministry. An encouraging number have continued to learn and grow; they have been focused and disciplined, maturing in ministry. Continual learning and growing is the key.

It is both encouraging and challenging to remember that *no* leader becomes what he is destined to be without continual learning in life and ministry; and *no* effective leader ceases to learn until the day God takes him home to glory. Robert Clinton captures this well.

> Quality leadership does not come easily. It requires time, experience, and repeated instances of maturity processing. Mature ministry flows from a mature character, formed in the graduate school of life....A mature successful ministry flows from one who has both ministry skills and character that has been mellowed, developed, and ripened by God's maturity processing. Character formation is fundamental. Ministry flows out of being.[2]

In many ways these last two chapters will be a summary of the book because the lessons we learn throughout life are repeated to bring us to maturity. The basic foundation on which all Christian leadership is built is *character*. Those who write on Christian leadership are unified in this assertion that 'character and spiritual development are more important than competency.'[3] The African Christian leaders whom we have interviewed have said the same thing. The reason Christian leaders fail is character, not competency. Therefore, in this chapter we shall examine ways of growing in character so that no one drops out and fails in ministry because of flawed character.

Self-Examination

Are you growing? Are you all that God has designed you to be? Are you taking steps each day and week to mature in your Christian character? Following are some basic principles with questions that you should ask of yourself to help determine whether you are growing in your relationship with God. You may consider this a little test to examine how you are doing.

1. The Word of God Principle. Do I have a growing appetite to read, study, memorise and obey the Word of God? Have I developed a disciplined pattern of making the Word of God an integral part of my life? Do I apply God's Word to my life daily as I appropriate God's promises, commands, and directions from his Word?

2. The Prayer Principle. Do I spend meaningful time each day in communion with God in prayer – worshipping, confessing and interceding for others? Do I find joy and satisfaction in my relationship with God through praying and meditating on God's Word? Have I found an appropriate time and place to meet with God daily? Is this a well established habit?

3. The Humility Principle. Do others see me as a humble servant-leader whose primary desire is to serve God and others? Or am I proud and self-centred with selfish ambition? Can I accept opposition to my viewpoint without taking this personally and being offended by it? Do I depend on God or on self for effectiveness? Do I give glory to God for success or do I seek attention and praise of others?

4. The Love Principle. Am I ever jealous of others who have larger Churches, bigger salaries, 'higher' positions or greater 'success' in ministry? Do I become angry when someone offends me, threatens my position or opposes my desires and plans? Do I retain control of myself when things go wrong? Do I increasingly show the characteristics of love, including patience and kindness towards others? Do I possess tact? Do I feel resentment towards others?

5. The Holiness Principle. Is my life marked by a thirst for righteousness and holiness; and a desire to live in obedience to God's Word? Is my living consistent with my preaching? Do I practice what I preach? Am I truly growing in purity, honesty and integrity of life? Am I pure in heart? Am I in the grip of some lustful desire that consumes me?

6. The Self-Discipline Principle. Can others see that I am growing in self-discipline? Am I increasingly self-disciplined in my use of time so that I live a balanced lifestyle? Do I spend adequate time daily and weekly with the Lord, with my family, in my own personal development and in ministry?

7. The Faithfulness Principle. How well do I perform the ministries which God has given to me? Do I see all opportunities and responsibilities as coming from God? Do I serve with joy, offering all my service as unto God? Or do I see some responsibilities as unpleasant chores that are heaped on me by others? Do I only do what must be done or do I go beyond the call of duty and give my best to the Lord in ministry?

Since we are all learning and growing, it is doubtful that anyone received a 100% grade in the above test. In fact, a grade of A+ might suggest lack of personal honesty. We all fall short in one way or another. That is the reason we must keep growing. So take heart.

What can I do to keep on growing in my character?

Growing in Your Relationship with God

Jesus made this very clear. 'As the branch cannot bear fruit by itself, unless it abides in the vine, neither can you, unless you abide in me.'[4] Fruit bearing depends on a vital relationship with Jesus Christ. Worldly success can come without abiding in Christ; Church attendance may surge, institutions may grow, money may flow in and a large ministry may develop. But unless this is through a vital relationship with Christ, the outward success will be empty and without merit before God.

Are you growing in your prayer life?

Every Christian leader faces two challenges in his devotional life.

First, is the challenge of consistency in spending time with God each day in prayer. We are creatures of habit. Most of what we do in life is ingrained in our being through consistent practice over time. The when, where and how of entering your 'prayer closet' away from others depends on many factors. But the practice should become habitual so that it is part of your lifestyle.

From personal experience, I have found no substitute for meeting with God first thing in the day. Early in the morning is when interruptions from visitors and work responsibilities can be avoided. Early morning you are fresh, assuming you have been disciplined to retire early. By meeting with God first thing in the day, God can prepare your heart and mind to face the challenges of the day. To maintain this practice of meeting with God daily at a consistent time takes personal discipline. That is what an effective ministry is all about. How are you doing in this?

The second challenge is to keep your prayer life fresh. Beware of prayer becoming a habit, mouthing words that do not come from the heart, praying out of a sense of duty. Such prayers have no value. Several things have helped me keep fresh in my prayers. Of first importance in preparing my heart for prayer is meditation on the Scripture. When God speaks to you through his Word, he warms your heart and draws you to himself in adoration. My 'routine' has been to commence my devotional time with a brief time of prayer, entering into his presence and seeking God's blessing as I read. This is followed by thirty minutes of studying the Scripture. Such a reading then prepares my heart for prayer. Others have found singing of hymns as a way to prepare one to pray. Whatever you do, make sure that prayer time is not mechanical or routine but meaningful and precious as you pour out your heart to God in adoration, praise, thanksgiving, followed by confession, prayer for personal needs and intercession for others.

Are you growing in the Word of God?

God's Word is a treasure to be loved and cherished. 'More to be desired are they than gold, even much fine gold; sweeter also than honey and drippings of the honeycomb.'[5] Is this your experience or do you find the Word of God a bit boring or uninspiring? That is a major test that may indicate whether you are growing in your devotional life.

I began reading my Bible through from Genesis to Revelation as a teenager. Before entering Bible School I had read the Bible through several times. Reading the Bible through in one year is doable if you read three chapters daily and five on Sunday. It is a discipline well worth your effort.

But I find serious limitations in this when doing it repeatedly, year after year. I need variety, a bit of spice in life. So my pattern of Bible reading is different each year.

Sometimes I do read the Bible through in one year. On occasion I read the Bible through chronologically but take as long as needed to do it – up to two years or more. By reading the prophets and writings at the appropriate place when reading the historical books, a person can understand the flow of redemptive history. Sometimes I just read a book through over and over again. Once I studied a Bible book along with the reading of commentaries. Some years I spend all my time reading the Old Testament; other years the time is spent reading the New Testament. I have read the life of Christ with *A Harmony of the Gospels*. One of the greatest experiences was to read the whole Bible through by asking the question, 'What does the Bible say about God? What is God like?' Every time I read some attribute of God, I wrote the whole verse on a paper with separate pages for each of God's attributes or works. That was a life changing experience. Some years I read the Book of Acts or the New Testament Epistles looking for certain truths. But I have always found the reading of a Study Bible, like *The NIV Study Bible,* to be so helpful. My desire is to hear from God, not through some spiritualising or allegorising of Scripture, but through an accurate understanding of Scripture.

How well are you growing in your relationship with God? Only you can know. But many Christian leaders are not aware of weaknesses and failures because they are not being honest with themselves. Perfection is God's goal for everyone,[6] but divine acceptance depends on contrite humility. God says: '*This is the one I esteem: he who is humble and contrite in spirit, and trembles at my word.*'[7] If you know your weaknesses and are honest before God with humility and repentance, and desire to grow in your relationship with him, then you are becoming a Christian leader whom God can bless and prosper.

Growing Character through Adversity

'No amount of reputation can substitute for character.'[8] No amount of 'success' in ministry can substitute for character. In fact, nothing can substitute for character. What you are in the dark, not what people see in public, is who you really are. That is what God sees and rewards. Hence, a Christian leader must keep growing in his character before God in order to be approved by him.

There are two basic ways in which God helps his children to grow in Christ-likeness. First, is through developing a daily walk with God as mentioned above. Secondly, growth in character comes from adversity in life. We learn important lessons in life, not only from models and examples to follow, but from negative experiences.

What kinds of adversity may develop character?

There are many different kinds of adversity:

Conflicts arise in ministry for many reasons. Conflict may erupt from misunderstanding, clashing personalities, different values or interests, or simply from jealousy. Jealousy brings much heartache to the leader. 'It is much easier to *keep* the peace than to *make* peace where it has been shattered. An important function in leadership is conciliation – the ability to discover common ground between opposing viewpoints and then induce both parties to accept it.'[9] In the process, however, the leader may be caught in the cross fire and suffer; he may be maliciously attacked and falsely accused.

Life crises such as sickness and death, accident, violent robbery and persecution are occasions that demand trust in the sovereign, loving God to see you through. Many of these adversities are personal and private. No one shares or understands the pain that comes from such trials but you alone.

Financial distress due to famine, irregular monthly support, inadequate salary or unexpected expenses due to sickness can be discouraging. Distress may be especially sharp when the financial difficulties continue month after month, year after year. This can be exasperated when the reason for financial famine is due to unfaithfulness on the part of others or lack of concern by those in leadership.

Undesirable assignments in ministry can lead to great frustration and inner turmoil. Some are assigned to ministries by higher authorities without any consideration of gifts or calling. Others are transferred from thriving ministries to smaller, struggling ministries out of jealousy. In any case the spirits of the Christian leaders are brought low with frustration and bitterness.

Can God be in all these adversities?

We come back to that basic truth that is so difficult to learn; something that may take years to embrace and incorporate fully into your worldview. It did for me.

> When a leader has a lifelong developmental perspective, that leader expects God to shape him over a lifetime. The leader views the things that happen to him as God's sovereign way of developing him. That leader recognizes that all of life, while being vital and true for the moment, is also used to prepare him for all of the rest of life. Bad things happen. Good things happen. All things are used by God to shape the life and help the leader realize his maximum potential. A leader with this perspective views the events in his life in terms of the longer viewpoint. He asks such questions as: How is this incident shaping me to be more like Christ? How is it helping prepare me to do what God wants me to do? How will this help me reach my God-given potential?[10]

Before we went to Africa in 1966 I was preaching sermons on Romans 8:28. So I surely believed that God in his gracious sovereignty is working all things out for my good. But I wish that the reality of God's gracious and loving sovereignty had been embraced with more wholehearted acceptance on my part than I actually experienced. It would have saved me so much pain.

The most distressing and soul wrenching experience in my life occurred midway in our missionary service. It is best to speak briefly and generally. For various reasons our family needed to move to this one location, but several people worked behind my back to create obstacles. Housing was not available; neither was a ministry. I felt abandoned and embittered. Now that I can look back over that experience I can speak with greater insight and understanding. If any of those individuals, with whom I felt so embittered towards, had done what I had wanted them to do, the ministry which God had entrusted to me for the following ten years would have been unfulfilled. The very dream which God had given me, and entrusted to my hands by those in authority over me, would have been annulled if those individuals had not acted in the contrary way they had. In plain English, it is now clear that God used people, who in my opinion were jealous and unjust, to make possible a ministry which was ordained by God. A highlight of ten years of research and writing would have not been possible apart from these difficult people – and God's faithfulness.

Truly, every Christian leader must learn to see life in terms of the bigger picture, knowing that God in his sovereignty uses many things to develop our character and expand our ministry. 'For we are *his workmanship*, created in Christ Jesus for good works, which God prepared before hand, that we should walk in them.'[11] Every time you pass through some adversity, remember that God's hand is working on you, as a carver works on a block of wood, to shape you into the kind of person he desires to serve him in the place of his choosing. Adversity is God's means of growing your character so you can be his servant.

Just think of all the God-ordained, character-shaping that I had received, all because of those difficult experiences! I learned ever so feebly at first, little by little over time, to have greater love and a forgiving spirit in this crucible of testing. I learned the virtues of patience and humility and faith.

I urge you to review Romans 8:18-39. Read the Bible from cover to cover and discover how utterly sovereign God is in every detail of life. God is in control of every detail of your life. He not only knows and cares about your adversity; he has actually ordained your adversity so that you might grow in character. The people who are instrumental in your adversity are only secondary causes. God is the One who is actually behind everything, taking the sins of men and using them to accomplish his purposes – and develop Christ- like character in you. Learn to trust in the loving, sovereign God who is working out his purposes in every detail of your life. Learn to rejoice with Paul in your sufferings, 'because we know that suffering produces perseverance; perseverance, character; and character hope.'[12]

Growing through Others

We are not alone; nor do we grow on our own. We need others.

Seek out a prayer partner, someone to whom you can pour out your heart and unburden your soul. Depending on your location, this can be a challenge. But you will grow stronger if some prayer partner is in your life.

Seek to be accountable to someone. Find someone with whom you may develop an intimate relationship of sharing so that you can be held accountable for your words and deeds. This may be your prayer partner or someone else. But no one should serve without being responsible to another for his words and actions. Accountability is key for growth in character.

Seek a mentor, someone whom you admire, and someone from whom you may learn. Observe his life and ministry, visit him, discuss problems or issues with him and seek advice. If God so leads, become a disciple of his, learning his way of avoiding pitfalls and his secret of being effective in ministry.

Being a spiritual leader in the place of your ministry may limit your options. People may be nearby but are not the ones you feel free to confide in; nor those from whom you may learn. This should be an item of prayer because growth in character can be enhanced and strengthened when you connect with others.

CONCLUSION

Preparing for ministry in a Bible School or College is needful. But too many assume that they have no need for further growth and learning after graduation. The sign of life and health is spiritual growth. Character either deepens or diminishes. You cannot maintain the same character constantly.

Remember, as you grow, remain faithful. Faithfulness to God is the true measure of success as a Christian leader. How well do you perform your ministries? Do you serve joyfully in all that is assigned to you? Do you simply endure or do you thrive as you serve God? Do you go beyond the call of duty and do more than what is assigned to you? Do you see what needs to be done and then step forward to do it without being ordered to do it? Do you voluntarily take on extra duties to help when the workload for others is heavy? Do you work only when the 'boss' is around or are you faithful when no one sees you?

Growing in character is the bedrock for Christian leaders. However, you can have the best Christian character but falter in ministry because you lack competency in leadership skills. Growing in competency of leadership skills is the topic of the final chapter.

SEARCHING THE SCRIPTURE WITH APPLICATION

J. Oswald Sanders in his classic, *Spiritual Leadership*, offers the following questions to help individuals measure themselves.[13] How do you stand?

1. 'Have you ever broken yourself of a bad habit? To lead others, one must be master of oneself.
2. Do you retain control of yourself when things go wrong? The leader who loses self-control in testing circumstances forfeits respect and loses influence. He must be calm in crisis and resilient in adversity and disappointment.
3. Can you handle criticism objectively and remain unmoved under it? Do you turn it to good account? The humble man can derive benefit from petty and even malicious criticism.
4. Can you use disappointments creatively?
5. Do you readily secure the cooperation and win the respect of others?
6. Are you entrusted with the handling of difficult and delicate situations?
7. Can you accept opposition to your viewpoint or decision without considering it a personal affront and reacting accordingly? Leaders must expect opposition and should not be offended by it.
8. Do you find it easy to make and keep friends? Your circle of loyal friends is an index of the quality and extent of your leadership.
9. Are you unduly dependent on the praise or approval of others? Can you hold a steady course in the face of disapproval?
10. Are you at ease in the presence of your superiors or strangers?
11. Do your subordinates appear at ease in your presence? A leader should give an impression of sympathetic understanding and friendliness that will put others at ease.

12. Are you really interested in people? In people of all types and all races? Or do you entertain respect of persons? Is there hidden racial prejudice? An anti-social person is unlikely to make a good leader.
13. Do you possess tact? Can you anticipate the likely effect of a statement before you make it?'

Endnotes

1 Eph 4:15 NASB
2 Clinton 1988:167
3 c.f. Barna 1997:135
4 Jn 15:4
5 Ps 19:10
6 1 Pe 1:15ff
7 Isa 66:2b
8 Wiersbe 1980:81f
9 Sanders 1980:44
10 Barna 1997:156f
11 Eph 2:10
12 Ro 5:3; c.f. Jas 1:2ff
13 Sanders 1980:44-46

40
GROWING AS A LEADER IN COMPETENCE

'Be diligent to present yourself approved to God as a workman who does not need to be ashamed…'[1]

You cannot be a leader with *character* alone; you also need *competence*.

Half this book stressed the fundamental need for godly character in order to be an effective Christian leader. But godliness alone does not make a leader. You need competence with skills in order to lead. Not everyone who wants to be a leader can actually lead. In order to be a workman divinely approved, who does not need to be ashamed when standing before God, we need to develop our gifts so that we can faithfully serve to the best of our ability.

Let us remind ourselves of what a leader is. According to Robert Clinton, a leader is 'A person (1) with God-given capacity, and (2) with God-given responsibility to influence (3) a specific group of God's people (4) toward God's purposes for the group.'[2]

'*God-given capacity*' refers to spiritual gifts for leading. Each person must access his or her gifts. We may not be doing our best because we are not in the place for which we are gifted. A person gifted to teach but not to shepherd will be frustrated if assigned to pastoring a Church. '*God-given responsibility*' refers to a divine call for that ministry. Some people have gifts of leadership as elders in the local Church but not to serve as the pastor. Some pastors have gifts for shepherding a local congregation but do not have gifts to oversee many pastors and Churches. Some have gifts to lead a denomination but not to lead a theological institution. When God assigns a ministry responsibility to us, he also equips us with the appropriate gifts. All that God requires of us is to use our spiritual gifts and abilities to their maximum in the place of God's choosing. 'Each is unique. Another's success is not our standard. Bigger is not better, nor is a greater sphere of influence.'[3]

The Christian leader must *influence* a group of people toward *achieving certain God-given purposes.* Thus a leader must have various skills, such as relational skills to motivate; organizational skills to help people work together; and ability to shepherd the flock toward achieving the mutually agreed upon goals. In other words, a leader must be competent to lead.

In this chapter we shall examine ways of growing in our competence as leaders, so that anyone with godly character and gifts will grow in competence.

Self-Examination

What steps are you taking to grow and develop your skills of leadership? Before outlining several suggestions for growth, let us ask some questions to find out your strengths and weaknesses in leadership skills.

1. The Gifts Principle. Am I aware of areas where I am gifted and those areas where I am lacking? Do I experience confidence in exercising those gifts where I am strong? Do I recognise and accept those areas where I am lacking in needed gifts for leadership? Am I willing to learn more so that my gifts can be better developed? Do I manifest humility in accepting my limitations and am I willing to enlist others to help me in my areas of weakness?

2. The Team Principle. Am I consciously developing a team of workers who can compliment each other in fulfilling our dream? Do I solicit feedback from others to learn how well I am doing personally and how we as a team are doing in fulfilling our objectives? Can I accept constructive criticism or do I resent suggestions from others? Do I fear others in their strengths or do I welcome their contribution in order to strengthen the achievement of the team? Do I delegate freely or do I fear that others may steal the limelight and eventually take away my position?

3. The Relational Principle. Do I have a trusting and cordial relationship with every member of my team? Does everyone feel comfortable in talking with me? Am I seen as their friend or do some fear me? Do I communicate well or do misunderstandings arise frequently? How do I handle misunderstandings? Is the team happy with the level of communications they receive? Do those who have grievances or concerns feel free to speak to me openly about them? Do I succeed in making sure the performance standards are met and handled in an appropriate manner?

4. The Vision Principle. Am I future oriented? Do I plan for the future? Am I driven by a God-given vision of future accomplishments? Is this vision mutually shared by the team? Who participated in the development of the vision and goal setting, and what process was followed in setting the goals? What steps do I take to communicate this vision to the team? How do I motivate the team toward achieving the vision and goals? Do I demonstrate effectiveness in thinking through a problem, securing the relevant facts and reaching sound conclusions? Do I accept the value of ideas from others?

5. The Implementation Principle. Am I able to take a vision and measurable goals and implement them practically? Am I a great dreamer with big ideas but poor at implementation? Do I fully understand what is required of me in my ministry? Do I manifest ability to organise myself and discipline my self to accomplish daily or weekly tasks? Can I motivate others to do their work? Do I take the initiative to take effective action or must I wait on others to tell me what to do? Am I dependable? Do I attend all the meetings on time? Can others rely on me to carry out my responsibilities faithfully?

Many other principles and questions could be written. But these are sufficient to give you an idea how well you are doing on leadership competence. The first step in growing is to be honest with yourself. Half the battle is won if you recognise your strengths and weaknesses. Be willing to accept help and grow. A leader keeps on growing until the day he enters glory. There is nothing to be ashamed of when admitting that you need help in a certain area. But there is a lot to be ashamed of when you deny any need for growth. Such an attitude is a sure indication of failure.

Following are some suggestions to help you grow in leadership competence. We know that giftedness is not sufficient. Spiritual gifts and abilities can remain underdeveloped. Christian leaders need to grow through education.

Growing in Competence through Education

Education is no substitute for gifts of leadership. But giftedness without education is a squandering of talents given by God. Robert Clinton writes:

> We can develop as persons using spiritual gifts and natural abilities right up to the level of potential that God intends. Skills that enhance our gifts and abilities should be learned and used. Knowledge that will make us more effective in our use of gifts should be sought. If we do not do so, we will have to account to God. And we will have to account for what we actually did, whether or not we developed to the potential that God intended. Hebrews 13:17, James 3:1, and the judgment passages certainly make it clear that leaders are accountable for their influence.[4]

A clarification and caution, however, must also be given to this advice.

The clarification is this: Leadership training comes at many levels. Seminars on leadership can be attended. Individual courses can be taken in school. Degrees can be earned in leadership. You can take in-service training or take up residence in a residential programme. Correspondence courses are available. Books and literature can be bought and read. It is not necessary to spend years in residential training to develop leadership skills.

In other words, obtain sufficient training for the calling you have received. Assuming one has had basic Bible training in Bible School or College, is it really necessary to obtain a graduate degree in leadership to serve as a pastor? That would be overkill and could lead a person away from his calling. On the other hand, if experience has proven to others that you are uniquely gifted in leadership and have the potential of providing top-level leadership for an institution or an organisation, then it may be wise to pursue a further degree in leadership.

The main issue is your calling and gifts. What is God's call upon your life and what gifts has he entrusted to you? Keep that as your focus. Education should not be an end in itself. Education can take you away from your calling. People can be perennial students in institutions. We all should be growing continually but learning can take place informally at home through reading, attending seminars, learning by doing, apprenticeship and learning from others. Clinton's advice is sound. We should all be learning in order to fulfill our calling and enhance our gifts. But formal education, when unrelated to our calling, can be a detour away from God's will.

A caution should also be given. While we must develop those gifts graciously proffered to us by God for leadership in his Church, we need to take care lest we be led away from God's calling in our lives. Seek not to be a leader. Many who want to be leaders often prove to be spiritual failures. Let God's Spirit stir the hearts of *others*, God's people, to lay the mantle on you.

As a young man, God gave me a clear and unmistakable calling to serve overseas in the training of pastors and Church workers. So clear and definite was that call that on several occasions I refused opportunities of ministry because I feared they would detract me from my calling; or at least, they would delay my serving overseas. But since God had called me to train others, I figured that sufficient education would be necessary. So the Bible School education was followed by a College degree, then followed by an M.A., then followed by a Master of Divinity.

As I concluded my Master of Divinity, I began to consider a Ph.D. However, I realised that my clear and distinct calling with a sense of urgency was fading. After nine years of education my sense of urgency was diminishing. As I prayed over this, I feared loosing my sense of call. How could I ever appear before God and give an account of my unfaithfulness if I would fail him? As a result, all further consideration for a doctoral degree was laid aside so I could pursue my call. How many times have I thanked God for this! Teaching at Scott Theological College in those early years required me to be a 'jack of all trades' as I filled in urgent needs. I taught New Testament, Old Testament, Greek, Homiletics, Christian Education, Theology and Church History; I was Field Education Director and Librarian. If I had pursued my PhD, I doubt if I would have been patient enough to serve humbly wherever I was needed. In God's providence, doctoral studies became an asset in mid-life in order to prepare me for a new ministry.

All education should be with your specific calling in mind.

Growing in Competence through Experience

Training in the classroom will never make a leader. The best form of leadership training is field experience that is built on some kind of training. We learn best by doing, and we learn from our mistakes.

Learning by doing

Learn from mentors: Seeking out a mentor to coach you in your leadership position is advisable. Blessed is the young leader who is tapped by a mature leader to mentor the younger. A mentor is simply a person with more experience who desires to encourage, guide and help a younger leader to grow and reach his full potential. Mentors see the potential in others and are willing to come along side to encourage. They are patient and tolerate mistakes; they are not judgemental and critical. They advise and help.

Even if a full-blown mentoring relationship is not realised, a young leader may visit colleagues to seek advice and gather tips. Young pastors may seek counsel from older, experienced elders in the local congregation. We learn not merely from books; the best learning is through personal discovery while serving as leader. Be alert, listen, observe and use some creativity.

Learn by applying lessons from school: If a course on leadership or management was taken in Bible School or College, review the notes frequently. Milk the course dry. Learn and apply in practice what was learned in theory in the classroom. Buy books on leadership to help you in practice.

Learn from every ministry task: Learn from every opportunity of service given to you. Learn to be loyal and reliable to those over you; be faithful in performing the task. Clinton speaks of 'The Little-Big Principle,' meaning that 'Faithfulness in a small responsibility is an indication of probable faithfulness in a larger responsibility.'[5]

Test your gifts and potential in those tasks assigned. Learn your strengths and weaknesses so that you will know in the future whether you have a God-given gift to accomplish certain tasks. As you faithfully apply yourself to the ministry assigned, you will gradually discover multiple gifts and multiple weaknesses. The more you do what appears to be your strength, the greater confidence and competence you will experience.

> It is important to recognize the ultimate source of ministry assignments. From a human perspective the task may appear routine or insignificant but ultimate accountability is to God even though the assignment came through human authority. Knowing this can bring great fervor and give a sense of accomplishing God's purposes.[6]

Learn from negative experiences: Negative experiences can become learning experiences. Do not assume you will be 'mistake free.' When mistakes are made, humility will go a long way in restoring faith. How do you respond during crises in ministry when mistakes are made? Nothing can compare with learning in the field. You may forget the notes crammed for a test in school, but you will never forget lessons learned in the field.

Learn by stretching: Eight years after commencing our teaching ministry at Scott, the Chairman of the Board asked me to become the next Principal. Fearing failure, I hesitated. I tried to help him find others more capable than me. Eventually, I consented. After eight years of serving as Principal of Scott Theological College, I believe everyone would agree that God's favour had rested upon this leadership because Scott moved forward in so many ways. Yet the *only* training I had received in administration and management was a weekend seminar a few years *after* becoming the Principal! The seminar was a wonderful learning experience but it was only a weekend.

This experience has shaped my thinking about leadership skills and training. Piano lessons cannot teach someone to play the piano if he doesn't have the musical ability. I have seen this in action. Neither will a degree in leadership make a leader. Leadership requires relational skills, ability to organise, attention to details, faithfulness, diligence, and a servant's heart. You can and should develop those God-given talents but you cannot create them.

Learning to develop relationships

In order to be an effective leader you must be both people-centred and goal- oriented at the same time. If you are not good in developing relationships (being people-centred), you are a non-starter as a leader. But neither can you be a successful leader without being future-oriented, focusing on goals to achieve. In this section we are concerned about developing relationships.

How are your people skills? In this, and so many other leadership skills, issues of character enter the picture. Developing healthy relationships with others is impossible if you sometimes speak rashly, slander, gossip or engage in loose talk. If you do not exercise self-control over your tongue and your emotions, you will do very poorly in developing relationships. Love is the key.

In the midst of ministry you should develop that ability to step back and look at yourself objectively. Does my attitude or do my actions tear down relationships? Do team members feel excluded when I disregard their advice? Do I show partiality? Examine yourself critically. Be honest with yourself. Being aware of problems you cause is half the battle won. Learn to cultivate good relationships using the guidelines set forth in earlier chapters in this book.

Learning to develop a team

No leader can do all the work himself. Any leader who seeks all the glory will fail before God and people, because ultimately the glory belongs to God; and secondarily, the whole team needs to be recognised and appreciated. Leadership is not a one-man task. Once you learn how to develop cordial relationships with your teammates, you are on the way to developing a team.

Where are you in building a team? Do you have any difficult members on the team? Learn to step back and not feel personally offended or attacked, though this can be hard to do. Nevertheless, it is important for you to remain detached so you can see things more objectively. If you are having struggles, review the principles of developing relationships in chapter 31. Learn by doing.

Learning to plan

If building relationships and a team are fundamental to all leadership, planning is not far behind. Leaders should ask these questions: Where are we? Where do we want to go? What may help us to get there? How are we going to get there? When will the results be achieved? Who is going to do it? How much of our resources will it require? These are basic questions to be asked.[7]

The greatest problem many face is planning with marvelous vision, but without practical understanding of how to reach the goals. How much will it cost? Who is needed to do the work? How will you organise the people and motivate them? How long will it take? These are basic questions that must be answered if your planning is going to result in practical accomplishments.

How is your planning? Has your goal setting helped you to accomplish anything? What lessons have you learned from your experience? Though the team should be engaged in planning, the burden rests on the leader who needs time to think, pray and reflect ahead of time; he must gather information from many sources. Planning comes natural for some; others require more learning.

Learning to implement the plans

In what aspects of implementation are you weak? Organising? Delegating? Motivating? Communicating? Correcting? Achieving the goals? How can you improve in any of these weak areas? Do some of the suggestions in Chapters 33-35 help? If not, can some elders or colleagues or more experienced leaders advise from their experience?

Consult with others and see if your denomination, institution or Para-Church organisation might be able to organise a management seminar?

There are many ways you can keep growing and learning so that you reach your full potential. Remember, comparing yourself with others is neither spiritual nor practical. Each person is unique, just as each face and fingerprint is unique. God's plan and purpose for you is unlike that of any other person in the world. Comparing yourself with others can only lead to jealousy. Furthermore, it is unprofitable. It accomplishes nothing but breeds discontent.

Become all that God has planned you to be; nothing more and nothing less. Be faithful in all your service and God will reward you richly.

CONCLUSION

How well I remember those exhilarating days when as a young person, I first graduated from Bible School, a liberal arts college, then a graduate school and a seminary. Those were expectant days for all of us graduating. The whole of life lay before us. The sky was the limit. We were full of dreams that we all hoped would be brought into reality some day. Somehow dreams can be dashed on the rocks of reality. Middle age crisis can threaten one's ego, as we begin to understand that our youthful dreams and visions may never come to pass.

It is wonderful to arrive in the golden years of life and look back with confidence, knowing that you served the Lord faithfully and for his glory. There is no reward greater than to hear from Jesus, '*Well done, good and faithful servant. You have been faithful over a little; I will set you over much. Enter into the joy of your master.*'[8] I trust that at the end of your life, you will have the same joy as you faithfully and perseveringly serve unto the end.

SEARCHING THE SCRIPTURE WITH APPLICATION

We shall use this final chapter to help you reflect on what you have learned from studying this book on leadership.

1. Review Chapters 2, 11-25. Which seven godly characteristics do you feel are the most essential for a Christian leader? Explain why you think so.
2. How well are you growing in these seven areas of godly character? In what ways do you need to grow more?
3. Review Chapter 7 on 'Spiritual Disciplines.' Consider how effective you are in practicing those Spiritual Disciplines necessary to grow godly character?
4. Review Chapter 9. Why is a forgiving spirit so essential for a leader?
5. Review Chapters 26-27.
    a. Discuss the distinguishing marks of an effective Christian leader.
    b. What is the difference between leadership and management?
    c. Why should a Christian leader be competent in management skills?
6. Review Chapters 31-35 on the management skills required of Christian leaders.
    a. In which aspects do you feel strongest?
    b. In which aspects do you feel weakest?
    c. What steps can you take to strengthen those weak areas?

7. Review Chapters 36-37. Self-discipline and a Balanced Lifestyle are intertwined. Why is self-discipline necessary to serve as an effective Christian leader? Why will an imbalanced lifestyle undermine the effectiveness of a Christian leader?
8. Review Chapters 29 and 38. No one can succeed as a leader unless he is an agent for change, and yet change can bring about disunity. How does one go about bringing change without causing disunity? Compare with Chapter 31.
9. Review Chapters 8-10. How does confidence in the sovereignty of God help one to persevere and forgive others?
10. Assess your own gifts for leadership. Wherein do you need to grow? List the steps you can take to develop those gifts more.

Endnotes

[1] 2 Ti 2:15
[2] Clinton 1988:201
[3] Clinton 1988:198
[4] Clinton 1988:198f
[5] Clinton 1988:95
[6] Clinton 1988:85
[7] c.f. Richards 1980:179
[8] Mt 25:21

SELECT BIBLIOGRAPHY

The books from which quotations have been drawn are copyright and duly acknowledged in the chapter endnotes.

Adams, Jay E.

1972 *Godliness Through Discipline*. Grand Rapids: Baker Book.

1973 *The Christian Counselor's Manual*. Phillipsburg: Presbyterian and Reformed.

Adeyemo, Tokunboh

1993 *The Making of a Servant of God*. Nairobi: CLMC.

American Heritage Dictionary of the English Language

2000 NY: Houghton Mifflin Co.

Anderson, Leith

1999 *Leadership that Works*. Minneapolis: Bethany House Pub.

Anderson, Neil T.

1994 *A Way of Escape*. Eugene: Harvest House.

Armerding, Hudson T.

1978 *Leadership*. Wheaton: Tyndale House Pub.

1992 *The Heart of Godly Leadership*. Wheaton: Crossway Books.

Arnold, Johann Christoph

1997 *Seventy Times Seven*. Sussex: The Plough Publishing House.

Arterburn, Stephen and Fred Stoeker

2000 *Every Man's Battle*. Colorado Springs: Water Brook Press.

Ashford, Ray

1977 *Loving Ourselves*. Philadelphia: Fortress Press.

Augsburger, David

1970 *The Freedom of Forgiveness*. Chicago: Moody Press.

Baker, Kenneth

1985 *Zechariah: The Expositor's Bible Commentary*. Grand Rapids: Regency.

Baldwin, Joyce G.

1972 *Haggai, Zechariah, Malachi: The Tyndale Old Testament Commentaries*. Downers Grove: InterVarsity Press.

Barber, Cyril

1987 *Nehemiah and the Dynamics of Effective Leadership*. Neptune: Loizeaux.

Barna, George

1992 *The Power of Vision*. Ventura: Regal Books.

2002 *A Fish Out of Water*. Nashville: Integrity Publishers.

Barna, George ed.

1997 *Leaders on Leadership*. Ventura: Regal Books.

Barnes, Albert

1949 *I Corinthians: Notes on the New Testament*. Grand Rapids: Baker Book House.

Barr, Allan
1950 'Love in the Church: A Study of I Corinthians.' *Scottish Journal of Theology*. III: 421.
Bauer, Walter
1957 *A Greek-English Lexicon of the New Testament*. Translated by William Arndt and Wilbur Gingrich. Chicago: The University of Chicago Press.
Baxter, J. Sidlow
1973 *A New Call to Holiness*. Grand Rapids: Zondervan Pub. House.
Beasley-Murray, Paul
1990 *Dynamic Leadership*. Eastbourne, UK: MARC.
Behm, Johannes
1965 'καρδια,' in the *Theological Dictionary of the New Testament*. Gerhard Kittel ed. Translated and edited by Geoffrey W. Bromiley. Grand Rapids: Eerdmans Pub. Co.
Benjamin, Martin
1990 *Splitting the Difference*. Lawrence: University Press of Kansas.
Benner, David and Robert W. Harvey
1996 *Understanding and Facilitating Forgiveness*. Grand Rapids: Baker Books.
Bernard, Abbot of Clarivaux
1940 *The Steps of Humility*. Cambridge: Harvard University Press.
Boehme, Ron
1989 *Leadership for the 21st Century*. Seattle: Frontline Communications.
Bonaventure, Philip O'Mara
1993 'Tests of a Leader's Character.' *Leadership*. 14 Fall, 38-42.
Bonn, Wellington
2002 *The Low Road to New Heights*. NY: Doubleday.
Bounds, E.M.
n.d. *Power Through Prayer*. Chicago: Moody Press.
Branner, John Ky
1983 'Chinese Leadership Patterns and Their Relationship to Pastoral Ministry Among Taiwan's Urban Masses.' D.Miss. Dissertation, Fuller Theological Seminary.
Bridges, Jerry
1985 *The Pursuit of Holiness*. Colorado Springs: NAV Press.
Brokke, Harold J.
1963 *The Law is Holy*. Minneapolis: Bethany Fellowship.
Bromiley, Geoffrey ed.
1982 *The International Standard Bible Encyclopedia*. Fully Revised. Vol. III. Grand Rapids: Wm. B. Eerdmans.

Brown, Francis, S.R. Driver and Charles A. Briggs
1983 *The New Brown-Driver-Briggs-Gesenius Hebrew & English Lexicon.* Christian Copyrights Inc.

Buchsel, Rudolf
1965 'θυμος,' in the *Theological Dictionary of the New Testament.* Gerhard Kittel ed. Translated and edited by Geoffrey W. Bromiley. Grand Rapids: Wm. B. Eerdmans.

Bukusi, Alan
2004 *Thinking Leadership in Africa.* Nairobi: Management Decision Information.

Burton, Ernest DeWitt
1920 "A Critical and Exegetical Commentary on the Epistle to the Galatians." *The International Critical Commentary on the Holy Scriptures* edited by Briggs, Driver and Plummer. NY: Charles Scribner's Sons.

Chalke, Steve with Penny Relph
1998 *Managing Your Time.* Great Britain: Kingsway Publishers.

Chapman, Gary
1999 *The Other Side of Love: Handling Anger in a Godly Way.* Chicago: Moody Press.

Chima, Alex
1984 "Leadership in the African Church," *AFER.* 26 Dec.: 331-337.

Clinton, Robert
1988 *The Making of a Leader.* Colorado Springs: NAV Press.

Cole, Victor
1991 'The Training of Leaders for the Ministry.' *African Journal of Evangelical Theology.* No. 2: 33-43.

Collins, Gary R.
1988 *Christian Counseling.* Revised Edition. W Publishing Group, A Division of Thomas Nelson, Inc.

Cremer, Hermann
1977 *Biblico-Theological Lexicon of New Testament Greek.* Edinburgh: T. & T. Clark.

Cribbin, James J.
1972 *Effective Managerial Leadership.* U.S.A.: American Management Association.

Cunneen, Joseph
1978 'Learning from Africa.' *Cross Current.* 28 No. 4 Winter: 385-461.

Danker, Frederick William
1979 *A Greek-English Lexicon of the New Testament and Early Christian Literature.* Third Edition, based on Walter Bauer's. Chicago: The University of Chicago Press.

DePree, Max
1989 *Leadership is an Art.* NY: A Dell Trade Paperback.

1992 *Leadership Jazz*. NY: A Dell Trade Paperback.
Douglass, Steve, B. Cook and H. Hendricks
1981 *Ministry of Management*. San Bernadino, CA: Campus Crusade for Christ.
Edwards, Thomas C.
1903 *A Commentary on the First Epistle to the Corinthians*. London: Hodder & Stoughton.
Eims, LeRoy
1996 *Be a Motivational Leader*. Chariot Victor Publisher.
1996 *Be the Leader You Were Meant to Be*. Wheaton: Victor Books.
Elliston, Edgar
1983 'Masai Leadership Development.' *African Journal of Evangelical Theology*. No 3: 20-31.
Ellul, Jacques
1984 *Money and Power*. Downers Grove: InterVarsity.
Engstrom, Ted W.
1979 *The Making of a Christian Leader*. Grand Rapids: Zondervan.
1987 *Integrity*. Waco: Word Books.
Engstrom, Ted W. and Edward Dayton
1976 *The Art of Management for Christian Leaders*. Waco: Word.
Engstrom, Ted W. and R. Alec Mackenzie
1977 *Managing your Time*. Grand Rapids: Zondervan.
Erickson, Millard
2002 *Christian Theology*. Second Edition. Grand Rapids: Baker.
Finzel, Hans
1994 *The Top Ten Mistakes Leaders Make*. Wheaton: Victor Books.
Ford, Leighton
1991 *Transforming Leadership*. Downers Grove: InterVarsity Press.
Fortes, Meyer and E.E. Evans-Pritchard eds.
1940 *African Political Systems*. NY: Oxford University Press.
Foster, Richard J.
1998 *Celebration of Discipline*. San Francisco: Harper San Francisco.
Gallagher, Steve
2000 *At the Altar of Sexual Idolatry*. Dry Ridge, KY: Pure Life Ministries.
Gangel, Kenneth O.
1974 *Competent to Lead*. Chicago: Moody Press.
1997 *Team Leadership in Christian Ministry*. Chicago: Moody Press.
Gardner, John W.
1990 *On Leadership*. NY: Free Press/Macmillan.
Gehman, Richard J.
1987 *Doing African Christian Theology*. Nairobi: Evangel.

Gitari, David M.

2005 *Responsible Leadership*. Nairobi: Action Publishers.

Godet, Frederic

n.d. *Commentary on St. Paul's First Epistle to the Corinthians*. Translated by A. Cusin. Edinburgh: T.T. Clark.

Groundmann, Walter

1972 "ταπεινος," in the *Theological Dictionary of the New Testament*, G. Kittel ed., Translated and edited by Geoffrey W. Bromiley. Grand Rapids: Wm. B. Eerdmans.

Guinness, Os and John Seel eds.

1992 *No God but God*. Chicago: Moody Press.

Guinness, Os, compiled by Mooney, Virginia ed.

2000 *When No One Sees*. Colorado Springs: NAV Press.

Gunderson, Denny

1997 *The Leadership Paradox*. Seattle: YWAM Publishing.

Guthrie, Donald

1977 *The Pastoral Epistles; Tyndale New Testament Commentaries*. Grand Rapids: Wm. B. Eerdmans.

Haas, Howard G.

1992 *The Leader Within*. NY: Harper Business.

Habecker, Eugene B.

1987 *The Other Side of Leadership*. Wheaton: Victor Books

Harder, Kenneth

1985 'Kenyan Church Leaders.' PhD Dissertation, Michigan State University.

Harrison, Everett F. ed.

1960 *Baker's Dictionary of Theology*. Grand Rapids: Baker Books.

Hendriksen, William

1973 *The Gospel of Matthew*. Edinburgh: The Banner of Truth.

Hess, J. Daniel

1978 *Integrity*. Scottdale: Herald Press.

Hestenes, Roberta

2001 'Public Spirituality.' *Leadership*. Spring: 38-41.

Hocking, David L.

1983 *Be a Leader People Follow*. Ventura: Regal Books.

Honeycutt Jr., Roy L.

1966 *These Ten Words*. Nashville: Broadman Press.

Howard, J. Grant

1983 *Balancing Life's Demands*. Portland: Multnomah Press.

Hughes, R. Kent and Bryan Chapell

2000 *1 and 2 Timothy and Titus*. Wheaton: Crossway Books.

Hunter, Rodney J. ed.
1990 *Dictionary of Pastoral Care and Counseling*. Nashville: Abingdon Press.

Hwang, Tom Yonghyun
1992 'Confluence and Conflict: Biblical and Cultural Influences on Leadership of Korean Churches.' D.Miss. Dissertation, Trinity International University.

Hybels, Bill
2002 *Courageous Leadership*. Grand Rapids: Zondervan.

Jacobs, Donald R.
1991 *From Rubble to Rejoicing*. Pasadena: William Carey Library.

Janvier, George and Bitrus Thaba
1997 *Understanding Leadership: An African Christian Model.* Jos, Nigeria: published by G. Janvier.

Jones, Geraint V.
1954 'Agape and Eros.' *Expository Times.* LXVI, October: 3ff.

Kamau, Francis Mugarami
1996 'Toward a Contextualized Leadership Approach for the Pentecostal Church in Kenya.' PhD Dissertation, Fuller Theological Seminary.

Kapena, Sumbye
2000 *How to be a Wise Leader*. Nairobi, Kenya: Paulines Pub. Africa.

Kittel, Gerhard
1951 *Bible Key Words.* Translated by J. Coates. NY: Harper & Bros.

Klag, Michael J. ed.
1999 *Johns Hopkins Family Health Book*. HarperCollins Publishers.

Kofele-Kale, Ndiva
1978 'The Politics of Development and the Problem of Leadership in Africa.' *Cross Currents.* 28 No. 4 Winter: 432-452.

Kohls, Paul
1998 'A Look at Church Leadership in Africa,' *Africa Journal of Evangelical Theology,* No. 2: 107-123.

Kouzes, James M. and Barry Z. Posner
1993 *Credibility*. San Francisco: Jossey-Bass Pub.

Kreeft, Peter
1986 *Back to Virtue*. San Francisco: Ignatius Press.

Laaser, Mark R.
1992 *The Secret Sin*. Grand Rapids: Zondervan Pub. House.

Lester, Andrew D.
2003 *The Angry Christian*. Louisville: Westminster John Knox Press.

Lewis, C.S.
1943 *Mere Christianity*. NY: Macmillan.

Love, J. Richard
1994 *Liberating Leaders from the Superman Syndrome*. NY: University Press of America.

Lundy, J. David
2002 *Servant Leadership for Slow Learners*. Waynseboro: Authentic Lifestyles.

MacArthur, John F.
1998 *The Freedom and Power of Forgiveness*. Wheaton: Crossway Books.
1998 *The Pillars of Christian Character*. Wheaton: Crossway Books.

Malphurs, Aubrey
1993 *Pouring New Wine into Old Wineskins*. Grand Rapids: Baker.
1996 *Values-Driven Leadership*. Grand Rapids: Baker Books.

Marshall, I. Howard
1999 *Critical and Exegetical Commentary on the Pastoral Epistles*. Edinburgh: T & T Clark.

Marshall, Tom
1989 *Right Relationships*. Chichester: Sovereign World.

Martin, Joe
2002 'On Leading by Serving.' *Let Your Leadership Speak*. Paxton: The Future is Yours to Create! Company.

Mbiti, John
1971 *New Testament Eschatology in an African Background*. London: Oxford University Press.

Mbogori, Elijah
1999 *Conflict Management*. Nairobi: Evangel.

McDonough, Reginald M.
1979 *Keys to Effective Motivation*. Nashville: Broadman Press.

McKenna, David L.
1989 *Power to Follow, Grace to Lead*. Dallas: Word Publishing.

McQuilkin, Robertson
2005 'In Sickness and in Health.' *Decision Magazine*. June: 18-21.

Means, James
1989 *Leadership in Christian Ministry*. Grand Rapids: Baker.

Miller, Calvin
1987 *Leadership*. Colorado Springs: NAV Press.

Mugania, John
1994 'A Study of the African Process of Mediation for Christian Ministry.' MA Thesis, Daystar University and Wheaton College.

Mushanga, Musa
1971 'Church Leadership in a Developing Society.' *AFER*. 13 Jan.: 33-40.

Munroe, Myles
2005 *The Spirit of Leadership*. New Kensington, PA: Whitaker House.

Mutinda, Paul
1991 'Understanding Church Leadership: An Analysis and Assessment of the Africa Inland Church, Kenya.' D.Min Dissertation, Biola University.

Mutunga, Stanley
1993 'Contextual Leadership Development for the Church: An Investigation into Rural-Urban Migration to Nairobi.' PhD Dissertation, Fuller Theological Seminary.

Myra, Harold ed.
1987 *Leaders: Learning Leadership from Some of Christianity's Best*. Waco: Word Books.

Norton, Ellen
n.d. 'Toward an Integrated Theory of Human Motivation, Psychology and Theology.' Unpublished Lecture Notes.

Nouwen, Henri J.M.
1994 *In the Name of Jesus: Reflections on Christian Leadership*. NY: Crossroad.

Oliver, Gary Jackson and H. Norman Wright
1992 *When Anger Hits Home*. Chicago: Moody Press.

Osei-Mensah, Gottfried
1990 *Wanted: Servant Leaders*. Achimota: African Christian Press.

Payne, Roland J.
1968 'The Influence of the Concept of Traditional African Leadership on Church Leadership.' *Africa Theological Journal*. 1: 69-74.

Perkins, Bill
2000 *Awaken the Leader Within*. Grand Rapids: Zondervan.

Perry, John
1983 *Effective Christian Leadership*. London: Hodder & Stoughton.

Phillips, J.B. Translator
1962 *The New Testament in Modern English*. NY: The Macmillan Co.

Popkes. W.
1981 'ζηλοω,' in the *Exegetical Dictionary of the New Testament*. Vol. 2, Horst Balz and Gerherd Sheider eds. Grand Rapids: Eerdmans.

Random House College Dictionary
1988 NY: Random House.

Redpath, Alan
1958 *Victorious Christian Service*. Old Tappan, NJ: Fleming H. Revell.

Reith, George
1948 *The Gospel According to St. John, Part II*. Edinburgh: Clark.

Richards, Lawrence O.
1985 *Expository Dictionary of Bible Words*. Grand Rapids: Regency.

Richards, Lawrence O. and Clyde Hoeldtke
1980 *A Theology of Church Leadership*. Grand Rapids: Ministry Resources Lib.

Richardson, Alan ed.
1950 *A Theological Word Book of the Bible*. NY: Macmillan.

Rima, Samuel D.
2000 *Leading from the Inside Out*. Grand Rapids: Baker.

Robertson, Archibald and Alfred Plummer
1911 *A Critical and Exegetical Commentary on the First Epistle of St. Paul to the Corinthians. The International Critical Commentary on the Holy Scriptures*, C.A. Briggs, S.R. Driver, and Alfred Plummer eds. NY: Charles Scribner's Sons.

Rush, Myron D.
1983 *Management, A Biblical Approach*. Wheaton: Victor Books.
1987 *The New Leader*. Wheaton: Victor Books.

Ryle, John Charles
1979 *Holiness*. Second Edition. Grand Rapids: Baker Book House.

Sanders, J. Oswald
1980 *Spiritual Leadership*. Revised Edition. Chicago: Moody Press.

Shults, F. Le Ron and Stephen J. Sandage
2003 *The Faces of Forgiveness*. Grand Rapids: Baker Academic.

Smedes, Lewis B.
1991 *On Being Truthful*. Prepared by the Center for Applied Christian Ethics, Wheaton College. Address presented at Wheaton College.

Smith, Fred
1986 *Learning to Lead*. Waco: Word Books.

Spears, Larry ed.
1998 *Insights on Leadership*. NY: John Wiley & Sons.
1998 *Servant Leadership: Essays by Robert K. Greenleaf*. NY: Paulist Press.

Spicq, Ceslaus
1959 *Agape*. Paris: Librairie Lecoffre.

Stott, John
1979 *God's New Society: The Message of Ephesians*. Downer's Grove: InterVarsity Press.
2002 *Basic Christian Leadership*. Downers Grove: InterVarsity.

Stowell, Joseph M.
1997 *Shepherding the Church*. Wheaton: Victor Books.

Strong, James
n.d. *The Exhaustive Concordance of the Bible*. McLean: MacDonald Pub. Co.

Stumpff, Albrecht
1964 'ζηλος, ζηλοω,' in the *Theological Dictionary of the New Testament*. Gerhard Kittell ed. Translated and edited by Geoffrey W. Bromiley. Grand Rapids: Wm. B. Eerdmans.
Swindoll, Charles R.
1978 *Hand Me Another Brick*. Nashville: Thomas Nelson Pub.
1987 *Living Above the Level of Mediocrity*. Waco: Word Books.
Thayer, Joseph Henry
1983 *The New Thayer's Greek-English Lexicon of the New Testament*. Christian Copyrights.
Trench, Richard Chenevix
1953 *Synonyms of the New Testament*. Grand Rapids: Eerdmans.
Trobisch, Walter
1976 *Love Yourself*. Downers Grove: InterVarsity Press.
Van den Toren
2004 'The Christian God and Human Authority: A Theological Exploration with reference to Africa's Principal Worldviews.' *Africa Journal of Evangelical Theology*. No. 2:161-186.
Vine, W.E.
1981 *Expository Dictionary of the Old and New Testament Words*. Old Tappan: Fleming H. Revell.
Vincent, M.R.
1972 *Word Studies in the New Testament*. Wilmington: Associated Publishers and Authors.
Wallace, Ronald S.
1965 *The Ten Commandments*. Grand Rapids: Wm. B. Eerdmans.
Walters, Richard P.
1981 *Anger*. Grand Rapids: Zondervan.
1985 *Jealousy, Envy, Lust: The Weeds of Greed*. Grand Rapids: Zondervan.
Watson, Thomas
1965 *The Ten Commandments*. London: The Banner of Truth.
Webster's New International Dictionary of the English Language.
1959 2nd Edition, Unabridged. Springfield: G. & C. Merriam Co.
Wengst, Klaus
1988 *Humility*. Philadelphia: Fortress Press.
Westermann, John
1997 *The Leadership Continuum*. Deer Lodge: Light House Pub.
White, John
1986 *Excellence in Leadership*. Downers Grove: InterVarsity Press.

Wiersbe, Warren W.
1980 'The Principles are the Bottom Line.' *Leadership*. Vol. 1, No. 1, 81-88.

Wigram, George V.
1980 *The Englishman's Hebrew and Chaldee Concordance of the Old Testament*. Grand Rapids: Baker Book House.

Wilkes, C. Gene
1998 *Jesus on Leadership*. Wheaton: Tyndale House Pub.

Williams, J.R.
2001 'Holiness' in *Evangelical Dictionary of Theology*. Second Edition. Walter A. Elwell ed. Grand Rapids: Baker Academic.

Wofford, Jerry
1999 *Transforming Christian Leadership*. Grand Rapids: Baker.

Youssef, Michael
1986 *The Leadership Style of Jesus*. Wheaton: Victor Books.

Zartman, I. William ed.
2000 *Traditional Cures for Modern Conflicts*. London: Lynne Rienner Pub.

Zokoue, Isaac
1990 'Educating for Servant Leadership in Africa.' *Africa Journal of Evangelical Theology*. No. 2: 3-13.

ADDITIONAL BOOKS WRITTEN OR EDITED BY AUTHOR

African Traditional Religion in Biblical Perspective, 2005 Revised Edition
East African Educational Publishers, PO Box 73476, Nairobi, Kenya.

African Traditional Religion in the Light of the Bible, 2001 First Edition.
Nigeria: Africa Christian Textbooks. (Copyright by ACTS)

Who are the Living Dead? A Theology of Death, Life after Death and the Living Dead, 1999.
Evangel Publishing House, PvtBag 28963, Nairobi, Kenya.

Doing African Christian Theology: An Evangelical Perspective, 1987
Evangel Publishing House, PvtBag 28963, Nairobi, Kenya.

A Biblical Approach to Marriage and Family in Africa, 1994.
Copyright by TAG (The Theological Advisory Group)
Scott Theological College, PO Box 49, Machakos, Kenya.

The Holy Spirit and the Church in Africa, 2000.
Copyright by TAG (The Theological Advisory Group)
Scott Theological College, PO Box 49, Machakos, Kenya.

'Come, Let us Bow Down…' Worship in the Christian Church in Africa, 1991.
(A Bible study booklet with twenty chapters developed by questions and suggested answers, complimenting a Work Book for students.)
Copyright by TAG (The Theological Advisory Group)
Scott Theological College, PO Box 49, Machakos, Kenya